HONORING ELDERS

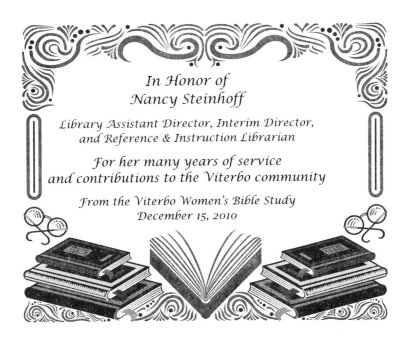

In Honor of
Nancy Steinhoff

Library Assistant Director, Interim Director,
and Reference & Instruction Librarian

For her many years of service
and contributions to the Viterbo community

From the Viterbo Women's Bible Study
December 15, 2010

The Religion and American Culture series explores the interaction between religion and culture throughout American history. Titles examine such issues as how religion functions in particular urban contexts, how it interacts with popular culture, its role in social and political conflicts, and its impact on regional identity. Series Editor Randall Balmer is the Ann Whitney Olin Professor of American Religion and former chair of the Department of Religion at Barnard College, Columbia University.

HONORING ELDERS

Aging, Authority, and Ojibwe Religion

MICHAEL D. McNALLY

Columbia University Press *New York*

Permission to reprint previously published materials in chapters 4–5 has been granted as follows:

Gertrude Kurath, Jane Ettawageshik, and Fred Ettawageshik, *The Art of Tradition: Sacred Music, Dance, and Myth of Michigan's Anishinaabe, 1946–1955*, ed. Michael D. McNally (East Lansing: Michigan State University Press, 2009), pp. xvii–xviii, 15–18. Reprinted with permission of Michigan State University Press.

Michael D. McNally, "Ogimaakweg/Boss Women: Women Elders in 20th Century Ojibwe Christianity," in *Deeper Joy: Laywomen and Vocation in the 20th-Century Episcopal Church*, ed. Fredrica H. Thompsett and Sheryl Kujawa-Holbrook (New York: Church Publishing, 2005), pp. 41–55. Reprinted with permission of Church Publishing.

Michael D. McNally, "Honoring Elders: Practices of Sagacity and Deference in Ojibwe Christianity," in *Practicing Protestants: Histories of the Christian Life in America, 1630–1965*, ed. Laurie Maffly-Kipp, Leigh Schmidt, and Mark Valeri (Baltimore: Johns Hopkins University Press, 2006), pp. 77–100. Reprinted with permission of the Johns Hopkins University Press.

Columbia University Press
Publishers Since 1893
New York   Chichester, West Sussex
Copyright ©2009 Columbia University Press
All rights reserved

Library of Congress Cataloging-in-Publication Data

McNally, Michael David.
Honoring elders : aging, authority, and Ojibwe religion / Michael D. McNally.
p.   cm.
Includes bibliographical references and index.
ISBN 978-0-231-14502-2 (cloth : alk. paper) — ISBN 978-0-231-14503-9 (pbk.)
1. Older Ojibwa Indians.   2. Ojibwa Indians—Religion.   3. Ojibwa Indians—Social life and customs.   I. Title.
E99.C6M346   2009
305.897—dc22
2008031541

Columbia University Press books are printed on permanent and durable acid-free paper.

This book was printed on paper with recycled content.

Printed in the United States of America

c 10 9 8 7 6 5 4 3 2
p 10 9 8 7 6 5 4 3 2

References to Internet Web sites (URLs) were accurate at the time of writing. Neither the author nor Columbia University Press is responsible for URLs that may have expired or changed since the manuscript was prepared.

For Devon Anderson, with whom I aspire to grow old.

CONTENTS

Contents

ILLUSTRATIONS

Illustrations

PREFACE

It is readily apparent in Bob Dylan's voice on recent albums: youth is evading the baby boomer generation. And as boomers age, their parents are joining the ranks of the very old. Many are trying to reimagine the latter stages of the life course and to reevaluate what elders in their midst have to offer. Ill nourished by a popular culture that valorizes youth, that lives in denial of its own aging, and by an economy and society that relegates the old and retired to the margins, many of us hunger for fresh ways of imagining aging as a meaningful process, on the one hand, and for evaluating afresh the worth and relevance of what the old and their ways of knowing have to offer the common good.

We might hope to discover a golden age of American religion when the young fully respected their seniors, but a closer reading of the American past finds people of faith fraught with a deep perennial ambivalence concerning the spiritual meaning of their own aging and about how they ought properly regard the spiritual authority of the old. For Christians, while the Fifth Commandment's injunction to honor father and mother grounds this most basic of kinship obligations in God's will, it has never been clear how the authority of elders should square with other configurations of religious authority: that of the learned, the clergy, the prophet, or the born again.[1] What is more, never has old age uniformly lived up to the wisdom and venerability that are so consistently expected of it.

Still, one can find rich veins of practice within American communities that distinguish themselves in their disciplined regard for the authority of old age, resources that can help reimagine the possibilities of what the old and their wisdom have to offer the common life.

Anishinaabe people (plural: Anishinaabeg, comprised of Ojibwe, Odawa, and Potawatomi "nations") indigenous to the upper Great Lakes region are tribal communities with an age-old regard for old age, its religious significance, and its authority.[2] For the Anishinaabe, to be called "that old man" or "that old woman" is an honorific, a term of the utmost respect in English. In Anishinaabe languages like Ojibwe, there are a wealth of terms denoting elder, with inflections that frame old age in terms of moral excellence and supernatural power and proximity to the spirits. Indeed the spirits themselves are addressed as "grandparents," the relationship between people and the spirits framed in terms of the intimacy as well as codes of respect involved in ideal relationships between grandchildren and their grandparents. Children are repeatedly taught to "respect their elders" as perhaps the most important social ethic, and the maxim is on display in virtually any public gathering or representation of Native culture. Those identified as elders are conspicuously given pride of place in assemblies, are authorized to speak at will, without interruption. And if their utterances are not uniformly heeded, as can of course be the case, Native communities must reason their way around the authority of elders.

This book focuses on the significance and authority of old age in Anishinaabe *tradition*, but it also focuses on the significance and authority of eldership as it has changed in Anishinaabe culture and history. The focus on one Native community is, I think, necessary in order to move beyond cliché to undertake the kind of sustained, grounded analysis of the religious authority of eldership that neither Native American Studies scholarship nor the academic study of religion have sufficiently accomplished to date. I begin the discussion of that scholarship in the introduction. But as specific as I must be about the intricacies and sophistication of Anishinaabe practices of eldership over time, this book is emphatically *not* fueled by scholarly concerns alone. It springs from my experience with a coterie of elder hymn-singers in the work of my first book, which was about how Minnesota Ojibwes took hymns translated by nineteenth-century missionaries in an effort to root out Indianness and made them their own, such that Ojibwe-language hymn-singing today at funeral wakes is, for many at least, emblematic of tradition.[3] Because the hymn-singers with whom I worked were also regarded as elders, I became in the fieldwork for that project profoundly impressed by the countercultural way that many Ojibwe people, today and in the past, come into their own in old age, expanding horizons where others occupy increasingly smaller worlds. This extends deeper than professed ideals of eldership, as important as they are; it concerns the capacity and fortitude of older Anishinaabe women and men to lay claim to the social space that those Anishinaabe ideals have made available to them (and that American economy, society, and culture, in turn, diminish) and to improvise their way to positions of authority, some with only partial training in their language and tradition; in sum, to grow into their positions of authority, to have their often difficult life experiences honored as valuable, and all this driven not by concerns for their own vital aging but for community well-being.

This impressed me as being one among many lessons that non-Native people could learn and take to heart from Anishinaabe communities. Although the examples of Anishinaabe elders in this book surely inspire, the lessons are, I don't think, ones of the spirituality of aging or simply how to age well versus how to age poorly (the obsession with the distinction itself being an outcome of our demeaning of aging) but about the health, wholesomeness, and sustainability of communities that create social space for the authority of age.

So, while the book is grounded firmly in Anishinaabe traditions, the potential lessons I think are neither wholly culture-bound nor tied to some inaccessible past, for today's Anishinaabe people live in multiple worlds and as such are more than familiar with a demeaning of aging in America, the disproportionate poverty of the old in communities of color, and the accentuated gender inequality facing the aged. I'm interested in how such traditions have been and still are put into practice in the context of Anishinaabe communities and amid these shared challenges. To get a better handle on these shared challenges, and in turn to place the contribution of this book to literatures in American studies and American history generally, let's turn to consider the major contours of the cultural history of aging in America.[4]

The Demeaning of Aging in America

Cultural historian Thomas Cole has traced the contours of a protracted, halting, and complex transformation in the meanings of aging in American cultural history, a transformation that he designates "the de-meaning of aging." For Cole, the demeaning is twofold. Old age is demeaned in terms of being stripped of its existential significance, on the one hand, and demeaned in terms of the diminution of the authority of old age with respect to other structures of authority, on the other.[5] It takes place in a transformation from old age as an existential problem, the ken of moral and spiritual commitment, to old age as a scientific problem to be managed by medical and social scientific specialists.

Cole takes as his baseline an early modern recognition of old age as a religious calling, the final stage of a spiritual journey on which all people found themselves. For Puritans, Cole notes, "hope and triumph were linked dialectically to decline and death since all were seen in light of eternity." "The aging pilgrim was a figure esteemed," Cole writes, for drawing closer to God on the sacred pilgrimage that was the life course.[6] Through such practices as prestigious seating in church, restriction of church membership to those old enough for self-examination, and providing public witness of the workings of grace in their lives, Puritans placed stock in the religious significance of becoming old even as they acknowledged its bodily difficulties. Even eighteenth-century Americans experienced old age as a trial, characterized by the loss of health and self-control that await all human beings, but Cole finds that those trials were considered existential mysteries laden with spiritual meaning. By the early twentieth century, old age was no longer an existential problem, but had become defined as a scientific problem pertaining to a discrete segment of the population—the old—and to be rationalized and contained if not solved by bureaucrats and social scientists.

Although Cole lets on that it would be tempting to make it so, the narrative arc from old age as a human experience facing all of us to a scientific problem facing a discrete group and to be managed by professionals was neither a simple one nor was it foreordained in the metanarratives of secularization or modernization. Instead, the demeaning of aging happened by fits and starts, and religious practices and institutions played a role in that narrative.

Of particular interest is the attention Cole pays to religious history—and here his work stands in sharp contrast to other histories of the same terrain. The demeaning of aging in terms of the transmission of its negotiation from religion to scientific and medical authorities wasn't a process that *happened to* American religion, as a wooden secularization thesis might suggest. In large part, it happened because of changes internal to American religion, especially Protestantism, itself.[7]

Specifically, Cole attends to how aging became a problem to be solved, not a mystery to be probed, by a nineteenth-century mainstream Protestant tradition that revised orthodox Calvinism into an ideal of self-control, an ideal that would ground such varied expressions as the great reform, antivice, and hygienic movements of mainstream nineteenth-century evangelicalism to perfectionist movements and alternative healing traditions of Christian Science and New Thought. Because old age represented the predictable loss of the very control that evangelicals made their moral ideal, the specter of extreme old age threw a wrench in the heart of their system.

The evangelical response, Cole teaches us, was to assert "in place of ambiguity and contingency" a tidy moral distinction between "good," healthy, virtuous, civilized aging and "bad" aging. Indeed this became an obsession in Victorian culture, iterated and reiterated in a burgeoning literature of aging manuals and other images sentimentalizing old age while stripping it further of its relevance and respect. Good aging, predictably, involved no small measure of denial of its eventual realities: "Men were to 'master' old age rather than yield to it, to eliminate rather than explore the final stage of life."[8]

The moral distinctions of this dualism, along with its contradictions, extend well beyond the highpoint of Victorian evangelicalism. Through health reform and what Cole calls "the legitimation of longevity," social and medical science joins technologies of healthy aging to its moral ideals. "Longevity and cheerful self-reliance, not decay and dependence, crowned the life of those who followed the Christian way. Instruction for healthful aging invariably turned on the benevolence of natural law."[9]

Later, in the early decades of the twentieth century, scientists absorbed the moral distinction between good and bad aging in their transmutation of *normative*, or good aging, into "normal" aging and, by turns, their pathologizing of bad aging. The constitution of old age as a scientific problem appears around the time of the naming of adolescence as a problem requiring scientific inquiry and careful management. Indeed, the early-twentieth-century psychologist who introduced the term *adolescence*, G. Stanley Hall, was also the author of *Senescence: The Last Half of Life* (1922), and this book serves as the culmination of the process tracked by Cole even as it discloses the deep ambivalence that remained. For while the aged were being made *other*, cast as a discrete segment of society, more and more of the people who had thought them into that box were entering it themselves.

Scholarship on Aging in America

No lack of scholarship on aging has been produced in the twentieth century, schooled by the emerging field of gerontology. Yet precisely because gerontology grew out of the social scientific attempt to control and manage aging that Cole identifies, humanities scholarship into the meaning and value of aging has only recently begun to emerge from the outskirts of the overall literature. There have been some very important exceptions to this rule. Beginning in the late 1970s, a handful of scholars were each trying to train the sensibilities of a "new social history" on the social distinction of old age. Animating these studies was a concern that older, more wholesome ways of regarding old age had somehow been lost in the course of modernity, particularly under the influence of urbanization, industrialization, and democratization. But what animated the studies curiously became the object of their animus as historians laid claim to the complexity of the past from the sweep of nostalgia.

Keith Thomas and John Demos in early modern English and Anglo-American history wrote generative articles that disclosed the ambivalence about the aged that accompanied early modern deference to elders in a traditional hierarchy.[10] Andrew Achenbaum, David Hackett Fischer, and Carol Haber each wrote book-length treatments of old age in the sweep of American history, emphasizing different aspects of the transformation.[11] Fischer emphasized the place of democratic values and ideologies of liberty and equality undoing traditional hierarchies supporting the authority of age. Haber argued that the transformation was less clearly bounded, but relied still on processes of urbanization and industrialization to frame new attitudes toward and realities facing older Americans. Similarly,

Achenbaum was reluctant to place the transformation too precisely, with "no one decade or period emerged as *the* decisive turning point," but stressed the late-nineteenth-century medicalization of old age and the rise of corporations, ideals of efficiency, and increasingly elaborated structures of retirement.[12]

Although there is more of a humanities sensibility in U.S. scholarship than has been seen until recently in social histories of aging by demography-driven Europeanists, Cole characterizes this early work in the late 1970s as fundamentally driven still by an approach to the aged "almost exclusively as objects of society's veneration or contempt, recipients of its benevolence or neglect, and as products of the historical forces of demography, social structure, and political economy. Sadly, we have not approached older people as centers of meaning and value."[13]

Cole's own study shows the value of stitching the cultural history of aging into the history of religion, not simply as the emblem of the traditional society prior to modernization and secularization when elders were authoritative and old age was significant, but as a complex of institutions, ideas, and practices crucial to the history of aging. But with a number of important exceptions, scholars of religious history have yet to reciprocate the cultural historian's interest in religion with a religionist's interest in the cultural history of aging,[14] and a fully developed literature using age as a category of analysis on a par with gender or ethnicity has yet to come into bloom. As I elaborate in the introduction, even the ethnographic literature on Native Americans can make frequent reference to the importance of respecting elders without sustained inquiry into what that might mean within the social and cultural fabric of specific Native communities.

Could it be that the lack of sustained scholarly attention to the meanings and existential experience of old age—outside the circles of gerontological social science or the therapeutic "how to age well" manuals shown by Cole to be so closely related to the gerontological management of old age—is itself related to the culturally shaped denial of the realities of old age within the world of scholarship itself? Perhaps so.

• • •

I offer the current study as an exhaustive theoretical correction neither to the literature on aging in North America nor to the place of age as a category of analysis in historical studies. Neither do I offer this study in the spirit of a simplistic "discovery" or "recovery" of Native American aging for a self-help project about "playing Indian-elder," though it remains my hope that the consideration of what constitutes Anishinaabe elders' ways of knowing, especially found in chapter 6, can be helpful in the constructive task of rethinking the significance of aging for an aging North American population and of appreciating what the old in our midst have to offer the common good.[15]

Instead, I offer it as a theoretically informed, but firmly grounded, elaboration on what I see as the key features of eldership in Anishinaabe communities over time. I trust that the general reader, as well as the scholar, will find something to engage them in the pages that follow, and I would be honored if others, including the book's critics, would carry on to deepen this important conversation.

ACKNOWLEDGMENTS

As I trust is clear from its pages, this book is rooted in life-changing relationships I've had with a number of Ojibwe elders in Minnesota. The late Larry Cloud Morgan and his family took a considerable risk on my education, and this book emerges largely through my own observation of Larry's becoming esteemed as an elder over the years I came to know him. At White Earth, I am indebted to the elders of the White Earth Ojibwe Singers, especially the late Josephine Degroat, who modeled courage, compassion, and a taste for life. Other White Earth singers, since died, taught by example: Lowell Bellanger, Margaret Hanks, Marge McDonald, Jack Potter. Ethelbert "Tiggums" Van Wert and Charles "Punkin" Hanks continue to inspire.

Since the death of many of these singers, I've been particularly shaped by conversations and relations with Joe Lagarde, Paul Day, Sylvia Gale, Jerry Morgan, Juanita Jackson, Paul Schultz, the late Philip "Danny" Kier and Vernon Bellecourt, and especially Erma Vizenor. To the degree I get things right in this book, I owe it to the tutoring and example of these and other Anishinaabe teachers. To the degree I sway from their teachings, I claim responsibility. To them I say, *miigwech*.

If the book is rooted in those relationships, it has matured through the good graces of a circle of academic teachers and colleagues. David Hall, the late Bill Hutchison, Robert Orsi, and Inés Talamantez remain important

Acknowledgments

teachers and models of scholarship and teaching. A wide circle of colleagues has shaped the work, among them Paula Arai, Susan Ridgely Bales, Shahzad Bashir, Mary Farrell Bednarowski, Courtney Bender, Ann Braude, Chris Coble, Bruce Forbes, Tracey Hucks, Roger Jackson, Jeanne Kilde, David Lamberth, Jay Levi, Jim Lewis, Stephen Marini, Louis Newman, Jim Notebaart, Susannah Ottaway, Anne Patrick, Lori Pearson, Steve Prothero, Asuka Sango, Monica Siems, John Soderberg, Craig Townsend, Tom Tweed, and Robert Two Bulls. My fellow scholars on the American Christian Practices project were particularly encouraging, especially Leigh Schmidt, Laurie Maffly-Kipp, Mark Valeri, Anthea Butler, Heather Curtis, Roberto Lint-Sagarena, Kathryn Lofton, Tisa Wenger, and David Yoo.

A special debt is owed to those commentators on the manuscript or conference presentations who were both tough and generous: Dorothy Bass, John Borrows, Jennifer Brown, Richard W. Fox, John Grim, Larry Gross, Rebecca Kugel, Charles Long, Joel Martin, Jim McClurken, John Nichols, Jim White, and especially Cathy Brekus and Larry Nesper. Bruce White was also extremely helpful in finding photographs. I wish to acknowledge a circle of writers and scholars whose work has been especially helpful and to whom I feel personally indebted even though I have yet to know them well: Jeffrey Anderson, Eddie Benton-Banai, Brenda Child, Alan Corbiere, Regna Darnell, Basil Johnston, Jim Northrup, Anton Treuer, and Elizabeth Tornes. At Columbia University Press, I'm grateful to the efforts of Wendy Lochner, series editor Randall Balmer, and all those who helped with the book's production and printing. I should recognize the good graces of the baristas and regulars at the Linden Hills Dunn Bros. Coffee Shop, who put up with me at window tables over the course of two years.

Financial support for the writing of this book has been generously provided by the National Endowment for the Humanities (Sabbatical Fellowship #FB-50179) and the American Philosophical Society Sabbatical Fellowship, as well as Scott Bierman and the late Shelby Boardman, Deans of the College at Carleton. My gracious colleagues in the department of religion took up no small amount of slack on behalf of this work. In the spirit of those who freely invested themselves in my work, a portion of the royalties from this book, modest as they surely will be, will go to the Migi-mi-gi-way-win Elders Program of the White Earth Reservation Tribal Council.

xx

Acknowledgments

Finally, support of the most intimate, and important, kind has been provided by family. Octogenarian newlyweds Miles McNally and Carolyn Linner quickened my sense of the possibilities of love and vitality in old age and, having since died, of the accomplishment of leaving the world on the top of one's game, ill health notwithstanding. My children, Svea and Coleman, have been my tutors in embracing the best parts of my own aging. Above all, I am grateful to my wife, Devon Anderson, who has commented on the work but, as importantly, has encouraged and inspired me to do scholarship that matters. It is to her, and to the prospect of growing old with her, that this book is dedicated. Thanks, Devon.

HONORING ELDERS

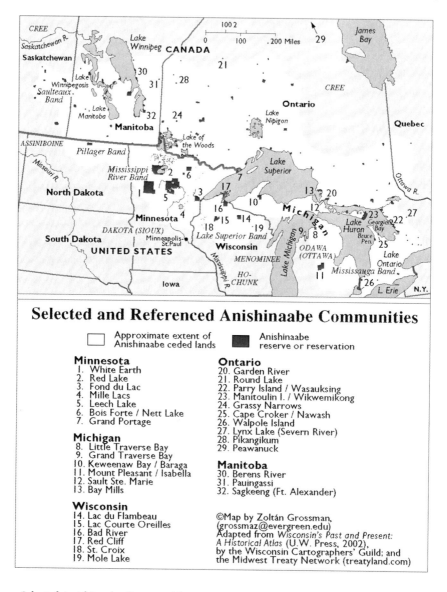

Selected and Referenced Anishinaabe Communities

☐ Approximate extent of Anishinaabe ceded lands ■ Anishinaabe reserve or reservation

Minnesota
1. White Earth
2. Red Lake
3. Fond du Lac
4. Mille Lacs
5. Leech Lake
6. Bois Forte / Nett Lake
7. Grand Portage

Michigan
8. Little Traverse Bay
9. Grand Traverse Bay
10. Keweenaw Bay / Baraga
11. Mount Pleasant / Isabella
12. Sault Ste. Marie
13. Bay Mills

Wisconsin
14. Lac du Flambeau
15. Lac Courte Oreilles
16. Bad River
17. Red Cliff
18. St. Croix
19. Mole Lake

Ontario
20. Garden River
21. Round Lake
22. Parry Island / Wasauksing
23. Manitoulin I. / Wikwemikong
24. Grassy Narrows
25. Cape Croker / Nawash
26. Walpole Island
27. Lynx Lake (Severn River)
28. Pikangikum
29. Peawanuck

Manitoba
30. Berens River
31. Pauingassi
32. Sagkeeng (Ft. Alexander)

©Map by Zoltán Grossman,
(grossmaz@evergreen.edu)
Adapted from *Wisconsin's Past and Present:
A Historical Atlas* (U.W. Press, 2002),
by the Wisconsin Cartographers' Guild; and
the Midwest Treaty Network (treatyland.com)

Selected Anishinaabe Communities

INTRODUCTION

Not all magicians have been old nor have all aged persons been shamans; but superannuation and the supernatural have been very commonly linked.

—Leo Simmons, *The Role of the Aged in Primitive Society*

 In the Ojibwe language, a number of terms apply to elders. The primary one is *gichi anishinaabe* ("great person"), nothing short of the paragon of humanity, a Mensch. An "old man" is an *akiwenzii*, glossed by one Ojibwe source as "long dweller on the earth"; to call a woman "an old woman," *mindimooyenh*, is a huge compliment. An elder is also known as a *gichi-aya'aa* ("a great/old being there" or "s/he that is greater"), a term that can also be applied to impressive or aged animals, trees, and plants. Even the verb denoting the plain fact of being aged, *gikaa-*, can be closely related by Native speakers to the root term for understanding or wisdom, *gikendam-*.

In Ojibwe social life, there are few relationships as important or intimate as that between grandchild and grandparent. Grandparents have been, and importantly still are, the primary educators of the young people in matters of ethics and tradition. In Ojibwe kinship, anyone of one's grandparents' generation is potentially their *nookomis* ("grandmother") or *nimishoomis* ("grandfather"). This relationship is so significant to Ojibwe life that grandparent becomes the primary symbol for imagining the divine and guiding how one is to relate to the divine. Prayers address the spirits as grandfathers and grandmothers, and thus lay claim to that privileged relationship in relationships between people and the spiritual sources of existence.

Perhaps it is unsurprising that a Native American community should make such claims, given the romantic image of the wise old Indian that film and popular culture reinforces.[1] But if Anishinaabe people do succeed in distinctively honoring elders, it is emphatically not because they *naturally* do so. Instead, honoring elders has required hard work, the disciplined labor of moral teaching, and the ritualized decorum that constitute the authority of elders through practices of *deference*. Practices of deference, in turn, have created conditions fostering the exercise of a way of knowing in practices of *sagacity*, also performed in the idiom of ceremonious decorum: practices of speech, silence, and wisdom.[2] While oral history and early accounts suggest that eldership thus constituted and exercised surely held sway in aboriginal days, more striking still is how Anishinaabe communities have doggedly held onto—even accentuated—their maxim to "honor elders" amid the momentous and rapid changes since contact with Euro-Americans. Indeed it is a major contention of this study that improvised practices of eldership have proved a key resource in the artful survival of dispossession and assimilation. This juncture between a timeless tradition of honoring elders and the timely value of that tradition amid the deep challenges of contemporary Native life could be no clearer than in the words of White Earth elder Gladys Ray:

> I think the main reason I have stayed with my own culture and religion is because of my grandparents. I respected them. They were such a large part of my childhood. I was very fond of these beautiful old people. I've always felt that if I could be the kind of grandma that my grandma was to me, then I really had succeeded in my life. My grandma and grandpa had time for us. They were our teachers and counselors, a constant reminder of who we were—who I was.[3]

Gladys Ray's comments are not extraordinary, but in my view, they signal an extraordinary truth: recognized elders have not only served as models of proper behavior, they have effectively become embodiments of a communal identity in a manner similar to the king in medieval European societies. Perhaps it is more than mere ceremonial language that drafters had in mind for article 22 of the 2007 United Nations *Declaration of the Rights of Indigenous Peoples*: "Particular attention shall be paid to the rights and special needs of indigenous elders, women, youth, children and persons with disabilities."[4]

. . .

"Honor the elders" is certainly a ubiquitous phrase in Indian country, but apart from a few notable exceptions, the academic literature of Native studies has yet to come to fuller terms with the rich cultural and historical contexts that give eldership depth and complexity over time in the context of specific Native communities.[5] Unfortunately the literature on religious studies, too, offers little sustained analysis, and this despite the fact that the authority of age and the figure of the elder are important features on the landscape of most religious traditions, and while indigenous traditions make this plain, they are by no means unique in assigning importance to the religious authority of age. One thinks of the recognized religious authority of aged *curanderas* in Mexican and Mexican American Catholicism, of "Mothers" in African American holiness and pentecostal communities, of the fourth life stage of Hinduism's Brahmin priesthood, of the shaikh in Islamic cultures of central and south Asia, and of course the often prominent authority of the aged in Confucian, Buddhist, and Taoist traditions of east Asia.

Drawing on archival and ethnographic sources, as well as my own cumulative two years of fieldwork, this book examines the significance of aging in an Anishinaabe understanding of the life course, the authority of eldership for Anishinaabe culture and religion, and the career of aging and eldership over time, especially as it fared in the context of Christian missions in the reservation era and again in the context of the renewal of tradition from the 1970s on. Anishinaabe eldership is complex in its own right and worthy of close study, but the book also aims, using this example, to put the elder in its rightful place in the sociology of religion adjacent to the priest, the prophet, and the shaman and to create a fuller appreciation for age as a category of analysis in the study of religion. Along the way, I trust these contributions to academic literatures will have helped nourish a broader aging readership of boomers concerned with the significance of our own old age and others to consider not just the meanings of an individual's aging but the importance of the authority of elders to the health and sustainability of communities. Finally, there is, I think, a central contribution to historical and Native studies in terms of the claim that since tradition is what elders say it is, any understanding of the complex relationship between tradition and change in Ojibwe history must come to fuller terms with the precise nature of the authority of eldership.

Tradition is, of course, a loaded term in modern thought; since the Enlightenment the term has designated the monochromatic background to the rationalism, progress, science, and secularization of modernity, on the one hand, or the font of timeless wisdom for modernity's discontents, on the other. Following in the "tradition" of sociologist Edward Shils and historians Eric Hobsbawm and Terence Ranger, there have been a number of supple analyses of tradition as a processual matter inevitably involving the contentious situating of "the past in the present," part and parcel of modernity, rather than as a discrete product prior to it.[6] As concerns Native American communities, the structures of orality and the history of colonialism mean that tradition carries a charge that should complicate any straightforward application of these more mainstream discussions of tradition to Native contexts. Here, Raymond Bucko's discussion of tradition as a dialectic between past and present is particularly helpful. Bucko's analysis is designed to account for both the continuity and the heterogeneity of practice of the *inipi*, or Lakota sweat lodge ceremonial complex, where the authority of experience leads, even within one linguistic and cultural group, to a heterogeneity of practice that is difficult to square with conventional wisdom surrounding "tradition."[7] My understanding of Anishinaabe eldership, however, goes further than merely declaring tradition to be a dialectic of the past and the present: I wish to identify the culturally and historically marked contours of a *tradition of authority* that molds and shapes the way that dialectic is to play out at any moment in time.

Coming to grips with eldership as a structure of the authority of tradition can, I contend, help rethink a stalemate of sorts that has beset for some time the academic study of Native American traditions, and with material consequences in legal and political processes for Native communities themselves. Ethnohistorians who wish to expose the historicity and discontinuities of "invented traditions" over time have challenged and been challenged in turn by scholars and Native leaders concerned to defend the profound continuities of Native American traditions against claims felt to undercut cultural legitimacy and even undermine Native sovereignty.[8] The evidence of this book helps contend afresh that, *since tradition is what elders say it is*, there has been in the persistent if changing recognition of elder's authority the possibility for negotiating change and continuity, tradition and history, indigenous religion and Christianity, on Native terms that cannot merely be chalked up to the "invention" of tradition. In exploring the practices of deference and wisdom that, over time, have created these dynamic conditions, this book brings a consideration of tradition and history together in a new way through a consideration of Anishinaabe eldership.

Eldership in the Anishinaabe Way, in Tradition and History

When Andrew Makade-bineshi Blackbird put pen to paper in the 1880s to describe the distinctiveness of his Odawa culture to Anglo-Americans, he identified an insistence on honoring elders as a central and distinguishing tenet. Importantly, Blackbird was also trying to assure his readers that Odawa culture would prove an asset, not a liability, to their continuing productive presence in northern Michigan, so he organized these tenets of Anishinaabe life "in its primitive state" in terms of twenty-one commandments or precepts that "were almost the same as the ten commandments which the God Almighty himself delivered to Moses." These precepts were oral in nature, "continual inculcations to the children by their parents, and in every feast and council by the 'Instructors of the Precepts' to the people or to the audience of the council."[9] They went well beyond the Fifth Commandment's injunction to honor father and mother, but they ultimately followed the logic of, and clarified the implications of, that Fifth Commandment. Three of Blackbird's twenty-one precepts concerned respect for the authority of one's elders:

6th   Honor thy father and thy mother, that thy days may be long upon the land.

7th   Honor the gray head persons, that thy head may also be like unto theirs.

9th   Hold thy peace, and answer not back, when thy father or thy mother or any aged person should chastise thee for thy wrong.

Blackbird offers a useful starting point for a cultural history of Anishinaabe eldership not only because he places the authority of age at the center of his representation of those traditions for an audience that he thought could actually admire that feature of Anishinaabe life. He also illustrates the presenting problem of this cultural history. A rendering of Odawa and Ojibwe tradition in terms of the distinctive regard for the "gray headed" makes meaningful reference to an Anishinaabe tradition that one Ojibwe consultant told me has "gone on for at least forty thousand years." It also bespeaks the historical position of Michigan Anishinaabeg in the 1880s, experiencing as they were a social cultural and demographic crisis that dramatically reduced the numbers of "gray heads" even while it accentuated their significance to the survival of the community and its distinctive culture.[10]

Blackbird's claim to the centrality of Anishinaabe eldership is at once timeless and timely, simultaneously a sounding into the deep continuity of Anishinaabe culture and an indicator of the juncture between his inherited cultural past and exigencies of his own historical moment, a juncture of what anthropologist Renato Rosaldo has called a "culture in motion."[11] This book's challenge is to do justice to both the continuity and the historicity of "honoring elders." If it is a tall order to fill, there is a certain necessity to it, for it will be my contention that an abiding facet of honoring elders in various phases of Anishinaabe history is that, in recognizing the capacity of elders in each successive generation to articulate for the following what Anishinaabe traditions are, Anishinaabe people have themselves negotiated continuity and change on indigenous terms that collapse the distinction. I'm asserting something more involved, I think, than the position taken by Edward Shils, Raymond Bucko, and others, that tradition represents a dialectic process of continuity and change. Instead, I'm arguing that eldership is itself a tradition of authority that frames that dialectic process in distinctive ways.

If, as Blackbird's appeal to twenty-one precepts shows, one cannot isolate a discussion of Anishinaabe tradition apart from its career in a series of historical moments, one can still distinguish shades of gray between continuity and change in such traditions. The first half of each of the thematically organized chapters is devoted to the project of attending particularly to deep continuities of eldership as a tradition. The second half of each chapter emphasizes historical changes to eldership and the practices surrounding it. Because both oral traditions and written sources involve both the continuities and the changes, the source materials for each discussion are largely the same: seventeenth-century observations by French Jesuit missionaries, eighteenth- and nineteenth-century travel and fur-trade narratives in English, nineteenth- and twentieth-century representations of indigenous customs by bicultural Anishinaabe figures (and often Christian clergyman) like Blackbird, ethnographic attempts by professional anthropologists in the twentieth century to isolate and document timeless Ojibwe traditions, transcribed oral narratives of myths and legends and "teachings," and contemporary oral exchanges with contemporary Ojibwe and Odawa people.

Since evidence for both continuity and change comes from the same pool of source material, the reader is encouraged to consider the first half of each chapter not as a clean representation of a traditional baseline to the historical change undergone by Anishinaabe communities and culture, but as one witness to a multifaceted phenomenon that can emerge in full only by considering its historical permutations as the chapter progresses, with particular interest at two moments in Ojibwe history. First is the early-reservation-era encounter with Christian missions—more particularly the way that Ojibwe people attempted, in the practices of what they termed *Anami'aawin* (prayer), to make room within the confines of missionary Christianity to continue practices of a meaningful Ojibwe lifeway. Second, eldership came again into pronounced relief a century later in the conscious turn to elders' authority by Native people in the rekindling of traditions in the 1970s.

A story from my own experience can further illustrate the historicity of this tradition and the traditionality of the historical. Ten years ago, I found myself in the packed gym of the Minneapolis American Indian Center, where then freshman Senator Paul Wellstone, along with the head of the Bureau of Indian Affairs, had arranged a town hall meeting with the local Native community. As one might expect, the senator had a number of places to be that afternoon, and his schedule afforded but one hour for this meeting, but in good Ojibwe custom, the meeting began with a tobacco offering and invocation in Ojibwe by Archie Mosay from Turtle Lake, Wisconsin. Mosay or Niibaagizhig, Sleeping Sky, a Midéwiwin and Big Drum leader, teacher, and activist who was in his early nineties, had been identified as the most esteemed elder present and had been approached in his wheelchair in the audience just moments before to do the honors. I trust that few in the room would have been able to fully comprehend the prayer, given the tragic loss of fluency in the language, but even if they knew Ojibwe, he carried on in the high register, rapid cadence, and sometime mumbling voice that typifies formal Ojibwe prayer: more intercession than invocation.

What was so striking is that he prayed, and prayed, and prayed ... and prayed for *over fifteen minutes* (such Ojibwe prayers are often careful catalogues of thanksgivings). More remarkable was that none of the Native organizers batted an eye, nor for that matter could they have broken the elder's momentum if they had wanted. The only ones nervously glancing at their watches were the twenty-something Senate staffer and then Wellstone himself. When the prayer was finished, the public officials had to rush through their remarks, and the town hall interchange was reduced to a few questions.

To the senator's aide, I'm sure, the old man was out of touch, oblivious of the fitness of things. But from another perspective, Mosay was masterful in his timing, completely in touch with what convention, and strategy, called for. He was laying claim to the space of the meeting by setting its proceedings in an indigenous idiom, syncopating its participants, including the "suits" on the dais, to other rhythms tied to other commitments and other reckonings of who has power over whom and whose time was important.

Some Considerations of Method

Personal experiences of such moments as this one at the Minneapolis American Indian Center have deeply impressed me as an ethnographic observer in Anishinaabe communities in Minnesota and have encouraged me to seek insight from oral traditional, archival, ethnohistorical, and earlier ethnographic materials in print as to how such traditions of eldership came to be, to change, and to survive. It will be helpful here to establish how my method of bringing ethnography and historical study into conversation in the same book works.

This project is rooted deeply in relationships at the White Earth Reservation with a group of elders, many of whom have since passed on, who organized and became identified by their White Earth Village community as Ojibwe Singers, revivers and custodians of a funerary tradition of singing Ojibwe-language hymns, which itself was an ironic outcome of colonialism, since hymns were translated and promoted by nineteenth-century missionaries as weapons to root out "Indianness" and inculcate patriarchal, agrarian, Christian values.

In *Ojibwe Singers*, I reflected at length on the authority and the limits of the authority of my own witness and interpretations of Anishinaabe events and lives over the course of the eight years that preceded that book's publication and that amounted to a bit less than two consecutive years. The relationships with Anishinaabe people out of which this current work emerges are largely congruent with those that gave rise to my observations in *Ojibwe Singers*, and so I won't recapitulate all the details, save my claim that my own perspectives on Anishinaabe culture are profoundly limited by the particularity of the relationships I have had with certain Ojibwe people. But on grounds of Anishinaabe ways of knowing, I submit that the contingencies of those particular relationships can serve not just as a constraint, but also a more secure grounding, for the authority of my observations and interpretations, especially as I aspire to place my writing and reflection in networks of accountability to Anishinaabe communities, especially on the White Earth and Leech Lake Reservations and in the Twin Cities community. In this book, as was the case in *Ojibwe Singers*, my narrative of Anishinaabe culture and history is "avowedly fragmentary, local, interested, collaborative, and accountable," and I refer the reader to the more extensive discussion of this method in the preface to that book.

If the ethnographic research and reflection of this book springs from that of the previous book, these relationships are considerably more temporally removed in this current work. My principal teacher and consultant, Larry Cloud Morgan, whose impact will be clearer in these pages, died shortly before the publication of *Ojibwe Singers* and well before my ideas for this book began to crystallize. Other elders who deeply impressed me in the years of traveling with Larry have also passed away and inform this study deeply, if through the mediation, perhaps obfuscation, of my own memory and field notes. But that temporal remove has also had some benefits for the current study. Although raising a family and taking on demanding teaching positions have made more difficult the kind of lengthy, grounded fieldwork that animated my first book, the relationships

I have with Anishinaabe friends have matured with time and with new circumstances. The reach of these relations has expanded to new circles of Anishinaabe people, especially to those colleagues in the academic community. I aspire to present my own ideas but also to vet and temper them with Anishinaabe consultants and readers, not simply for the purposes of accuracy, but for the purposes of relevance and ethical reflection. At the time of this writing, there admittedly remains more work on my part to solicit those conversations, and I invite elders, scholars, and community people to pose questions of this book, to me and more publicly, in hopes of an ongoing conversation that is more accurate still.

As for the historical research that supports this book, I have reread much of the missionary correspondence archived in the Minnesota Historical Society, both in the Protestant Episcopal Diocese of Minnesota papers, the extensive Henry Benjamin Whipple papers, and the American Board of Commissioners for Foreign Missions papers relevant to the Great Lakes region archived in Harvard's Houghton Library but mercifully copied and catalogued in the Grace Lee Nute collection at the Minnesota Historical Society. I have also read with great interest published travel narratives, collections of myths and oral traditions, "self-representations" of Native culture and life by the likes of Andrew Blackbird and George Copway in the nineteenth century and Ignatia Broker and Edward Benton-Banai in the twentieth century, as well as the quite extensive ethnographic record on Anishinaabe communities amassed by social scientists like A. I. Hallowell, Frances Densmore, Ruth Landes, and Inez Hilger.

It is my conviction that the archival and textual research has usefully framed my reflection on ethnographic observations and experiences by suggesting both the profound continuities, but also historical changes involved with traditions of honoring elders. By turns, I'm also convinced that the cumulative time I've spent visiting with Anishinaabe friends and consultants, and the observations I've made, have sharpened my focus on the significance of certain details, perhaps committed to the historical record only in passing by missionaries, travelers, or casual observers. It has also made me even more perplexed about the surprising lack of analysis in the less casual observations of professional ethnologists in the ethnographic record.

Finally, I should speak to the scope of the research. I was encouraged by another publisher to consider writing a book about eldership across Native

American traditions, limiting my work on the Anishinaabe to one chapter. I took umbrage, frankly, that that publisher could overlook my obvious point that Anishinaabe traditions of eldership, and the history in which eldership has played out over time, are sophisticated enough to warrant a book-length treatment. That said, my analysis extends at points beyond the Anishinaabe proper to related Cree, Oji-Cree, and Algonquin communities, in order to draw on important scholarship and resources focused on eldership in those community contexts.

Elders: Seen But Not Heard in the Ethnographic Record

Anyone having traveled in Indian country knows it: "honoring elders" is perhaps the most emphatic maxim of Native social teaching, and if it is not uniformly practiced according to the ideal, a distinctive regard for the aged is no less tangibly present in Indian country. And it has a deep history. Peter Jones wrote, for example, in the 1830s, "No people reverence old age more than the Indians. The advice of the uhkewaihsee, or long dweller upon the earth, is generally listened to with great attention."[12] Any number of such references to the importance of elders to Anishinaabe communities are made in the extensive ethnohistorical and ethnographic record on the Ojibwe.[13]

Given its ubiquity now and in the past, it is perplexing just how seldom eldership receives sustained analytic or interpretive attention in that ethnographic record, even as it receives frequent mention in passing. When eldership does get more than a sentence of treatment, it is in discussions of an individual's passage through the life cycle, but seldom do these observations inform their more pressing analyses of social structure, authority, or religious leadership.

Diamond Jenness, Ruth Landes, and Frances Densmore directly discuss the life cycle of the Ojibwe, but none of them includes even a sentence about the period of life between marriage and death. Even Landes, who clearly tried to organize *The Ojibwa Woman* in terms of the life cycle, sequenced her chapters in this way: "Youth," "Marriage," "Occupations," and "Abnormalities." In effect, she made no structural provision to consider the place of age in one of her key findings: the capacity of women like elder Maggie Wilson (her primary consultant) to freely cross the gendered boundaries of spiritual vocations in particular.

Where old age does appear in discussions of the life cycle, as it does in the work of A. I. Hallowell, E. S. Rogers, and Robert Ritzenthaler, it pales in comparison to the treatment of puberty, marriage, and death.[14] The most expansive treatment is Hallowell's on the "terminologically distinguished age grades corresponding to maturation status" in his 1937 essay on Ojibwe temporal orientation.[15] But the selfsame scholar who lifted up *bimaadiziwin*, "the good life"—life and longevity in the fullest sense—as an Ojibwe ultimate concern, contents himself with a brief discussion of the ultimate stage of life (what by his own account could be identified as a religious attainment in its own right) by documenting the terms for old women, men, and people: *mindimooyenh*, *akiwenzii*, or *kete anishinaabe*.

Jenness and Hilger make more substantial reference to eldership in the life cycle, but do so in discussions of other stages of the life cycle, especially as they remark on the crucial role of grandparents in the ethical training of youth[16] and in offering impetus, preparation, and subsequent spiritual direction to young people undertaking their vision fast.[17]

When discussions of old age appear occasionally also under the rubric of kinship, the relational nature of eldership comes through with further clarity as a matter of social organization. This makes a certain sense since ethnologists affirm generally the central role of kinship in a social world that lacks other strong structures beyond the family. In these treatments, mapped of course by kinship terminology, older people appear in their aspect as ego's grandparents or great-grandparents. Rogers makes detailed observations about the special relations effected in this bond. Landes and Hallowell go further to follow relationships effected beyond bloodlines between grandchildren and all members of that class of elders of the grandparent generation, or *gichi anishinaabe* ("great people").[18] But curiously such observations remain confined to discussions of kinship, which clearly are not also discussions of social organization beyond the familial.[19]

Even Landes's four-page disquisition entitled "Political Organization" in *Ojibwa Sociology* makes only terse, and apparently self-evident, reference to a "council of elders" that obtains in spring and summer *odenas* (bands comprised of three to fifteen families) whose male members are accorded "a conventional respect" and who assemble to discuss anything that may be "of communal import," such as puberty fasts and war parties.

Even more overt studies of Ojibwe political organization make frequent reference to *ogimaag* ("chiefs") and shaman leaders, but fail to make of their consistent old age a matter for inquiry. Persuaded by the ethnographic record's attention to the link between a leader's authority and the accrual and exercise of dream power, I don't mean to suggest here that age is the only or even the primary determinant of a leader's authority; but reviewing the literature from the perspective of the contemporary significance of elders begs the question of why the ethnographers so frequently reference the extreme age of the highest status individuals without making anything out of that observation.

As with the specific ethnographic record on the Ojibwe, anthropological attention to old age generally has confined itself largely to discussions of an individual's passage through "the life cycle"—and thus largely left unexamined the place of age in matters of authority and social structure. Interest has been aging, not eldership. Similarly overlooked is how complexly old age can mute gender distinctions. Eldership is, of course, profoundly gendered itself, especially insofar as gender norms are "aged." The Ojibwe ethnographic record is representative of that on other peoples for whom elders are significant features on the social and religious landscape. Even ethnographies of societies with clearly demarcated age-grading pay surprisingly scarce attention to the shape of the authority of oldest age-sets.[20]

How and why this is the case surely carries implications for considerations of other Native peoples like the Anishinaabeg. It could mean one of at least three possibilities. The first is that ethnologists like Jenness, Densmore, Landes, and Hallowell together missed the significance of eldership even though it was right under their noses. The second is that eldership as we know it is principally a twentieth-century invented tradition, a product of colonizing encounters, as Sam Gill has argued was the case (rather problematically in my view) with the concept of Mother Earth.[21] A third, more plausible, middle position finds that Anishinaabe eldership has been in considerable historical motion, taking on a force in the late twentieth century that dramatically accentuated what went before. But this is not to speak of an invented tradition.

For a variety of reasons, early ethnographers did not assign adequate significance to what they heard and observed about the authority of age.

They made many scattered references to aging and eldership, but these references never really went anywhere because of a taxonomy where eldership is seen as a facet of the *natural life cycle of individuals*, not a structure of social relations beyond the family or a domain of significance to religion or worldview. If references to eldership occasionally elude this classificatory scheme, they are ultimately eclipsed by the controlling ideas that captured the interpretive imaginations of early ethnographers and established the framework for subsequent sociological interpretation of the Ojibwe: namely what Victor Barnouw termed Ojibwe "atomism" or Landes called Ojibwe "individualism," or by a focus on the shamanic dream authority that Mary Black-Rogers and others referred to tersely as "power."

Ojibwe atomism and individualism were largely derived from considerations of Northern Ojibwe social life and were, as Harold Hickerson observed, embroiled in a theoretical move that Hallowell, Landes, Barnouw, and other American anthropologists were keen to make: that so-called primitive societies were not plainly communal in orientation, as Lewis Morgan and, significantly, Marx and Engels had believed.[22] Despite the criticisms of Hickerson, Vivian Rohrl, and Theresa Schenk, such correctives have yet to breathe analytical life into how eldership might be part of the equation.[23] As this book makes clear, I think, for example, that observed respect for elders was then as now more than a concern of interpersonal etiquette; such codes of respect in effect configured authority in ways that gave Ojibwe communities a significant if noninstitutionalized structure of authority that extended beyond the bloodlines of family or the centripetal draw of charismatic authority around the powerful medicine person.

Hallowell took this sociological understanding of Ojibwe atomism/individualism and explained it in psychological terms. In the tradition of Landes's insight that Ojibwe life was predicated on the accrual of individual power from dreams and visions and noting that such power could be used for good or evil, Hallowell found its antisocial implications. "It is impossible for people to get together," he wrote, "when their outlook is colored by the possibility of malevolence, particularly when there are no social institutions."[24] Religious power (dream power) and social power are aligned most prominently in the figure of the powerful medicine men. In Weberian terms, these figures would be wielders more of the dynamically flowing *charismatic authority* than the *traditional authority* one might associate with eldership, and to be sure one cannot say that chronological age alone conferred authority, much less respect, in Ojibwe communities. Still, medicine people so captured the imaginations of early ethnographers up through Hallowell, his students, and their later readers (e.g., John Grim), that their status as dreamers has wholly obscured their frequent status also as elders.

To be sure, dream power was profoundly generative in the religious and social life of Ojibwe communities aboriginally and thereafter. But what do we make of a certain confusion in the early ethnographic record about the relationship between the sacred power that sustains and prolongs life in this world and the length of lives lived by virtue of it? Landes came to the conclusion that power, like the person wielding it, matures. "Hence," she wrote, "the mighty shamans are 'old' and always termed so in deepest respect and fear. To say 'old man' was synonymous with saying 'great shaman.'"[25] This makes a certain kind of sense in a tradition that regarded the relationship between humans and spirits of all sorts in terms the relationship between grandchildren and grandparents. But the respect that animates those relationships, which she documents in *Ojibwa Sociology* and *The Ojibwa Woman*, yields in Landes's reckoning to pathological fear of the antisocial possibilities of the most potent shamans' power. Rogers is more honest in his confusion about whether individual power increases over lifetime. He reported that his sources suggested that power dissipates, not matures, with age.[26] In a footnote to the observation, however, Rogers acknowledges that the position conflicts with the sense that power increases, and he observes that this was a tradition undergoing "violent change."[27] Dunning's 1959 study of that change suggests a general devaluation of the "charismatic prestige of the magico-medical expert" to the more dispersed and mundane "rule of implicit and impersonal gossip groups."[28] In light of Hallowell's keen insight into the ultimacy of the good life well lived and long lived, it is especially ironic that aging and, more particularly, eldership should receive such short shrift in the ethnologists' more sweeping interpretations of Ojibwe life, worldview, and social order. Atomism, individualism, and the power that drives them involve little room for the more social, and mundane, authority of age and eldership—an unremarkable stage, if identified as a discrete stage at all, in the natural life cycle.

On this point of power, we can account, I think, for the lack of attention in the extensive ethnographic record to eldership as such, for what has captured the imagination of ethnographers (Hallowell, Densmore, Landes) of the Ojibwe and religious studies interpreters who read them has been the shaman, the medicine men and women affiliated with the ceremonial Midéwiwin society or with the healing and divination arts of the *jiisakii* shaking tent ceremony, labels that mark them as religious specialists and thus as worthy of the attention of the sociology of religion. But while there is a contrast between the shaman's more identifiably charismatic authority and the elder's traditional authority and while the latter has waxed in the twentieth century as the former has waned, the distinction seems to be more one of degree than kind, as Weber's framework would suggest. First, by virtue of their accrual through dreams of ritual, medicinal, and clairvoyant knowledge/power, these medicine people (like elders) have come to exercise authority associated with political and social life as well as with ceremony. Second, the more powerful of medicine men and women were coded in terms of old age: addressed by indirection and honorific titles like *akiwenzii* and *mindimooyenh*, translatable as "that old man" or "that old woman." Even here, power is no mere function of religious virtuosity but rather a kind of maturation. If the more powerful shamans are old, why has their agedness (admittedly itself a cultural construction, but a significant one) gone unremarked in shaman studies?

If it remains too subtle and isolated to fully integrate an understanding of the authority of age, religious power, and the life cycle, perhaps a nod in the right direction can be found in the one other place that elders qua *elders* receive consistent mention as ritual specialists: the naming ceremony, which I examine in detail in chapter 5. "In nearly all cases," Jenness wrote, "the parents commissioned an old man [other sources mention older women as well], whose age indicated that he had enjoyed the favour of the supernatural world, to discover a suitable name for their child. . . . The old man generally devised a name from some incident in the vision that had come to him during his boyhood fast, but occasionally he sought a special dream for the occasion, or accepted the name suggested by some dream of the baby's parent or relative."[29]

Ethnographers found deeper significance in the sociology of this practice than they could identify without reference beyond purely social or material terms. According to Landes in *Ojibwa Sociology*, the reference concerns the powerful fictive kin relationship formed between namesakes, *niiawe*, but she notes that the situation of terminological identity between namer and named "is incomprehensible in terms of behavior or associated with the kinship system." Instead it "must be viewed as related to another system of thought, the securing of supernatural power."[30] Barnouw carried the conversation further in the direction of relating life cycle, kinship, and the acquisition of power by noting that the naming ceremony constituted the only instance for the sharing of "supernatural power," an otherwise "private resource."[31] Where Jenness discussed infancy in the "Cycles of Life and Death," he observed that good names were crucial to a baby's physical and spiritual survival, and he understood the ceremony as a kind of exchange of life force or power that may have suggested the double possibility for power's maturation and dissipation in old age.

Although the insights here remained locked up in a discussion of the naming ceremony and in the life cycle, they render visible a comprehensive understanding of proper passage through the life cycle, requiring power variously shared and gifted through dreams and properly exercised, as an Ojibwe ultimate concern. The elder offering the name and its power— often her or his own dream power—could extend through this gift nothing less than what anthropologist Jeffrey Anderson calls "life movement." This is no narrow story of infancy alone. Neither is it a mere detailing of a notable kinship relation between namesakes. Neither still is it an offhand remark about the etiquette of respecting one's elders: it is an insight into the way that social relations, ritual, cosmology, and life cycle come together.

Anderson observed among the Northern Arapaho that, as "people matured, they became more and more 'human' and thus more and more Arapaho."[32] If this is also the case among the Ojibwe, as I believe it was and is, then how are we to regard anew the significance of age and the authority of eldership in Ojibwe life? Hallowell, the most likely of the ethnologists to make these interpretive connections, was apparently beginning to do so on this particular issue late in his career. In a posthumously published 1976 essay entitled "Northern Ojibwa Ecological Adaptation and Social Organization," Hallowell concludes with a series of three observations, and since these are prospective as much as conclusive, a reader can reasonably conjecture that, had he lived longer, Hallowell would have paid even more attention to their elucidation. First, Hallowell observes, the kin terms pertaining to grandfather and grandmother extend to the entire generation of one's blood grandparents and always carry "overtones of respect associated with advanced age, experience, and presumed wisdom." This observation segues to a discussion of the naming ceremony and elders' distinct role in it, which in turn occasions a discussion of the authority that comes from elders' proximity and more frequent contact with other-than-human persons. Here Hallowell reiterates a point he made in a previous essay about the homology between the kinship terms for grandparents/elders and the terms of address for spirits, or other-than-human persons. Implied is a claim on Hallowell's part that kinship terminology, ceremonial activity that privileges elders' authority, and elders' special proximity to the world of other-than-human persons are of a piece and should be reckoned with in a larger understanding of the Ojibwe worldview, culture, and society. Given that, "collectively, other-than-human persons were referred to as 'our grandfathers,'" Hallowell concludes, "the relationship between grandparents and grandchildren leads us directly from a consideration of the interrelated roles of the Ojibwa social structure to their traditional worldview. An understanding of their cognitive outlook is necessary for a comprehension of the functioning of their sociocultural system as a whole."[33]

The Absence of Elders in the Study of Religion and Anthropology

If the ethnographic record on the Ojibwe and other Native American peoples offers little sustained analysis of the elder, neither do the canonical interpretive texts in the sociology and anthropology and history of religions, and for related reasons. At best, the aged are a subheading of the individual life cycle. As such, they are segmented off from the weightier discussion of social organization, authority, and religious specialization.

Neither the first nor second edition of Mircea Eliade's *Encyclopedia of Religion*, the reference work of record for the history of religions, includes an entry for elder.[34] An entry in Jonathan Z. Smith's *Dictionary of Religion* includes only several sentences about elders in Presbyterian polity. Arnold Van Gennep's generative *Rites of Passage* omits any discussion of life passage between marriage and death, and one is hard pressed to find in other treatments of the life cycle a consideration of seniority and old age—this despite a number of "great traditions" for which the period of old age is ritually marked and religiously significant.

Even Max Weber, with all his interest in varieties of religious authority, entertains no sustained discussion of the elder: this despite his own observation that "gerontocracy" is among the "most elementary types" of traditional authority.[35] That Weber should not attend to the nuance or variety of traditional authority is unsurprising, for we know it interested him primarily as a sort of foil to the contrastive charismatic and bureaucratic authority associated with differentiation, rationalization, and modernization.[36]

Trying to deepen Weber's work by paying closer sociological attention to the nuances of so-called primitive societies, Joachim Wach, while noting in passing the significance of age in the allocation of authority in small-scale societies of which he was an ethnographic omnivore, failed to assign a discussion of elder in his concluding discussion of figures of religious authority.[37] For Wach as for Weber, the elder falls under the radar of a sociological interest in religious *specialists* and virtuosos whose authority signals the differentiation of the religious from other aspects of society and culture. The specifically religious authority of eldership has never been thus cleanly differentiated from the political, social, and cultural authority. If the figure of the elder is crucial to understanding the dynamics of authority in most indigenous religions, and if religious authority pertaining to old age stands in complex relation with other sources of priestly, charismatic, and experiential authority in the lived reality of all religious traditions, there is a curious lack of sustained interest in it in the sociology of religion and the history of religions rooted in this earlier sociology.

How then, one asks, can there be so many indigenous societies around the globe organized significantly around the authority of elders with so little sustained analysis of the figure of the elder. An outlier perhaps, anthropologist Leo Simmons, who had himself been deeply impressed by the figure of a Hopi spiritual leader whose biography he authored, sought to identify a broader contribution for the anthropology of aging in the 1940s. He combed through references across the Human Area Resource Files, a compendium of ethnographies of the world's societies that was thematically indexed to enable cross-cultural study of human phenomena, and produced a magisterial study, *The Role of the Aged in Primitive Society*. Simmons drew on ethnological materials from more than seventy societies and put an empirical mark on a commonplace: "The most striking fact about respect for old age is its widespread occurrence [in primitive societies]." Although the particulars in each culture were varied, "some degree of prestige for the aged seems to have been practically universal."[38] Of course his work took rather unproblematically as "data" the ethnographic products of early ethnological encounters, themselves significantly shaped by colonialism.[39] Still, Simmons made a number of observations that tied the authority and significance of old age to the concerns of the religious: "Not all magicians have been old nor have all aged persons been shamans," Simmons observed, "but superannuation and the supernatural have been very commonly linked."[40] For Simmons, the link between superannuation and the supernatural had to do with the control the aged tend to exercise over resources of sacred knowledge and sacred paraphernalia associated with interpreting mysterious phenomena and addressing difficult circumstances. Simmons writes, "Truly have [the old] been the guardian's of life's emergencies, the custodians of knowledge, and the directors of ceremonies and pastimes. In possession of such great influence, they have been the chief conservators of the status quo. And finally, after death, they have become supernatural agents themselves."[41]

Some thirty years later, a more robust anthropology of aging began to emerge, resulting in a number of collaborative volumes drawing on a range of ethnographic material to assert some broader comparative insights.[42] In the Native American literature, Pamela Amoss considered the way that assimilation and culture change has accented the authority of elders in the Pacific Northwest, and she documents their continued importance in community political and cultural life.[43] Observing that the old fare best in societies when they contribute or control resources that are vital or desirable to the group, the literature notes that cultural resources, rather than economic and political capital, are more typically significant to old age. In primarily oral traditions, elders are the libraries of cultural memory, myth, ritual, and ethics, and because they maintain, allocate, and distribute this knowledge, elders bring something important to the well-being of community.

This anthropology of aging literature hastens, perhaps following Simmons's lead years before, to tether the authority of age to the allocation of resources necessary to community well-being. Culture, and particularly the sacred knowledge, practices, and paraphernalia associated with religion, is seen in subtly functionalist terms, just as the religious

Kahbenagwiwens, or John Smith, of the Leech Lake Ojibwe, was often depicted on postcards as a commodified symbol of the old Indian, billing him as a wizened man who lived in three centuries characterized by tragedy and loss. The 1919 postcard on the left thus isolates Smith and his age as a curio for the region's summer tourist industry. By contrast, the 1919 photograph on the right shows him as people would have encountered him on the street, often accompanied by family and community. *Photographs courtesy of Minnesota Historical Society.*

authority of age is a function, objectively viewed, of the religious and cultural knowledge they control in an economy of resource allocation. Religious phenomena are resources, reduced to their value to community survival.

A number of ethnographic efforts in the late 1970s and early 1980s began to provide a richer, less tidy, view of the place of old age in culture and society. Among the most artful of these was Barbara Myerhoff's *Number Our Days*, an ethnography of a Jewish senior center outside Los Angeles. Myerhoff shows how Jewish tradition, perhaps especially the emphasis on lifelong learning, equips the members of the *Aliyah* center with a profound sense of dignity and purpose late in life, but she also captures the contradictions as a generation of Yiddish-speaking holocaust survivors tries to make due amid the isolation from family, the loneliness, and the poverty that stand in such relief to expectations based on those official cultural traditions.[44]

But it was not until the 1990s that a broader number of anthropologists would come to write head-on about the place of the aging and eldership in Native communities in a manner that did not reduce the authority of age and eldership to some other terms. Two works in particular stand out, one a collaborative book on grandmothers in a range of Native communities assembled and edited by Marjorie Schweitzer, and the other a masterful ethnographic study of old age, society, and cosmology in Northern Arapaho culture and history by Jeffrey Anderson.[45] Insights from Anderson, in particular, will help give depth at moments throughout the present analysis. At this juncture, it is useful to heed Anderson's observation about the perils of cultural anthropology's failure to deliver an adequate account of the authority of elders. "Only a few of the oldest people," Anderson writes," possessed at any given time knowledge of the total cosmological order. Out of that fact has arisen one of the greatest barriers to understanding the so-called worldviews of North American Indian cultures."[46] Anderson adds that this also may explain the lack of sustained examination by ethnologists of eldership and age generally.[47]

In sum, the anthropology of aging, including that concerning Native American traditions, is only beginning to reckon with the religious authority of the elder, with considering old age not simply as a part of the life course but as a salient social distinction pivotal for social relations. And while there are a number of important recent efforts among historians of religion to establish *age* as a significant category of analysis in religious studies, there remains much work to do with respect to older stages of life.[48]

Toward an Understanding of the Elder via the Anishinaabe Example

Grounded as it is in the details of Anishinaabe cultures and histories, this study perhaps can serve as a more purposeful step toward identifying the place of age and its authority in our reckoning of religion. I turn now to introduce the primary arguments I make about eldership in Anishinaabe tradition and in the context of the major turning points in Anishinaabe history. I trust such a condensed overview of the book can suggest at the outset what can be gained by taking age as a category of analysis in our reckoning of the authority of indigenous traditions, and perhaps any religious tradition at all.

As a starting point, taking age as a category of analysis must move beyond the study of individual aging and the characteristics or demographics specific to the old as a group to encompass the social relations in which the old find themselves. Any adequate study must work to interpret indigenous ways of idealizing eldership and its authority while also denaturalizing eldership, the better to come to grips with its practice as a social fact in place and over time. This study attends both to largely enduring cultural ideals of eldership but also to the historical changes to the practice and meanings of those cultural ideals. In this sense, this study of eldership is not simply a study of elders, but is also a study of ideals and practices of Anishinaabe sacred community that turn on the authority and example of eldership. Any study of this authority of eldership, in turn, must consider how old age is marked in three inseparable but distinguishable frames: how the authority of age is marked bodily, how old age is marked culturally, and how both are marked historically.

THE AGE OF ELDERSHIP

First, the Anishinaabe example instructs the student of eldership to consider how eldership is marked by and on aging bodies. While Ojibwe eldership is not age-specific, no mere function of biological age, crucially it remains age-related, a form of religious authority that acknowledges the maturation of the person over time and that values the ways of knowing such persons can master. Put succinctly: there have been, and are, old people who are not Elders with a capital E; but there are no Elders who are not also older, or who at least evidence the comportment and ways of knowing customary to old age.

There can be no shortcuts to eldership, for it rests in no small part on the maturation of Anishinaabe bodies and the maturation of the knowledge and power those bodies carry, not to mention the authority of experience accrued, tried, tested, and tempered over time. As indicated in the discussion of the controlling idea of power in the ethnology of the Ojibwe, elders as such are not the only—perhaps not even the primary—figures of religious leadership. Anishinaabe tradition privileges the authority of knowledge and power gifted by the spirits through visions and dreams to medicine women and men in a manner that is hardly age-specific. Indeed much of the authoritative ritual and healing knowledge/power classically comes through dreams in late youth or early adulthood. Religious specialists distinguished by this knowledge/power, or those they take as their apprentices and heirs, are seldom distinguished by their old age alone.

But again, the charismatic authority of what the literature often calls the shaman stands in a complex relationship with the traditional authority of age. Dream knowledge/power itself, though perhaps gifted in late youth, is seen by many to mature with the body of its owner. And the more powerful of medicine people were/are conceptualized in terms of age. To speak of "that old man" or "that old woman" classically was to acknowledge not simply the traditional authority of age, but also the more powerful wielders of charismatic authority. In the end, the charismatic authority of vision and dream is more closely connected with the accrual of traditional authority by aging and maturing Anishinaabe bodies/minds/souls than Max Weber's classic analytical distinction allows.

THE CULTURAL CONSTRUCTION OF LIFETIME AND OLD AGE

While aging is a physical phenomenon shared by all humans across culture and time, the life cycle, including the particular significance and authority assigned to aging bodies in a given society, is culturally constructed, and any study of eldership in any religious tradition must pay close attention to this aspect of the cultural imagination. In the Anishinaabe case, how the life cycle is marked relates closely to cosmological convictions about the processes of the universe and as a consequence frames the religious authority of eldership in those terms. Because the life course itself is a matter of ultimate concern, the biological facts of old age signify ethical rectitude, mastery of harmonious relations, and the exercise of spiritual power. The life cycle of an individual is a microcosm of the universal circle of life, encapsulated in the Ojibwe term *bimaadiziwin*. Hallowell glossed *bimaadiziwin* not as life, but as the "good life," encompassing the moral, aesthetic, and religious associations of the term. To live on the land, one must *live well* on the land, showing not only hard work and economic prowess but also a mastery of right relations with all other persons—which in an Ojibwe taxonomy includes nonhuman persons of the natural world (animals, plants, geological and weather phenomena) and of the spiritual world (ancestors, spirits, myths). Aging through the life passage here is no mere natural process; it is a moral attainment as well. On Ojibwe terms, as people mature, they stand the possibility of becoming more and more human, more and more Anishinaabe. In this scheme, the elder woman or man, commonly called *gichi anishinaabe* ("great person"), is the ethical paragon, the emulable practitioner of proper relations.

If old age could represent *ethical* attainment, it could also represent a *religious* feat, for Ojibwe tradition teaches that humans must rely on spiritual helpers for gifts of knowledge/power to live. "Ojibwe religious behavior," Hallowell wrote, "can be identified as any activity . . . that helps to promote a good life for human beings by making explicit recognition, direct or indirect, of man's faith in and dependence upon other-than-human persons.[49] In this aspect *bimaadiziwin* connotes a notion of power that is both rooted in relations with supernaturals while remaining an embodied biological and social fact as well. "A more telling gloss of *bima.diziwa.d*," writes Mary Black-Rogers, beyond "those who are alive," might be "those who have power."[50]

Anderson recently has understood the Arapaho community's version of *bimaadiziwin* as "life movement," a principle that the cosmos persists in ongoing motion by virtue of an ongoing generational exchange: elder generations pass on power and knowledge toward life to younger generations in return for respect.[51] *Respect*: no simple straightforward concept this. Indeed, because teaching respect for all things is the first and last word of Ojibwe people when speaking of their value system, a number of Ojibwe people have wondered how I could generate an entire book simply on respect for elders. In response, my second chapter places the virtue of respect for elders not simply as a matter of sentiment, etiquette, or blind deference to patriarchy, but as a *paradigmatic* ethical relation that grounds all other relations in the social, natural, and spiritual realms. In this it is comparable in depth and reach with Confucianism's "filial piety" (*xiao*), which over time came to be identified as the root of all other virtues, a matter of everyday etiquette and social ethics that has also been theologically elaborated into a kind of principle standing behind the ongoing universe. Although honoring elders in the Ojibwe tradition has not been the subject of extensive commentarial traditions as has Confucian filial piety, I think there is something comparably ultimate about that relationship worth exploring, something that links the moral, aesthetic, and cosmological.

Crucially, there is in Anishinaabe traditions a parallel, or homology, between the kinship terminology for one's elders and the terms of address for the spirits, including the all-encompassing *gichi manidoo* ("great spirit/mystery"). In the Ojibwe language and social world all members of one's grandparents' generation are addressed by and claimed as my grandfather (*nimishoomis*) and my grandmother (*nookomis*), extending the claiming of relationship to a grandparent to all elders of that generation. Although the Ojibwe tradition has no formal ancestor cult, the whole class of supernatural "persons"—drums, mythical beings, dream visitors, and spirits—is claimed by homology as one's elders, one's grandparents; conversely, one's elders/grandparents are regarded by homology in similar fashion as the spirits who take pity and offer gifts of ritual, practical, and medicinal knowledge/power. Following Clifford Geertz, scholars of religion have paid ample attention to how the symbol (in this case kinship term and thus mode of relationship) employed for the divine is both a "model of" and "model for" the iconic relation between grandchild and grandparent, between junior and elder. More recently, Robert Orsi has directed the study of religion to pay closer attention not simply to the "meaning" of such symbols, but to the social relations, the obligations and privileges of kinship, asserted in religious imaginations and realized as presences in social worlds that extend "between Heaven and Earth."[52]

If there is a generational distance implied in a grandparent/grandchild relationship, there is also a remarkable social proximity implied in that relationship among Anishinaabe people, for whom grandparent and grandchild are considered almost, if not wholly, social equals. There is nothing short of an Anishinaabe vocation of grandparenthood. The oral tradition by which grandparents teach and grandchildren learn through this relationship gives grandparents leeway for improvising on the traditions they've inherited, making them not only as conduits of some stuff called tradition but creative agents of it, gauging the grandchild's needs and circumstances and teaching with conspicuous cultivated intention.

In primarily oral traditions, elders are the libraries of cultural memory, myth, ritual, and ethics, and because they maintain, allocate, and distribute this knowledge, elders bring something important to the well-being of community. All true. But the authority of elders does not just *follow from* orality, their prestige no simple function of their lifelong accrual of cultural capital in an oral tradition's economy of knowledge. Such a formula may appear to make sense today, when linguistic and traditional knowledge is scarcer than ever, but it is not nimble enough to gauge the subtlety of Anishinaabe practices of deference and sagacity. It presumes a decidedly non-oral, reified notion of tradition such that tradition and traditional knowledge can be seen as a thing.

Here, Weber can be helpful for his sociological insight that traditional authority is less the authority of tradition than the authority of those authorized to speak on tradition's behalf, to articulate tradition. If Weber was rather uninterested in the varieties and complexities of this authority in small-scale egalitarian societies, he nonetheless argued that unlike the bureaucratic authority that seems to us moderns so axiomatic, the legitimacy of traditional authority rests legitimacy only partly "in terms of *traditions* which themselves directly determine the content" of a leader's "command." It also refers to "the traditional prerogative" of the authoritative leader in the rather ample sphere "which tradition leaves open to him."[53]

Crucial here is a Weberian turn from an objective approach to tradition or culture to the situational constitution of traditional or cultural authority in social life. Cultural authority does not rest simply on those with an authoritative command of some thing called culture but the prerogative of people invested by the community with the authority to articulate culture. To be sure, the authority of elders has to do with the acquisition over time of both cultural knowledge and judgment, augmented and tempered over years of life experience, but eldership in the sense that Ojibwe people tend to speak of it is less a function of biological age than of community recognition. It is the prerogative of an Ojibwe elder to improvise, within bounds scrupulously maintained by the community, on cultural knowledge to address new circumstances facing the community.

In turn, the measure by which successive generations of elders determine what is "within bounds" makes reference not so much to some fixed content of tradition that can be isolated independently from the utterances of elders, but to the standards established by *their* elders who entrusted the teachings to them. In other words, the claim of *cultural* fidelity to tradition is in truth a *social* fidelity to the elders' own elders.[54] Here also is the basis for contention around tradition, rooted as much in social networks of fidelity to elders as in competing understandings of what constitutes tradition.

Anishinaabe Eldership in Historical Motion

History is thus hard-wired into Anishinaabe traditions of eldership, making provision for the incorporation of new historical circumstances into the timeless authority of tradition. But history has also transformed those very traditions of Anishinaabe eldership in ways that are of as much interest to this study as the putatively timeless traditions themselves, and such markings of the authority of old age represent the third aspect that any consideration of the religious authority of eldership must contend. Before signaling what those major changes are, it will be helpful to sketch briefly a meaningful periodization of that history.

The specific historical narrative that frames Anishinaabe eldership is one that is deeply shaped, though not determined, by a history of interactions with Euro-Americans and by the reach into and regulation of Anishinaabe lives by U.S. and Canadian Indian policy.

FUR TRADE

The framework begins with fur-trade period from the early seventeenth century through the early eighteenth. Driven by strong European demand for fur, especially beaver fur, French fur traders and the Jesuit missionaries that accompanied them reached into Anishinaabe territory in the early seventeenth century. Even prior to their arrival, however, diseases borne by Europeans to which Native Americans had insufficient immunities wrought devastation on Native populations in the Great Lakes region, in turn introducing untold social chaos and fostering new ways of asserting peoplehood.[55] The aged in this period were a population particularly vulnerable to disease. At the same time, they remained a force to be reckoned with, as attested by Jesuit missionaries who found certain elders as gatekeepers to the inroads toward conversion of extended families and as the

European powers found as they sought to negotiate favorable relations among Native peoples who could still play one against the other.

As control was consolidated in the region by Britain, the United States, and later Canada, and as a fur-trade economy transformed into encounters with timber companies, settlers, and more sustained missionary efforts, Anishinaabe elder leaders, or *ogimaag* ("bosses") and *ogimaakweg* ("boss women"), were ironically not simply bastions of the old ways against the new, but were at the forefront of strategic accommodation to American, Canadian, and missionary interests, exercising diplomacy and the making of treaties. This in turn fueled a generational challenge from younger "warrior" leaders convinced instead of the urgency of militant anticolonial resistance that came to further define and delimit the authority of eldership.[56]

By the 1870s, as most Anishinaabe people found themselves living on reservations, governmental regulation of Native life and missionary efforts intensified. Confined by law to reservation lands, which were themselves depleted of resources by timber companies, dam projects, and policies of land allotment, the seasonal round that supported and constituted the Anishinaabe way of life became all but impossible to effect. Disease, dislocation, and poverty framed Anishinaabe efforts to survive by engaging new missionary and bureaucratic policies of religious conversion, cultural assimilation, and education, and for others to continue to resist in both overt and subtle ways.

The strength of the religious and cultural authority of elders was particularly problematic to the assimilationist designs of missionaries and bureaucrats, and so efforts such as residential boarding schools were devised to sever the strong bonds of kin and land and in no small part the moral and cultural pedagogy of grandparents and elders. Dances, giveaways, and ceremonies deemed inimical to progress and assimilation were suppressed, even criminalized, further undercutting the authority of elders and other spiritual leaders typically in charge of them. For their part, while they continued to have to reckon with the persisting authority of older Anishinaabeg, missionary churches like the Episcopalians, sought to raise up a younger generation of indigenous clergy leadership. Still, Anishinaabe elders did not simply turn away, instead asserting their authority in newly improvised ways.

Indeed this is one of the two main historical moments by which this book tries to denaturalize Anishinaabe eldership by attending to how elders were instrumental in cultural innovations for the sake of cultural continuity.[57] In chapter 4, I examine how Ojibwe people newly settled on Minnesota's reservations began to engage the Christian practices proffered by Episcopalians in new ways, making them their own in tension with missionary intentions. Although the Episcopalians' efforts to ordain young Ojibwe men deacons have been celebrated as the reason for this marked engagement with Christianity, it was in fact older men and women who gave sanction to affiliation with Christian communities and who authorized young deacons to lead in a manner continuous with tradition.

REORGANIZATION

In the United States, assimilation policies were formally reversed in 1934 with the passage of the Indian Reorganization Act (IRA). Here the United States acknowledged the failure of policies designed to erase tribal distinctiveness and communal property and reasserted the rights of Native peoples to govern their internal affairs through tribal governments newly created on the model of bureaucratic efficiency and on constitutions, referencing, if not delivering, democratic rule and the separation of powers. If the act did not altogether stem the tide of subtler incorporation of Native communities into the American economy, society, and culture, it did at least formally affirm rights to tribal exercise of religions, languages, and cultural practices. Still, the legislative innovation of tribal governments, today often referred to by many as "IRA governments," made few if any gestures to tribal traditions of governance, including the political authority of elders, and this mattered. Likewise, in Canada, a series of twentieth-century amendments to the controlling Indian Act of 1876 similarly softened, if they didn't eradicate, the assimilation aims of nineteenth-century policies, and elected tribal leaders there as in the United States stood in considerable relief to the elder leaders of Anishinaabe tradition. Canadian

Ojibwe even came to distinguish in their language the elected tribal leader (*ogimaakan*) from the traditional community elder leader (*ogimaa*) by means of a suffix (*-kan*) suggestive of artifice, perhaps even imposture. If there was, through tribal elections, a novel shortcut to leadership, it was not recognized as eldership per se.

TERMINATION AND RELOCATION

Following World War II, the United States again tried—through policies of termination and relocation—to privilege Native people's status as U.S. citizens (legislated by Congress in 1924) over their membership in distinctive tribal nations and cultures. Although Ojibwe tribal governments were not, as were the Menominee in Wisconsin, formally terminated (the Menominee were later reinstated in the 1970s), the financial incentives of relocation policy were sufficient to persuade many poor Indians to leave reservation communities for jobs in American cities flush with a postwar economic boom. If working-class Anishinaabe did not fully share in the economic opportunity advertised to them, and if they did not or could not blend into cities organized along racial lines, by the 1970s fully half the U.S. American Indian population could be found living in the cities.

Along with the increasingly felt ramifications of sustained assimilation policies a generation previous in terms of loss of language and cultural knowledge, urbanization severed continuous ties to reservation lands and the many elders who stayed home, but Anishinaabe people were resourceful in the ways they maintained ties to reservation communities, going home at important times. Urbanization brought Native people of various tribes into close proximity, creating conditions for the further shaping of an intertribal "Pan-Indian" identity that had already begun to emerge through new religious movements, the boarding school experience, and the political organizing of groups like the National Congress of American Indians. Elders in the cities became crucial figures in the survival of the reconstituted Anishinaabe communities in places like Detroit, Chicago, and Minneapolis. Beyond mere survival, a number of these elders served as advisers and mentors to the younger leaders of the American Indian Movement, helping to give spiritual and moral direction to their movement, even if this direction was not uniformly recognized as authoritative among other circles in reservation communities.

With the forceful assertion of tribal identity and distinctiveness and the renewal of public traditionalism in the American Indian Movement, the United States recognized expanded possibilities for political and cultural tribal self-determination beginning in the mid-1970s. Native leaders claimed increased tribal control over social services and education on the reservation and to a degree in the urban communities. Tribes asserted their presence in new media and in larger political processes to assert greater control of representation of culture, religion, and tribal life. Many Anishinaabe people returned to traditions that had gone underground in their communities, seeking out certain elders with the linguistic and cultural knowledge and authority necessary to the renewal of those beliefs and practices. And such elders themselves took the reins of public community leadership, in stark contrast to a larger American culture that dismissed the authority of age. More recently, many tribal communities have returned to their founding legal documents, reimagining their formal governance, revising constitutions, and writing tribal codes in ways that affirm Anishinaabe traditions of the authority of elders.

The Sacralization of Eldership

The second major historical focus for my denaturalizing of eldership is actually a series of turning points hinging on the 1970s, when a generation of elders—many of them denied the full continuity of traditional knowledge as survivors of boarding school educations, relocation, and other facets of forced assimilation—were actively sought out by young, urban leaders of the American Indian Movement to give direction to the resurgence of Native traditions. If tradition is what elders say it is, as I am arguing here on Anishinaabe terms had long been the case, then these elders came to speak with a force, with a traditional authority, that defies the commonly held logic that renewed interrupted traditions are invented traditions.

This authority of elders was newly configured amid historical and social conditions that gave rise to the resurgence of traditionalism even as they made it more difficult to arrive at a consensus about what was traditional and who could speak as an elder. The plain statistics of life expectancy bespeak how the age of recognized eldership, or at least the potential recognition of it, had decreased significantly. In light of the forces of urbanization and factionalism in reservation communities, elders were recognized by smaller circles of family, if still more extended than the nuclearizing families of broader American society. And the devastating loss of language, and narrative and cultural knowledge in that language, created conditions for the recognition of eldership among people defined more in terms of age and not solely in terms of cultural knowledge or moral stature.

Because so much has been at stake, these same forces gave rise to an accentuation of eldership and its authority. Indeed, as I discuss further in chapter 1, while one can find evidence of the English term *elder* being referenced earlier in the twentieth century, its usage carried an increased force in the latter twentieth century even as it became more difficult to agree on who could be considered an elder. Among the Northern Arapaho, Anderson notes, these same forces, especially those of age, mute earlier Arapaho distinctions of age-grading and occasioned no small amount of talk and disagreement among his Native collaborators about whether just anyone should be regarded as an elder. Older Wind River consultants told Anderson it was the language-revitalization programs in the 1980s that elevated certain figures as elders according to novel criteria related to those revitalization programs and the grants that drove them, and these were typically younger than those distinguished by initiation into the more advanced age-sets. Concerning the term *elder*, Anderson identifies key contrast among "Arapaho, Pan-Indian, and Euro-American ideologies of knowledge and life development":

> To the first it is all about demeanor, observed life history, and knowledge. Identity as an "elder" is constructed by other elders and the age structure overall. To the second, it is about language fluency, public identity, and leadership roles in ceremonial life as defined by emerging pan-Indian culture not always grounded in Arapaho tradition. With the neo-traditional revival since the 1970s people of decreasingly younger age have had to take on more and more leadership roles in ceremonies in order to meet the demand for participation by more young people in a growing population with increasing interest in tradition.

Anderson is, at the time of this writing, at work on contrasting cultural construals of time that will surely improve even further on the analysis offered here. But Anderson is right on in observing that "defining eldership has become less and less tied to local control through age structured processes of decision making based on the traditional life cycle and more a matter of both bureaucratic processes, pan-Indianism, and self-identification. Locally, most folks try to follow the old ways, such as always going to the oldest people first for decisions, consulting, and inquiries, but there are so many other conflicting forces that push things in other directions."[58]

In the present study, I attempt to document the ways that demographic realities—grim life expectancies and a younger Native population relative to the U.S. population as a whole—and cultural realities—especially those of language loss and programmatic efforts to institutionalize the teaching of language and culture—have resulted in the recognition of a greater number of younger Anishinaabe women and men as elders. If the authority of eldership among Anishinaabe communities is pushed in many directions, as it is in the Arapaho case, and if the social tensions that arise stand in considerable relief to a more consensual model of authoritative eldership in the Anishinaabe past, it is also clear that contemporary Anishinaabe people, especially those variously regarded as elders, have muted open discussion of those tensions in their public discourse. Inasmuch as I have tried to denaturalize Anishinaabe eldership by laying claim to its contested nature, I must also acknowledge a telling silence, or at least reticence, about this contestation, likely the result of self-censorship in Anishinaabe self-representation and very possibly an artifact of the very structures of the oral tradition itself.

As chapter 5 elaborates, I understand the story of Anishinaabe eldership since the 1970s in terms of a process of *sacralization*, one that inherits previous traditions about eldership and accentuates them even as it newly configures them. Although elders as such had long served as ritual specialists in naming ceremonies, sponsorship, and spiritual direction, the interruptions to Anishinaabe ceremonies, traditions, and languages through assimilation policies and processes and the renewal of pride and interest in tradition since the 1970s have accentuated the authority of elders as elders. As tradition and culture have become reified and more sacralized precisely because they were so threatened with oblivion, and as Anishinaabe languages have gone from being everyday languages to everyday languages that are also *holy* languages, the elders who still speak them, and who are esteemed by virtue of their access to these traditions, have exercised an authority not unlike that of priests.

The highly conscious return to tradition with the Indian power movement in the 1970s was fueled in large part by the zeal of those starved from access to tradition by adopted or urban upbringings and with the politicized intensity of the American Indian Movement. That's how we can understand the moment in historical and sociological terms; in the idiom of Ojibwe teachings, the contemporary day marks the watershed where, after several generations of oppression, younger Anishinaabeg must turn away from the seductions of the present day to elders and to traditions and where, importantly, elders who had fallen asleep to the urgency of their vocation must wake up and teach traditions and values.

Waking up to tradition is an apt image here; it is a rekindling of something there all along but a rekindling that takes place in a new day all the same. That new day is characterized by a dramatic differentiation of an integrated Anishinaabe way of life into religion, politics, economics, and so on that has been an internal force of the legacy of colonialism and linguistic cultural, economic, and bureaucratic incorporation into dominant North American society. But the zealous call to wake up to tradition is at least in part a gesture to reintegrate the lifeway and to consciously privilege the authority of elders, not ethnographies (the present one included), about what tradition has been and can be for this moment.

These circumstances muted the distinction between spiritually powerful medicine people and elders as elders, between the authority of dreams and the authority of age. What is more, the bureaucratization of authority in Canadian and American tribal governments based on democratic and business administration models, and the differentiation of the religious and cultural from the political and economic, have shrunk the reach of the authority of elders and medicine people alike from a broadly integrative political-economic-religious-cultural authority to one pertaining largely to the religious and the cultural. One can thus acknowledge the significance of "elders' circles" proliferating on reservations, at urban Indian centers, and in intertribal convocations even as one notices the primarily cultural and religious mandates of such groups. If a "spiritual proclamation" of an elders' council is a far cry from a deal struck between a tribal council and the federal government, the spiritual direction that most Anishinaabe elders bring to bear is hardly a matter of religion alone but about a return to an integrated way of life. In part because of persisting deep traditions of Anishinaabe eldership, in part because of the plain courage of elders, even the sacralization of eldership has not entirely succeeded in confining their authority to a purely religious or cultural realm.

The Integration of Bodily, Cultural, and Historical Studies of Eldership

Understood in terms of a cosmology of *bimaadiziwin*, the "grandparent-hood" of the spirits, and the narrative authority of the elder, old age in Anishinaabe culture is marked by cosmological and ethical associations of great import. Indeed, it follows from this that the figure of the elder has become the preeminent emblem of Anishinaabe peoplehood. It should be said that the cultural construction of old age is not itself unrelated to the biological aging of Anishinaabe bodies. For bodies, as we know from cultural studies, themselves incorporate cultural expectations into their sinews and actions. In the case of Anishinaabe eldership, the embodied performance of eldership in terms of gait, carriage, and speech practices demonstrates how the cultural and natural marks of eldership cannot be so easily distinguished, much less separated. And although this is by no means uniformly the case as Anishinaabe communities are incorporated into the poverty, racism, and ageism of contemporary American life, cultural expectations for the authority of old age can make for tremendously vital—"peppy" to gloss an Ojibwe term—old age. Cultural and physiological aspects of old age must be seen in this relation. So, too, must the marks of historical change be incorporated into any analysis of the religious authority of old age.

The current study attempts to pay attention to the shared human realities of the aging body and mind and the maturation over time of experience; it also attempts to place that maturation in terms of cultural constructions of the life course, and all this in historical motion. It is a tall order to fill indeed, and so I commence with the full knowledge that further scholarship on the religious authority of eldership, in the Anishinaabe tradition or in any religious tradition, can only improve upon my efforts here.

Eldership in Theory and Practice

In the Spring of 2005, as I was writing chapter 3, which concerns grandparents as teachers, the tragic shootings of Ojibwe students and staff of the high school on the Red Lake Reservation unfolded. In the worst case of school violence since Columbine in 1990, a 16-year-old Anishinaabe boy killed first his grandfather (a 58-year-old tribal policeman), then his grandfather's companion, and then trained his grandfather's weapons on more than a dozen fellow students, a teacher, a security guard, killing a total of ten people and stunning an entire nation.

The boy, Jeff Wiese, had slipped through the cracks. He grew up in the Twin Cities, but he moved to live with his grandfather and aunt after his father took his own life and his mother was incapacitated in an automobile accident. Red Lake High School is, in many respects, anyone's high school, more like Columbine than like anything that has struck an Indian community, and the incident is more a function of a wider culture of violence than representative of dysfunction on an Indian reservation. Still, as part of the desire to probe an unthinkable crime like this, the media searched his family background and the life on the reservation for clues. One wishes the boy's story leading to his act of desperation was less representative still than it was.

Because I had just completed a draft of a chapter about grandchildren and grandparents, I was exceptionally disturbed about the violence turned first on the boy's grandfather, the man raising him along with aunts and others. Of course, a kid could act out on the people he thought were not embracing him enough. If the incident is necessarily part of the cultural history of Anishinaabe eldership—and this book will reckon with such moments as evidence of the difficulty of putting into practice such virtues of Anishinaabe tradition in history—so, too, is the way that Red Lake elders responded, far from the cameras and microphones of the press, gathering together in prayerful consultation and then in action to bring healing to their community. In a word, it is important to view such tragedies not simply as evidence for the failure of Anishinaabe traditions of eldership but also as evidence for their urgency to Anishinaabe people trying to lead their lives in a good way.

Indeed such a moment places in starkest relief what Edward Benton-Banai, citing the widespread prophecies of the seventh fire, has identified as the charged nature of the current moment among Anishinaabe communities and the crucial importance of traditional practices of elder-ship. Benton-Banai places the difficult history of the Anishinaabe people under colonialism within an organizing framework of a series of prophe-cies. The fifth fire, which involved the promise of great things to be had if the Anishinaabe would abandon the teachings of elders, turns out to be a "false promise" that did much to destroy the community:

> Those deceived by this promise will take their children away from the teachings of the chi'-ah-ya-og' (elders). Grandsons and granddaughters will turn against the elders. In this way the elders will lose their reason for living . . . they will lose their purpose in life. At this time a new sickness will come among the people. The balance of many people will be disturbed. The cup of life will almost be spilled. The cup of life will almost become the cup of grief.[59]

The sixth fire leads directly up to the watershed moment of the seventh fire, presumably pointing to the present:

> In the time of the Seventh Fire a Osh-ki-bi-ma-di-zeeg' (New People) will emerge. They will retrace their steps to find what was left by the trail. Their steps will take them to the elders who they will ask to guide them on their journey. But many of the elders will have fallen asleep. They will awaken to this new time with nothing to offer. Some of the elders will be silent out of fear. Some of the elders will be silent because no one will ask anything of them. The New People will have to be careful in how they approach the el-ders. The task of the New People will not be easy.[60]

If they "remain strong in their quest," ceremonial life will resume and "there will be a rebirth of the Anishinaabe nation and a rekindling of old flames." But the prophecy also presages a crossroads facing Euro-Americans, one interpreted to be the slower path of spiritualism that "traditional Na-tive people have traveled and are now seeking again" and the other one of technology and destruction. "If they choose the right road, then the Sev-enth Fire will light the Eighth and Final Fire—an eternal Fire of peace, love, brotherhood and sisterhood."[61]

If Benton-Banai's relation of this prophecy indicates the need for elders themselves to awaken and not simply others to awaken to the teaching of

Norval Morrisseau, "The elderly lady spoke and said I have replacements all over my body. Meanwhile the wounded healer had his first replacement. He spoke to the lady in esoteric words: 'Daughter, you are indeed the role model of life, with all the pain you go through in order to appreciate life and a great inspiration to all.'" Acrylic on canvas, 36 × 48 in., 1996. *Courtesy Gabe Vadas*

elders, it also conspicuously points to the urgency of recovered traditions of eldership that are also demonstrably spiritual. Returning to eldership, both through practices of deference and practices of sagacity, is aligned in Benton-Banai's reckoning with Anishinaabe peoplehood and well-being.

Elders as Representation of Communal Self

In a sense, as I'll show, elders as *gichi anishinaabe* serve their communities as embodiments of the ideal person, but they also have come even to embody the Anishinaabe social body, becoming representations of peoplehood itself in ways not dissimilar from kings in medieval and early modern Europe.

This symbolic life of eldership has been placed in heightened relief as Anishinaabe communities have become integrated into a Euro-American economy, society, and culture that does not thus honor or respect the authority of the old. With this integration, a newly articulate Anishinaabe consciousness about eldership has developed. In time, this consciousness came to assert a significant contrast with a precontact Anishinaabe tradition of eldership from its historical demeaning, as does Wub-e-ke-niew (Francis Blake) in an interesting book that he claims to be the first written from a sovereign "Ahnishinahbaeotjibway perspective":

> Our elders, both male and female, have always been deeply respected in the Ahnishinahbaeotjibway community. This is very different from European culture, in which age and gender polarization makes families more amenable to state control, and creates discontinuity in oral history. Our family relationships are harmoniously balanced, there is no authoritarian head of the family, and so there is no need for role reversal. The foundation of our egalitarian family inter-relationships includes mutual respect and a language which is both male and female. Because we have no hierarchy, there is no competition for authority in the family. . . . Our elders were wise and loving teachers who knew our history and genealogy, and who knew about medicines and other herbs. They had a clear and useful understanding of community dynamics and practical psychology. We did not warehouse our old people, nor segregate them away from the rest of their *Dodemian* [clan].[62]

Wub-e-ke-niew's book, though deeply informed by the author's fluency in Ojibwe, is written in English, and the reference is to the English word *elder*. The rise of this English term as it has come increasingly to be applied to esteemed older Anishinaabeg, which I discuss at the end of chapter 1, is itself an index of this new consciousness about the authority of age in this cultural history of eldership.[63] By the late twentieth century, authors from Native writers like Ignatia Broker to non-Native writers Theresa Smith and Melissa Pflüg had begun to capitalize the term when designating its weightier honorific sense.[64]

This newly articulate consciousness has also come to be seen as a crucial link in the rebuilding of an Anishinaabe future made possible by a return to such traditions. Jerry Morgan, a youth wellness counselor and drum-keeper at Leech Lake, urged a group of gifted and talented Native high school students in a summer college-prep program to put this respect for elders into practice. He taught them to sing a rather simple Ojibwe song with his drum. The Ojibwe text was simply repeated over and over, a translation of which is "children listen to elders."[65]

So peoplehood and the sovereignty or integrity of a distinctively Anishinaabe future have come increasingly to hinge on beliefs and practices of eldership, both practices of deference on the part of younger people and the public exercise of sagacity or wisdom on the part of elders. Each chapter that follows is concerned with the remarkable persistence over time of seemingly timeless traditions of eldership even as each is also about the peculiarly timely nature of such calls as Benton-Banai's about the urgency of the honoring and exercise of eldership here and now.

1

AGING AND THE LIFE CYCLE IMAGINED IN OJIBWE TRADITION AND LIVED IN HISTORY

Once there was a young person who had reached the customary time to prepare himself for a fast, so that he could dream about his future life. So this young man went into the forest and made a little lodge where he could fast. He thought very highly of himself, this young person, and he wanted to be well thought of when he returned. Thus it was that on the tenth day of fasting, he had a dream. He saw a very old man walking toward him, smiling, and the young man recognized that this was himself in his old age. But he did not like this vision, and so he thought he would continue fasting in order to have yet another. But he did not have another dream. Later on, he was missed in the village, and some others came to look in the lodge to learn what had happened to him. They found him lying there, having already starved to death, but they did not immediately remove him. His flesh was drying up very rapidly on the bones, but they did not bother that skeleton. Later on, during the night, a big wind came up and blew the bones into the branches of the trees where they began to howl. So now that is why the trees are said to howl in the wind: "Bagag! Pambiso!" ("Skeleton, flying about!")[1]

—Fred Ettawageshik, *Art of Tradition*

"When I was young, I used to hear the average age of death for Indians was forty-four years. I adopted an attitude that anything over that many years was pure gravy, just juice. It was a bonus for trying to live a good life."

—Jim Northrup, *Rez Road Follies*

The Life Cycle Lived and Imagined

Life cycles are imagined even as they are lived, and our experience in living them is importantly shaped by those ways we imagine the life cycle. Whatever our culture or moment in time, as humans, our bodies commonly are born, mature, age, and die. But our respective experiences of that process (and even our bodies themselves) are as much inflected by culturally specific imaginings of the life cycle and its meaning as determined by the biological facts of our aging. For example, the category of adolescence, which we take to be such an axiomatic and natural demarcation of the transition years to manhood and womanhood, is a designation of early-twentieth-century developmental psychology and marks a more pronounced anxiety with the transition that faces modern industrial societies. Just as these cultural imaginings mark the biological progress of our bodies and their ultimate demise in death, so too do they place our physical existence in larger spatial, temporal, and cosmological frameworks. Human communities variously imagine the self—body, mind, soul (or souls)—variously imagine lineage, and variously imagine an afterlife or afterlives that assign particular significance to existence in here and now. To be sure, different communities at different times and places imagine old age in so many ways, so coming to terms with Anishinaabe traditions of eldership must first involve placing old age in terms of Anishinaabe understandings of the life cycle and of the person who passes through it. But first: a word about the basic status of the life cycle in a this-worldly religion, for the process of aging, and old age itself, poses the most challenging of questions as to the ultimate worth of this world and the bodies that inhabit and experience it.

Dominant culture in the modern West at least since the Enlightenment has assumed a posture toward the body and its aging that is fundamentally different from the one that Anishinaabe tradition has taught. This has been in no small part possible in the modern West because of dominant philosophical and religious traditions that assigned a provisional status to the body and its progression through the life stages of this world toward its ultimate demise. Even before Christianity, Platonic cosmology asserted a strong distinction between the privileged spheres of *being* and the flux of change and imperfection of *becoming* that characterize existence, or "becoming" on this world's plane. To this basic framework, Christianity added that the decay and death of bodies were anomalous to God's original design, a moral outcome of human disobedience in the fall, and preached the urgent need for *salvation* from nature and death, locating ultimacy and harmony not in this world, but in the next. Modern influences on Western Christianity saw to a process of what Weber famously, if too univocally, called the disenchantment of this world. By turns, dominant Western philosophies following Descartes located human freedom and subjectivity not in the body, but in the mind. In the modern West at least since the Enlightenment, the dominant language with which the aging of bodies through the life course has been imagined has been the materialistic language of physiological science, itself a product of culturally specific understandings of what the human consists of. As cultural historian Thomas Cole has argued, the field of gerontology emerged in the context of this twentieth-century scientific moment in large part to understand and *manage* the process of aging.

In stark contrast, traditional Anishinaabe reckonings of the life cycle and the phase of old age within it make such integral reference to metaphysical and ethical matters that we cannot understand them without making extensive reference to the domains of Ojibwe religion. The Ojibwe life cycle is, as we shall see, a matter of ultimate concern, not simply a preamble or proving ground for a good or bad eternity. This does not mean, as early missionaries thought it did, that Ojibwe had no conception or concern for an afterlife, that Ojibwe people lived in a state of nature as Christianity had rendered it. Instead, Ojibwe life proceeded in a world that was imagined as itself an expression of profound relationality, of what Zen Buddhists strive to experience as the ultimate "suchness" or "thusness" of a world that does not at first glance appear thus. But before we graduate to such subtleties in Ojibwe thought, let's begin with the more grounded Ojibwe anthropology or understanding of human being.

Ojibwe Understandings of "Persons"

In traditional Ojibwe religion, human persons are comprised of a material body, which is born, ages, and dies and with which is associated two distinct souls. Importantly, these souls do not stand for the Ojibwe in the dichotomous relation to the body that dominant Western thought since Descartes has instilled, even if they can survive a body, and neither of the souls constitute the whole person.[2] The first soul, the *jiibay*, a seat of intelligence and experience apparently situated in the mind, is capable of leaving the physical body during sleep and trance, and at death this soul lingers for a time after what would be described in the modern West as physical death. The term is sometimes glossed as "ghost," but clearly involves a range of associations not commonly shared by that term. The second soul, the *ojichaag*, was seated in the heart and remained stationary in the body that it animated, until death. This was what Christopher Vecsey, following Åke Hultkrantz, refers to as an "ego soul," the "seat of the will," which "experienced emotions." This soul passes on alive, immediately upon death, eventually to be rejoined by the *jiibay* after some period of its lingering.[3]

A question arises: do souls age and mature? According to Diamond Jenness:

> there was a definite period or crisis in childhood, the Ojibwa believed, when the soul and shadow attained to the proper stage of awakeness or maturity for receiving the vision and revelation from the supernatural powers. Roughly the crisis coincided with adolescence, but often it arrived before that period, and sometimes, though much more rarely, a little after. The exact time seems to have depended on what we would term the psychological development of the child, which the parents studied closely. A boy who fasted at too early an age, before his soul and shadow had become fully "awake," obtained only an imperfect dream which, being not fully intelligible, left him a prey to sickness.[4]

As souls and body were not bifurcated, this notion of a proper "age" of the soul clearly was not divorced from a notion of a body's age, and as we'll see at a number of points there is a sense that "power" matures along with the maturation of the person.

Importantly, Ojibwe language and tradition provides for the possibility of transformation, whereby the immaterial seats of the self can assume various material forms, and in many cases such transformation is believed to be so common that an encounter of say, a bear, does not authorize one to speak in the language, with the utter certainty implied by the English verb *to be*, that what they've heard or seen *is/was* a bear, ontologically speaking.[5]

Vecsey writes of several other "extensions" of the person, including the physical extensions of the living body, such as blood and hair, that remain associated with the person even after they lose contact with the embodied person, as well as the material presence of the deceased, especially bones. What a modern Western perspective might regard merely as human remains, an Ojibwe perspective would regard as associated with the ongoing person and thus worthy of an elevated standard of respect.[6]

Names, too, constitute what Vecsey calls extensions of the self. Ojibwe persons had, and still often have, multiple names: associated with a naming ceremony at birth, names bestowed as "gifts" through visions, baptismal names, family legal names, nicknames, clan names, and what Frances Densmore referred to as "a euphonious name." Vecsey notes the particular necessity of the first two names to the "essential person," often held in secret and guarded as with other bodily extensions of the person.[7] As we'll see in an extensive discussion of the naming rite in chapter 5, the viability of a healthy life in part depended on the receipt of a ceremonial name from an elder, because the name confers crucial power.

Importantly, Vecsey frames this entire discussion with an observation that the "metaphysical topic" of the ontology of the person "rarely found ready expression by the Ojibwas. It usually took white observers' questions to bring the subject into discussion."[8] I would add that thus isolating a discussion of the ontology of the person cuts against the fundamental grain of Ojibwe thought. For where the terms of the previous discussion suggest the person as a self-sustained entity, Ojibwe personhood was and is decisively relational in nature. Subjectivity and identity remain functions of a person's relations to other persons, a state of affairs that makes more comparative sense to a Confucian understanding of the human than a modern Western, to a world where the collective, not the individual, is the basic unit.

Anishinaabedoog: *Becoming Human in a Sacred Community*

Instead of with "Ladies and Gentlemen," formal addresses in the Ojibwe language commonly begin with *nindinawemaaganag* ("those of you who would/may be relatives") or the greeting *Anishinaabedoog* ("those of you who would/may be Anishinaabe, who would be the people, who would be human"). Although it may be simply a convention by which a speaker conspicuously does not presume to be declarative, instead saying "you who might be my relatives," one could also read the convention as signaling that the word *Anishinaabe*, at least in certain usages, does not merely describe descent from or belonging to a particular Native American nation but prescribes the very goal of living.[9] Indeed it could commit any occasion of the exchange of ideas to the ongoing process of becoming more fully human. It is against this backdrop of imagining the life course as a process of learning to become more human that I think one can appreciate the fuller resonance of aging and old age. One of the common Ojibwe terms for referring to a class of people regarded as elders is *gichi anishinaabeg* ("great persons"). Although one would not want to rely solely on etymological evidence, in light of other observations, one could justly infer from this usage a suggestive relation between attainment of old age and approaching a lifelong goal of becoming human.

Following the cue of John Grim's comparative insights on Ojibwe religion, I am emboldened to make such claims upon reading scholars of east Asian religions, particularly Tu Weiming, who address the ultimacy or religiousness of Confucian social ethics.[10] In the Confucian scheme, according to Tu, "from childhood to old age the learning to be human never ceases."[11] As with the Confucians, becoming Anishinaabe, becoming fully human, is no mere matter of individual self-fulfillment. As among the Confucians, a person is no island unto herself but a busy intersection of relationships. Self-realization is a lifelong discipline of cultivating proper relations. And I think there is an instructive analogy to be made with Herbert Fingarette's famous observation that in the proper ordering of the human, natural, and heavenly realms, Confucians seek the transformation of the secular into the sacred by making a "holy rite" out of the practice of authentic human community.[12] Of course, what distinguishes the Ojibwe from the Confucian approach to the practice of a sacred community is the extension of that community well beyond the realm of human society to include *the nonhuman persons* of the natural and spiritual realms. Still, the analogy is a strong one, and it is this notion of community, I submit, that is at the heart of Ojibwe religion more than is acknowledged in a scholarly literature that has been trained on the "individualistic" pursuits of dream-seeking, shamanic divination and healing, and ceremonial initiations into medicine societies.

For Confucians, babies are not born fully or wholly human as much as they begin to be at work on the process of becoming human, which for the Confucians is nothing short of disciplined labor. Among Confucians, learning can be conceived as the cultivation of "sincerity" or "authenticity" that "fulfills possibility for cosmic and natural relatedness within the human order."[13] To me, the translated notion of sincerity in relations carries resonance with Ojibwe understandings of the fully human person.

Among the Ojibwe, too, learning is more than the acquisition of empirical knowledge about objectified things: it is a matter of learning one's relatedness to other subjects—the subjectification of things, really—and learning how to behave in light of that relatedness. Notions of relatedness abound in conventional understandings of Native American cultures, and rightly so, but not because Indians are *naturally* one with nature. Precisely the opposite: cultivating the knowledge and practice of relatedness is *hard work*, a lifelong matter of human discipline and culture. Such learning requires humility, economy, restraint. It requires listening, watching, and learning of proper ritual relations that markedly distinguish Anishinaabe idioms of learning. In this regard the Anishinaabe person, like the Confucian, is trained to habituate the self to the terms set by a system of relations. Honoring or respecting elders in such a system is among the more important expressions of this practice of relationality. As I shall demonstrate in chapter 3, it is characteristic of the teaching of elders that gaining knowledge and gaining facility with the proper relationality go hand in hand. On Ojibwe terms, as people mature, they stand the possibility of becoming more and more human, more and more Anishinaabe.[14] In this scheme, the elder woman or man, a *gichi anishinaabe*, is the ethical paragon, the honorable, emulable student, and practitioner of proper relations.

• • •

Bimaadiziwin: *The Ultimacy of the Good Life*

If old age could represent *ethical* attainment by the *gichi anishinaabe*, it could also represent a kind of *religious* attainment. Put in more accurate terms, longevity for the Ojibwe (as for the Confucians but perhaps even more plainly so) was as resonant with a religious as with an ethical vision of the profundity of life in this world. By this, I don't mean to make too much of a distinction between religion and ethics, but to note the significance of Ojibwe convictions that moral relations extend beyond the human not only to nonhuman persons in what the West would call nature—plants and animals and weather phenomena—but also to nonhuman persons in the realm of the spirits.

This is crucial to understand about Ojibwe "religion," a term that most Anishinaabe people I've met have rejected as a representation of what they have consistently preferred to call "our way of life" or "our way." Indeed the this-worldly focus of Ojibwe beliefs and ceremonial practices has proved a stumbling block for missionaries and scholars of religion alike. Rather than starting with "religion" or simply "nature," let's begin with the indigenous category that has served anthropologists, historians, and community people alike, as a coherent organizing concept of this Ojibwe way of life: *bimaadiziwin*. *Bimaadiziwin* is a substantive form of a verb that indicates to "move by" or "move along" and that serves as a verbal root for terms that refer to things and people that are alive. *Bimaadiziwin* can be rather flatly translated as "life" or "living," but a richer rendering shows it to be a window into the traditional goal of Ojibwe religion: to live well and to live long in this world, and this in contrast to eschatological traditions stressing the afterlife for the transformation of the natural order. *Bimaadiziwin* orients the natural ordinary workings of this-worldly existence to an ultimate order of things. Translating it as "the good life," A. I. Hallowell placed the concept of *bimaadiziwin* at the center of the Ojibwe religious project, noting the moral, aesthetic, and spiritual connotations carried by the term. "Ojibwe religious behavior," he wrote, can be identified as any activity by an individual or a group of individuals that helps to promote a good life for human beings by making explicit recognition, direct or indirect, of man's faith in and dependence upon other-than-human persons.[15] This good life required more than competence and skill in hunting, fishing, growing, and gathering; it required proper ethical relations with the plants, animals, and their spiritual "owners" and proper relations within the human community.

Bimaadiziwin refers not simply to the natural movement of life, to *nature*, but also to the practices of an Ojibwe *way* of life, to *culture*. In the first major Ojibwe dictionary, Slovenian Catholic missionary Frederic Baraga glossed the term as "the Savage Life," thus opposing the life to which it referred to a civilized or religious life. We would appropriately recognize the missionary's bias in this wordsmithing, but Baraga was onto something when he recognized how closely the practices and conception of an Ojibwe way of life, an Ojibwe culture, conformed to the seasonal rhythms of nature: the lakes, swamps, and forests. Where he went wrong was his insistence that, absent the beliefs and practices of the Christian tradition, Anishinaabe people and their culture were tied to nature, incapable of abstracting themselves from the natural life. Ironically, many contemporary non-Natives who strenuously disagree with Baraga's observation that the Ojibwe way was devoid of religion—those who might see with longing a kind of nature-religion or spirituality of the woods—are similarly misguided in their lack of appreciation for the religious and ethical hard work that can result in a life thus attuned to natural cycles.

And it is not just ethical. According to Mary Black-Rogers, *bimaadiziwin* also connotes a notion of "power" or "power-control" that is both rooted in relations with supernaturals but remains as well a biological and social fact. Humans are by nature "pitiful," born helpless but always standing in need of reliance on supernaturals for the power and knowledge necessary to live. She glosses *bimaadiziwad* not as "living things" but as "those who have power."[16]

This all suggests a this-worldly religion, a way of life oriented profoundly to living well in this world. The English term *religion* as it is used commonly in the West is as much worth keeping as it is worth discarding, for just as an Ojibwe way of life refuses at every turn a tidy dichotomy between the supernatural and the natural, the spiritual and the material, the sacred and the profane, so too does it keep in play at each turn the first term in each pair. Vecsey was careful to define the Ojibwe religion as follows, "Conceptions of and relations with the sources of existence. . . . By existence I mean life itself. In some religious traditions, this may translate as 'being,' transcending existence; however, traditional Ojibwa religion did not articulate concern for matters beyond 'existence,' beyond life. Survival in this life, this 'existence,' was the Ojibwa's ultimate concern."[17] "The central goal of life for the Ojibwa," Hallowell concluded, "is expressed by the term *bimaadiziwin*, life in the fullest sense, life in the sense of longevity, health and freedom from misfortune. This goal cannot be achieved without the effective help and cooperation of both human and other-than-human persons, as well as by one's own personal efforts."[18]

In his study of the understanding of the life cycle among Wyoming's Northern Arapaho, a community that speaks an Algonkian language related to Ojibwe and one whose social and cultural life is significantly directed by marked age-grades, anthropologist Jeffrey Anderson draws deeply on Hallowell's insight about the centrality of *bimaadiziwin*, glossing the cognate Arapaho concept as "life movement" in a way that is suggestive for a deeper understanding of Ojibwe conceptions of the life course and, indeed, life as movement.[19] Of the Midéwiwin ceremonial society, Densmore observed, "the principal idea of the Midéwiwin is that life is prolonged by right living, and by the use of herbs which were intended for this purpose by the Midé manido ['Midéwiwin spirit']." "The ethics of the Midéwiwin are simple but sound," Densmore continued, "they teach that rectitude of conduct produces length of life, and that evil inevitably reacts on the offender."[20]

As to the flow of power, there is a relationship between age and power; as several sources suggest, power grows or ripens with age. Citing Peter Jones's comment about the advice of the "uhkewaihsee, or long dweller on the earth," Victor Barnouw observed that the Ojibwe granted old men "ceremonious respect" and "most respected of all" old medicine men, "for their power was believed to grow with age, rather than to weaken."[21]

In *bimaadiziwin*, the ordinary and the sacred, the natural and the supernatural, the life cycle and the ultimate reference point for life commingle in sharp contrast to other-worldly traditions such as Christianity. Indeed the tradition is profoundly oriented to life in this world: but in so doing it imbues the material existence of this world with a moral, spiritual, and aesthetic profundity. *Bimaadiziwin* incorporates both nature and culture, the "is" and the "ought," since the goal of human life is to exercise through proper relations a good and beautiful contribution to the flow of life.

This larger understanding of *bimaadiziwin*, the good life as not simply what is but what ought to be, has weighty implications for how an individual's life course is imagined and valued. Carl Starkloff, a Jesuit scholar interested in interreligious dialogue with Native traditions, reflects on the distinctive and crucial importance of what he calls "the ritual of the life cycle." He privileges this discussion at the end of a chapter on the ritual dimension of Native traditions generally in order to distinguish its significance vis-à-vis a presumed Christian audience:

> I have reserved this discussion for the end of this chapter because of its profound significance, particularly for the white Christian, who might well ask himself how his own tradition deals with the "life story." Or, does life simply pass the Christian by without commentary, save for a birthday or an anniversary. Does the mystery that is called life demand to be symbolized and mythologized—in sum, integrated into a whole?[22]

Undergirded by a relationality so encompassing and so profound that an entire lifetime is scarcely long enough to cultivate a full appreciation, old age itself marks a kind of religious attainment, and eldership carries a

John Kakaygeesick, a spiritual leader from Warroad, was said to be 124 when he died in 1968. He attained considerable renown in the non-Indian community as a result of his age, but is pictured here at home with his pipe, in 1960. *Courtesy of Minnesota Historical Society*

corresponding religious prestige and authority by virtue of the mastery of relatedness. The authority also implies the obligation to pass along knowledge/power for the furtherance of life.[23]

Ojibwe "Lifetime"

In an important essay entitled "Temporal Orientation in Western Civilization and in a Preliterate Society," Hallowell noted that among Manitoba Ojibwe communities in the 1930s, the life cycle was not reckoned by "a chronological year count," but rather "was divided into a number of terminologically distinguished age-grades corresponding to maturation status."[24] The first age, "childhood," extended from the time of a viable fetus until puberty. Terms distinguishing temporality within this stage included the generic term for child, *abinoojiinh*, the term *oshkaa-abinoojiinh* ("fresh child" from birth until it begins to walk), and the gendered diminutive terms for boy and girl, *gwiiwizens* and *ikwezens* respectively.

The second terminologically distinct stage of "youth" included males and females between the onset of puberty and marriage (itself a fairly fluid category). Male youth were *oshki-inini* and *oshkiniigikwe* respectively. For Rebecca Kugel, Ojibwe associations of childhood and youth, the *oshki-* ages (i.e., being "fresh, new, green, young, in process") stand in direct contrast with the authority of maturation. "Youth," she writes, "should not, in other words, be expected to act with the wisdom of age."[25]

Still, the long period from marriage through old age, Hallowell noted, was not marked linguistically.[26] The latter was recognized by the terms *akiwenzii* ("old man") and *mindimooyenh* ("old woman"), and "extreme old age" could be signaled by adding to those terms the prefix *gichi*.[27] In contrast to age-grades in other Native American societies where demarcations were clearly made through *rites of passage*, for the Ojibwe the linguistic distinction between elders and other adults did not emerge from a clearly defined moment in life. "Men and women move gradually into the period of old age," E. S. Rogers said of the Northern Ojibwe of Round Lake, Ontario, "there is no ritual or event which marks the transition. Years and a diminution of physical ability tend to delimit this period. Old men with many, perhaps ten, grandchildren are referred to as kihci'yaha' ['great being'] or nimishsho'm ['grandfather'] while very old men and women who have turned grey and have many, perhaps, twenty, grandchildren are referred to as kihci-nimishsho'm ['great-grandfather'] and kihci-ko'hkomina'n ['great-grandmother'] respectively out of deference."[28]

Later, I will explore further the connotations of the various Ojibwe-language terms pertaining to old age, as well as others that refer to the old in Native-inflected English. At this point, however, I'd like to acknowledge the significance of the fourness of this periodization, for it resonates with and corresponds to other temporal and spatial schemes of cosmic significance.

The Circle of Life: Life Cycles in Bimaadiziwin

If passage through the life cycle to old age in classic Ojibwe thought bespoke living in proper ethical and ritual relations with other persons, human and nonhuman, "lifetime" was also imagined, demarcated, and thus understood by reference to other cycles, dimensions, and practices of time and space. In addition to the spatial imagining of a linear journey "forward" over four hills, the time of life is also imagined with respect to the geometry of the circle and circular motion. Indeed, this is perhaps the more recurring spatial representation of the times of life and perhaps incorporates the fourness of the linear hill passage motif as well as the four seasons into the four directions and colors with which the circle as symbol is demarcated. Here, the life of the individual is a microcosm of the larger circle of *bimaadiziwin* and calibrated to its rhythms of seasonal and diurnal time. Old age is figured as the evening or winter of life, with confidence in the cyclical upturn that places it in a larger prevailing framework.

Given the fecundity that autumnal decay and winter sleep confer on the vernal earth, and accustomed to the renewal in these other natural circles to which lifetime corresponds, it is perhaps unsurprising that an Ojibwe kinship code should understand grandparents and grandchildren as exceptionally close. Larry Cloud Morgan poetically likened the shrinking frames and hunching backs of elderly persons as embodied preparations on the part of human beings to rejoin the earth. The earth that buries is also the earth that brings forth life. In the rendering of the circle of life—the life cycle—old age and the death that surely follows it are imagined in a seamless proximity to the birth, infancy, and new life that follows in the continuous circular motion of *bimaadiziwin*. Compared to other great traditions from south and east Asia that similarly chart the cycle of life on a great wheel of birth and rebirth, the Ojibwe tradition does not teach with surety about the reincarnation of souls into new lives on earth, but still shares with those traditions the conviction that death (and by extension old age) is part of life, not an anomalous interruption of it or a moral consequence of sin.

I've been repeatedly struck by how Ojibwe elders presenting their culture and traditions to non-Native audiences begin not with a historical narrative or an outline of religion, economy, kinship, and so on, but instead with accounts of seasonal cycles and the activities that traditionally follow those cycles in the seasonal round of Ojibwe life: making sugar from the running sap of maple trees in early spring sugar camps, spearing fish during spring spawning runs, gardening, fishing, and berrying in summer lakeside villages, wild ricing and hunting ducks in the early fall, and hunting big game in scattered family groups over the winter. More than a convenient outline for introducing culture, this seasonality has offered a framework of time and space for an Anishinaabe way of life. As Priscilla Buffalohead has observed, even the sociology and political governance of a traditional Ojibwe community on the move looks different at different times of the year.[29] And although the number of Ojibwe who can make a subsistence entirely on the land has dramatically diminished with their land base and with other draws, these activities and the seasonal cycles on which they are based remain important, perhaps even accentuated markers of identity for a people with a particular relationship to a particular land.[30] Even today's Ojibwe people—including those living and working in distant cities—can feel the pull of certain seasonal activities, especially ricing (*manoominike*) and maple sugaring (*ziinizibakwadijige*), and can organize vacation schedules in order to practice these traditional activities.

SYMBOLIC AND CEREMONIAL REITERATION OF THE CIRCLE

In the Smithsonian's National Museum of the American Indian exhibit "Our Universes," Canada's Sagkeeng Ojibwe community represents its spiritual traditions through a circle layered with meaningful correspondences.

Sunwise (clockwise) passage from east to south to west to north finds the north referencing, respectively, Elders, North Wind, Bear, Cedar, and Winter.[31]

Ojibwe ceremonial life reiterates the circle and draws from its perceived generative power. From today's "talking circles" to circular councils to pipe ceremonies wherein the pipe is rotated in four directions and raised and lowered above and below to the ubiquitous circular motions of dance traditions, Ojibwe ceremonial and social life reiterates the generativity and resonance of the circle.

As a visual cosmological symbol, the circle concentrates the totality of everything that is from all directions and the four colors to which it points. Drums, which serve as perhaps the most emblematic symbol of Ojibwe religion and as powerful vehicles for prayer and exchange with the *manidoog*, are uniformly, significantly round.

Ritual performances prescribe in gesture and step the circular motions of the cosmos. Dance steps of various types, except those associated with funerals, proceed in the elemental sunwise (clockwise) direction of the cosmos. In Odawa storyteller Larry Plamondon's telling, following the great flood, the Trickster and a handful of creatures dance the ordered world back into being in a clockwise direction. The sweat lodge, too, reiterates the power of the symbolic circle in its orientation. The spatial orientation of the lodge, the prescribed movement within it of bodies and prayers, reiterates and thus draws on the powers of correspondence with the seasonal, directional, and cosmic cycles. The lodge reiterates in spatial movement the four stages of life, with the privileged place of old age in the direction of the north and adjacent the door facing east.[32]

THE MIDÉWIWIN "PATH OF LIFE"

One of Densmore's consultants at White Earth, Maingans, told her the Midéwiwin view of the life course "from youth to old age" was a path—not a straight and obvious one, but a zigzag that seven times presents the individual with a choice: continue straight ahead, the seemingly easiest choice, but in actuality one of a series of seven temptations, one that leads on a tangent away from the goal, or take the turn, which puts one ultimately on a tack leading closer to the goal.[33] Maingans was cryptic concerning the first and second tangents, each of "which comes to a young man. If he yields to it he will not live long." "With the third temptation," Densmore recorded, "the element of religious responsibility appears, and the man is asked: 'How did you act when you were initiated into the Midéwiwin? Were you respectful to the older members, and did you faithfully fulfill all obligations?'" The fourth temptation, which "comes to a man in middle life," appears to be even less obviously the wrong choice, occurring right after the person has already chosen to take the correct turn (and presumably believing him/herself beyond the temptation). "With the fifth temptation the man begins to reflect upon his own length of days, and asks himself: 'Have you ever been disrespectful of old age?'" The sixth temptation "returns to the religious idea, and asks whether all religious obligations have been fulfilled." The seventh temptation, Densmore was told, is "the hardest of all, and if a man can endure it he will live to the allotted age. At this time an evil spirit comes to him, and if he has even so much as smiled during a Mide ceremony, he must reckon with it then."[34]

THE FOUR HILLS OF LIFE

In addition to the circle of life and the path of life, Ojibwe people have used, as apparently have other Native communities, the metaphor of spatial passage over four hills to imagine the temporal passage through life. The hills correspond to infancy/young childhood, youth, adulthood, and old age.

Basil Johnston, a scholar and educator from southern Ontario's Rice Lake community, renders such traditions through artfully written creative narratives and presents his community's teachings about life stages by means of an exchange between a perplexed dreamer and a medicine man to whom he brings a dream of the entirety of life. In his dream, Weegwauss sees in their entirety four hills, which he and others on the life course will travel and which he experiences in his own life. The first hill was covered with infants making a "steep and rugged" climb, and only half the number who began completed the ascent.[35]

The second and third hills were less rugged. On the second were boys and girls, who evidenced the same "compelling irresistible motion toward the top of the hill" with calamities that made some perish along the way. "There was life; there was motion," Johnston's narrator relates, "there was death; there was no stopping."[36]

The third hill was much like the second in terms of the indifference to the stricken and the onward surge of life, but there were no infants or youths, "few games to be witnessed, little laughter to be heard. Men and women began to travel in pairs, although there were solitary travelers, both men and women. All . . . were bent upon reaching the top. Little else mattered, pleasures were few and short lived." "In between the tasks and the infrequent joys, there were shouts of anger and hatred. There were battles between peoples over matters of little importance. Too frequently quarrels ended in pain, injury, and death." "No calamity, no impediment, no pleasure halted that surge of human beings. There was only one motion, forward."

Far fewer were present to ascend the fourth hill, which like the first was towering and difficult. "With faltering steps, halting strengths, gasping breaths the decrepit struggled on. Some inner strength of spirit urges us on; some outer force pushed or enticed us onward, forward, upward." But "old men and ancient women crumbled to the ground and were engulfed into the mountain soil to become one with it. Unlike the people on the other hills, those ascending the fourth hill heeded the fallen around them." "Those living on looked back, shouted encouragement to the fallen, to the faint. They shouted even to those on the third hill." Only a precious few reached the summit, which in the dream was shrouded in mist. "Those of us who continued to live slowly vanished into the shroud that hid the crest."[37]

Unsure of whether the dream betokened good or ill, Johnston's Weegwauss takes the dream to a wise man, and presumably an elder himself. After smoking a pipe, the wise man offers a lengthy teaching:

In the evening of life, the aged give way to decrepitude and must accept the loss of strength, the lessening of endurance, and the wane of agility as part of life's destiny and the consequence of continuing to live. A former way of life must be forsaken; a new mode of living accepted. But to give up the old and embrace something new has always been difficult. For labors, pursuits, habits, manners, and pleasures that have become part of a man or woman are not easily cast off. The more familiar and cherished former ways, the more difficult the parting. Though former modes can no longer be exercised, they live on in memory. By their very sweetness and worth they call out for living on; they deserve to be repeated in life again and again. To resurrect the past in forms already done, is to negate survival. The same flower does not live, die, to live again. It lives, dies, and is no more. After death and passing it leaves a memory of loveliness and a promise of a renewal of that beauty in another flower in another spring. To resurrect former times and to relive them would end the fulfillment of visions and growth in the new order. Perhaps it is the knowledge that what was can never be again—can never be restored except in fresh modes that render old age most difficult. Men and women know that death is inevitable. No wish can defer it. Men and women are destined for it from birth. The end must be accepted as part of life.[38]

Old age is "to be cherished, not disparaged," as a gift from the Great Spirit that is also a vocation:

Even in old age, life's work is not finished. There is still much good that can be done for brothers in life. By living through all the stages and living out the visions, men and women know something of human nature and living and life. What they have come to know and abide by is wisdom. This is what they must pass on to those still to traverse the path of life and scale the mighty hills. Only when they finally vanish into the mists is the work over.[39]

The fourth hill of old age in Johnston's imagining is distinguished in terms of its proximity to death and whatever comes afterward but that remains shrouded in mist from the perspective of those along the way. In this sense, the old one is constrained to live, think, and teach from a profound appreciation of death's certainty. But the image of the other hills, particularly the first, reminds that old age is not alone in its proximity to death and thereby not wholly determined by this proximity. Old age is also, in the rendering of the four hills motif, distinguished by the distance/time one has traveled and the wisdom gleaned along the way.

The "four hills of life" motif was also alluded to by my late teacher, Larry Cloud Morgan, who spoke repeatedly, if cryptically, of facing that moment when he would be situated somewhere on the slope of that final hill of life, looking both backward with knowing and upward with the need for extreme courage. He was fond of a poem he wrote about this last hill, a poem that I had the privilege of reciting at his burial:

> Our dreams must tell what we cannot speak,
> Like footprints to Ishpeming [heaven]
> Weaving the winds to sing
> Fanning the stars to shine
> Lighting the trail to the sacred mound
> Where we say, "Mountain, you are beautiful
> And I am not afraid."

Passage through the four hills of life may, as Johnston describes it, be the pursuit of individuals in obedience to their particular vision and calling in life, but there is something irreducibly collective about the life motion in this process, and this is perhaps where the linear image of a lifetime and the profound circulate on which it is, in reality, mapped and with which it is syncopated come together.

Anderson observes that for the Northern Arapaho, whose tradition includes clearly bounded age-grade demarcations through initiations between the stages of life, it is exceedingly clear that "life movement" hinges on intergenerational exchanges of respect and deference for elders' gifts of knowledge/power. The passing on of wisdom and ritual knowledge that empowers subsequent generations to live and live well is, in classic Arapaho understanding, more than education; it is a discarding of the old and embrace of the new that animates life movement. Anderson's observation of the Arapaho is much like Johnston's above of what the fourth hill requires of the Ojibwe: "Through life one must discard the burden of the previous stage while keeping its life giving force before entering the next."[40] Proceeding through life stages is more than a physiological process: it is a function of a previous generation's releasing of power/knowledge specific to the life stage it leaves behind even as it enters the next with the benefit of the same from the generation elder to it.

To each generation of Arapaho pertained a distinctive "way of knowing" that was regulated by controlling access to particular kinds of cultural and ritual knowledge in the age-grade initiatory system. An Arapaho elder described these ways of knowing to Anderson in these terms, which echo how Cloud Morgan described to me his own understanding of Ojibwe ways of knowing particular to life's passages:

Childhood: "the age of listening"
Youth: "the age of doing"
Adulthood: "the age of giving it back"
Old Age: "the age of sacred learning"[41]

It is for the Ojibwes, I think, as Anderson observes it is for the Arapaho: "The life cycle was modulated with respect to the transmission of knowledge. Elders ultimately controlled the process. They made certain that forms of knowledge were conveyed only at certain times in the life trajectory and in appropriate contexts."[42]

Here one can see the ultimate convergence of the linear image of the lifetime and the basic circularity from which it draws and to which it contributes motion. What is imagined from the perspective of the self as a linear movement from there to here is seen, in truth, to be a completion of a circle from here to here, and the duration of the lifetime by turns is seen to be subsumed into the ancient and eternal rhythms of *bimaadiziwin*.[43]

From "Old Age" to the Honorific "Elder"

Just as passage through all of life's stages has been imagined by Ojibwe people as more than a natural or biological process, so too the imagining of elderhood has been related to, but no straightforward function of, biological age. This point is crucial to my purposes here. Although all older people in Ojibwe communities are deserving of some respect as elder, age alone does not determine one's position as elder. Indeed, keeping track of an individual's precise age is a rather recent phenomenon among the Ojibwe. Even today, I meet people whose understanding of their own life cycle and time did not generate enough concern to be readily able to say how old they were. Eldership rests more firmly still on community recognition. As Theresa Smith observed about Manitoulin Island Ojibwe, "You do not become an elder there because you have reached a certain age but because people see that you are 'living right.' Thus not all elderly people are elders and some extraordinary middle-aged persons are, in fact, included in this honored group."[44]

One certainly cannot pinpoint the moment when a given person is regarded as an elder. For example, the Ojibwe tradition contains no formal rite of passage that marks off the final stage of life from the rest of adulthood or that secures an elder's social status. Indeed, community recognition of eldership in part seems to rest on an individual's carriage: the way that one comports oneself as an elder. One term that a dictionary project looking at the Mille Lacs dialect translates as "elder," *gikaajig*, is a substantive formed from the verb stem to be grave or respectable: those who act respectably or gravely. The expression brings together both the individual's comportment and the community's response: respect.

I would put the matter this way. All elderly people, on Ojibwe terms, are worthy of respect befitting an elder: they are not to be interrupted, they are to be served first, seated in places of advantage, publicly recognized, and generally treated with conspicuous deference. At the same time, as I once heard it put: "there are elders and there are Elders," the latter distinguishing those older women and men who are spoken of and addressed in deferential and honorific usages of elder terminology. In my experience, many of these people, too, refer in respectful language to their own elders or to "what the elders say." In sum, the term *elder* seems to be something that, perhaps like the Confucian sage, is never fully attained. Confucius himself purportedly disclaimed his own sagehood, and a similar dynamic is at work in Anishinaabe life: respected elders themselves will rarely speak directly of themselves as elders. For to claim it vociferously would be to deny it in the doing—a kind of spiritual arrogance perhaps not unlike declaring oneself to be "enlightened" or "free of sin" altogether. As one Native educator put it: "My rule is anyone who says they are an elder isn't."[45]

Unsurprisingly, a wealth of expressions in Ojibwe can give utterance to the term *elder*, along with a number of Ojibwe inflections on English and French usage. A variety of terms draw on the term *gichi* to indicate elder status. Along with *gichi anishinaabe*, or its variant *gete anishinaabe*, found by Hallowell in northern Manitoba, a man or women elder could be referred to as *gichi aya'aa* ("great being"; lit., "greatly s/he is there")[46] or *getazid*.[47] Baraga, the Slovenian priest who from the 1830s on worked on grammars and dictionaries of the Ojibwe language, glossed *Kitchi Anishinâbe* as "old person" and *Kitchi Aiaa* as "great being; a big, great, noble, mighty or elevated person; an old aged person; also, a large, big or old animal." Baraga's gloss on *Kitchi* (*gichi*) helps us appreciate the semantic range and force of this honorific adjectival or adverbial particle. It can mean "great, grand, large, big, extensive; preeminent, principal, old aged, much, well very; arch—," a particle that modifies verbs and substantives but that cannot stand grammatically on its own.[48]

John Nichols and Earl Nyholm gloss yet another term as referring to an elder, *gikaajig*, a substantive of the verb *gikaa* ("to be elderly").[49] Baraga glossed a term related to *gikaa*—*gikâd*—which combined with other verbs indicates "grave; respectable" and ties in this understanding of age not so much as one of biology or chronology, but of comportment.

Mindimooyenh ("old woman") and *akiwenzii* ("old man") are among the more respectful ways of referring to a person in the complex decorum of Ojibwe parlance, though Ruth Landes noted that these polite terms applied in casual conversation.[50] Even among those Ojibwe who do not speak the original language with proficiency, the English terms *that old man* or *that old woman* are the respectful and socially acceptable way to speak about esteemed persons, more respectful certainly than referring to them by their given name. Contrast that with the senses such terms have in contemporary American parlance: evocative of obsolescence, irrelevance senility. The nineteenth-century eastern Anishinaabe circuit-riding preacher Peter Jones glossed *akiwenzii*, "uhkewainsee," as "long dwellers upon the earth."[51]

Kinship terms for grandmother and grandfather, *nookomis* and *nimishoomis* respectively, are also used with frequency to address those taken as one's elders. In the system recorded by Hallowell in Manitoba in the 1930s, kinship terms for grandfather and grandmother extended to all generation in a kin and stood apart from other kinship categories for their intimacy. They also establish a potential kin relationship to all elders, whether or not related by blood or overt adoption.

Elders, the Afterlife, and the Spirits

If Ojibwe thought frames in supernatural terms what might be called "material" existence in the modern West or "earthly" existence in the Christian, so too does it extend the notion of the "natural" cycle of life into what the modern West and Christianity would construe as the afterlife. Much ink has been spilled by fur-trade observers, missionaries, and anthropologists, trying to fix the precise nature of Anishinaabe teachings about the afterlife, surely more than members of different Ojibwe communities themselves, thinking in terms of the dynamics of orality and shaped by different oral lineages, have given to systematizing the same. Teachings include, variously, an arduous journey by the soul to a land in the south (or west) that may, or may not, include the passage over a treacherous river whose outcome is shaped by one's moral conduct in life, to a kind of transmigration and rebirth of the soul in this world,[52] to prophetic and/or Christian teachings about heavens and hells, to the attainment of a status of ancestor, who continues to take an interest in the affairs of those who follow, appears to them in dreams, and in some cases can be summoned as *manidoog* who can bring power to bear on the affairs of this world.

Whether or not such teachings need become fixed or systemized in the complex dynamics of an oral tradition, the latter reference to ancestors is of particular interest to us here, for there is a consistent conviction that old age in this world, in this life, is but a stage along the way to a subsequent existence and that the old live in a kind of temporal *and mystical* proximity to these ancestors/spirits. I choose the word *mystical* here to indicate at once the communicative proximity understood to obtain between those of advanced age—and especially those with mature power—and in terms of a kind of nebulous identity between the elder and the ancestor, the elder and the spirits, recalling Johnston's image of the fourth hill's summit being shrouded in mist.

This proximity gives elders—both men and women—a kind of status as familiars with powerful *manidoog* ("spirits") who have passed on. What is more, there is a crucial homology between social kinship and spiritual kinship that places human eldership directly in a larger framework of the sacred. Hallowell notes that to fully understand the relationship established between grandfather/mother and grandchild, one must appreciate the relationship between human persons and nonhuman spiritual persons, and vice versa, for in an Anishinaabe worldview, human beings relate to the spirits as a grandchild relates to grandparents. Collectively, the other-than-human persons we might call the supernaturals or the spirits are known as "our Grandfathers."[53] In Midéwiwin teachings, the Seven

Grandfathers in particular are significant *manidoog* who are charged with looking after early human beings after the flood and who gift the Anishi-naabe with knowledge of how to live well with one another and creation. The term can also be applied more personally to particular stones, trees, or, more generally, to "Grandmother Earth." When Hallowell asked an Ojibwe consultant why he kept referring to a particular ceremonial drum associated with a Dream Dance as *gimishoomisan* ("our Grandfather"), he took the response at face value and offered an additional gloss. The consul-tant explained it was "due to the fact that it is one of the oldest things known to the Indians. But since, 'grandfather' is commonly used, not only as a term of respect for any old man but also in addressing or referring to spiritual helpers of all types, it has probably a deeper significance in this context."[54]

In a 1942 book on Ojibwe "conjuring," Hallowell noted that the generic term for spiritual being, in addition to the term *pawaganag* ("dream visi-tor"), was *grandfather*, "which conveys an attitude of respect in addition to any connotation of relationship" implied.[55] Citing Rogers's description of the grandchild/grandparent relationship, Smith noted "he could be de-scribing the human/manitou relationship.[56]

As Clifford Geertz and others, following the philosopher Suzanne Langer, have understood about other symbols for the sacred, a reflexive operation is at work here: the terms for grandparents (Hallowell refers to "grandfather" but elsewhere references are made to "grandmother") evoke the figure of ultimate respect in the social world, akin perhaps to the king in Israelite religion.[57] The ultimacy of social respect, however, is also tem-pered by the social intimacy that obtains in human grandchild-grandparent relationships, the subject of chapter 3.

In her more conventional study of Ojibwe kinship at a Canadian re-serve earlier in the twentieth century, Landes noted that the general term to speak of any elder is *gichi anishinaabe*.[58] *Gete Anishinaabeg* ("old peo-ple" as referred to in English) is also the collective term to describe the gen-eralized dead or the ancestors. In an essay entitled "The Spirits of the Dead in Saultaux Life," Hallowell noted that *keté änicinábek*, which he translated "old Indians" or "Ancients," could refer to the *jiibayag* or souls of the dead living in the southerly land of the dead, *jibaayakiing*, where the "drum-ming of human beings can be heard" giving them pleasure and where "the spirits of the dead themselves sing, dance, and drum." Hallowell here was tracking the spiritual sponsorship by these spirits of the dead of a Drum Dance that had been gifted to Kwtc in a dream.[59]

On numerous occasions I have heard Ojibwe people at White Earth refer to visits or experiences of "the old people." When spoken of this way, the old people were not specific personages who had passed on and visited them in dreams, but rather generalized ancestors. While there is no elaborate system of ancestor veneration in Ojibwe tradition, the *gete anishinaabeg* are considered to be *manidoog* active in the affairs of the living.

Ceremonialized offerings of tobacco offering to the spirits parallel decorum expected when juniors offer tobacco to ask elders to tell stories, perform ceremonies, or pray. As Leo Simmons noted in what he considered "primitive communities," "superannuation and the supernatural have been very commonly linked."[60] Elders occupy a privileged place between the living and the dead relatives, between human and nonhuman persons, between persons of exceptional power and those in need of it for the furtherance of the good life.

Bimaadiziwin/*Life Movement and the Exchange of Power*

The incessant forward movement of beings up and over the four hills of life, in Johnston's character's dream, or the recurrent cyclical movement of the seasons and the life of each person underscores, as does the verbal basis of the concept of *bimaadiziwin*, a connection between life and movement.[61]

As I indicated in the introductory review of the extensive anthropological literature on the Ojibwe, ethnologists made frequent passing mention of the power and authority of old age in the communities they visited and studied, but consistently failed to make anything of significance with those observations. References to aging and eldership never really go anywhere in that literature, I argued, because of a taxonomy where eldership is seen as a facet of the natural life cycle of individuals, not a structure of social relations beyond the family or a domain of significance to religion or worldview.

I also noted that late in his career, in a posthumously published essay, Hallowell was beginning to place respect for elders in the social realm with other domains of Ojibwe thought and practice. His observation that all members of one's grandparents' generation are worthy of that honorific segues to a discussion of the naming ceremony and elders' distinct role in it, which, in turn, occasions a discussion of the authority that comes from elders' proximity and more frequent contact with other-than-human persons, implied in the homology between grandparents and spirits. To Hallowell, kinship terminology, ceremonial activity that privileges elders' authority, and elders' special proximity to the world of other-than-human persons are of a piece and should be reckoned with in a larger understanding of the Ojibwe worldview, culture, and society.[62] Hallowell here began to reckon with the significance of the flow of power implied in an elder's ceremonial "giving" of a name, often that same elder's own name, and thus an extension of themselves, for the furtherance of life, *bimaadiziwin*. Subsequent chapters will elaborate on this framework, both in terms of the value of the power/knowledge that Ojibwe elders have to teach and preach, as well as the particular nature of the power/knowledge that Ojibwe elders gain by virtue of their social location and the posture, comportment, and ways of knowing culturally prescribed for eldership.

More Than a Footnote on Ambivalence Toward Old Age

As I write about these lofty ideals, I know well how easy it would be to overlook a decidedly human ambivalence about one's own aging and about the authority of old age that appear in clear if undeveloped references in the historical, ethnographic record, as well as in my own experience with members of the community.

While Hallowell and other ethnographers made too much of the social and psychological dimensions of what they called Ojibwe "atomism," especially as it concerns what they viewed as a dysfunctional fear of witchcraft/sorcery, they bore witness to occasional resentment of elders' authority. Hallowell cites Jenness on the Parry Island Ojibwe: "Every man suspects his neighbor of practicing the nefarious art to avenge some fancied grievance, and the older and more conservative the Indian, the more he is held in suspicion."[63]

But the emotive aspect of fear could also be seen as part and parcel of an overarching concept of respect: one that was not simply a matter of sentimental esteem or trust in a domesticated, predictable other, but a principled matter of good judgment with regard to one with more power. For sacred power is morally ambiguous, and the power to heal is simultaneously the power to harm. This ambivalence, too, must be part of the story. (Chapter 2 will help illuminate how respecting elders is a matter of respecting the power associated with accrued age.)

· · ·

Bimaadiziwin *in Historical Motion: Historical Demographics*

If *bimaadiziwin* characterizes healthy, long lives nourished by proper relations among people, land, and spirits, it has proven increasingly difficult for Ojibwe people to realize in the years since contact with Euro-Americans, their diseases, and their dispossession of Anishinaabe lands, languages, and cultures. I turn now to consider both the persistence of an ideal of *bimaadiziwin* as well as these new challenges to its unobstructed flow.

Archeological analysis has suggested that prior to 1492 the life expectancy of Native North Americans was comparable to that of European populations of the day.[64] Although it is difficult to identify what such numbers might have been for the Anishinaabeg specifically, scholars have noted that humans of the Western Hemisphere generally were "remarkably free of serious diseases before European and Africans arrived" and in particular in the colder environments of the subarctic and woodlands of the north and northeast.[65]

Citing an array of widely ranging 1492 population estimates, historical demographer Russell Thornton estimates that in 1492 more than five million Native people occupied lands of what is now the United States (of seventy-two million in the Western Hemisphere). In "one of the more important demographic events in the history of the world," this number dwindled—to use a completely inadequate expression—to roughly 600,000 by 1800 and further to its low point of 250,000 by 1890.[66] Importantly, Thornton makes clear, this means more than the untimely death of five million people: with negligible population loss through out-migration, such dramatic decline is produced by the ratio of mortality rates and birth rates. Since declining birth rates could have accounted for only a small part of this enormous decline, one must contend with astounding increases in mortality rates. Because diminished life expectancy typically can suggest a younger population and a smaller number of elderly people in a given population, and because those elderly comprise segments of a given population particularly vulnerable to such diseases, surely these conditions made a dramatic impact on the numbers and nature of eldership.

Deadly microbial exchanges predated the Anishinaabeg's actual encounter with European explorers and traders in the seventeenth-century fur trade, and thus the earliest written European witnesses to Anishinaabe life were describing not aboriginal communities on the verge of cultural change, as conventional wisdom might have it, but communities already reeling from prior waves of disease owing to exchanges with European and African populations. Henry Dobyns identifies 1520 as the year of the first major smallpox epidemic among Native peoples of the northeast.[67] Anishinaabe and other Native communities were also beset by measles, bubonic plague, cholera, typhoid, pleurisy, scarlet fever, diphtheria, mumps, whooping cough, gonorrhea, pneumonia, malaria, and yellow fever. These microbial exchanges did not simply run their course in the early years of contact, but revisited their destruction in waves, resulting in as many as ninety-three major pandemics of diseases owing to exchanges with European and African populations.[68]

Nor were these epidemics the result of purely natural causes; disease was deployed in a highly intentional way. During Pontiac's revolt against British colonization in 1763, which involved a good number of Odawa and Ojibwe warriors, the commander in chief of British forces, Sir Jeffrey Amherst, suggested deploying smallpox-infected blankets. "You will do well," Amherst wrote to a field commander, "to try to inoculate the Indians by means of blankets as well as to try every other method that can serve to extirpate this exorable race." He was later informed by another field commander that "out of our regard for them [i.e., two Indian chiefs] we gave them two blankets and a handkerchief out of the smallpox hospital. I hope it will have the desired effect."[69] Many contemporary Native people regard alcoholism and other forms of substance abuse in the same category as chemical warfare.

Waves of epidemics and pandemics led to nothing short of social chaos for many local Native communities, upsetting the family and clan structures of many Anishinaabe groups and producing among survivors new and resilient forms of social organization. Ethnohistorian Richard White has understood that the communities that formed the fur-trade and mission outposts in New France were busy polyglot intersections of communities reeling from these results.[70]

The social chaos was accompanied by a crisis of spiritual power. Ethnohistorians have studied extensively the impact of diseases and circumstances that taxed and outpaced indigenous apothecaries and healing methods and in turn cleared ground for a regard for the powerful Jesuit missionaries and their God, but sufficient attention has not yet been paid to the age-specific implications of smallpox and other outbreaks. If it is reasonable to conclude that the old, especially the very old, along with the very young, fell victim in disproportionate numbers,[71] the disruption would, it follows, have an impact on the authority structure of the communities whose oral traditions privilege the authority of key elders and their wisdom. If authority resided among elders, as seventeenth-century *Jesuit Relations* suggest, this raises further questions about the nature of social chaos. Were one to assume the analytical posture that Calvin Martin took concerning the social and cultural ramifications of decimated beaver populations for the fur trade, one could reasonably expect that the social and ecological chaos would generate a revolt against the established authority of elders and traditional ways in favor of prophetic critiques of the same, and to be sure various prophetic movements emerged amid these disruptions and displacements.[72]

Epidemics could also disrupt the familial networks that cared for the physical and economic needs of grandparents and great-grandparents. Documents left behind by missionaries from the seventeenth-century Jesuits on through nineteenth-century Episcopalians suggest that a disproportionate number of the reliable catechists were elder women and men either unable to take up the rigors of the seasonal round or who had no recourse for care within debilitated families. Perhaps, one could conjecture, the harder it became to care for the elders who did survive the scourge of disease, the greater the resentment of their presence. Still, if one takes seriously the claims in subsequent chapters about the nature of the authority of age in oral traditions generally and Anishinaabe communities in particular, one could just as well conclude that an emerging demographic scarcity of elders served to reinforce, if not increase, their authority and prestige. Since honoring elders had never been an easy or natural priority for Native communities to live up to, some measure of both increased resentment and redoubled efforts to honor and respect elders were likely in play.

Importantly, the nadir of Native American population generally came not in those first few years after the encounter with unfamiliar pathogens with origins in Europe and Africa but in the waning years of the nineteenth century, and this on the watch of the U.S. government, which had turned considerable attention toward resolving what it glibly called "the Indian problem." Early in the century, the incipient nation continued policies of treaty making that had been past practice under the colonial rule of the English and Spanish. From the 1820s until the United States put an end to its treaty making in 1871, Anishinaabe people made a series of formal treaties (and with Canada for several more decades) ceding lands and committing to peace in exchange for annuity payments, capital infrastructure, and, after the 1850s, discrete tracts of reservation lands. With a few exceptions in the case of Michigan communities, most Anishinaabe people did not face, or refused, the formal policies of "removal" that relocated many eastern and southeastern nations to distant and unfamiliar landscapes, but Anishinaabe people perhaps no less felt the sting of displacement, with shrinking land bases increasingly unable to sustain the seasonal round that provided not just a living, but that defined *bimaadiziwin*. Beginning in 1868, many Minnesota and Red River Anishinaabeg were relocated to the White Earth Reservation, established in the country that straddles the boundary between northern forest and prairie, chosen for how it might draw its residents from the attachments to the seasonal round to the sedentary agriculture that policy makers and missionaries alike viewed as necessary to civilization.

It is against the backdrop of the presumptions of the "reforms" of assimilation policy and on the premises of reservations closely administered by civil and religious authorities that one ought properly to measure the violence of the demographic disaster in the nadir of the Anishinaabe population.

On Minnesota's reservations, waterborne diseases, tuberculosis, and other diseases, including alcohol abuse, that thrive in impoverished, overcrowded circumstances were the rule. Diseases endured by the strong proved fatal for young children and the elderly. Smallpox afflicted Ojibwes in large numbers as recently as 1883 and again in 1899–1900.[73] In his informal census of the White Earth Reservation in 1880, an Episcopal priest remarked that there were "fifty more deaths than births." "The Indian of today," he wrote, "does not reach the same old age of the red man of 100 years ago. . . . There are now but five or six old men on the reservation."[74] More formal reports by the Indian Agents among Minnesota Ojibwes show that, by the 1890s, birth rates were outrunning death rates by two to one, perhaps because provision had been made for resident physicians at the two Indian agencies at White Earth and Leech Lake. But such gains were fragile, as suggested by Leech Lake and Red Lake in 1902, where deaths outnumbered births two to one and four to one respectively.[75] Even given the dramatic growth in the birth rates, epidemics of untimely death still beset Minnesota's Ojibwe and impacted the number and status of community elders.

Although aggregate census figures for all Native Americans have consistently obscured the particular devastation for Anishinaabeg in Minnesota, the 1900 census recorded only 13.1% of the Native population over the age of 50. Ten years later it rose to only 13.6%. In 1920, the share of the Native population over 50 was 14.1%; in 1930, it was 13.5%.[76] The 1920 and 1930 censuses recorded median ages of 19.7 and 19.6 among Indians respectively, compared to 25.2 and 26.4 for all races.[77] As Thornton notes, these early-twentieth-century census reports took a peculiar interest in tracking distinctions among self-reported "full blood" and "mixed blood" Native populations and documented consistently younger populations among the full bloods, signaling "differences in socioeconomic conditions, particularly health care, between the two groups."[78]

Those who survived to old age were difficult to support in the lean years of the late nineteenth century and early twentieth century. Seasonal rounds were more difficult to obtain. Congress routinely failed to apportion the treaty annuities due Ojibwe people. Timber companies were leveling the habitat for game. A series of dams on the headwaters of the Mississippi for the benefit of navigability downstream flooded entire villages and, more

An elder woman, Ma-key-dence, sits, unmoved, with blanket and crucifix on Minnesota Ojibwe lands apparently denuded by timber companies, ca. 1910. *Courtesy Minnesota Historical Society*

ominously, destroyed the wild rice beds that provided their staple food.[79] Again, these circumstances placed incredible stress on the care structures within kin networks for meeting the needs of elders and may have forced many Anishinaabe people to provide for elders by letting them reside near mission stations and in Indian agencies.

TWENTIETH CENTURY

The twentieth century saw a steady gain in Native American population, from one quarter million in 1890 to just over 2 million in the 1990 census and 3.5 million in the 2000 census (the latter census enabled self-reporting of multiple racial identifications). Indeed, by late in the twentieth century, this population was among the fastest growing of U.S. populations, a fact that counters popular notions of the "vanishing Indian" and suggests the profound resilience of Native American communities. Still, any visit to an Anishinaabe community reveals that all is not completely well in this state of affairs. Indeed much of the growth of the population can be understood as dramatic increases in the birthrate with unremarkable decreases in mortality. A 1997 in-depth U.S. government survey of Indian health made plain statistics of untimely preventable deaths that are as troubling as they are consistent with the previous century's injustices.

Indeed, old age can be considered a rare accomplishment in Indian country. Thornton observes, "The American Indian population has been and is far younger than the non-Indian population," with leading causes of death that are not typically associated with old age and thus do not mirror the U.S. population as a whole.[80] Only 6% of Native people were 65 or older in the 1990 census, less than half the percentage of similarly aged Americans as a whole (12.5%).[81] In 1970, only 5.7% of Native Americans were in that aged category.[82] Of course, a younger population could be a function of burgeoning numbers of young people more than one of the difficulty of attaining a full age, but it is also true that life expectancy is a problem. Life expectancy at birth for American Indians and Alaska Natives between 1939 and 1941 was only 51. Between 1972 and 1974, life expectancy at birth was only 63. Between 1992 and 1994, it was 71, four and half years younger than the population as a whole.[83] The particulars are as troubling as the broader figures.

Between 1992 and 1994, nearly one third of deaths among Native Americans took people before they reached 45, and this against a national average of 11%. In part this is a direct result of disproportionate violence: murders among Native Americans occur 40% more frequently than among the population as a whole. Teenage suicides run at levels nearly three times the national average.[84] But more typically the violence of death and illness is less direct, more insidiously tied to conditions of poverty and racism. In these years, Native Americans suffered mortality from heart disease at rates twice the national average, diabetes at rates three times the national average, and alcohol-related accidents at rates seven times the national average.[85]

These stark conditions have meant that more Anishinaabe people have arrived at what is considered "old age" at younger and younger chronological ages, and this with considerable implications for the shape and texture of eldership. A Stanford study summarized the scene in the mid-1990s as follows: "Most American Indian/Alaska Native elders are living in worse conditions than the majority of older persons in the United States, and might be considered 'elderly' at a younger chronological age than other U.S. populations." This was not simply for reasons of cultural valuing of eldership but "because of the onset of problems of associated with old age at an earlier point in life."[86]

The maladies to which these statistics point inscribe on individual bodies what many White Earth residents view as the historical wounds inflicted on the Anishinaabe social body. Here illness, chemical dependency, and violent death are seen as part and parcel of historical dispossession of land, language, and culture that still affect Ojibwe lives. Since the 1867 treaty that established its boundaries as sacrosanct, White Earth Ojibwes, as individuals or as a tribe, own fewer than 7% of its land base. And after a century of assimilation policies and English-only boarding schools, only 4% of Ojibwe young people (aged 5–17) speak the original language in their home.[87] According to a 1994 study, fewer than thirty Minnesota Ojibwes aged 35 or younger were fluent in the language.[88]

Neither have policies of assimilation and integration into the cultural, social, and economic life of the United States worked to bring justice to White Earth. The 1990 census showed that more than half of the Native people on the reservation live below the poverty line, compared to 13.1% of all U.S. races. Today, only 2% of reservation residents hold college degrees, and nearly half did not complete high school.

Amid these ills, today's elders, like those of prereservation days, evidence uncommon power by virtue of their very survival, and living a long time can be associated with intelligence, resilience, and wherewithal. If, in the seasonal round of prereservation Ojibwe life, elders by their very longevity demonstrated a resourcefulness toward life and some measure of a mastery of ethical and religious relatedness that empowered them to live well and to live long, so too have elders in the early-reservation era and through the twentieth century garnered worthy stature as resourceful survivors, beating the odds of statistical life expectancy and impoverished conditions, and navigating the displacements and discouragements that can come with integration into racist educational, economic, and political structures. To describe the prowess of today's elders, contemporary Ojibwe people may not use the vocabulary that early ethnologists learned from their consultants concerning dream visitors and the power gifted by guardian spirits/*pawaganag*, and given the numbers of people stricken

Five generations of Leech Lake Ojibwe women are pictured in this 1943 snapshot by John Clement Beaulieu: Dorothy V. Hodder, Mrs. Henry Buffalo, Mrs. John Rabbit, Nadine Hodder Chase, and Elsie R. Beaulieu. *Courtesy Minnesota Historical Society*

early in life by disease and violence, they may not as readily correlate old age with moral accomplishment or spiritual acumen, but today, as of long ago, attaining old age amid these circumstances is a notable accomplishment and tangible evidence that old people can be persons of peculiar muster, if not extraordinary power.

The Accentuation of and New Challenges to the Authority of Eldership

If the authority of eldership has proved surprisingly persistent in Anishinaabe history, its significance has not remained static. It appears that eldership has grown in stature, and honoring elders has taken on a new urgency in light of the demographic and cultural tragedies of the last two hundred years. The knowledge and example of older Anishinaabeg have been viewed increasingly as safeguards to, and perhaps even antidotes for, contemporary social ills. That knowledge is perhaps quite different in content from that of long ago, but it remains structurally similar for its value to future generations of Anishinaabe young people. For example, the very brokenness of health and well-being of Native communities suggests that surviving to old age cannot be a sure indication of upright living or spiritual blessing, and the Christian tradition and science give Anishinaabe people other lenses through which to view the significance of old age. But surviving conditions that the statistics indicate all too few Anishinaabe people survive, elders' very presence can thus be highly charged with connotations of strength, character, intelligence, perseverance, resourcefulness, bravery, and judgment that today, as in aboriginal times, are celebrated and emulated traits. In this, their very presence can inspire younger people in family networks and in larger circles of community with some version of a vision of *bimaadiziwin*, and what they have to say about navigating the difficulties of living in a racist world, in a discriminatory job market. But the difficulties have been so ominous that this should not be romanticized to be uniformly true.

Grim life expectancy rates have meant that more Anishinaabeg are arriving at recognition as elders at younger ages, and this has presented new challenges to community consensus in the recognition of eldership. Recognized eldership has never been a mere function of age, but as a result of these demographic changes, and in light of generations facing concerted cultural assimilation, recognition of eldership has come to be perhaps even less closely tied to length of years and experience or to cultural and linguistic competence that previous generations had associated more consistently with old age. Perhaps, too, this younger threshold of eldership recognition has resulted in the potential for increased tensions surrounding varying interpretations of tradition among recognized "elders" of different age-groups. Indeed, because the English term *elder* has gained traction in and through these circumstances, it is fitting to reflect on its etymology and contemporary usage.

A History of the English Term Elder

This chapter has considered traditional Anishinaabe ways of marking old age and rendering significant old as well as the increasing difficulty of achieving old age under colonization. Because those difficulties generally have accentuated, rather than diminished, the authority of culturally recognized old age, it is worth augmenting our earlier consideration of the variety of indigenous terms denoting old age with a discussion of the emergence of the English term *elder*.

If not used as an honorific itself, the English term *elder*, as opposed to "old man," "old woman," or "old person," has accrued associations of maturity and venerability rather than irrelevance and feebleness. This may owe to the English-language history of the ecclesiastical position of elder, from the Greek New Testament's *presbyteros*, which various Christian groups have accorded various official tasks.

In some Protestant denominational polities, the elder is a figure of religious authority with a variety of official roles. In the Presbyterian denomination, ruling elders are chosen as the legislative leaders of a congregation. Once one's term has been served as a ruling elder, one technically retains the title, though the connection between church eldership and old age became severed during the eighteenth century. In the Methodist tradition, the presiding elder refers to those ordained clergy who are in positions of regional authority over others, but again, the relationship between the title and chronological old age is at best associational. The elder as authority figure extends to the polity of many other churches as well. In liturgical traditions like the Roman Catholic and Anglican/Episcopalian, it should be said, the elder is no official figure of religious authority.

Seemingly, it would follow that the English term *elder* might appear in Anishinaabe English parlance as most honorific in the most missionized communities, but I have found no clear evidence to support this; indeed as I discuss in chapter 4, there is evidence to suggest that Protestant missionaries felt deeply ambivalent about the kind of authority that aged Anishinaabe people held in their communities. Nevertheless, there is evidence to suggest that the honorific associations developed around the English term *elder* from its career as an ecclesiastical designation made it suitable as a term of choice for Native people wishing to reference their older relatives in this manner. Also, its gender neutrality as a term calls attention, more than "old man" or "old woman," to an authority of age that mutes gender difference.

The earliest Euro-American references to older Anishinaabeg are French, found in the seventeenth- and eighteenth-century *Jesuit Relations*, the extensive body of published correspondence from French Jesuit missionaries in the Great Lakes regions. Very frequently, there are French references to *les Anciennes, les vieillards* ("old men"), and occasionally *les vielles femmes* ("old women"). In his masterful translation, undertaken between 1853 and 1913, of ninety some volumes of the *Jesuit Relations*, Reuben Gold Thwaites translated *les Anciennes* as the gender-neutral "Elders" (note capital E) and *vieilleurs* as "Older Men," These two designations frequently appear with references to the impressive formal gatherings, or councils, that the Jesuit missionaries addressed.

The English term as we know it begins to appear in the mid-nineteenth century, and the earliest usages I could find are in the published writings of the Ojibwe Methodist clergyman Peter Marksman in Michigan in his description of pre-Christian Anishinaabe life, complicated as it was with both Christian criticism of pagan customs and a strategic Christian appreciation for the genius of certain indigenous values:

> We obtain our names when young, by our parents making a feast to the **elder** of our tribe, or some man or woman who professes knowledge of the gods of the heaven or of the earth or of the waters, and have blessed him or blessed her; and these persons receive the feast prepared and offered to their god, whoever he is . . . and after the offering is over, the guests of the feast answer the person, who pronounces with a loud voice, saying, "He shall be called by his generation." The guests say, Ha, which means Amen. . . . Then the food is distributed to every person who was called to this feast. After the child receives a name, he is known by that name.[89]

Perhaps this rhetorical bind informed Marksman's own reference to the reckoning of eldership by date of initiation in the Midéwiwin, which of course he had formally dispensed with as a Christian leader. Calling into question the indigenous logic of Midéwiwin initiation, Marksman wrote, "I was only a boy when I was classified as an elder."[90]

The term gains further traction as a term of choice in ethnological descriptions for designating not simply any Anishinaabe person of advanced age, but those who are recognized older people serving a public function in the community. The 1860 translation of German travel writer and ethnologist Johann Georg Kohl's *Kitchi-Gami: Life Among the Lake Superior Ojibway* recorded Kohl's observation of a treaty payment: "If the turn has arrived of a tribe whose members have not come in yet, the statistics are temporarily compiled from the memory of elders."[91] William Warren makes occasional reference to the term as it applies to men in council, as in the case between Ojibwe and Dakota where "a lasting peace was discussed between the elders of the two camps."[92] But such writings make ample reference elsewhere to "old men" and "old women" without appeal to the term *elder* in this sense, and so *elder* doesn't emerge as a term of art in ethnographic literature as it develops in the early twentieth century, perhaps because presumptions to scientific objectivity in description cautioned against the usage of a term that still carried ecclesiastical associations. Or perhaps it was a term useful primarily in designating relative age. For example, Densmore appealed to the term *elder* only when making distinctions of relative age generally such as in the custom of younger people who "must pass their elders in entering or leaving" a wigwam.[93] Here the word carries no particular freight. According to Jenness, whose work among the Parry Island Ojibwe was published in 1935, "Children were taught certain rules of conduct, and frequently punished for their infringement. They should never tell lies. They should be respectful to their elders and not walk in front of them."[94]

But it does appear with greater frequency by the mid-twentieth century, as demonstrated first in the important ethnographic writings of Ruth Landes and Inez Hilger, each of whom paid further attention than their male cohort to the life cycle and its significance. Perhaps Landes was shaped by the Thwaites translations of *Jesuit Relations* in her 1937 discussion of governing councils in *Ojibwa Sociology*: "All old men are called giche anishinaabe, ancient, elder, and are accorded a conventional respect. Along with the mature males of the village, they constitute the council, the 'smoking place.'"[95]

In 1937, Hilger made occasional reference to "elders" to help distinguish the public role of the age-set of older Anishinaabe from specific grandparents in a family line: "The moral code," she wrote, "was taught to boys and girls at puberty, usually by the grandparents or, in their absence, by elders living in the community."[96] But by 1951 Hilger was making frequent and decisive reference to older Ojibwe by the term *elder*, the term appearing fully fifteen times in references like this: "A favorite diversion of elders was visiting, children sitting by and listening in. Topics of conversation might be gossip, legends, historic events, travels, or visits of other tribes."[97]

By 1962, Rogers's ethnography of Ontario's Round Lake Ojibwe could boast fully thirty-six references to elder or elders, typically in this larger sense: "Children are taught to aid others and to listen to the advice of their elders."[98]

I suspect that these ethnographic references to *elder* were themselves serving as indices of increased use of the English term in indigenous speech to reference those carrying an even accentuated authority of age. And the gender-neutral reference, rather than appealing to gendered translations of *akiwenzii* or *mindimooyenh*, suggests the striking way that age mutes gender distinctions in this authority structure.

2

ELDERSHIP, RESPECT, AND
THE SACRED COMMUNITY

Our elders were wise and loving teachers who knew our history and genealogy, and who knew about medicines and other herbs. They had a clear and useful understanding of community dynamics and practical psychology. We did not warehouse our old people, nor segregate them away from the rest of their Dodemian [clan].

—Wub-e-ke-niew, *We Have the Right to Exist*

 Several Native people to whom I have introduced this project have been curious whether I could generate enough material on the subject of elders to fill an entire book. In part, their curiosity owes to the fact that honoring elders is so axiomatic in today's Ojibwe communities. In part, though, it may derive from an Anishinaabe conviction that honoring elders cannot be divorced from respect for all others: human others, but also plants, animals, weather phenomena, rocks, ancestors, and spirits. As Thomas Peacock puts it, "As with our ancestors, the path to wisdom really comes down to simple things, simple yet complex at the same time: honor the Creator, honor elders, be kind, be peaceful. Live in a gentle way."[1] This chapter will situate the respect for elders in the larger framework of an ideal Anishinaabe *sacred community*, one held together by bonds of honor and respect.

If the last chapter placed the significance and authority of eldership in the context of Ojibwe imaginings of the life course, this chapter shows how the practices of deference for the old, which along with practices of sagacity constitute eldership, take their place among the more important practices recognizing and promoting the subordination of the self to a web of relations, practices that can be said to create and sustain a sacred community. In this light, an insistence on respect for elders suggests the junior-elder relationship as the paradigmatic relationship for a harmonious social, and ecological, ethic. I will unpack the concepts of "honoring" and "respecting" elders and examine attitudes and ritualized practices of decorum, deference, and care with regard to elders. It is through such practices that Anishinaabe people in the past and present strive to recognize and sustain community, the ultimacy of which compares well to that imagined by the Confucian tradition. In short, the logic of honoring elders is not simply the logic of deference to the old in merely patriarchal terms, but the logic of producing and maintaining a relatedness that contributes to, even as it taps into, *bimaadiziwin*. Here, as in the neo-Confucian tradition, the respect toward one's elders is a paradigmatic, iconic relation grounding other interpersonal relations (human, ecological, and spiritual) in a relational cosmology.

Even as the analogy to Confucianism helps elicit the sacred urgency of Ojibwe social and ecological ethics, the comparative work helps establish just how the more prominent features of Ojibwe religion may not be in the ritual life of shamans or in the beliefs about sacred power, as prevailing studies have suggested, but instead in the insistence and practice of sacred community, toward which those ritual and belief structures are means. Indeed, the prevailing academic literature on the Ojibwe (and other Native traditions) has missed the forest for the trees in contenting itself with shamanism, power, and ritual. If it seems commonplace to examine a relational harmony ethic among Native societies, the interest in ritual and shamanism has eclipsed a fuller reckoning of the centrality of social ethics to Native religions. This chapter will not endeavor to fully restore that vision, but a focus on the ceremonious ethics of respect, of which respect for elders is paradigmatic, can help connect the seemingly disparate fields of ritual, ethics, and social relations.

As with other chapters, this chapter will also examine the historical career of these practices of decorum, deference, and provision for the needs of elders, especially as care provision for elders has become increasingly institutionalized under federal, state, and tribal programs. Even with the assault on community and eldership by assimilation policies, missionization, educational structures, and market capitalism, a persistent emphasis on honoring and providing for elders and community has been negotiated by improvising with the resources of government programs and the institutional frameworks of tribal governments.

Kinship, Not Atomism

I know that I am not alone in being puzzled by the tyranny of the organizing idea of "Ojibwe atomism," to use Victor Barnouw's language, or
"Ojibwe individualism," to use that of Ruth Landes.[2] Explications of individualism or atomism consume page after page in the ethnographic record
on the Ojibwe. In such a view, Ojibwe people, especially in the far north,
but also Southern Ojibwe, lacked any significant social structure beyond
the family, and this resulted in a striking degree of autonomy in social,
economic, religious, and ethical matters. A.I. Hallowell even offered his
own "psychological explanation" of "atomism or individualism of Ojibwe
society." Hallowell took as his starting point the observations of Diamond
Jenness: "Every man suspects his neighbor of practicing the nefarious art
to avenge some fancied grievance, and the older and more conservative the
Indian, the more he is held in suspicion. Probably there is not a single
adult on the island who has not been accused of sorcery at some time or
another." Hallowell continues in this vein:

> It is impossible for people to get together when their outlook is colored by
> the possibility of malevolence, particularly when there are no social institu-
> tions that demand a high degree of cooperation. Since covert malevolence
> is always potentially present in one's dealings with others and the only de-
> fense against it is one's own supernaturally augmented powers, psychologi-
> cal security can only be achieved by the enhancement of confidence in
> one's power to stand alone. Close kin are important because identification
> with them is possible. Religion is a system of obtaining individual power
> for individual ends, originally dependent upon the individual's ability to
> attain it.[3]

In time, the spread of this organizing idea produced its critics in Ojibwe
studies. Harold Hickerson pointed out in the late 1960s that Landes and
Hallowell had tailored their mid-twentieth-century interpretations of the
Ojibwe social ethos, perhaps even beyond recognition by the communities
with whom they lived, to correct the excesses of social anthropologists'
contentions that primitive societies were perforce communistic in economic orientation and communal in social orientation.[4] Following Hickerson, Vivian Rohrl and historian Theresa Schenk argued that atomism or

individualism misses the social structural force of the *doodem*, or clan, system, its traditional delineation of labor and of leadership (as in the Crane *doodem*).[5] Eldership adds yet another layer of extrafamilial social structure to the equation, for the authority of eldership crosses familial and clan boundaries. For example, Rohrl was surprised to find at Mille Lacs no such "individualistic relational orientation . . . inasmuch as older people were respected."[6] E. S. Rogers noted how an overly individualistic approach to Ojibwe religion distorts the relationality at its heart: "The native religion is more than simply a means of dealing with the supernatural. It is involved intimately with medical problems and with interpersonal and to a certain extent with intercommunity relations."[7]

More elementally, the organizing idea of Ojibwe atomism or individualism has wholly failed to touch on the profound relationality at the center of traditional and historical Ojibwe understandings of the person or the self. One could even argue that Ojibwe social and ecological ethics, ritual, and even humor are principally oriented toward the humbling of the self by methodical, ritualized folding of the individual into various layers of the collective: social, natural, and spiritual.

Ethical emphases on kinship and practices of kinship terminology offer clear examples of this presumption away from a sense of the individual to relationality. Polite conventions of everyday Ojibwe-language speech emphasize the subordination of the self at nearly every turn, including word order, by placing references to oneself conspicuously at the end of the sentence. While these conventions may be, according to some views, just that—arbitrary conventions with no encoded meaning—for contemporary bilingual people like Larry Cloud Morgan, they have been important parts of what has distinguished speaking the Ojibwe language and the worldview to which that language provides access and articulation.

Again, formal Ojibwe-language address involves the greeting, akin to "Ladies and Gentleman" in English, *nindinawemaaganag*, a dubitative form that could be translated "you who might be relatives." The shape of the expression is, again arguably, pure convention. But in the view of some Ojibwe people, it also speaks to a posture toward the social, natural, and spiritual world that presumes relationality, that prioritizes the subject's place in a web of relations, and that vigilantly reminds the subject ever to place her/himself in terms of that web of relations. Put another way, the kinship system is less a map of Ojibwe conceptualizations of social order than it is a document of practices of relationality. The question is not "am I kin?" but "how am I kin?"

Landes discussed the complex schedule of Ojibwe kinship terminology in northern Ontario and Minnesota as variations on the basic category of "relative," the generic term for which she identified as *nindako-maagan* or *indinawamaagan*, to which, she found, "the associated generic obligation is kindness. The term is also used towards any non-relative who behaves kindly."[8] Part of this kindness involves, according to Landes, a speech convention of using the appropriate kinship term when addressing anyone save one's own offspring, uniquely for whom use of proper names was appropriate. As Landes puts it, "this is said to be out of considerateness, 'pity.'"[9] Such speech practices framed ordinary interactions in terms of expectations, responsibilities, and benefits associated with a particular relationship, say with one's older brother or one's mother's sister's daughter. The convention served to remind, numerous times each day, of one's place in a web of relations and obligations, and to shape the disposition that looks expectantly for relationship. When Ojibwe "strangers" encounter one another, they often begin by ascertaining how they might be related, "placing" one another in terms of family, clan, band, and lineage.[10]

Extension of Respect in Social Realm to Natural and Spiritual

Kinship terminology is also conventionally applied beyond the realm of human society to the myriad of nonhuman persons who make up the natural environment and the spiritual beings that people and animate the web of *bimaadiziwin* ("life movement" or "life").[11] Through such media as Disney's *Pocahontas*, American popular culture has trivialized Native American practices of addressing, for example, bear as brother, as a mark of a natural propensity to be at one with the natural world, but the fuller religious and ethical force of such practices should not be thus taken for granted, taken as natural. To make a habit of addressing any animal or plant or weather phenomenon with a kinship term is not to claim "oneness with nature," but to claim "nature's" subjectivity, indeed to claim that "it" isn't some abstraction known as "nature" to which humans are in some problematic relation, but rather a society of nonhuman persons, to

Norval Morrisseau, "Our duty is to teach our grandchildren to share the fruits and berries of the land with the birds and the animals." Acrylic on canvas, 60 x 40 in., 1990. Morrisseau's is a modern representation of a traditional Ojibwe view that animals and plants can teach human persons about how to live, including how to be elders. *Courtesy Garfinkal Publications*

use Hallowell's important words, who have moral status, sacred power, and in some cases sentience, independent of what humans confer upon them. In this light, the use of kinship terminology when addressing nonhuman life is anything but a mark of a "natural" Native American affection for nature or oneness with nature; it shows the hard work involved with living well in relation to the web of life.[12] Significantly, the animals, plants, and weather phenomena that constitute nonhuman persons are considered "elder" siblings in a kinship sense and thus claim a certain level of age-related deference. Old animals can share the designation *gichi-aya'aa* ("great being") with human elders and can even model and teach ethics to human people. A painting entitled "The Duty of Elders" by the Canadian Ojibwe artist Norval Morrisseau depicts a grandmother showing a grandchild how to pick blueberries, opposite a bear and bear cub who are doing the same. Morrisseau subtitles the piece, "Our duty is to teach our grandchildren to share the fruits and berries of the land with the birds and the animals."

What is more, kinship and society extend beyond the circle of human relations not only to the nonhuman persons of the natural world, but also to the nonhuman persons of a spiritual nature. As Hallowell famously argued in his examination of an Ojibwe worldview, there is no clear conceptual, or even perceptual, distinction between the natural and the supernatural. Given the expectation that what we might call spiritual or supernatural presences could transform themselves into natural phenomena, in the Ojibwe language, what one experiences as a bear, or a tree, or an eagle is never with certainty asserted to be such; at best it "very reliably is a bear."[13] Kinship terminology and the concomitant sense of society extend to these spiritual presences as well.

Still, the posture of respect is more basic than any particular term that would refer to it in the Ojibwe lexicon. One might even say it is grammatical. The Ojibwe language observes no masculine/feminine/neuter gender distinction but instead makes a distinction between animate and inanimate genders, him/her and it, respectively. This is more than a matter of pronouns; Ojibwe speakers learn and assert in everyday speech a sharp distinction between actions done toward a him/her and actions done to an it, drawing on a different verb form and in some cases a different transitive verb entirely to say, for example, "I carry him/her (a drum)," versus "I carry it (a piece of hide)." Animate nouns include people, spirits, animals, and plants; they also include ceremonial items like drums, pipes, and nouns that English speakers would construe as things: stones, thunder, ice, snow.

Now, to be sure, a linguist could point out that such gender distinctions in the structure of a language do not perforce indicate conscious awareness of the distinction. But Ojibwe speakers like Larry Cloud Morgan hasten to point out the significance of the reach of the animate gender and how it constrains the Ojibwe speaker to think of plants, animals, weather phenomena, and ceremonial items as presences, subjects, rather than the mere transitive objects of human thought and action.[14] Even as she acknowledged that "there is no particular reason why some objects would be included in the animate class," Ojibwe-language educator Patricia Ningewance put the force of the animate gender this way:

> I remember this as a child: when a household object broke and couldn't be fixed again, I was told to go hang it on a tree in the forest. This was like giving it a dignified burial at the end of its life as a useful object. Or, maybe its

life could be extended by being planted in the arms of a living tree. The fact that it was "just a thing" made no difference. It was still as important as an actual living thing. We all have importance—human, animal, plant or inanimate object. One is not worth more than the other.[15]

Ningewance's subsequent difficulty deciding whether "an inanimate verb should be listed before the inanimate in the glossary (and toss[ing] a very animate coin to decide)" struck her anew as evidence that "the consideration runs deeper than we would think." No small grammatical matter, this is so because it was keyed to a pervasive insistence on *respect*. She concluded: "I guess that's an illustration of one of the Anishinaabe teachings: respect for everything."[16]

This digression is not peripheral, but central, to a fuller understanding of eldership, Respect for elders, I will now turn to show, can be seen as the paradigm for these other relations. To help lay the groundwork for such a view, we turn to further examples from Confucian history to amplify the nuances of the Ojibwe case.

Filiality, Honoring Elders, and Sacred Community: Insights from Confucian Tradition

If Ojibwe sacred community is peopled by so many nonhuman persons and presences, then an Ojibwe ethic of respect rests on very different cosmological foundations indeed from those of the Confucian tradition, with its overriding concern for human relations and emphatic distinction of the human from nonhuman life of "Earth."[17] Still, there is much to gain by analogy to a tradition with a similar orientation to the resonant universal harmony of well-ordered relations as that of the Anishinaabeg to *bimaadiziwin*, but a tradition that has well-documented internal conversations about the meaning, significance, and shape of these practices of community over several thousand years of commentary traditions on sacred texts.

First, the analogy is helpful in terms of the ultimacy, the religiousness, so to say, of Confucian understandings and practices of sacred community. As Herbert Fingarette famously argued, in the proper ordering of the human, natural, and heavenly realms, Confucians seek the transformation of the secular into the sacred by making a "holy rite" out of the practice of authentic human community.[18] Fingarette was trying to address the view that the Confucian tradition was no religion at all, but merely a system of ethics and philosophy.

The Confucian way doubtless has changed considerably over two and a half millennia of development, but it has remained steadfast in its insistence on the need for "self-transcendence" toward the fuller realization of humanity and an appreciation of the difficulty of learning and decorum that lead toward this fuller humanization. Confucius, or Master Kung (551–479 B.C.E.), began a transformation of Chinese society by recasting the ritual sacrificial traditions believed crucial to the proper functioning of cosmos and society into ethical norms for conduct in a web of social relations, later represented in terms of a series of key relationships: father/son, husband/wife, elder/younger brother, sovereign/minister, friend/friend. In effect, Master Kung transformed Chinese ritual traditions of ancestor and deity worship into ethical traditions of reverence toward one's living ancestors, both familial and extrafamilial.[19] But in Fingarette's view, by improvising on the key category of li ("ritual, propriety"), Confucius was less a figure who transformed ritual traditions into an ethical one, but rather one who came to ceremonialize ethics, noting the highly ritualized, even aesthetic dimensions of codified ethical conventions. Moving out in concentric circles, the exercise of ritualized propriety in li begins with cultivating personal life, regulating family relations, ordering affairs of state, and ultimately bringing peace to the world.[20]

If the Confucian analogy helps appreciate the fuller spiritual resonance of the proper exercise of ethical relations in a sacred community, it can be even more specifically helpful in appreciating how a principled regard for those of old age is paradigmatic of this larger, ultimate scheme of things, and thus of how respect for elders need not be seen as blind deference to patriarchy.[21] As part of his effort to reclaim Confucian traditions from the caricature that they are plainly authoritarian, Tu Weiming has called attention to the "creative tension" between the inner ethical drive of jen ("humaneness") and the outward propriety that is li. If not animated by jen, li becomes empty formalism, mere ethical convention. Tu glosses a famous passage from Confucius's Analects that notably ties moral self-cultivation to the process of biological maturity: "At 70, I could follow the dictates of my own heart, for what I desired no longer overstepped the boundaries of right [li]." "This does not mean he had become a virtuoso of *li*," Tu comments. It suggests, instead, that he was "able to bridge the seemingly unbridgeable gap between 'what is' and 'what ought to be.' He was so versed in self-cultivation that he could operate in a specific social setting with an artistic maturity."[22]

Over the centuries of the Confucian tradition's complex development in China, Japan, Korea, and elsewhere in east and southeast Asia, Confucius's ideas were refined and theologically elaborated, interpreting earlier classic texts in terms of a correspondence between "heaven," "earth" and "human community." Two of the classical "five relationships," those between younger and elder brother and between son and father, were extended to represent all relationships of juniors for their elders. Indeed the many relationships came to be seen as each stemming from *xiao*, the filial piety (variously "filiality" or "filial devotion") of the child for the parent. These elaborations were ensconced in the *Xiao Jing*, or *Classic of Filial Piety*, an eighth-century text that swiftly gained scriptural status in the Confucian canon. "Filial piety is the root of (all) virtue and (the stem) out of which grows (all moral) teaching," declares the *Xiao Jing's* opening chapter.[23] The text's fourteenth chapter extends the younger/elder brother relationship to encompass relationships between any junior toward their elder: the "fraternal duty with which [the superior man] serves his elder brother may be transferred as submissive deference to elders."[24]

As filiality, thus enlarged, became identified as the "root" of all the other virtues, this sure foundation of authentic community became grounded in the dynamic structures of the universe itself. Confucians came to see filiality not just as a human convention but something coded into the moral landscape of the universe: a principle animating the cosmos. In Thomas Berry's translation, the *Xiao Jing* declares: "Filial devotion [*xiao*] is the interior pattern of Heaven itself, as well as the ultimate norm of earth and guide of the people. When people follow the design of Heaven and earth, which leads them by the brightness of Heaven and benefits of earth; then the whole world is at peace."[25]

Yao Xinzhong identifies the centrality of filiality as caught up in a Confucian notion of this worldly eternity and immortality through the furtherance of a family line,[26] but Berry understands the special nature of filial virtue as a result of its connection to origins: "This capacity to stand forth magically out of a prior nonexistence into existence is always related to another existence. To this prior existence a unique and absolute reverence is due. This virtue is a metaphysical and ontological as well as a moral mode of being. Without filiality, there would be nothing. The phenomenal universe exists in itself and in all its relations, only by the power of this virtue."[27] Mary Evelyn Tucker extends the discussion of the thoroughly cosmological, religious vision of an ethic of filial piety:

> Through civility, beginning with filiality, one could repay the gifts of life to one's parents, to one's ancestors, and to the whole natural world. Through humaneness [jen], one could extend this sensibility to other humans and all living things. The root of practicing humaneness [jen] was considered to be filial relations. The extension of these relations from one's family and ancestors to the human family and to the cosmic family was the means whereby these primary biological ties provided a person with the roots, trunks, and branches of an interconnected spiritual path. The personal and the cosmic were joined in the stream of filiality. From the lineages of ancestors to future progeny inter-generational connections and ethical bonding arose.... By analogy, through developing reverence for Heaven and Earth as the great parents of all life, one came to realize one's full cosmological being.[28]

A seventeenth-century Japanese neo-Confucian, Nakae Tōju, put it this way: "Filial piety dwells in the universe as the spirit dwells in humans. It has neither beginning nor end; without it is no time or any being; there is nothing in all the universe un-endowed with filial piety." In Confucian east Asia, as Berry observes, "interrelatedness is grounded not in any religious covenant, nor in any social contract, but in the very origin, structure, and functioning of the universe."[29]

Beyond Blind Deference

Something similarly cosmic and religious is at work in the traditional and contemporary Anishinaabe emphasis on ethical respect for elders, and these larger references make its workings more complex than mere blind obedience to the old. Although its orality distinguishes the Ojibwe tradition from Confucianism's long textual development and philosophical elaboration enabled through that textual practice, and although the Chinese state over the centuries has conscripted Confucian filial piety to its own purposes, Ojibwe tradition too can be seen to understand respect for elders as more than one among many ethical conventions.[30] In a "teaching" for an oral history project, Lac du Flambeau elder Ben Chosa makes explicit how honoring elders is at the very core of Ojibwe religion: "Have religion. That's about it. Listening to your elders comes with religion. In the Indian religion, the first thing they teach you is to respect your elders. If somebody older than you is talking, don't interrupt them. That comes with the religion: you respect your elders."[31]

Proper regard for elders is elemental to the proper functioning of *bimaadiziwin*. It is modeled on and, in turn, serves as a model for relations with spiritual beings, since the ethical and ritual practices honoring elders are congruent to those honoring spirits, the "grandfathers." The specific practices of decorum toward elders, then, are not just good manners, but constitutive of *bimaadiziwin*, the harmonious, beautiful, natural, circle of life. An elder from a neighboring Manitoba community, the Swampy Cree, explicitly linked the specific respect for elders with an appreciation of the cosmic, religious, implications of the subordination of self:

> That is why the young people are told, "Never say 'I am my own master'!" It is [the Spirit] who rules over our lives. We will never be able to do anything and keep it hidden, such as gossiping about one another. When we gossip about our fellow man, or if we were to laugh at someone who looks pitiable, then we are in fact gossiping about ourselves; that is what the old people always used to say. That is why the old people, the old men, warned them about it, for they, of course, had come to understand things. Never laugh at an old woman, in particular, for old women are held to be dream guardians and they, of course, make our life as humans go on. If it were not for women, we who are humans would not be alive.[32]

The Gendered Respect for Age and Gender

The particular urgency of respecting old women here can be read as this Cree elder's reference to the increasingly countercultural gender norms of respecting elders as Cree and Anishinaabe communities have become further integrated into Canadian and American society. Indeed in a different address, the speaker made this more explicit still:

> Truly, Our Grandmother is kind, "Old Woman Spirit" as she is called. If it were not for that kind, if women had not been put here on earth by the powers, we would not be sitting here; who would give birth to our existence as humans? No one; that grace was given to women. That is why the old people used to say, "Think of one another with compassion, you women! You all, think of the women with compassion!" There is not excuse for "man" as he is called to be abusive to women he is watched from over there, and when he is abusive to a woman, he is being mean to himself.[33]

But it also may register a truth that the social distinction of old age significantly configures the actual shape of other social distinctions, especially gender. As will be elaborated in chapter 4, Anishinaabe people traditionally have understood gender distinctions as complementary distinctions of labor and role rather than hierarchical relations of power, and relatively fluid distinctions at that. The fluidity of gender roles is made clear in the twentieth-century lives of Maggie Wilson and Landes's other consultants in northern Minnesota discussed in chapter 4. But especially in the prereservation days, historian Priscilla Buffalohead has found that gender roles were fluid with respect to the changing sociological shape of the seasonal round. "Leadership had a wide variety of contexts in the yearly round of Ojibway life," Buffalohead writes. "Groups to be governed could be as small as a single family or berry-picking party or as large as intertribal war parties or the people who came together for village ceremonials. In general, men led male-oriented pursuits such as the hunt or a war party, while women leaders supervised activities within the female domain. There were occasions, however, when elderly women were chosen as spokespersons for hunting bands. These women managed the products of the hunt and negotiated deals with the traders."[34] Consider one such woman encountered by Henry Schoolcraft early in the nineteenth century. Blue Robed Cloud, a prophet, "acquired her power in a youthful vision quest coincident with her first menstruation. In subsequent years, she used her gift of power to help her people find game in times of great need. After her first success, she recalled to Schoolcraft in later years: 'My reputation was established by this success, and I was afterwards noted ... in the art of a medicine woman, and sung the songs which I have given to you.'"[35]

Even as women and men age in gendered ways, and as that transformation in status looks different for aging men as for aging women, as "elders" they share some status in common that has dampened an emphasis on their differences. Ethnohistorian Rebecca Kugel writes that among the Anishinaabe in the eighteenth and nineteenth centuries, "age trumps gender almost all the time. In Ojibwe society, the aged, if they are wise, have power (social, political, spiritual) that transcends all other categories. The young, in contrast, whether male or female, are rarely wise. They are, in the Ojibwe language, 'oshki,'—fresh, new, green, young, in process—and they should not be expected to act otherwise. ... One's age or youth is more important in allocating power & status than one's gender."[36]

As we shall see, although Native peoples found themselves increasingly absorbed into a Euro-American society that emphasized gender distinctions, these Anishinaabe traditions did not go away; instead they stood in even sharper relief as the distinguishing of women elders by age supercedes their gender distinction, in turn contributing to the sacralization of eldership.

The Shape of Respect

If respecting elders in Anishinaabe tradition is similar to Confucian filiality in the way it epitomizes and models an overarching ethic of relationality, respect is given highly specific shape in Anishinaabe teaching. According to teachings of the Midéwiwin lodge as represented by Ojibwe author Edward Benton-Banai and the Sagkeeng Ojibwe curators of the "Our Universes" exhibit at the National Museum of the American Indian in Washington, D.C., respect is one of the seven cardinal virtues that characterize living well, the virtue itself considered a gift from the spirits. Respect, *manaajitowin*, is one of the seven gifts for living bestowed on a little boy, who is taught by the Seven Grandfathers left in charge of creation. In Benton-Banai's terms, "to honor all of the Creation is to have *respect*."[37] Gauging the shape and texture of Anishinaabe respect as applied to elders must be informed by this larger sense of respect for all things.

The terms *respect* and *honor* in Native English usage are condensed terms signifying a broad web of interconnected of ethical and ritual attitudes and practices.[38] Their use is hardly exclusive to that deference directed toward elders; it includes honor and respect toward all beings. Still, they are certainly used with frequency in that paradigmatic context, and it will be useful to unpack their dense meanings and associations by reference to their Ojibwe-language counterparts, but a word study of the Ojibwe alone will not convey the force of the use of these terms in English. Indeed, the force of the English terms in Native parlance today may register the accentuation of a particular, distinctive regard for elders, gaining semantic concentration (compared to a wealth of expressions translatable to respect or honor) and force in its contrast to a wider society that does not thus respect elders. What's more, amid these changed inflections of meaning, there has been a marked persistence in the practices of deference that constitute respect for eldership, and though more extensive discussions of these practices appear in subsequent chapters, they will be enumerated here as well to help sketch the shape of respect.

A number of Ojibwe expressions can be translated "to respect." The most important cluster of terms for respect involves the verbal root, *manaaji-*, glossed by Nichols and Nyholm as "spare someone, go easy on someone," and by Ningewance as being "gentle" or "respectful" of someone (bear in mind that "someone" grammatically could refer to any animate object, including animals, plants, and weather phenomena).[39] The form of the verb taking inanimate objects, *manaajitoon*, similarly, is glossed by Nichols and Nyholm as to "spare something, go easy on something" and by Ningewance as "to be gentle with," to "try not to use it up." Baraga glossed this form of the verb, *Manâdjiton*, as "honor or respect it; save or spare it, use it sparingly, economically; take care of it."[40] Michigan Odawa Fred Ettawageshik added the gloss "glorify it, make it beautiful" to the term as it applied to the phrase *O miskwim manadjitoda* in a Christian hymn involving veneration of Christ's body and blood.[41] If respect in this sense carries liturgical associations that seem in contrast with those listed above, one could observe a variety of ritualized actions toward other persons, human, animal, and plant that fuse the ethical associations with the ritualized actions pertinent to *manaaji-*.

Indeed, the range of this term for respect implies not simply an interior affection or regard toward the person, plant, animal, or thing, but a form of outward conduct toward him/her/it that takes into account the integrity and dignity of the other. *Manaaji-* is cited by Benton-Banai to refer to the respect on which a relationship between husband and wife ought to be based.[42] I think it would be accurate, though not exhaustive of the semantic range of this Ojibwe term, to say that one takes another person, animal, plant, or thing as a subject rather than an object and acts toward it accordingly.

AN ETHICAL ATTITUDE/SENTIMENT

But the Native English parlance of respect can make reference to other Ojibwe concepts as well. One of those, *zaagi-*, illuminates an aspect of respect that is an interior sentiment, an affection of attachment to the person respected. Minnesota's Ojibwe Language Society translates respect/honor elders with the verb root *zaagi-*, a root that leads to a cluster of terms more commonly glossed as "to love" but that carries the force of "to treasure someone." One of the phrase-a-day calendars produced by the society to promote language revitalization around seasonal activities and core values glosses *zaagi gikaajig* as "treasure the elders," indicating the depth of feeling that issues in proper behavior. Hallowell included *sagia* (*zaagi'aa*) in a list of "emotional words" and glossed it thus: "as I am attached to him/her."[43] Hallowell also glossed as "I honor him, I respect him" a construction in Manitoban dialects that involves esteeming, thinking well or highly of someone: *minadeniwa*—a construction that Nichols affirmed as possible if not typically used in Minnesota Ojibwe.[44] Anton Treuer has also glossed *izhinaw-*, a verb that appeared in some Minnesota Ojibwe narratives he documented, as "to think of someone a certain way, think of someone respectfully."[45]

In the 1950s, Rogers found in a Northern Ojibwe group that "advancement" to old age raised the status of individuals. "In general elders are loved and respected. One old man was referred to by one informant as the 'finest man I ever knew.' Other informants were of the same opinion."[46] Such words may not be ebullient, but they are consistently a pattern in Anishinaabe parlance concerning special elders in their community. References and memories of elders are savored in a tangible way, tangible sometimes by how few words are equal to the task of the often tender regard inside. An elder of the Swampy Cree community, related to the Anishinaabe, conjoined respect and compassion:

The old men used to say, "When all the plants have come out and all the creatures have had their young, just see, go outside! Sit down where the ground is really clean! [Hold] the blades of grass up like this [gesture]! There you will see an insect crawling along, populating the earth, therefore think of it with compassion! Especially the birds, Our Father thinks highly of them, and when you see a bird with its young, never bother it!" the old men used to say, that is why one should treat things with respect. He himself thinks of them with pity. For example, behold, you have been given a baby so that you might think of that one with compassion, you are to think of it with compassion.[47]

Still, respect is more than a straightforward function of compassion or interior sentiment. Treasuring someone indicates an important aspect of Ojibwe teachings about respect: the concern for the worth of a person, plant, or animal. When Mary Black-Rogers, in her efforts to map a hierarchical taxonomy of power in an Ojibwe worldview, inquired of a Round Lake Ojibwe man how he would rank high or low fish, she was rebuffed. "His response in Ojibwa: 'I like all fish.' In English: 'We respect all fish. We treat those fish the way they should be treated. It's too dangerous to make fun of those fish.'"[48] Here, the respect and cultural imagining of age are linked, for Anishinaabe people consider plants and animals elder brothers in their understanding of the order of the world.

A VIRTUE, NOT JUST A SENTIMENT

Indeed, from another view, respect can be seen as the opposite of a sentimental attachment or conduct determined by such an attachment: it is a kind of posture of distance from the one respected. In her intensive scholarship on the associations and ramifications of Ojibwe "power"— "essentially coterminous with 'living' for it signifies among other things, the power to be alive and make a difference in the world"—Black-Rogers has argued that the behavioral code of "respect" is rooted not in an affection or sentiment but in the dispositional "caution about known or potential power" of any living things.[49] "In the old days," an unidentified Ojibwe elder told her, "people had to show respect for everything living." She continued, "I submit that living refers to power . . . for it is further learned that something called 'respect' is the appropriate behavior toward all those

who may have the power to affect or control one's life."[50] The proper behavior "is simply to leave others alone and concentrate on steering one's
own ship. Behavior, then, is strongly geared toward noninterference with
another's autonomy, that is, toward avoiding actions that could be interpreted as attempts to control others. At the same time, care is taken not to
offend any 'living thing' since all may have the potential to affect or control."[51] On this score, elders classically could be expected to possess more
relative power and would warrant deference not simply because they are
old.

But this train of thought can go too far, missing the ethical urgency of
respect as a cardinal virtue, as a matter of proper action, of habit and conduct and not simply disposition or element of a survival strategy: "It looks
as though Ojibwa 'respect,'" she writes, "boils down to respect for 'power,'
and the whole matrix is what I have referred to as the 'Ojibwa power belief
system' or 'power-control belief system.'"[52] In this regard, Black-Rogers
misses the hard work associated with the cultivation of respect. Less a
natural survival instinct than a difficult discipline of learning, *manaajitowin* is profoundly ethical in nature.

On this point, I am reminded by how taken aback I was when, on a particularly mosquito-infested still summer evening in the woods of the
Leech Lake Reservation, as a boy declared "Gotcha!" as he swatted a mos-
quito that landed on his arm, his father, the late Warren Tibbets, said in
his characteristically calm, teaching voice, "Don't say that!" It was no moment of deep treasuring of mosquitoes, for they can annoy Anishinaabe
people like they can annoy anyone on such evenings, but it struck me as an
example that, for people trying to raise their children with Anishinaabe
values, no occasion was too small to teach respect for life.

The practices of deference that habituate this virtue are many, and all
involve a conspicuous subordination of the self. It has been important not
to laugh at or at the expense of elders. This goes beyond too much mirth in
their presence—it involves restraining any impulse to laugh at their mis-
fortunes or frailties. Melvin Eagle related, in Anton Treuer's translation, a
story that dramatized for him the importance of this teaching:

> There was one young boy whom I accompanied all the time—we were al-
> ways together, and we went to school together too. One time we were stand-
> ing around near the road, laughing with one another, as we were talking

and laughing together there. Well that elder man named *Zhimaaganish* came walking by, and we were laughing together, letting ourselves say whatever [came to mind]. *Wa*, as that old man was walking, he turned around just startled there when he saw us. And he was holding onto those canes too. As he saw us, he thought we were laughing at him. "So why are you guys laughing," that old man says to us. As he pointed at us with [his cane], we were scared. I didn't tell that old man anything as he just stared at us the whole time, so we started to run away to go home. But no. I told my father and mother where they were, "That old man *Biindige-gaabaw* and I were talking by the road. We were laughing together and that *Zhimaaganish* walked by. He thought we were laughing at him, he said. You shouldn't laugh at elders; that's what I was thinking. Then that old man got mad at us. Then he saw us again by the tree." "Oh no," my mom tells me. "Come quick, hurry up, go over and give that old man tobacco telling him you were not laughing at him. Hurry up. Go on. As fast as you can, go over to his house. Go inside," she says. And so I went inside, wanting to be as timid as possible. As I entered I nudged that old man where he was sitting. Boy he just stared at me, and kept an eye on his cane. So I told him, "Hey *Zhimaaganish*. You weren't being laughed at over there. We were just laughing at one another again." He was given tobacco then, "So I won't be thought of in a bad way because I wasn't laughing at you." Boy then that old man laughed too. "Ho, ho ho ho, grandson. It's good, in a good way that you come to do this," he said. "I don't know you. But I think you guys were laughing in a good way," that old man said. So for the first time again I was happy when I prepared to go home. Golly, I laughed with him and I was singing again as I left.[53]

Even though the boys had only inadvertently laughed in a way that could be misunderstood to come at the elder's expense, it was seen as an infraction worthy of a strident lesson. "*Giche-apiitenimad gichi-aya'aa*," his mother and father told him. "Never ever laugh at those old men and old women when you're standing around someplace," they admonished, "'hold the elder in high regard. . . . One time the elders are going to watch over you. They'll take care of you in various endeavors,' he told me. And they spoke the truth."[54]

Respect for elders is often a matter of regulating speech. "Respect for older people," Inez Hilger's Ojibwe consultant told her, was "evidenced in speaking to them in a civil way and in listening to them attentively, [and] was well impressed upon children."[55] I will explore in chapter 4 the relationship between these speech practices and the dynamics of authority. For now it is important to recognize them not simply as etiquette and good manners, but as practices that formally privilege the words of elders, and by extension their ways of knowing, above those of younger people.

Young people have been taught that respect is constituted by remaining quiet, not loud or boisterous, in the presence of elders, waiting for elders to initiate exchanges, and refraining, above all, from any interruption of an elder's speech. Rogers observed at Round Lake that "elders are listened to in silence no matter what they may have to say. No one interrupts."[56] Questions can be posed of elders, of course, but as Regna Darnell has observed in Cree interactional etiquette, there are demonstrable rhythms of appropriate questioning of elders. Politeness involves waiting for conspicuous pauses in elders' speeches before even posing questions of them.[57]

Even speech practices referring to elders are matters for ethical teaching. Third-party references to respected elders are politely coded by choosing honorific terms like "that old man" (*akiwenzii*) or "that old woman" (*mindimooyenh*) over direct references to their names, considered quite impolite.

Polite indirection extends beyond speech practices. Restrained eye contact and maintenance of appropriate physical space are also important. Among Severn Ojibwe, Lisa Philips Valentine observes, "Direct eye contact with another is considered to be bold, to the point of challenging another." In her description of ritualized hymn-singing, she observes that "young people, whose heads are usually bowed when talking with elders, extend this behavior with their books, or by turning their backs, which is not considered to be rude, but a posture of modesty. Among the women singing, the younger adults have their books closer to their eyes, ready to shield them if they make an error, ready to show humility." By contrast, Valentine observes, "The older women hold their books at waist level: they have earned the right to be front and center publicly, regardless of the quality of the performance."[58]

Elders are often conspicuously recognized and honored through spatial practices of respect. Larry Nesper observed in the context of contemporary Wisconsin Ojibwe community organizing what many have observed over the centuries in treaty negotiations, payments, and ceremonies. In meetings, elders were conspicuously invited to be seated in the front of the gathering. This is consistent with practices of seating the aged in sweat lodges and around ceremonial fires. Such arrangements visibly align the proceedings according to indigenous ways of valuing elders' speech and wisdom and create clear boundaries calling attention to other expected practices of ethical respect.[59]

Lac du Flambeau elder Cecilia Defoe relates these codes of respect and the notion of life journey as she described the grounding for respect of elders in terms of hospitality to wayfarers on a long journey: "Because anybody I talk to [says] be good to the older people. Because they came a long way, you know. They were on a long road. You don't answer them back. If you want to answer them back, keep it to yourself. Its always good advice."[60]

A RITUAL, NOT JUST ETHICAL, MATTER

Again, respect is a matter of profound ethical import: as much a matter of recognizing the worth and subjectivity of the other through inward thoughts and outward practices constituting respect. But each of these practices are not merely ethical; they are profoundly ritual in nature, concerned with the ceremonious shape of respect and rooted in the cosmological ground that gives it fuller force and informed by an aesthetic sense of the beauty of harmonious relations. On this point one appreciates the nuance of the English term *honor*, which in contemporary Ojibwe parlance is interchangeable with respect when it comes to proper relations toward elders. The Ojibwe term presumably anchoring the English usage, though not necessarily defining its semantic reach in English, stems from the root *kitchitwa-*, which Baraga and other translators have conflated with the same regard expected of saints, translating it as to recognize as "holy" or "blessed," as in the Blessed Virgin Mary.[61] Although Baraga may have had missiological aims in his own translations that distort the indigenous sense of *kitchitwa-*, there are important practices of honoring elders that have, even prior to Christianization, linked in practice the respect for elders and respect for the spirits to which they are related by homology as "grandfathers." The offering of tobacco to spirits has been, and continues to be, a crucial ritualized gesture of honor to the spirits or to Christian understandings of God, Jesus, Mary, and the saints. To offer an elder tobacco is not just an economic act or merely a gift, but also a ritual extension of an appropriate relationship between supplicant and grandparent, one that ritualizes the authority of the elder even as it can, if accepted, come to define responsibilities that flow in both directions of the relationship. In Melvin Eagle's story, he was forthrightly admonished by his parents to offer tobacco to the elder at whose expense he and his friend were seen to laugh. It began as a gesture of restoring a relationship that had gone awry through the faux pas and was recognized as such by *Zhimaaganish* who laughs himself and declares, it is "in a good way that you come to do this." And as Melvin Eagle later remembered, it was only "the first time I gave him tobacco."[62] No casual act or mere pleasantry, the offering of tobacco to elders.

Even more than respect, honor has come to carry the charge generated in contrast to a larger society that arguably does not thus honor elders, or the earth, or women. But honor also calls attention to a ceremoniousness to the work of respect, the ritualization of ethical relations that the theorist Catherine Bell, herself a student of Chinese religions, has identified as often at the heart of ethical systems.[63]

Ritualization here refers to the practices by which people strategically if habitually mark and effect proper relations through careful attention to formalities of interaction, gesture, speech, spatial organization, and so on. Importantly, the ritual dimension of Anishinaabe ethics is also a profoundly aesthetic matter, where the creation of proper relations effected have an artistic as well as moral force. To do something "in a good way," as Melvin Eagle did in offering tobacco and an apology, is more than a recognition of doing the right thing, it is an affirmation of doing the graceful thing, doing the beautiful thing.

To recognize the simultaneously ritual and ethical nature of decorum around and toward elders is to affirm, on the one hand, its constitution through the scripts of everyday ritualized interactions and, on the other, its ethical force as more than manners or etiquette. Importantly, both ritual and ethical resources are brought to bear in emphasizing respect for elders because, contrary to a stereotypical understanding of Native eldership, one does not naturally honor or respect the other; one ritualizes the practice of it in order to make it so.

BEYOND CHARITY: AN ECONOMY OF RESPECT

If respect in Ojibwe tradition is notable for the way it integrates the ritual and the aesthetic with the ethical, it is also distinctively—profoundly— economic in character. Providing for the needs of one's elders is less a charitable sentiment, disposition, or duty toward the least among us than it is an aspect of a mutual exchange of resources between generations. As we saw in chapter 1, a classical generational exchange between elder and younger generations was part of survival. Elders provided subsequent generations with guidance, wisdom, and knowledge of the land, of culture, and of religion that was crucial to the survival of the group, in exchange for economic, ethical, and ritual respect. Dramatic changes to the livelihood of Ojibwe people changed the content of that exchange, but did not do away with its structure: perhaps especially today, elders are those who have survived incredible demographic odds and as a consequence can share the guidance, resourcefulness, and example necessary for younger generations to negotiate harsh conditions of contemporary life: racism, poverty, alienation, interruptions of tradition, and the like.

Ojibwe economic ethics have been characterized less by the accrual of personal wealth tempered by a charitable impulse than by an insistence on general generosity rooted in reciprocity and respect for others' rights to basic needs. Johann Georg Kohl wrote of Wisconsin Ojibwe in the 1850s:

> Next to the liar, no one is so despised by the Indians as the narrow hearted egotist and greedy miser. The Indians might possibly give a murderer or the sinner the seat of honor in their lodges, but a man known as a "sassagis" (mean [stingy] man) must sit at the doorway. As long as a man has anything, according to the moral law of the Indians, he must share it with those who want; and no one can attain any degree of respect among them who does not do so most liberally.[64]

But generosity in provisioning one's elders with the food, shelter, energy, and other necessities of life has long been paradigmatic of codes of social respect generally. Kohl wrote, "Lately I saw, in front of a wigwam, great affection displayed towards a very aged woman, who was lame, blind, and half dead, who longed for the sunshine. The way in which the daughters and daughters-in-law prepared her bed in the fine warm sunshine, and then led her carefully out—to notice all this did me good. They told me they had brought their grandmother one hundred and thirty miles in a canoe, because there was no one at home to take care of her."[65]

As Kohl's observations suggest, provision for elders was firstly a familial responsibility, but it was crucially a communal responsibility as well,

Mah-zoonc and Indian boy, Mille Lacs, 1897. Mah-zoonc was said to be a century old at the time of the photograph, though in those days, many Ojibwe did not think in terms of keeping track of precise chronological age. *Courtesy Minnesota Historical Society*

for all members of a grandparent's generation could be considered grand-parents. A White Earth consultant told Hilger in the 1930s, "Mother would . . . tell us that if we met a blind man, to lead him; if a hungry man, to feed him; or if we found an old person alone, to help him."[66]

Of course, providing for the aged involved ensuring the basic needs of housing, food, medicine, and companionship, but also involved lavishing them with offerings of tobacco and other gifts and going out of one's way to ensure that elders feel no misgivings about being thus provisioned or voicing their needs, desires, or preferences. It has become an emphatic tradition to publicly serve elders first at public and private feasts and meals. At most gatherings I've attended, food and coffee are presented buf-fet style for the assembly, but elders often remain seated as younger people scurry about and serve them. Often the children are conspicuously tasked to do so, but just as often, elders cups are refilled and their plates cleared, whether or not an announcement is made to remind young people of this duty. This is a ritualized indicator of an essentially economic ethic in which honoring elders gives priority not only to the meeting of their basic needs, but to offering them food and drink that gives them pleasure.

The Ambivalence of Deference

It remains to be said that as emphatic as is the ethical maxim to respect or defer to elders, this has hardly led unambiguously to good outcomes. The ethic is rooted in the ambivalent realities of human relations, not in a utopian faith that all will always turn out well as a result. Perhaps it is not surprising that such deep ambivalences are given voice in traditional sacred narratives.

At a crucial moment prior to the great flood in several versions of his story cycle, the trickster Nanabozho seeks to avenge the underwater *manidoog's* murder of his adoptive brother, Wolf.[67] When he wounds, but fails to kill, the two leaders of the *manidoog* and sets out to find them, he encounters their mother singing a song of revenge against him, collecting basswood bark for a vast net in order to catch him. At first, she is afraid, believing him to be Nanabozho, but he persuades her that were he Nanabozho, he already would have killed her. When he subsequently addresses her with the familiar term of respect and endearment, *nooko* ("grandma"), she lets down her guard and reveals the whereabouts and condition of her sons, whom she is doctoring. Here, the story focuses attention on the trickster's false deference, but it continues with the dangers of duplicitous eldership. Nanabozho kills the frog woman and assumes her clothing, her song, and her feeble mannerisms, in turn playing on the trust that the *manidoog* have for the guileless sincerity of their aged mother. Pretending to doctor her with a new ceremony, he asks the siblings to close off all light from the wigwam and to leave the premises for a new curing ceremony, after which he finishes the *manidoog* off and triggers thereby the great flood from which the standing order emerges.

Indeed, Anishinaabe narratives are shot through with examples of old women and old men who exploit the code of respect for their own gain. If the stories uniformly tell of honoring old people, they do not uniformly tell of honorable old people, but with notable frequency present the figure of "bad old men" or "old witch grandmothers" who take advantage of younger people.[68] Such transgressions suggest by their conspicuous presence in the narratives the conventionality of respecting elders, along with its difficulty and its potential cost/danger. For in these various stories, with the notable exception of the trickster, who is able to rise above convention—or alternatively unable to rise to it—the protagonist consistently gestures respect to the older man or woman. These ambivalences about deference do not lead to equivocation in the insistence on the teaching. One story, whose widespread appearance in transcribed collections of Ojibwe narratives indicates its continued importance into the late nineteenth and early twentieth centuries, concerns a boy whose fast for a vision was so zealous and extreme that he ended up starving himself and became transformed into a robin. Importantly, the desire to overfast was not his own, but his parents' ambition for him, and although he became hungry to the point of starvation, he "agreed to fast more, because he had never thought to disobey his parents."[69]

Perhaps these narratives suggest an important cautionary note even as they teach the rule: "uniformly respect, but do not uniformly trust the respectability" of elders. If the Anishinaabe ethic, like the Confucian, insists on a principled ceremonious deference to old age across the board, it does not insist, as the Confucian does not, that old age itself ensures the worthiness of eldership. As Confucius famously castigates the aged peasant who has done little to improve his life over the years, Anishinaabe narratives point out that there are older people of whom proper respect is called for, but not the community esteem of eldership, the latter a function of community regard and not age alone. Doubtless this crucial distinction has produced, over time, considerable contention within Anishinaabe communities even as it has not altered the insistence on an ethic of respect for old age.

· · ·

Etiquette and Economy of Eldership in Historic Perspective

Wub-e-ke-niew (Francis Blake) identifies the tradition of eldership as a distinctive feature of what he calls an Anishinaabe-Ojibwe point of view: "We did not warehouse our old people, nor segregate them away from the rest of their Dodemian (clan)."[70] In large part, Wub-e-ke-niew is right, not only in his insistence on care for the elderly as a distinguishing feature of Anishinaabe ethics and economy but also as an accurate historical claim. In the first decade of the 1900s, Alanson Skinner went out of his way to observe of the Northern Ojibwe, "older people were treated with respect and cared for, if necessary," and went equally out of his way to note from the early fur-trade documentary history that it had not always been that way.[71] From what he could learn, Skinner wrote, "the aged and infirm were well taken care of, but this was not always the case according to some of the older observers."[72]

Skinner apparently was right about numerous details in the earlier historical record. In light of the clear evidence that an economy as well as a ritualized ethic of respect for elders has been a reality as well as vocal insistence in Ojibwe tradition, we must reckon with a series of observations that suggests that Ojibwe history also has borne out evidence to suggest otherwise. But these observations, frequent as they are, appear in a predictable pattern that reflects as much on the position and prejudices of the observers as on the actual practices of the observed. Moreover, to the extent they did occur, past observations of what today's parlance would identify as elder abuse reflect the aggravating conditions of social chaos in the wake of disease and dispossession—often occasioned by bouts of intoxication. Importantly, this is not to explain away any counterexamples to the overall argument of the chapter and book; it is rather to appreciate just how difficult it could be to continue respecting elders according to traditional norms amid the increasingly difficult social and economic conditions of Ojibwe history.

ABANDONMENT OF THE VERY OLD

One striking pattern of early observations concerned the abandonment of the very old. Peter Grant wrote at the outset of the nineteenth century of practices of elder abandonment among Canadian Ojibwe, with thinly veiled moralizing typical of the day:

> If the mind dwells with pleasure on those proofs of sincere attachment to the memory of departed friends, it cannot but deplore their cruel prejudices and inhuman conduct towards their aged and infirm. They indeed greatly

respect their old men while they are of some use in society, but if from extreme age or other infirmity, they become incapacitated to follow them in their encampments, they are then considered as dead to society, and their nearest relations think themselves no longer bound to maintain them; in this case a temporary shade is provided for them, with provisions and necessaries to prolong their miserable existence for a few days, and they are abandoned forever. Any kindness or assistance to those poor wretched exiles would meet with the utmost ridicule from their relatives; they would think it a more meritorious action to knock them out of the world at once. Some indeed, with more humanity, prefer leaving their condemned relatives with the white people, but are quite indifferent about what becomes of them afterwards.[73]

Among Ojibwe in northern Wisconsin, Kohl also remarked on rumors of such a practice: "Parents gradually grow a burden on the children. It never happens among the Indians that an infant is exposed, as is the case among our urban population, who deny the impulses of nature. On the other hand, you may often hear—at least of the very savage tribes—that they expose their old people in the desert, and leave them to their own resources."[74] John Long told in far more detail (worth recounting in toto) an eighteenth-century account of ritualized euthanasia he encountered in one Canadian Anishinaabe community:

Death among the Indians in many situations is rather courted than dreaded, and particularly at an advanced period of life, when they have not strength or activity to hunt: the father then solicits to change his climate, and the son cheerfully acts the part of an executioner, putting a period to his parent's existence. Among the northern Chippeways, when the father of a family seems reluctant to comply with the usual custom, and his life becomes burdensome to himself and friends, and his children are obliged to maintain him with the labor of their hands, they propose to him the alternative, either to be put on shore on some island, with a small canoe and paddles . . . or to suffer death according to the laws of the nation, manfully.

As there are few instances where the latter is not preferred, I shall relate the ceremony practiced on such an occasion. A sweating house is prepared in the same form as at the ceremony of adoption, and whilst the person is under this preparatory trial, the family are rejoicing that the Master of Life

has communicated to them the knowledge of disposing of the aged and infirm, and sending them to a better country, where they will be renovated,
and hunt again with all the vigor of youth. They then smoke the pipe of
peace, and have their dog feast: they also sing the grand medicine song, as
follows:

*Wa haguarmissay Kitchee Mannitoo kaygait cockinnor nicshinnorbau
ojey kee candean hapadadgey kee zargetoone nishininnorbay mornooch kee
tarpenan nocey keen aighter, O, dependan nishinnorbay, mornooch tow-
warch weene ojey mishcoot pockcan tunnockay*—The Master of Life gives
courage. It is true, all Indians know, that he loves us, and we now give our
father to him that he may find himself young in another country and be
able to hunt.

The songs and dances are renewed and the eldest son gives his father the
death stroke with a tomahawk: they then take the body, which they paint in
the best manner, and bury it with the war weapons, making a bark hut to
cover the grave.

Thus to the unenlightened part of mankind assume a privilege of de-
priving each other of life, when it can no longer be supported by the labor of
their own hands, and think it a duty to put a period to the existence of those
to whom they are indebted for their own, and employ those arms to give the
fatal stroke which in more civilized countries, would have been exerted for
their support.[75]

Of course, euthanasia practices that were so publicly scripted, and so obviously ceremonialized, could very well serve as evidence of the very respect
for eldership and confidence in a life cycle that stressed elders' proximity
to the *manidoog*, in direct contrast to Long's reading the custom as a representative sign of Native savagery. But the reference does beg further
questions about a potential slippage between professed regard for the authority of age and incidents that puzzled even those Euro-American observers trying to square such observed incidents with their sense that deference and respect for the aged often carried the day. Kohl wrote, "If the
Indians generally neglect their old folk, as they are accused of doing, it is,
at any rate, not always the case."[76]

In the later reservation era, missionaries, reformers, and governmental
bureaucrats frequently made mention of ambivalence concerning Native
regard for the aged. A White Earth consultant told Hilger in the 1930s that

respect for elders was a central teaching for children: "It was one of the main things taught us; we were told no one would respect us if we did not respect older people."[77] But Hilger took pains to observe that "assisting the aged in a material way, however, does not seem to have been part of the training of the Chippewa children. On all reservations old persons were seen to shift for themselves; their able bodied sons felt no obligation to assist them. Daughters, more often, seemed to feel a responsibility. Old parents seemed indifferent to their neglect; none offered any complaints against their children."[78]

Apparently, Hilger's observation was rooted in the prejudiced perspective of the archdeacon in charge of northern Episcopal missions, Joseph A. Gilfillan, for she substantiates her interpretation of the dynamic by saying "Gilfillan found this condition to exist in his time." Hilger continues, quoting Gilfillan:

> But it seems to be an unwritten law among them that an old man, and especially an old woman, must shift for himself or herself somehow. They have a contempt for the aged and useless, like all heathen. The son never seems to think he is under any obligation to do anything for his aged father or mother. Nor do they make any complaint of him, for they do not seem to expect anything. And one always hears the complaint that food given by the government, or by charitable persons, does not get to the old persons for whom it was intended but is eaten by the well and strong.[79]

Later in the twentieth century, an ethnographic literature informed by depth psychology and social-scientific research on Indian substance abuse began to argue that Indian violence, including abuse of elders under inebriated conditions, was not anomalous antisocial behavior but eruptions of pent-up resentment that were suppressed as a byproduct of demanding Ojibwe ethics.[80] In 1950, at Pekangikum, Ontario, R. W. Dunning heard of the brutal beating of Old Birchstick, an elder who had been a traditional *ogimaa* who was ousted in an election after forty years of traditional leadership. "When the old man walked into a camp having a brew party and single handedly 'upset the brew pot,'" Dunning reported, "he testified he was attacked by two of his own grandsons as a result of a drinking party, partially stripped of his clothing, and beaten."[81] The anthropologist interpreted the scene in terms of generational tensions emerging with the creation of band governments that rested on rational, bureaucratic authority rather than on the traditional authority of the elder/medicine person/ chief. The change in authority to Dunning "reflects a general decline in the authority of the leader of a co-residential group," and one infers along his line of reasoning a kind of liberation to younger men within an extended kin network vis-à-vis their elders.

Hallowell, who did much to bring the discourses of psychology into the field of cultural anthropology, went even further in his interpretation of such violence. Hallowell thought "the conduct of the Indian when drunk, was, in a sense, a natural experiment, a cue to his character. If his basic emotional structure was one that led to the suppression of a great deal of affect, in particular aggressive impulses, then we would expect that these might be released in a notably violent form under the influence of alcohol. This seems to have been what happened."[82]

How are we to regard such observations about Ojibwe life that seemingly contradict the depth and consistency of an Ojibwe respect for elders? First we must note the rhetorical purposes of the authors involved. Authors of early manners and customs portraits, like Long in his *Voyages and Travels*, were writing accounts of sensational adventure for European audiences, and as is clear in the passage quoted, their janus-faced observations of Native peoples' nobility and savagery were drenched with unstated moralism: either Indians were noble in respects that served to criticize European mores as uncivilized, or they were savage in ways that invited the civilized mores of Europe as refinements, rather than as matters of invasion.[83] A related moralizing purpose appeared in the twentieth century, in the trope of the "degraded" Indian who, often drunk, disheveled, indolent, and at home in squalid conditions, was unable to live up to the expectations of the noble savagery of precontact days. Such a dynamic can be seen to animate and color Archdeacon Gilfillan's observations. His writings are shot through with venom toward some Native people in his purview that was matched only by the intensity of his praise for other Native converts. His comments are part and parcel of a great concern to distinguish the worthy poor—Indians deserving of mission charity and advocacy—and those whose lives he thought were becoming degraded by their reliance on either mission charity or government programs.

But as much as the consistent patterning of such observations suggests a trope at work, the observations are doubtless more than rhetorical inventions. It is a consistent contention of this book that honoring elders has never come *naturally* to Native people; it has rather been a matter of hard work, detailed attention in moral education, and disciplined ethical labor. If respect for elders or honoring elders has become axiomatic in Indian communities, part of the proverbial air that one breathes, this is so only because those communities have struggled much toward its continuance, even when colonialism has made its practice ever more difficult. In this light, that an ethical teaching's opposite—elder abuse, for example—could appear ought not to strike us as suggestive of the irrelevance of the entire teaching. If it suggests a kind of subterranean resentment for the honoring of elders, that in itself is not a sign of intrinsic dysfunction and ought not obscure the efforts made on the part of the community to live up to these ideals amid conditions exceedingly hostile to them.

THE PARADOX OF AGING IN NATIVE AMERICA

In her study of grandmotherhood among American Indians, Marjorie Schweitzer frames this conundrum usefully in terms of a thoroughgoing "paradox of aging" in Native American communities, where on the one hand, Native people age in cultural contexts that are "rich and supportive" alongside "demographic and statistical data" that "show depressing hardships facing elderly Indians."[84] In a sense this paradox is written into the biological processes of extreme age among humans: regardless of social position, we all begin at some point to lose abilities and faculties. But there are important ways in which Native American elders have faced a paradox more consistently dangerous, even lethal, and more consistently at odds with cultural expectations for old age. As a result we must reckon both with the refreshing possibilities and expectations for full life in old age as well as the realities facing older Anishinaabeg as a result of colonizing processes, broken families, and increasingly institutionalized patterns of care.

As the fur trade waned in the nineteenth century, and the land base dwindled to smaller and smaller reservations increasingly leveled by logging interests, the seasonal round that could underwrite traditional practices of families providing for their elders, yielded to new patterns where provision for shelter, food, and other basic needs of older Anishinaabeg fell upon bureaucratic institutions. These institutions were responding to newly arising needs, but they were, in turn, creating new patterns of need.

While it was never a stated goal of U.S. assimilation policy to interrupt indigenous people's provision for their own aged, it had that effect for communities whose traditional economy privileged meeting the needs of the collective over the accumulation of individual wealth and who understood the provision for the needs of elders as a shared community responsibility. The policies, and the Indian agents who administered them in countless discretionary decisions, set out to replace tribal allegiances and economies by engendering a sense of property ownership whose principal unit was the patriarchal nuclear family. The policies of land allotment, which were formally applied to Minnesota's Ojibwe under the 1889 Nelson Act, broke up those reservation lands into individual parcels eventually to be owned by male heads of households. In a series of Indian Bureau directives, dances, feasts, giveaways, and other ceremonial practices were deemed inimical to the aims of "civilization" and its proper regard for the value of private property and were discouraged and even forbidden by Indian agents through the enormous discretionary authority granted them in the system of treaty annuity payments and access to other services. Some, especially those concerning the giving away of valuable property, were even singled out in Indian bureau circulars, like this one of 1921:

> The sun-dance, and all other similar dances and so-called religious ceremonies are considered "Indian Offences" under existing regulations, and corrective penalties are provided. I regard such restriction as applicable to any [religious] dance which involves ... the reckless giving away of property, ... frequent or prolonged periods of celebration, ... in fact any disorderly or plainly excessive performance that proposes superstitious cruelty, licentiousness, idleness, danger to health, and shiftless indifference to family welfare.

Importantly, such official codes made explicit the link between civilizing policies and interrupting deferential relations to elder generations, especially those shaping cross-generational relations framed in ceremonies. The Commissioner of Indian Affairs in 1921 strongly recommended to his agents in the field:

That the Indian dances be limited to one in each month in the daylight hours of one day in the midweek, and at one center in each district; the months of March and April, June, July, and August being excepted. That none take part in the **dances or be present who are under 50 years of age**. That careful propaganda be undertaken to educate public opinion against the dance.[85]

The system of government and mission schools, especially boarding schools, was established in the 1870s and 1880s with an even more explicit purpose of isolating Native young people from hearth, home, language, and kin, not the least of which the grandparents, who were their customary educators.

In these circumstances, distinctions of gender, age, lineage, and band accrued new meanings and new ramifications. Factions emerged. Skirmishes among kinsmen aggravated by alcohol proved deadly. Men and women interacted in ways that weren't recognizable to previous generations.[86] Tensions among generations, too, took on new valences with greater ramifications in the reservation era. Generation gaps appeared, and regard for the elderly met with glaring examples of its opposite.

Pauline Colby observed the tangible results of these policies on the Leech Lake elderly whom she served as a missionary in those years: "In many respects the old people are the greatest sufferers by this onward sweep of progress. They cannot . . . adapt themselves to the new order, and yet the old is vanishing from their grasp. . . . I have looked in vain for the reverence for the aged that is accorded [the southwestern Indians]. Our aged ones, especially the women, expect but little consideration, and get less."[87]

Colby's language invites our skepticism about a timeless romanticized image of venerable elders revered by their people; but it also bears witness to the difficulties facing Ojibwe people trying to honor their elders in those difficult years of tuberculosis, hunger, and broken promises. The uphill battle of meeting the basic needs of children and younger people in these lean, difficult years, and the coercive practices of missionaries and Indian agents bent on assimilating Anishinaabe people to other patterns of living and caring, were perhaps conditioning some Anishinaabeg to regard their aged in less traditionally "respectful" ways, beginning to evidence a slippage between rhetoric and actual practice. Or perhaps it is more accurate to say that desperate economic conditions and increasingly bureaucratized patterns of care for aged Ojibwe drove a wedge between an economy and an etiquette of honoring elders. For even as it marked a governmental response to identified needs in the community, the institutionalization of care for the aged was part of the larger package of programs and policies designed to dissolve the bonds of extended kin networks toward assimilation to land-owning, agrarian, patriarchal nuclear families. Because of the cultural importance of caring for elderly, few Anishinaabe families were so desperate as to fully concede the care of their older members to these institutions, and elders themselves resourcefully drew on these institutional sources in their artful survival, but institutions took an increasing share in the provision for the elderly, with consequences for the structure of families and the integration of elders' authority in family and community life.

HONORING ELDERS AND THE BUREAUCRATIZATION
OF PROVISION FOR THEM

In the last decade of the nineteenth century, the Indian bureau inaugurated a modest "Homes Policy" by which it created a network of old-age homes on reservation communities, including the one at Leech Lake of which the Episcopalian missionary Pauline Colby was named matron. She observed that even after a government "poor house" had been established, aged Ojibwe sought "a liberal amount of pork, flour, tea, and sugar" from the mission and similarly shared donations expressly given them toward larger collectives. "This they carried to any house or wigwam where they thought they would be welcome, and in return for the privilege of sharing their fire and shelter, gave them part of the provisions. If they found they were not treated fairly the next month they took their pack somewhere else. It worked admirably."[88]

With old-age pension programs of the New Deal, Hilger noted at White Earth that the elder generations (aged 66–102) "accept old age assistance graciously and with independence" in that they fully believed "it's what the government promised us for our lands."[89] In her study of 130 White Earth families in the 1930s, Hilger found one in five not only housed, but were headed by, elders between the ages of 66 and 102. Born between 1839 and 1872, they were all, Hilger observed, in their teens at the time of the 1867 treaty establishing White Earth.[90]

Dunning, who taught summer school in a Canadian Ojibwe community in the 1950s, noted the importance to community survival of public assistance for senior citizens. He found that since "the rations at Pekangekum by the Christian mission there in the 1930s were insufficient to support a person for a month, it makes a difference that old people are there to get their ration. However, as aged and destitute persons normally lived within a family group, this quantity of rations issued in their name helped to secure a place for them especially during times of extreme shortage of food."[91]

Contemporary Economic and Social Conditions of Ojibwe Elders

More recently, as a result of the bolstering of assistance to the aged under Great Society programs and subsequent programs, like specific amendments to the Older Americans Act, which were expressly designed to respond to the needs of older American Indians and Alaska Natives, Native elders enjoy a variety of health and assistance programs available through federal, state, local, and tribal governments. Still, according to one study, these programs often involve a wide range of "bureaucratic barriers" to entry, and "more and more older American Indian/Alaska Natives officially remain undercounted and undocumented, making them invisible and ineligible for needed benefits and services."[92]

The study, sponsored by a geriatric center at Stanford University, summarized the scene in the mid-1990s as follows: "Most American Indian/Alaska Native elders are living in worse conditions than the majority of older persons in the United States, and might be considered 'elderly' at a younger chronological age than other U.S. populations" not simply for reasons of cultural valuing of eldership but "because of the onset of problems of associated with old age at an earlier point in life."[93] The statistics of their life circumstances as a whole bespeak extremely difficult circumstances and are often accentuated in the contexts of Ojibwe reservations and urban communities in Minneapolis, Chicago, Detroit, and elsewhere.

Native elders are poorer. According to the 1980 census, more than one quarter (27%) of American Indians between the ages of 65 and 74 lived below the poverty line, roughly three times the rate of older Americans generally (10%). For those of extreme age, 75 and older, 33% of Indians lived in poverty, about twice as many as among the general population in the same age range.

Native elders live with more health difficulties. A greater percentage of Indian elders consider their health to be fair or poor (48%) than elders in the general population (34%). Well more than half of Natives 65 and older, the highest rate for any older ethnic group, reported functional disabilities.[94] Diabetes, in particular, has devastating and disproportionate consequences for older Native people. With two of five Indian elders afflicted with diabetes, the longer lives they enjoy are burdened with the difficulties of dialysis, wound care, amputations, and other concerns frequently encountered in the advanced stages of the disease.

Native elders live in disproportionately difficult conditions. A 1980 study found more than 26% of Native elders were living in "substandard housing," many "lacking telephones, indoor sanitary facilities, and electricity."[95] By 2002, almost 30% of Native American elders were living alone.[96]

Native elders have fewer educational resources. In the late 1980s and early 1990s, 12% of Native elderly had no formal education, compared with 2% of white elderly,[97] they had a mean educational level of only eight years, and only 22% of elders had completed high school.[98] And finally, Native elders have been subjected in disproportionate numbers to elder abuse of various kinds. Although studies have been spotty and local in nature, a survey of urban Indian elder abuse in Seattle found 10% of older people had definitely or probably been abused, with women nearly ten times as likely to be abused as men.[99] Risk factors for financial and physical abuse and neglect of older Native Americans include poverty and financial dependency, gender, mental health problems, and substance abuse, along with social and historical conditions.[100] Those conditions are central, according to a social worker with South Dakota Adult Protective Services. "One of the prices we pay for Indian country modernization is assimilation," observes Chris Horvath. "On a social level, [assimilation] has had some pretty disastrous effects, because some of the natural systems that they wanted people to move away from were better than what anybody else could offer as substitutes. That's how you wind up with things like elderly abuse."[101] "I think a lot that happens today is related to drugs and alcohol," the late White Earth elder Saraphine Martin reflected (then in her 80s), "Things get stolen and broken, and the old people don't get as much respect as they used to."[102]

A PARADOX OF LIFE SATISFACTION

Despite the odds that these objective realities of life circumstances represent, a significant number of Native elders show a remarkable subjective affirmation of life satisfaction. Here again, we are met with what Schweitzer has identified as the paradox of aging among American Indian people. With considerable disparity among tribes, suicide rates for Native elders aged 65–74 were less than half the rate for all U.S. races in that age range and dramatically less than the troublingly high rates among younger Native Americans. An intensive study of elderly Natives on two midwestern reservations found "self-perception of life satisfaction" measured by "congruence of mood, zest, and fortitude . . . and mental health were more highly correlated than objective ratings on these two variables."[103]

These indices point in no small part to the continued vitality of practices and beliefs about Anishinaabe eldership, a cultural resource that imagines possibilities for old age and its importance to traditional community life even in the face of difficult economic, social, and physical conditions. They also register the importance of Native communities' creative efforts to provide for elders collectively and in their own culturally meaningful ways. Tribal sovereignty affirmed in judicial decisions from the 1960s onward have equipped tribal government with the resources of public programs for the elderly as contracting government agencies; it has also enabled those communities considerable control over the shape of such programs, equipping them to meet needs in a more locally responsive and culturally more meaningful way. And although gaming revenues since the early 1990s have had uneven and easily exaggerated effects on Anishinaabe reservation communities, they have also helped equip tribal governments to meet more needs of more elders in more creative ways.[104]

PROVIDING FOR ELDERS TODAY

If older Americans generally have high rates of malnutrition, the problem has been more difficult still among Native elders. Nutrition programs were extended to older Native Americans and Native Hawaiians beginning in the 1990s under an express provision of the Older Americans Act, with some meals delivered by contractors with the U.S. Administration on Aging to the elderly in homes and other elderly served in community centers, like "the Congregate" in White Earth, so named for the moniker of the legislation itself.[105] That "the Congregate" has entered the everyday parlance of White Earth life as the reference to where the housing, nutrition, and social needs of many older reservation members are met indicates how pervasively such bureaucratic programs influence reservation life.

But federal contracts are not alone responsible for the delivery of food and other services to community elders. Tribal governments, which themselves contract with the federal government to provide many local services, also allocate tribal resources toward feeding, housing, clothing the elderly, and meeting needs through formal events and programs and through informal payments and programs. Through powwow committees and informal networks of service provision, elders will often receive the choice leftovers from events and the like. But there are also in many communities formal benefit programs to which member elders are eligible. In this regard chronological age—with 55 or 60 as typical thresholds—is the delimiting factor.[106]

Not infrequently, other programs expressly for elders arise, such as the annual deer hunt at Wisconsin's Red Cliff Reservation to feed elders. Since the mid-1980s, the Great Lakes Indian Wildlife and Fisheries Commission, the agency created out of the spear-fishing disputes in northern Wisconsin, has sponsored the hunt by tribal members. "For the elders, many who are accustomed to venison in their diets but no longer able to hunt, it's a real treat when those packages arrive at their doors ready to become a meal."[107]

Still, older Natives were less likely to be living in homes for the aged (3% compared to 5% in the general population),[108] which suggests that family networks continue to provide the principal care for Native elders. This makes considerable sense in light of the tradition, but in the absence of support programs to enable such informal care, it places added stress to lives and families already under duress compared to the U.S. population as a whole.

In a 1993 study of 1,400 Native elders participating in Social Security programs, the National Indian Council on Aging found only 37% involved in retirement benefits, 9% in disability benefits, 12% in survivor's benefits, and 45% in supplemental security income.[109] Given the high rates of poverty, such low participation could reflect, according to Melvina McCabe and Jose Cuellar, lack of physical access, language barriers, knowledge of such services, and "possible racial discrimination or lack of cultural sensitivity when individuals do apply for services."[110]

MEETING LONG-TERM CARE

At White Earth, most nursing-home care has taken place one half hour south of the reservation boundary in Detroit Lakes, and while this may seem quite local, for rural people lacking reliable transportation and devoid of public transportation options, the distance can be a deal-killer. David Baldridge testified in a 2002 Senate hearing about the urgency of more federally funded long-term care facilities on reservations:

> As American Indians and Alaska Natives grow older and have more disabilities, one of their greatest fears is being placed in a nursing home far from their families and friends, where no one speaks their language, where the food is unfamiliar and where they are left alone to die. The need for long-term care services in Indian Country is great and continues to grow. The Indian Health Service has never included long term care as part of its mission and it does not operate or fund any long term care facilities. We need to think creatively about enhancing existing resources to meet the needs for home and community based long term care.[111]

Indeed, of late, many tribal governments are beginning to do so, but as of 2002, only twelve tribally run long-term eldercare facilities were in operation nationally, with 90% of long-term care on reservations being provided by families, already stressed by poverty and isolation from services for seniors.[112]

Conclusion

Amid all these changes in the institutionalized care for aged Native people, there is also the clear persistence of traditional practices of looking after community elders, whether or not they are directly familial relations. Elder Susan Jackson said, according to Anton Treuer's translation: "And the ones still living today, I can't put them in a nursing home. I can only take care of them myself. There was one old man, he was called *Bezhig-oogaabaw*. I looked after him myself as he became an elder. Then too I didn't feel bad about that old man's passing. I loved that old man as he was like a grandfather to me. He was over one hundred years old when he died. That's how much I loved him; I loved that old guy."[113] Similarly Josephine Degroat took under her care a neighbor widower who was suffering from diabetes and Ethelbert Vanwert, an elder man scarcely older than she. Taking care of elders in this way, instead of a nursing home, would seem to be part of the exercise of eldership by those financially and physically able. The practices of these community leaders may be conspicuous, but they are not loquacious. They are just part of the resolve of Anishinaabe people to look after their own in responsible ways.

If there is an accentuated concern for deference to and care of elders in Anishinaabe communities today, it is not solely because of the increased historical difficulty of recognizing the authority of age or providing that care in an American society that does not thus regard elders. It is more significantly a function of a deeply running tradition of evaluating the health of sacred community in terms of how the young and old are cared for. Article 22 of the U.N. Declaration on the Rights of Indigenous Peoples, approved by the General Assembly in 2007, specifies that "particular attention shall be paid to the rights and special needs of indigenous elders, women, youth, children, and persons with disabilities in the implementation of this declaration." The formal constitution of Michigan's Little Traverse Bay Odawa nation, representative of other Anishinaabe constitutions, specifies among its guiding principles "promoting with special care the health, education, and economic welfare of all the people, . . . especially our children and elders."[114] Such formal pronouncements emerge because of the resolve of numerous Anishinaabe men and women who, like White Earth enrollee and activist Sue Bellefeuille, relate the care for old people with community health: "I believe we need to start taking care of our old people. If we can't take care of our elders, our young will be neglected too."[115] Lac du Flambeau elder Cecilia Defoe remains optimistic about the future, although she appears to hold a position that others disagree with: "I don't care what you say or what anybody says. I think Flambeau has come a long ways. Like they're teaching the young now respect. If you can catch all of them kids, I think will get along better in school too. Teach them to respect."[116]

3

ELDERS AS GRANDPARENTS AND TEACHERS

The children of our people . . . are again honoring the Old People by asking them to speak, and I like other older people will search my memory
and tell what I know. I myself, shall tell you what I have heard my grandmother tell and I shall try to speak in the way she did and use the words
that were hers.

—Ignatia Broker, *Night Flying Woman*

 As the last chapter shows, eldership has less to do with the
maturation of individuals through the natural life cycle than
with the relational place and authority of older people in a
sacred community. This chapter considers the most elemen-
tal social role of old people in Anishinaabe communities, that of grandparents, but acknowledges the expansive notion of grandparenthood as apply-
ing to all people of one's grandparent's generation. There is, I will show, a
vocation of grandparenthood, a vocation organized around the work of
education through example, through reproof, and most powerfully through
stories. In other words, this chapter considers the elder as grandparent, the
grandparent as teacher, and the teacher significantly as storyteller. Traditional pedagogy and traditional families have had to adapt to rapid changes
and daunting challenges in the last century, and this too is part of the discussion of this chapter.

Grandparents at the Center of Anishinaabe Families

"Families are one of the blessings of the Anishinaabeg," writes humorist
Jim Northrup in commencing a collection of essays on his Ojibwe com-

Mrs. Frank Razor with Benedict and Herman Big Bear, ca. 1910. *Courtesy Minnesota Historical Society*

munity. "Living without family would be like trying to live without air and water. It can be done but not for very long."[1] Anishinaabe people today as ever emphasize the significance of family to their personal and social lives. In personal introductions, everyday conversation, as in more serious discussions of a person's reputation or character, they routinely seek to place individuals in terms of their family—"she's from those Pine Point Martins," or "Kingbird . . . are you a relation of the Kingbirds of Cass Lake?" "Family" or "relations" in Native parlance are considerably more fluid than is commonly the case in middle-class Anglo-America: it can reach out to an even more extended kin network to include aunts, uncles, cousins of various degrees, people considered family either ritually and legally through adoption or by means of informal adoption. But extended families have been and remain the key institution—arguably even the operative social unit—of Anishinaabe communities, and this in increasing relief over time with a wider society organized to consider the individual as the indivisible social unit.

Anishinaabe families emphatically have included, if they haven't revolved primarily around, elders who are grandparents and great-grandparents. That this has continued to be the case despite more than a century of forces privileging the nuclear over the extended family—be those forces ones of overt assimilation policy or subtler economic, social, and demographic pressures—suggests its priority and resilience in the life of Native communities. In many cases today, the relationship between grandchild and grandmother or grandfather can be seen as a central, not ancillary, social relation, whether or not a child is primarily or in part raised by grandparents, whether they be paternal, maternal, or adoptive.

In Ojibwe myths and other narratives, what is remarkable is how unremarkable is the grandparent/grandchild relationship. It is so prevalent, so conventional, so much the setting or subject of a story, that it defies even as it invites analysis. At the beginning of many stories, it appears almost as a stock phrase, "long ago there lived a boy with his grandmother" or an "old man and old woman lived alone with their child." In a collection from Wisconsin's Lac Court Oreilles and Lac du Flambeau reservations in the 1940s, edited by Victor Barnouw, stories often take as the elemental relationship that of grandson and grandmother. Four of the fifteen stories in the collection begin with a scenario of a grandson and a grandmother, and another two with an "old" man and nephew. Barnouw cites this as evidence of a truly "atomistic" Ojibwe social organization, since the stories depict Ojibwe people living in small, isolated groups.[2] That may be, but one could also observe that myths, like jokes, often begin with a charged relationship ("there was a priest, a minister, and a rabbi"). In so doing they are not necessarily aspiring to be *representative* of a social order, but configurations that situate an entertaining and edifying story around basic elements of social experience. It is certainly the case that the most significant character in Ojibwe narratives, the trickster Nanabozho, is raised by his grandmother—an archetypal grandmother—simply identified by her name *nookomis*, and this entirely in the absence of his birth mother and the sun, which fathered him.

The privileged place of grandparent/grandchild relations are not solely a function of the *mewinzha* ("the long ago") of traditional narratives. These relationships are often the setting for and subject of countless narratives of contemporary Anishinaabe families: recountings of the sayings and doings of storied elders in particular family lineages or appeals to the authority of a certain practice or belief by reference to that grandparent's teaching: "my grandmother used to say . . ." or "my grandfather always put out tobacco when the coming thunderstorm turned the sky became dark."

These narratives are not just framed as signals of the authority of a particular belief or practice, though that is certainly also the case. There can be a relish, a delight, in telling such stories that conveys the quality and ongoing significance of grandparental relationships even as they identify the source of a teaching. Larry Cloud Morgan loved to tell and retell stories of his summers with adoptive grandparents, the Clouds, near Cass Lake, who took him in after his birth mother died in childbirth. In particular, he told stories of how the old man had four dogs, each one of whom he called simply *animosh* ("dog"), but he called each with a differing inflection, and the dogs knew which one he was calling. His stories of his Red Lake grandparents too were animated in exceptional ways with delight and significance.

Elders as Everybody's Grandparents

Beyond the configurations of immediate family, be they biological or adoptive, older people in Anishinaabe tradition are categorized as *everyone's grandparents*, and certain elders especially so. Winnie Jourdain was a White Earth elder who lived fifty years in Minneapolis but who moved back to the reservation and died just shy of 100. White Earth tribal historian Andy Favorite described Jourdain, his own biological grandmother, as "the godmother of White Earth." "She commands respect."[3] Here, "godmother" implies the power, respect, as well as kindred feeling that are associated with Anishinaabe grandparenthood.

In the sense of a Winnie Jourdain, to speak of elders as grandparents begins with the familiar but extends to a much wider scope of social influence. But this is rooted in the basic structures of Anishinaabe kinship. The kinship terms for grandmother and grandfather, *nookomis* and *nimishoomis* respectively, were and are used in an expansively adoptive fashion to address those taken as one's elders. In the system as recorded by A. I. Hallowell in Manitoba in the 1930s, kinship terms for grandfather and grandmother extended to all members of a grandparent's generation and stood apart from other kinship categories by virtue of their intimacy. Ruth Landes found that Ojibwe from Emo, Ontario, could, with the right "personal feeling," make reference to a "grandparent by *doodem*" (*nimishoomis niwiiji doodema*) if they had a fellow clan member of a grandparent's generation. Of Ka'kapeanakwat, Landes wrote "one Christina Bombay and her children jested with the old man just as they would with classificatory relatives of those categories."[4] But one's "grandparents" could extend well beyond the kin group and the clan affiliation. They also establish a kin relationship to all elders, whether or not related by blood or overt adoption. Elders in this sense are everyone's teachers, everyone's resource, everyone's responsibility.

The Exceptional Relationship of Grandchild-Grandparent

To address another with the kinship terms for grandmother or grandfather is to claim a kind of special relationship, one marked by mutuality, intimacy, and trust, as well as respect. Practices of deference did not uniformly create social distance with a community's elders; indeed, just the opposite could be the case, were one to consider how the kinship relation between grandchild and grandparent fostered an emotionally proximal relationship of equals. Landes detailed the customary attributes of this kinship relation:

> Grandchildren are expected to assist grandparents when requested; and the grandparents serve as the guardians of the grandchildren whenever the occasion arises. Generally the mutual relation is good humored. Teasing can accompany the kind respect and services. Teasing or sternness can be adopted at will, the attitude can vary from one moment to the next, and the manner in which a person's complement must behave is not rigidly fixed. . . . The grandparent-grandchild relation is one of equals; but between a very young grandchild and a very old grandparent, the tenor in the reciprocal exchange is often set by the older person.[5]

This equality had its socially acceptable limits. Landes also noted that the joking among these equals could not be "pushed so far as to resemble" the joking between cross-cousins, riddled as it could be with sexual innuendo, nor she wrote, "should sternness become avoidance, as between mother in law and son in law."[6] E. S. Rogers, too, observed the joking characteristic of the proximity with grandparents, as well as its limits:

The grandparent–grandchild relationship has remained a crucial one through the difficulties of Ojibwe history. Richard Day, Mary Day, and grandchild at Walker on the Leech Lake Reservation. Photographed in 1941 by Monroe Killy. *Courtesy Minnesota Historical Society*

"There is a mild form of joking between grandparent and grandchild under certain conditions. A person may joke with his grandmother but only when she is very old."[7]

Still, given the highly "reserved and formal" relationships that he observed to be typical among members of adjacent generations, that "frequently" could be "fraught with hostility either implicit or explicit," Rogers remarked on how "the relationship between alternate generations," that is, between grandparents and grandchildren, tends to be more relaxed and easy going with little or no friction. "Between a grandparent and grandchild," Rogers wrote, "there is a strong bond of affection and a continual interest in the welfare of each other. This is especially true of the grandparent. It is shown in the kind behavior and indulgence a grandparent bestows on a young grandchild. When a baby is born both grandmothers attend the birth if possible and grandfathers immediately afterward. Thereafter they make frequent visits."[8]

At least in such Northern Ojibwe communities that remained based on the fur trade and life in the bush well into the twentieth century, this proximity was physical as well as abstract. Based on her interviews and fieldwork at Emo, Ontario in the 1930s, Landes wrote:

> The grandparents were storehouses of knowledge which they impart gladly to their adult children and to the grandchildren alike. The grandparents and small grandchildren are thrown very much together, for the grandparents no longer carry on sustained active work and the grandchildren are still too young to take it on; they treat one another with the camaraderie of equals. All this is particularly true of the girls, for they always remain about the lodge, while the boys are gradually removed for outdoor fasting, trapping, hunting, and war.[9]

Similarly, R. W. Dunning noticed that at Pekangikum, Ontario, in the 1950s "although a grandfather is in some ways superior in status to his grandchild, the relationship is almost a reciprocal one."[10]

The proximity and equality of grandparents and grandchildren are social conventions; but on Anishinaabe terms, they are conventions that correspond to more fundamental claims about the nature of life and time. If lifetime and other durations of time were matters of circles, it follows that the grandparent and the grandchild, the very old and the very young, are of a piece. As it was put by a 96-year-old Minnesota poet, Meridel Le-Seuer (who though non-Native herself moved frequently in Native circles), the very old and the very young can have this special relationship because neither is trying to "hang on" to much of anything.[11] Whether or not it was the case that they were thus existentially or morally of a piece, certainly it was often the case that grandparents and small grandchildren could find themselves left at home while the parents were engaged in other economic pursuits. Given the number of contemporary Native families headed by single parents, or in which economic realities and job possibilities find one or both parents away from home for long periods of time, or where kids return to grandparents' homes during summer vacation, this state of affairs often continues in the present day.

Between grandparents and grandchildren, the circumstances of this existential, moral, and spatial proximity within the homes of Ojibwe tradition—or, more recently, in the improvised networks of Ojibwe life—

geographic proximity has framed the distinctive nature of Ojibwe pedagogy. The special bond between elders and children created an important intergenerational context for the passing on of traditions and values, one that made room for a more careful, deliberate passing on of great matters of tradition, ceremony, and ethics by securing them from the distractions of daily life and economic priorities of the parents' generation.

In discussing the major influences in his life, Lac du Flambeau elder Ben Chosa relates that his father was "always busy trapping or guiding or trying to feed eight to ten kids. So he was always gone," including for protracted periods of time during the Depression on crucial cash-earning opportunities through WPA projects and CCC camps. He spent a great deal of time with his grandmother, from whom he said he learned much, but clearly Chosa grew up in a world with as many grandparents as there were community elders: "But many other people had an influence on my life, especially a lot of the older people. Older men. They taught me a lot. I don't know why they did it, but they would come over to the house and get me. Say 'C'mon, we're going, here' or 'we're going there.' . . . I don't know why. I think part of it was I was willing to learn about certain things. About everything."[12]

Importantly, the teaching and the learning go in both directions, as we learn from Northrup, a storyteller and self-described "apprentice elder" who learns much from his grandson:

Ezigaa continues to be a good Grampa teacher. He has been living with us since he was a week old. His mother, Dolly, calls him Aaron. . . . We call him Ezigaa. It means wood tick in Ojibwe and it describes the way he hugs. . . . He is just discovering the world. I feel young seeing the world through his eyes. He gets up early so he can old man around with his Grampa. He comes into the room and greets me with open arms. Still sleepy, he climbs in my lap and we sit for a few minutes, feeling each other's heartbeat. We call it the Morning Ezigaa Hug. Then together we look around the yard to see if night has changed anything. Without saying anything, we watch the birds flying by. We both turn to hear the train passing through downtown Sawyer. . . . Ezigaa and I share a walk almost every day. We go looking for rocks [agates] and find memories. . . . I remember my Ma or Gramma walking down these same roads looking for maybe the same agates.[13]

The Teaching Vocation of Grandparenthood

Because elders have been integrated fully into the life of the extended family, elders exercised broad authority in their capacity as the ones charged with the education and moral nurture of children. The early-nineteenth-century Ojibwe clergyman Peter Jones observes: "The advice of the 'long dwellers upon the earth' is generally listened to with great attention, as it is from them that the youth receive their instructions respecting . . . the traditions of their forefathers."[14] "Long dwelling" in itself, of course, bespeaks a certain credential of life education, but the credentials of old age are more ramified still in light of an Anishinaabe understanding of the life course, discussed in the first chapter, which ties length of life lived with the proper flow of knowledge and blessing from the spirits and across generations, as well as the ethical practice of right relations. The medicine man in Basil Johnston's colloquy related this dimension of Ojibwe pedagogy as follows:

> When men and women attain the last weary hill and climb toward the crest, they are sustained by the knowledge that they have lived out their visions and given a helping hand to their fellow beings. Old age is a gift of the Kitche Manitou. As such it is to be cherished; not disparaged. Even in old age, life's work is not finished. There is still much good that can be done for brothers in life. By living through all the stages and living out the visions, men and women know something of human nature and living and life. What they have come to know and abide by is wisdom. This is what they must pass on to those still to traverse the path of life and scale the mighty hills. Only when they finally vanish into the mists is the work over.[15]

Minnesota Ojibwe elder and author Ignatia Broker, too, tied in the grandparent/grandchild relationship and the teachings secured through that relationship with the larger generational exchanges that make for a continuation of *bimaadiziwin*. "We believe in the circle of life," Broker professed:

> We believe that all returns to its source; that both good and bad return to the place where they began. We believe that if we start a deed, after the fullness of time it will return to us, the source of the journey. . . . Because the

earth is our Grandmother and our Grandmother is old, the Old Ones of our dodaim are called grandmothers and grandfathers. Because they are wise and have known Grandmother earth longer, we hear their words and remember them, for they are the words of the grandmothers and grandfathers who were before us. Thus the young hear what they must teach when they become the Old Ones.[16]

The Shape of Traditional Pedagogy

"The purposes of traditional Ojibwe education were both to serve the practical needs of the people (to learn life skills) and to enhance the soul," writes Ojibwe educator and historian Thomas Peacock, following Basil Johnston.[17] One could add to these the extensive moral education that splits the difference in an Ojibwe worldview, teaching proper knowledge of relationality and modeling the proper exercise of right relations among humans and nonhuman "persons" of the land and spiritual world. In all cases, grandparents were the ones, in these regards even more than parents, charged with the education of the rising generation.

PRACTICAL LIFE SKILLS

Although education in life skills could rest on the teachings of a child's parents, it could often principally involve grandparents, at least one set of whom until recently lived in typical proximity to their children, if not under the same roof. "Grandmothers were especially important as caretakers of infants and small children when parents were busy at other tasks," notes Priscilla Buffalohead, adding "that this practice has some antiquity in Ojibway history [and] is reflected in legends and stories of children living in the lodge of their grandparents."[18] As the children grew, the teaching and learning was increasingly gender specific, with boys apprenticing with fathers and grandfathers and girls with their mothers and grandmothers. At puberty, Inez Hilger observed, boys and girls are instructed into what will be expected of them as men and women. A change of a boy's voice signaling puberty "gave notice . . . that he was to be instructed in the duties and obligations of manhood" by either a father or grandfather, and girls, in turn, by women of elder generations.[19]

ETHICAL TEACHING

If grandparents shared with parents the charge of teaching practical life skills, it was more specifically the grandparents who were responsible for moral education. Hilger observed, "The early Chippewa had no formal schooling such as we know it . . . but they did receive instructions from their elders in ethical standards, moral code, and vocational guidance and practice. . . . The moral code was taught to boys and girls at the age of puberty, usually by the grandparents or, in their absence, by elders living in the community."[20] "The ethical training was as rigid as the physical," wrote Diamond Jenness of Ontario Ojibwe at the turn of the twentieth century:

> Children were taught certain rules of conduct, and frequently punished for their infringement. They should never tell lies. They should be respectful to their elders and not walk in front of them. They should never stand around like beggars when others ate. Boys should avoid looking at girls, lest the girls' faces should appear in their way during their hunting. Children should not play too much, or climb too much, lest their souls should leave their bodies and some accident befall them. They should dream as much as possible, and try to remember their dreams. They should keep quiet in the evenings, or their parents would catch no game.[21]

SPIRITUAL EDUCATION

As with education in ethic and etiquette, much of the teaching of Anishinaabe spiritual heritage has been decidedly the province of older Anishinaabe. The work of elders as "spiritual directors" or "mentors" to the young will be taken up in some detail in chapter 5, and the teaching of certain esoteric ritual knowledge by medicine men and women was tied more specifically to ritualized teacher-novice relationships, often with the framework of initiatory societies like the Midéwiwin. Still, many Anishinaabe had spoken of the importance of learning not just ethics, but ritual propriety, healing, and spiritual knowledge outside the confines of initiatory societies.

Early in the nineteenth century, the Euro-American captive/adoptee John Tanner made frequent reference to the knowledge of proper ethical/

ritual action taught him by Netnokwa, the aged Ojibwe woman who adopted him as her son. When a young Tanner kills his first sturgeon, for example, he recalls that "the old woman thought it necessary to celebrate the feast of Oskenetahgwawin, or first fruits, though, as we were quite alone, we had no guests to assist us."[22] Of Swampy Cree tradition, elder Louis Bird told how it would be a grandparent or uncle rather than a parent who would serve as the mentor to a young person seeking spiritual direction and knowledge through dream fasting.

As much as spiritual education rested on the knowledge and discretion of the elder, the teacher/student relationship very much also depended on the sincerity and initiative of the young, as judged by the elder. Ben Chosa of Lac du Flambeau relates:

> Respect the old people for their knowledge. Ask them if you want to know, ask them. . . . They won't tell you if you don't ask them. You have to ask—about religion especially, about anything. If they see that you want to learn, they'll teach you. One of the things about religion specifically is any religious person will not tell you about religion unless you ask, but you have to ask.[23]

Indeed, Chosa's observation is borne of his sense of the urgency of young people's initiative here to complete the exercise of eldership. "A lot of the old ways," Chosa adds, "are being lost because of that, nobody asks. Nobody asks!"[24]

EDUCATION IN RESPECT AND IDENTITY

It is ultimately anachronistic to distinguish, as I have, the religious from the secular, or the practical from the ethical, in grandparental education. On Ojibwe terms, the work of teaching and learning religious and cultural knowledge necessarily cannot be a wholly secular, wholly dispassionate, undertaking. "The purposes of traditional Ojibwe education," Johnston writes, "were both to serve the practical needs of the people and to enhance the soul (to grow in spiritual ways). . . . To possess only the skills of living without knowledge of the spirit would be to live a life without purpose, depth, and meaning. To rely solely upon inner growth was to ignore the harsh reality of life in earlier times."[25]

Again a key concept linking the practical and ethical/spiritual dimensions of an Anishinaabe lifeway on the land is respect, *manaajitowin*. Many references to the teachings of grandparents refer to the respect articulated by grandparents through stories or admonitions and modeled by them. In a series of public "counseling speeches," a Cree elder related:

> A young woman listened most carefully to the things her grandmother, especially, warned her about. Of course the "old woman" . . . had come to be experienced in always treating everything with respect. That is what she used to pass on to her grandchildren, how the children and grandchildren would have peace of mind, so they would be given peace of mind.[26]

Public Grandparenthood

As intimate as relationships between grandparents and grandchildren could be, older Anishinaabeg could and did exercise their prerogative as "everyone's grandparent" beyond the intimacies of family. In her discussion of the educational work of Ojibwe grandparents, which she presumably learned at White Earth, Frances Densmore observed the public figure of the "crier," a public grandparent of sorts:

> When everyone had retired and the camp was quiet an old man walked around the camp circle, passing in front of the dark tents. This man was a crier and he made the announcements for the next, day, telling whether the people would go hunting or what would be done in the camp. He also gave good advice to the young people who were taught to respect him and obey his words. Only a man who was known to embody in his own life the excellent principles he uttered was allowed to act as crier. . . . He taught sterling principles of character and gave such advice as he thought necessary. Odinigun said that the old man emphasized the teaching that the young people must not steal, also that they must keep away from fire water, use very little tobacco, and never say anything disrespectful concerning women. He told the women that they must keep from quarreling, live peaceably and not say bad things about each other. The advice to young men and women was "obey your parents, take their advice, and respect them. If you live in that

way while you are among your own people you will be respected when you go to a strange village."[27]

Whether exercised in such public ways, or more frequently in family lineages, grandparental teaching took a variety of forms. As seen in Densmore's note about how the crier himself was expected to "embody in his own life the excellent principles" he taught, the pedagogy of example was as important as, perhaps even more than, that of pronouncement.

EXAMPLE

One Anishinaabe man summarized traditions in terms of the "3 Ls" of Ojibwe education: Look, Listen, and Learn. Today as doubtless of old, there is scarcely any community gathering or ceremony where children are not present and encouraged to look, listen, and learn. And the phrase *pay attention!* is so pervasive that in Indian country it extends beyond the conventional sense of the term to encourage a posture of learning even in situations where intentional teaching is not underway.

Elders taught and teach perhaps more by example than by words of instruction. Vernon Kinietz wrote that most crises of life were met "according to well established culture patterns . . . learned by absorption rather than direct instruction and the individual is often unable to formulate their nature."[28] Consider the practice of hospitality. Ojibwe narratives are shot through with old men and especially old women, who, from their typically sedentary place in stable, warm wigwams, go out of their way to take in the sojourning protagonist, providing him or her with warmth, food, comfortable lodging, advice, and special knowledge. One stock image of the myths is the ever hospitable *mindimooyenh* ("old woman"), whose kettle magically refills itself. *Biindigen! Biindigen!* ("Come in!"), *Namadabin! Namadabin!* ("Have a seat!"), *Wiisinin, wiisinin, wiisinin!* ("Eat, eat, eat!")—these are the Ojibwe phrases modeled as much as taught by hospitable elders today as of old. In his narrative of his life as an Anishinaabe, Tanner wrote about the striking nature of Anishinaabe hospitality: "This kind of hospitality is much practiced among Indians who have had but little intercourse with the whites, and it is among the foremost of the virtues which the old men inculcate upon the minds of children in their evening conversations."[29]

REPROOF

The ethnographic record suggests that as everyone's grandparents, charged as the role was with the moral education of all, elders also exercised their pedagogical prerogative through public reproof. The *Jesuit Relations* record a number of instances where elders (in French either *les Anciennes, les vieillards*, or *les vielles femmes*) appear to take charge as exhorters or rebukers of the young, particularly for acts of what the Jesuits took to be disrespectful acts toward them for that Anishinaabe elders, regardless of their interest in the missionary's religion, may very well have viewed as inhospitable conduct. "They even so esteem the holy places," wrote Père Beshefer of the Anishinaabe at St. Ignace (now in Michigan) in 1681, "that when a man threw a stone at the church windows, all the elders after holding a council . . . exhort[ed] all their young people to have more respect for the house of God, and for the persons who came on his behalf to give them sense."[30]

Kinietz wrote that John Pete, an Ojibwe consultant from Lac Vieux Desert in the 1940s, was "constantly reminding the younger generation of their remissions. He feels so strongly the errors of their present ways that he makes an ideal informant, for in telling of the old and correct customs, he invariably expostulates on the present shortcomings of various individuals."[31] Andrew Blackbird's ninth of twenty-one Anishinaabe precepts "by which they were governed in their primitive state" reads, "Hold thy peace, and answer not back, when thy father or thy mother or any aged person should chastise thee for thy wrong."[32] Because such commandments imply some occasions of the prohibited conduct, one can infer some measure of resentment could arise from public reproof by "any aged person." Indeed, the elders' prerogative to reprove could generate social tensions. Northrup spoke about something like this kind of resentment framed by the experience of language loss:

> Poet Adrian Louis said something like, "Respect your elder? They're the ones who got us in this mess." At times, I felt that way about Ojibwe language speakers. Most of us learned a few phrases because we were around Ojibwe speakers. We learned a little but not enough. We mostly learned the command words: don't, be quiet, sit down, don't cry, eat, or go to bed. It is hard to carry on a conversation using only command words. A cousin said for the first eight years of his life, he thought his name was *gego*, the Ojibwe word for don't.[33]

But while exhortation and even rebuke may be called upon in certain circumstances, the more conventional approach to elders' pedagogy would be that modeled through the close relationship between grandparent and grandchild.

Not all esteemed storytellers have been elders, but only rarely has a recognized elder not also been regarded a storyteller. It seems that where the instruction was explicit and not simply by example, it was through stories, and situated in storytelling moments in evenings, around campfires, and perhaps more intensive in the cold months when much more time was spent in such an otherwise nonproductive context. From her White Earth consultants, Hilger learned, "They were taught the ethical standards of their people around the campfires of the wigwam through the long winter evenings," and "these lessons," Hilger added, "were usually embodied in stories."[34]

The nineteenth-century Wisconsin Ojibwe writer George Copway tells of the lessons of his own childhood:

> Some of these stories are most exciting, and so intensely interesting, that I have seen children during their relation, whose tears would flow quite plentifully, and their breasts heave with thoughts too big for utterance. Night after night for weeks have I sat and eagerly listened to these stories. The days following, the characters would haunt me at every step, and every moving leaf would seem to be a voice of a spirit.[35]

At times the lessons conveyed through such oral narratives, as with reproof, could be plain and direct. "It is the custom of the old men to reiterate again and again that which they consider of importance," Densmore observed, "repeating it with a slight change of words. The same manner of speech is used in telling ancient stories."[36]

At other times the messages were far more subtle, far more demanding of continued reflection. "Our ancestors' stories," writes Broker, "were filled with both obvious, simple teachings and deeper, more subtle meanings." "The deeper meanings of stories were seldom directly conveyed," she continued; and "it was up to the listeners, who would go away from storytelling thinking about their meanings, to try to figure out the messages on their own. This subtle, indirect way of teaching remains an important cultural way among the Ojibwe today. Sometimes we are given advice without recognizing it as such."[37] Historian J. R. Miller relates: "There was never any shortage of inspiring examples or horrible cautionary tales in a family's store of myths and legends with which to teach, gently but effectively, what was and what was not acceptable conduct by the youngest members of the community."[38]

Artful teaching with stories, be it direct or indirect, has come from elders who were not only prodigious in their repertory but also judicious in their timing and economy of words. Ojibwe tradition and language recognize a number of different classes or categories of stories. *Aadizookanag*, arguably translatable as "myths" or known commonly as "winter stories," tell of the actions of the trickster and other beings of mythical proportion. Such stories are gendered animate in the language, "persons" capable of transformation and whose telling has been traditionally tied to the seasonality of winter (because snow on the ground muffles them so as not to offend spirits). The other class of narrative, *dibaadjimowin*, perhaps translatable as "legends" or "news," are by contrast inanimate in gender. These stories range from *mewinzha* ("the long ago") to the relatively recently historical and semihistorical relations of family and community lore. Together with these, one might add the artful crafting of new stories by such public figures as Anne Dunn or Jim Northrup, or other more locally known writers and performers. As Northrup puts it: "I have heard the old stories and continue to tell new ones."[39]

Much has been made by Hallowell and others in the ethnographic record of classificatory distinctions in narratives, but Northrup's phrase suggests that today, as in former years, the pedagogical action is less a matter of rules of classification and genre as one of the agency of the storyteller, as she or he conjures a story from an eclectic repertoire for a particular moment in time. Even in the ethnological attempts in the early twentieth century by Alanson Skinner, Paul Radin, William Jones, Victor Barnouw, and others to collect, systematize, and gloss Ojibwe narratives, the utterances they recorded defy oversystemization. These ethnologists' careful efforts to label the provenance of stories as "Indian" or "European" in origin, or as "Legends," "Myths," "Semihistorical," are resisted by the improvisation and fluidity of the uttered stories themselves, which when told can involve kings, castles, and *wiindigoo* (persons who become cannibals) without contradiction. Here the dynamics of the oral resist efforts on the part of abstract, texted analysis to fix them by category and purpose.

This is not to say that the stories themselves have no status aside from their usefulness to a storyteller. There is clearly an urgent commitment on the part of storytellers to remain true to the stories as they have been passed down, to honor the integrity of the stories. In this the animate gender of *aadizookanag* serves as an apt image for much of the larger repertory: the animate stories are not objects in a storyteller's toolbox, but subjects, "persons" within a moral universe, to whom one can do injustice. This complex relationship between storyteller and story is congruent with the nature of traditional authority that I will examine more fully in the context of the dynamics of orality in the subsequent chapter. But we gain further appreciation of eldership by lingering here on the distinctive features of that knowledge embodied not in propositions but in stories.

NARRATIVE KNOWLEDGE

"We may never have met the people in some of the stories," writes Kimberly Blaeser, "but they're part of our family history, and the stories have a moral [within them]—not stated—but sown through what someone did. Indian people don't *teach* their children. They *story* them."[40] Swampy Cree elder Louis Bird reflected on his own process of interviewing his elders for cultural knowledge and on the particular way of knowing that ties storied knowledge to the person of the elder:

> In our culture you cannot specifically . . . extract the story from a person, just one item. No, you can't do that. In order to have an understand piece or information, fully understood, you will have to listen to elder why he tells you the stuff. You have to listen [to] stories, a series of stories that he emphasizes this is what he's talking about. And that way you do not extract the particular information that you want from an elder. And that I find that out. So what I did then when I begin to . . . take notes or take the recording of the elder, is to allow them free run. What I mean to say free run, I just sit there in front of them and listen to them. Let them speak their mind, let them say whatever they want. If I have question about the hunting or special hunting, they will tell me the story about the hunting and in time I am supposed to get information from there. And if I ask them about some of

the stuff, they would do the same, they would answer a little bit first and then they would tell me a story. And for that it doesn't matter what kind of a story they tell me, but what they do is they give me an answer in a story. Not just a few word answer. No the interview would never work that way with the native people. It hasn't worked.[41]

Here the pedagogical prerogative of the elders as a structure of authority is woven into a pattern of knowledge that is embedded in stories and inextricable from their lives, land, and community.

Walter Ong discusses in theoretical terms the distinctive shape of cultural knowledge embedded in stories. Primarily oral societies, he avers, "do not generate durable abstractions," "and so they use stories of human action to store, organize and communicate much of what they know." Ong adds that stories, unlike proverbs, riddles, and other briefer durable forms, "can bond a great deal of lore in relatively substantial, lengthy forms that are reasonably durable."[42] Among other things, cultural or ritual knowledge cannot be segmented off from the relational and ethical matrix in which it is embedded in stories.[43] But what Ong takes primarily to be the "psychodynamics" of orality also has a social dimension, for as Louis Bird's experience relates, there is a kind of sovereignty retained by the elder in the process of "storying" a student. It shows how the process of cultural transmission was anything but "automatic," but shaped by the authority of the grandparent elder. Again, this authority is exercised in speech practices that are stylized in important ways.

In contrast to the question and answer conventions of teaching and learning in Euro-American contexts, among the Cree, Regna Darnell found "the speaking which is most highly valued is a monologue by someone who is wise (old) enough to have something to say that is worth listening to. A young listener may ask questions, but the segments of a monologue into which interjections are acceptable are controlled by the elder, not by the questioner."[44] Darnell also identified a distinctive "lack of interest in topic closure" in Cree teaching conventions, consistent with idioms of storytelling and with a confidence in cultural learning as a long process. The open-endedness stresses the "continuity of knowledge" rather than its "novelty." "Life itself is a cycle, within which individuals grow up listening to their grandfathers, come to be old themselves, teach their own grandchildren, become one of the ancestors, expect that their teachings will be assimilated by the next generation, providing eventual closure to old teachings and open-endedness to new ones."[45]

These idioms of teaching are again seen to be tied into a worldview in which individual lives and cosmic life move in corresponding cycles. "No one can comprehend more than their own understanding allows at a given point in the life cycle," Darnell writes, "therefore, words spoken by a teacher/elder/man of power are retained for future consideration, for growing into to the greatest degree possible. The Cree believe that there is time for things to come to fruition, that there are cycles both in the natural world and in individual human life. Wisdom and understanding are the natural consequences of living and attempting to maintain harmony of oneself with the world of living-ness."[46]

Anishinaabe pedagogy engineers firsthand learning situated in and implicated in a student's experience, at the direction of but not determined by the authority of the elder. Ojibwe children are refreshingly, boisterously present in every ceremonial and other community occasion I've experienced. They are taught skills of active watching and listening, not simply of the content of what to look or listen for. They are taught to take in cultural lessons experientially, to take them in over time, and not to expect spoon-fed segmented units of knowledge.

I learned this, I should add, the hard way. Until I began to develop a more discerning appreciation of such things, I took my own teacher, Larry Cloud Morgan, and other elders to be tentative or even passive educators. For example, fancying myself to have a facility with languages and trained in a pedagogy oriented to efficient, rapid acquisition of knowledge, I was eager to "pick up" the Ojibwe language and was often frustrated by the slow pace of Larry's instruction, which happened largely on the long drives between Minneapolis and the northern Minnesota reservations, the language instruction in exchange for the time and energy of helping Larry with his advocacy work at White Earth and Leech Lake. Given his age and the important and exhausting advocacy and justice work we were engaged with as liaisons for White Earth's Camp Justice struggle, we were predictably too tired to accomplish much. But it wasn't fatigue alone. On those long trips, I would learn at best the vocabulary for various animals and plants and would be antsy to get on to the more complicated conjugations of verbs and the like. Sensing my anxiousness, Larry would often simply close the lessons down, change the subject, and look out the window. Later

I would realize I was the epitome of *mindawe*, an Ojibwe term referring to the petulance of a child, or the impatience of a non-Native person with an undue sense of entitlement. I now see such moments as themselves teachings, thoughtfully proceeding in a deliberate Anishinaabe manner of teaching.

Anishinaabe religious and cultural knowledge has a temporal dimension in that it emerges concretely in "teaching moments," judged by the teacher or grandparent, and this temporal dimension is closely tied to the culturally constituted life cycle. It is for them, I think, as Jeffrey Anderson observes it is for the Arapaho: "The life cycle was modulated with respect to the transmission of knowledge. Elders ultimately controlled the process. They made certain that forms of knowledge were conveyed only at certain times in the life trajectory and in appropriate contexts."[47] Anderson follows this logic to criticize an ethnographic record that often fails to take into account that "only a few of the oldest people—whether Arapaho or other Indian—possessed at any given time, knowledge of the total cosmological order." "Out of that fact," Anderson concludes, "has arisen one of the greatest barriers to understanding the so-called worldviews of North American Indian cultures."[48]

TEACHING WISDOM IS MORE THAN "EDUCATION"

As personal as could be the teaching and learning, or the "cultural transmission," between grandparents and grandchildren, it would be wrong to miss the cosmic nature of it. To return to the theme of *bimaadiziwin* charted in chapter 1, Anishinaabe pedagogy can be fruitfully understood in terms of indigenous conceptions of life stages, the importance of exchanging knowledge/power between generations for the continuation of *bimaadiziwin*, and ways of knowing particular to them.

Perhaps it is for this reason that contemporary Anishinaabe people can feel so powerfully about the place of their grandparents, their elders, in the constitution of their deepest identity, of what we might designate as their total being. In their study of grandmothers in various Native American communities, Marjorie Schweitzer and collaborators found that "grandmothers-as-culture-transmitters may be one of the most significant contributions to the perpetuation of Indian communities."[49] Their study showed that despite the diversity of indigenous ways of conceptualizing grandmotherhood, in all cases, grandmothers engaged in periodic or seasonal childcare and even in many cases childrearing when parents were dead, ill, incarcerated, or unstable.[50] More than an obvious implication of grandmothers' key roles in childrearing and the inculcation of values, such a view suggests that distinctive identities of younger people as Anishinaabe, or any other Native people for that matter, have been and continue to be significantly fashioned around and through a relation with a grandparent—very often a grandmother. And although such terms as grandparent should be understood to apply broadly to adoptive and general intergenerational relations, there is a force to the grandparent/grandchild relationship that makes the connection with the past more intimate still.

White Earth Ojibwe Gladys Ray put it this way: "I think the main reason I have stayed with my own culture and religion is because of my grandparents. I respected them. They were such a large part of my childhood. I was very fond of these beautiful old people. I've always felt that if I could be the kind of grandma that my grandma was to me, then I really had succeeded in my life. My grandma and grandpa had time for us. They were our teachers and counselors, *a constant reminder of who we were—who I was.*"[51]

Since time immemorial, as previous chapters have shown, respected elders have embodied the ideal person and represent the social body. In that regard, Gladys Ray's quote could have come from the end of the eighteenth or of the nineteenth century. But her utterance bears witness to the timeliness, the urgency of the grandparent/grandchild relationship in the late twentieth century. I turn now to a more overtly historical consideration of the timeliness of grandparenthood and its pedagogical shape to a community increasingly incorporated into Euro-American configurations of family and systems of learning.

•   •   •

History

It is counterintuitive to imagine an accentuation of the vocation of grandparenthood over time as Anishinaabe communities have been increasingly incorporated into a Euro-American society that does not stress the value of grandparental wisdom. From the boarding schools that sought to remove children from their elders and, in turn, education and moral/spiritual formation from familial to institutional contexts, to relocation programs that served to divide extended Anishinaabe families and shrink them into nuclear units, it is all the more remarkable that the vocation of grandparenthood should retain such a robust force in Anishinaabe life.

Anthropologist Anastasia Shkilnyk traced the tragic lines of this history in the context of the Ojibwe of Ontario's English River Reserve. On the cover of the book is a striking photograph of a smiling extended Anishinaabe family, kids and elders among them, but the photograph is graphically torn in half, suggesting the total effect of what her subtitle identifies as "The Destruction of an Ojibwa Community" beset by poverty, alcohol, and environmental degradation.[52] This is surely representative of the experience of many Anishinaabe families and communities in these challenging times. But a consideration of difficult history must also attend to the crucial ways in which Anishinaabe people have artfully survived that history, often on their own terms.

ASSIMILATION POLICY

The churchmen, reformers, and bureaucrats who drew up and administered the system of assimilation policies from the 1870s through the 1930s considered the extended Anishinaabe family, anchored as it was to its elders and the seasonal round on the land, a key obstacle to their efforts. Consequently, their agenda took aim on this extended family, communal lands, and, it happens, the pedagogy and authority of Anishinaabe eldership.

Visiting White Earth in 1938, Hilger noted the fruits of assimilation policies, racism, and the "liquor and its concomitant evils" that dissolved an older social order in which elder grandparents exerted their influence by example and word. "The breaking down of the dominant social order of the old culture has done away with the institutionalized controls of social conduct," Hilger wrote, and the younger generation "is reaping the results."

> Such controls were exercised among the primitive Chippewa by the parents and grandparents. Today their control is gone; they feel dejected and discouraged and without resource in the present situation, for they are fully aware that the pattern they know so well does not coincide with that which

their children and grandchildren are being taught. "You are now citizens of the United States and no longer Indians. You must live like the white man," the children are told. The old guard is confused; it wonders what in the white man's civilization is worthy of imitation. It feels it has not been able to keep up with the times and hence retires discouraged and heartsick.[53]

Discouraged and heartsick: Hilger's language conforms to the experience of many older Anishinaabeg who were becoming resigned to the state of affairs and were regularly reminded by other elders of their duties to assume those roles of teacher. Kinietz, who visited Lac Vieux Desert in Michigan's Upper Peninsula in the 1940s, wrote of how his principal consultant, John Pete, "regrets the digressions from the old ways. He is constantly reminding the younger generation of their remissions."[54] Similarly, Hilger's elder consultants told her "unhesitatingly . . . that modern education has been no substitute for traditional parental training."[55]

BOARDING SCHOOLS

The "modern education" to which Hilger referred was significantly an education on the boarding school model. The idea, pioneered in an experiment at the Carlisle Institute in Pennsylvania by a civil war veteran who believed he had a formula to remake "hostile" Apache prisoners of war into "civilized" people, captured the imagination of assimilation era bureaucrats and continued through the mid-twentieth century.[56] These schools were to be totalizing institutions, militarily regimented ventures complete with uniforms and haircuts, that were designed to extract Native children from the ties of extended kin and land and remake them in the image of assimilation policy. Replacing Ojibwe and Odawa with English, replacing the seasonal round with vocational training toward market agriculture, wage labor, and the gendered structures of Victorian domesticity to fuel an American economy, and replacing fluid gender norms with disciplined middle-class Euro-American expectations for women and men, these schools are today criticized broadly for their crucial role in generating dysfunction in later twentieth-century Native communities. But from Native points of view, the story of boarding schools and their standing with respect to the pedagogy of family and elders is as complicated as the circumstances in which Anishinaabe families struggled to survive.

Anishinaabe children from Minnesota found themselves at boarding schools far away in southwest Minnesota at Pipestone, at Flandreau in South Dakota, at Wahpeton in North Dakota, or further away at Kansas's Haskell Institute, or Pennsylvania's Carlisle Institute. Other children, while attending government and residential schools on reservations, like the government school at White Earth's Pine Point Village or the Benedictine schools in the towns of Red Lake or White Earth Village, often had to stay with extended relatives near those schools in order to attend regularly, given that much reservation transportation was on foot and family compounds could be thirty or forty miles away from the school proper.

Especially in the early twentieth century, after the previous policy makers' obsession with forced assimilation had given way to a slightly more moderate approach to assimilation, boarding schools offered stressed Ojibwe families a useful way to meet the basic needs of many young people. Diseases like tuberculosis, combined with poor reservation health care, left many children without a parent, parents, or grandparents altogether. Historian Brenda Child observed, "As family life suffered during the early reservation, post-allotment, and Great Depression years, traditional methods of absorbing children into the extended kinship group were not always possible."[57] Child points out that even families whose parents and grandparents were intact faced daunting challenges to make ends meet in these years, and often enrolled children in boarding school as part of their strategy to survive. Eventual compulsory requirements, in any case, drew more children to the government or missionary schools that would compete with traditional idioms of familial education by grandparents and parents.

But while these schools institutionalized education away from the family, in most cases, the matrix of the Anishinaabe family never fully succumbed to the assaults on it. Child has shown masterfully how the seasonal and familial rhythms of Anishinaabe life continued to draw kids out of these institutional contexts on a regular basis and revived them with a sense of other commitments than those stressed in the straight rows of boarding school classrooms. Anishinaabe families knew well the stresses that long distance, strict rules limiting visits from family or travel back to the reservation (even in summers), and the prohibition on Native languages, might bring. And to be sure, as Child writes, "nothing less than a complete assumption of a new identity was expected of the boarding school student," signaled by the almost uniform practice of immediately replacing Anishinaabe names gifted them by significant elder *wen'enh* ("namesakes")—and freighted with familial and cultural and spiritual resonance—with more modern names supposedly "easier to pronounce." But Child's close reading of correspondence to and from reservation families gives an impression of considerable resilience and resolve, among children and their families, in spite of those stresses. "The power of home," Child writes in response to histories that tell only of the disjunctions in family life, "was so intense and comforting that few students left that world behind. Letters reveal the intimacy of relationship not always apparent in more formal documentation of the boarding school experience."[58]

Despite strict rules against home visits to reservation communities—only after 1933 did federal policies suggest that boarding school students be allowed to return for summer vacations—Child discovers from these letters how strong were parents' commitments to keeping their distant children connected to familial life. A Menominee father in 1924 appealed to the head of the Flandreau school to allow his deaf daughter to spend a summer at home while her aged grandmothers were still alive:

> Won't you please let me know if my poor girl is coming home this summer. I would very much like to have her come home. I know she is going to fail in examination. I know it. But for our poor sake please please let her come home this summer We have two old ladies here our mothers aged old ladies. Because if she don't come home this summer next year they might be gone. They old and sickly.[59]

If administrators' typical dismissals of such appeals indicated the thoroughgoing challenges to Anishinaabe communal life that boarding schools represented, boarding school graduates by and large returned, at least eventually, to communities of origin, many becoming holders of Bureau of Indian Affairs and tribal government jobs and not a few trading on the skills they learned as boarding schools in negotiating Euro-American systems and expectations to become tribal leaders, like Red Lake's legendary Roger Jourdain. Jourdain remained an outspoken critic of federal and state governmental interference in his community's sovereign affairs for more than thirty years as a tribal chairman and, upon retiring from formal public life, became an important elder consulted on a variety of matters by Red Lakers and other Ojibwe leaders.

As the concluding sentences of Child's study put it, "The schools designed to separate Indian families, dilute the influences of home, and impose a new set of cultural values ironically helped many Ojibwe families survive hard times and economic depression. . . . The boarding school agenda did not triumph over Indian families or permanently alienate young members of the tribe from their people. Descendants of boarding school alumni at Red Lake and other Ojibwe communities are still taught to know and value their relatives, as their families always wished."[60]

When Ignatia Broker's autobiographical character in *Night Flying Woman* returns to her family from the government school distraught that the teacher had insisted "our old life is bad. We must heed only what we hear in school to make us better people." Where her mother is upset that the young girl is not engaging the education, Christianity, and assimilation chosen for her by her parents, the grandparents offer a more comforting view that seeks to meaningfully integrate the two traditions. "Yes, my child," her grandfather tells her, "I can see why it is confusing. . . . But you must remember all the good our people have known and taught. Compare it to what you are now learning. Do not be ashamed of the good that we have taught and do not be ashamed of the good to be learned. Our way of life is changing, and there is much we must accept. But let it be only the good. And we must always remember the old ways. We must pass them onto our children and grandchildren so they too will recognize the good in the new ways."[61]

ELDERSHIP AND URBANIZATION

In the second half of the twentieth century, despite relocation policies and the increasing urbanization of the Native population, Anishinaabe familial leanings on grandparent-grandchild bonds persevered. By the 1970s, as a result of relocation policy incentives and other economic realities, fully half the Native American population could be found residing in cities. As sociological studies have shown, urban Indian people by and large have maintained a kind of translocal existence, traveling to and from reservation communities for important events like ricing, powwows, wakes, and other ceremonies.[62] But the racial, social, political, and economic realities of the cities in which they have worked and lived most of the year shaped identity and experience in profound ways. Often densely settled in particular neighborhoods with people of various tribal identities and often in close proximity to other communities of color, Native peoples in cities found themselves lumped together as "Indians." Individuals who relocated often married and started their families in cities. Other families who moved to cities together typically did so as nuclear units, spending much of their year—often the school year—at some remove from the grandparents and great-grandparents so central to Anishinaabe tradition and identity. Indeed it was arguably what one historian has called the "proletarianization" of the Ojibwe, rather than their internalization of assimilation norms, that dealt the deeper blow to the force of Ojibwe grandparenthood.[63]

Again, this didn't obviate the place of grandparents in the children's cultural and moral education, instead it became seasonally intensified during summer vacation. In this regard, the seasonality was not entirely new: in earlier reservation years and certainly in the prereservation era, wintertime was a season of intensified storytelling and teachings of culture from elders to children.

Larry Cloud Morgan is representative in this regard in the postwar era. His adoptive nuclear family, the Clouds, moved from Cass Lake on the Leech Lake Reservation to the Twin Cities, where his father obtained work as a bricklayer, yet stories of his youth were richer in details from summers spent with his Beaulieu grandparents at Red Lake and his Cloud and Morgan grandparents near Cass Lake.

Perhaps the shift of population to cities generated a state of affairs that accentuated the centrality of elders in keeping relations intact, both in the cities and with reservation communities of origin. In her study of urban Anishinaabeg in a Michigan automotive city she calls "Riverton," Deborah Davis Jackson found that much of the "community" life did not revolve around the official institutions of the local Indian center and the like, but was reassembled in informal institutions of extended kin networks, fashioned in no small part through the continued, if improvised, exercise of eldership. Through these practices, urban Indians "not only maintained what ties they could with their home communities, but also forged close bonds with extended family and others from their home reservations who were in the city."[64] Emerging in Michigan, Wisconsin,

Illinois, and Minnesota cities were grandparents of particular urban families who not only held their own immediate biological and adoptive families together but really did become the grandparents of extended networks of others who knocked on their doors seeking assistance for housing, transportation, protection, advocacy; for help navigating governmental or family systems; for guidance in language and tradition; and for spiritual direction. One towering example of this was Winnie Jourdain, a White Earth figure who lived many years in Minneapolis. She "kept Indian children in her home to make sure they stayed in school. She started a tutoring program for Indian students. She organized picnics, rummage sales and potluck dinners to help them buy books. When they graduated, she found places for them to live. Winnie and other Indian women made quilts, which they sold to buy books and eyeglasses for students."[65] She also earned respect of then Minneapolis mayor Hubert Humphrey, played a role in creating the Minneapolis American Indian Center, and gave direction and sometimes reproof to leaders of the American Indian Movement. In the Minneapolis area in the 1980s and 1990s, at least several Anishinaabe women and men came to have this status as elders: Bea Swanson, Roberta Brown, Ira Sailor, Larry Cloud Morgan, Porky White, Archie Mosay among them. Acting not simply as individuals, these elders also convened informally as elders' councils, in anticipation of elections and other political gatherings, and in response to community traumas such as in the wake of fatal police brutality.

Many of these urban elders have come back to the reservation to live out their final years. Winnie Jourdain put it this way: "I never thought about moving back to White Earth, because in my mind, I never left. I spent more than 50 years in Minneapolis, but White Earth was home. I had to get back."[66] Even in my relatively brief times spent at White Earth, I've been impressed with the frequent and sudden appearance on the reservation of older people who have returned after being away for twenty or thirty years, often far afield in California or Texas or the East Coast. Many surely return for the confidence they can have that their needs will be met in extreme old age by family and the home community. Perhaps others are drawn to return to fill out their days on landscapes and amid extended families with which and whom their identities have long been tied, if only from a distance. Some of these elders, by virtue of their distant travel, their honorable military service, or their plainly successful negotiation of the "White world" can assume places of honor and respect within kin networks and among reservation communities generally. Put another way, some return not just for what reservation life can do for them, but out of a strong sense of responsibility because they know it's time to take their place as elders.

If it is important to acknowledge such resilience of eldership, it is as important to bear witness to the truly devastating effects of later-twentieth-century conditions on its continued exercise. Beyond the geographical challenges of an increasingly urbanized population, reservations too have endured the conditions of poverty, racism, ill health, and the concomitant chilling effect on continued practices of Anishinaabe eldership and community, not to mention the larger society's embrace of a popular culture valorizing youth and a considerable erosion of intergenerational time. Researcher Darryl Zitzow interviewed 95 adolescents and 141 adults aged 55–70 on six Minnesota reservations to find that the "average amount of time American Indian adolescents spent with parents or elders had declined from 62 hours per week in the 1930s to 12.5 hours per week in the 1980s."[67] Perhaps the torn family photograph that serves as the cover art for Shkilnyk's study of dysfunction in a Canadian Ojibwe community does in fact represent much of the reality for contemporary Anishinaabe people.

The Promise and Challenge of Integrating Elders and Schools

But a truly representative story cannot stop there with such a picture. If Anishinaabe communities have demonstrated the resilience of grandparenthood amid these conditions, they have increasingly of late sought to incorporate the pedagogy of elders as everybody's grandparents into the public arena of schools, both in tribally operated schools, independent Native-run "survival schools" in cities, and in the urban and rural public schools that educate the large majority of Anishinaabe children. Since in many communities today, only members of elder generations speak the language fluently, bringing elders into classrooms boldly affirms the epistemological value of Ojibwe and Odawa languages and incorporates an elder's knowledge of the language that lives and breathes.

The integration of elders and their cultural and linguistic knowledge into institutions will have wider repercussions, for it incorporates not just Native individuals and their languages into the school environment. It can also incorporate what Alan Corbiere calls the "wholistic" epistemological orientation of Anishinaabe familial and community life with the orientation of the schools. "Wholistic education can effect cultural survival by providing an education that affirms indigenous worldviews and traditions, restores the role of the land and Nature as teachers, teaches history from a Native perspective, restores the Elders to their rightful place as transmitters of indigenous knowledge, reconnects the generations, and uses Native languages as the medium of instruction."[68]

Unless esteemed elders are telling the stories and offering the teachings, Corbiere writes, the teaching of Native knowledge can be segmented off from the rest of the curriculum such that Native "understandings of the world are irrational, nonlinear, and most of all 'unscientific,' that is, scientifically unverifiable. Approaching First Nations education from this orientation results in the rationalization and despiritualization of the [Anishinaabe] worldview."[69] The three "conduits" of indigenous epistemology, Corbiere argues, namely, "the land, the stories, and the Elders," are typically blocked in Euro-American and Euro-Canadian classrooms.[70] Incorporation of elders and their pedagogical authority in schools also can bridge the frequent and perilous "chasms" between generations that institutional schooling has created. "The purpose of wholistic education is to increase the level of shared meaning between the Elders and the young," Corbiere writes.[71]

The presence of an esteemed elder in the classroom also conveys a particular ethical responsibility to the process of learning toward community and environmental health. Alfred Manitopeyes, an Ojibwe elder from Canada, "uses the metaphor of good talking and good walking to indicate the ethical responsibilities of teachers."[72] And as we have seen, the lessons that elders teach are, in Anishinaabe contexts, taught by example as much as by pronouncement.

But it has not been easy to integrate the cultural authority of elders in classrooms, especially the majority of classrooms educating Native children beyond tribal control. Most elders with the necessary authority to teach language and culture lack the typical official credentials required of paid instructors in colleges and universities concerned about numbers of instructors with doctorates or, more commonly in public school systems, with collective bargaining agreements designed to protect organized teachers. It requires more work and more flexibility than is often difficult to come by among underpaid and overworked educators and administrators in public schools. If it is ironic that a non-Indian with little or no Ojibwe-language training is favored by such a system over an authoritative elder, it is also true, as Corbiere suggests, that the segmented and text-based idioms of instruction in classrooms do not square easily with indigenous idioms of elder's instruction in which culture and language and science and religion can together constitute a web of instruction. A number of tribally controlled schools, private nonprofit "survival" schools in urban environments, and charter schools have succeeded in bridging these idioms and more fully incorporating the instruction, example, and even counseling of elders in schools, but there remains the question of the majority of Native children being instructed in public schools where they remain a minority population.

There is also an issue of formally incorporating the dynamic process of elders' authority. A good number of paid "elder-in-residence" programs have been established recently that offer the stability of instruction and counseling that a continuously resident paid elder can provide. But this is not without issue. There are typically not as many paid positions as there are potentially recognized elders, and the institutional recognition, not to speak of the income, that comes with language programs or elders-in-residence programs can exacerbate community tensions concerning which elders should be recognized. And where the recognition of such elders can be fairly uniform in tribal college settings in reservation communities, it is more complicated at urban universities serving students from many different tribal communities and where, say, an Ojibwe elder's presence would not serve the same function for a Lakota student.[73] There also seems to be a concern that such elders are largely restricted by administrations to their roles as counselors and spiritual leaders and not integrated into the full curriculum.

Northern Manitoba's University College of the North, begun in 2004, serves a student body that is three-fourths indigenous.[74] A Council of Elders was chartered to "promote an environment at the university college that respects and embraces Aboriginal and northern culture and values. The Council of Elders is also to promote an understanding of the role of elders within the university college." To insure that their determinations are included in university governance and curriculum, both the governing council and the learning council in charge of the university curriculum include representatives from the elders' council.[75]

A different initiative tries to revive the intergenerational pedagogy of elders through formal master-apprentice relationships outside schools. A project at Cass Lake, called Anishinaabe Wi Yung, takes place outside of the schools and involves putting fluent elders together with Ojibwe young adults to "do everyday things like cooking, shopping or taking care of children," with elders receiving a small stipend for their time. Leslie Harper spent fifteen hours weekly with her "master," Josephine Dunn. "Where my baby-talk level of learning is at right now, she translates," said Harper, "but we try to get away from English as much as possible, and turn it into using real big, grand gestures and facial expressions, . . . so that you learn the language just like a little kid learns a language, by hearing that language all around him." Harper says elders are taking interest in what she's doing. "Now, they have this whole circle of friends, you know, these ladies and a couple of other guys at home." "And they know that's what I'm doing. So they test me whenever I'm out. I see them anywhere, I see them at the casino, if I see them at the post office, if I see them at the store, they'll talk Ojibwe to me, you know. Three years ago, these people would never have stopped in the store to talk Ojibwe to me, or to any young person. . . . I think it's bringing generations back together."[76]

To illustrate just how many important efforts like this are underway currently, as I was editing this chapter, by coincidence I received an email circular from Alan Corbiere announcing his Ojibwe Cultural Foundation's "Youth and Elders Gathering" for February 2008, with a rich assortment of teachings by respected elders on such topics as "Feeding the Clans, Feeding the Ancestors," "Teachings about the Pipe and the Colors," and specific "Teachings for Young Men" and "Teachings for Young Women."[77]

Whether in a community center, school, or grocery store, the personage of the elder, the distinctive idiom of their instruction, and its culturally rich content concerns the cultural survival, if not the very survival, of the Anishinaabeg. In a book with uncommon reach and influence within the Ojibwe community, Edward Benton-Banai described the series of seven "fires" that prophesy the signs of the times, identifying the penultimate sixth fire or generation, when young people have turned away from elders'

In 2002 the White House's Office of National Drug Control Policy tailored its *Parents: the Anti-Drug* campaign to Native American communities with this and two other frequently reprinted advertisements rendering elders as the antidrug.

instructions. The seventh fire, in which Ojibwe people currently find themselves, is characterized as the watershed when the healthy pedagogical relationship is restored between grandparents and grandchildren, or between young and their elders as everybody's grandparents.

A public advertising campaign running in Native newspapers at the time of this writing depicts an aged grandmother with her granddaughter with the prominent caption: "Elders: the Anti-Drug." Presumably this is a calling to elders to assume their traditional role as teachers and mentors to the young, and in particular to convey and model to the young the healthy, sober manner of living crucial to community survival. The image is as jarring as it is intriguing: a stock image of grandparent and grandchild so stereotypical of Native American life is set in relief to the harsh realities of despair and substance abuse that plague contemporary reservation and urban life. But in contrast to the broken family on the cover of Shkilnyk's book about the fragmentation of an Ojibwe community in the face of such poisons as alcohol and inhalants, the prognosis of this image is one of resilience.

Anishinaabe communities strive to maintain the vitality of grandparent/grandchild relationships and to assert in the midst of a larger society that has largely stripped the old of their role as teachers, especially of moral and spiritual values. Although there are surely Anishinaabe elders who do not assume this role and though there are surely many young people who do not heed those teachings, it remains tremendously important for harmony and balance to regard grandparenthood as a teaching vocation. Chapter 6 will take up just what might be distinctive about an elder's way of knowing.

ELDERS ARTICULATING TRADITION

Moving out from the familial/pedagogical authority of elders as grandparents, this chapter elaborates on the more public nature of elders' authority. Of course, given the expansive reach of grandparenthood described in the previous chapter, there can be no stark distinction between private and public authority. But we should consider more directly the dynamics of eldership as that form of public authority charged with defining what tradition is to be in any given situation. Elders can be seen as stewards of tradition, those who meet needs of those around them, as stewards do, with a judicious economy that implies fidelity to the stores over which they are charged or, more precisely, a fidelity to the previous generations of elders who entrusted the teachings to them. This chapter will identify the dynamics and range of the traditional authority of eldership, to gauge the precise nature of the meeting of the agency of elders and the body of tradition of which they are stewards and to survey the range of ways this authority has been exercised in a public realm.

For heuristic purposes, this chapter's focus on the *political* exercise of eldership contrasts with the subsequent chapter's focus on the more *spiritual* vocation of eldership. Still, the central concern here is not eldership as a political institution but rather the traditional authority of elders, an authority that transcends the conventionally political to include the religious and cultural. Examining speech conventions in this oral tradition and appealing to practice theory to speak of a "sense of tradition," I will trace how the authority of elders has produced improvised tradition so as to elude the conventional analytic oppositions of tradition/innovation, of culture/culture change, but also elude the tidy framework of the "invention of tradition" that shapes so much contemporary historical analysis.

Fittingly, the chapter engages that dynamic meeting of tradition and innovation in the authority of elders through the past several centuries of Ojibwe history. Elders as leaders have been authorizing change, and have been challenged for doing so, at a number of key moments in Ojibwe history: in making treaties, in conferring traditional status on certain Ojibwe Christian practices, and in a conscious "returning" to traditions from the 1970s on. More recently, because Anishinaabe communities have made concerted efforts to institutionalize the traditional authority of elders into codes and constitutions, I will also survey such attempts and what they might mean for the future shape of eldership.

In the paradigmatic work on the anthropology of aging, Leo Simmons drew the following generalization from a study of correlated traits from ethnographies of the world's small-scale societies: "Truly have [the old] been the guardians of life's emergencies, the custodians of knowledge and the directors of ceremonies and pastimes. In possession of such great influence, they have been the chief conservators of the status quo."[1] While such a view is not wholly inaccurate, it does justice to neither Anishinaabe elders nor the traditions of which they are ostensibly custodians. Though of course the structures of memory in primarily oral traditions promote the status of eldership, I want to challenge the conventional wisdom that the authority of elders is plainly a function of their years and the presumption of their steady accrual of oral knowledge. On the one hand, this perspective, elaborated in subsequent work in the anthropology of aging, reduces elders to the cultural resources they control. On the other, it views tradition (or culture, for that matter) in overly objective terms, as a kind of payload that gets carried or transmitted in the oral tradition, rather than as a social process itself, the work of regulated improvisation. But before one can fully appreciate such improvisations, one must first come to terms with the rules within which they take place, to acknowledge the conservative forces of orality and eldership.

Traditions of Traditional Authority

ORALITY AND AUTHORITY

The Anishinaabe tradition has always been, and remains today, profoundly oral.[2] Of this centrality of oral advice from "long dwellers upon the earth," nineteenth-century Ojibwe author Peter Jones put it this way: "Where there is no literature it cannot be otherwise than that they would think much of those who impart to them all the knowledge they most prize, and who are supposed, from the length of time they have lived, to have gained great experience."[3]

To be sure, orality itself has been a deep root of authority for elders in the tradition, and particularly so in this century, as the Ojibwe language has given way to English, as the seasonal round in the bush has yielded to incorporation into a cash-based American economy, and as a wealth of specific songs, ceremonies, and healing traditions tied specifically to economic practices in that seasonal way of life and to the language have become at worst endangered and at best folklorized. One can even argue that, amid a proliferation in print and electronic media of knowledge that designates Ojibwe tradition, and amid a ravenous if undiscerning, appetite in American popular culture for Native spirituality and wisdom, elders' traditional authority has appreciated in value for its identification with a living oral tradition. As communities zealously guard matters of ritual and sacred knowledge securely in the oral tradition, where ethical and ritual canons can be maintained in relations between teachers and those they authorize to receive teaching, there is an additional valence of "purity" ascribed to the knowledge of elders as compared to those in print. This is not to deny, of course, the more complex relationship that Anishinaabe people have with ethnographic sources: the Ojibwe-English dictionary by Roman Catholic missionary Frederic Baraga often graces bookshelves in Native homes, along with perhaps a reprint of Frances Densmore's *Chippewa Customs* or Ignatia Broker's *Night Flying Woman*. But to the extent that such books are deemed authoritative, this esteem typically refers to the author's personal reputation in the community rather than, say, to the academic credentials of the author or the evidentiary argument of the text. What is more, given the groundswell of Native interest in the renewal of traditions, the crucial generational position of today's elders connects them to a living past and frames the authority of their oral memories of that living past.

Anishinaabe people have placed an enormous amount of trust in the veracity and stability of oral traditions, and with good reason. Scholars like Jan Vansina have helped understand the remarkable fidelity with which oral traditions can account for the past.[4] Among the news reports about the recent tsunami in the Indian Ocean was a phenomenal story about the survival of the several hundred Moken Islanders off the coast of Thailand whose elders instructed them to take high ground immediately upon seeing the ominous low tide that betokened, according to their oral tradition, a devastating wave, and this despite no tsunamis of such proportion in historically documented times. Similarly, Joe Lagarde of White Earth has spoken with great enthusiasm and gravity about oral traditions of enormous beavers and great floods that he correlates to the retreat of the ice sheets from the last ice age.[5]

Such fidelity of communal memories sustained in oral exchanges over generations has, to be sure, required hard work and a principled regard for elders who serve as conservators of the knowledge. Walter Ong articulates a prevailing view of the dynamics of an oral tradition and the corresponding authority of old people:

> Since in a primary oral culture conceptualized knowledge that is not re-peated aloud soon vanishes, oral societies must invest great energy in say-ing over and over again what has been learned arduously over the ages. This need establishes a highly traditionalist or conservative set of mind that with good reason inhibits intellectual experimentation. Knowledge is hard to come by and precious, and society regards highly those wise old men and women who specialize in conserving it, who know and can tell the stories of the days of old. By storing knowledge outside the mind, writing, and even more, print downgrade the figures of the wise old man and the wise old woman, repeaters of the past, in favor of younger discoverers of some-thing new.[6]

Ong's observations pertain to our example to a degree but one would assume, following Ong's logic, that Anishinaabe elders would perforce lose cultural authority with time. Since this has not uniformly been the case, we must then locate the authority of eldership more nimbly in the dynamics, not the content, of oral tradition.

From the Authority of Tradition to Traditional Authority

The authority of elders does not simply *follow* from the orality of knowledge, their prestige is no simple function of the number of years they've had to hear and accumulate such traditional knowledge.

The very suggestion that one can accrue tradition as though it were a discrete content itself outside of memory bespeaks the base assumptions of a literate culture. In a primarily oral society, tradition's articulation is confined to what Ong characterizes as the "evanescent" moments of time that sound occupies. Ong argues that conceptual thought in primarily oral societies has always been more situational than abstract, tied to particular moments of human interaction rather than fixed in space through written or printed words, and as such has not yielded to elaboration in further abstraction.[7] Even if one hears routine reference to "tradition" and "culture" in English parlance of Ojibwe communities today, one searches in vain for translations of such abstractions in Ojibwe/English dictionaries that start with the idioms of indigenous parlance.[8] In the verb-rich Ojibwe language, such abstractions—if used at all—would emerge as substantives creatively composed from verbal forms; in Ojibwe idiom there is potentially *gikendamowin* ("knowing"—not "knowledge"), *izhitwaawin* ("doing things in a certain way"—not "culture"), *gaa-izhichigewad* ("as they did so"—not "tradition").[9]

Traditional authority is less the authority of tradition than the authority of those authorized to speak on tradition's behalf, to articulate tradition. The distinction may not seem so significant at first, but there is a weighty contrast to be recognized and demonstrated in the course of Ojibwe cultural history. The sociological understanding of traditional authority comes to us from Max Weber, whose distinction of three ideal types of authority—traditional, charismatic, and rational/legalistic/bureaucratic—fashioned the groundwork for his understanding of processes of modernization. To Weber, traditional authority is that which validates its "claims to legitimacy" on "an established belief in the sanctity of immemorial traditions and the legitimacy of those exercising authority under them."[10] Although he noted that "gerontocracy" is one of the two "most elementary types of traditional domination [*Herrschaft*, authority]," Weber, of course, was more interested in the kinds of traditional authority that underwrote stratified premodern European societies than with the varieties and complexities of traditional authority in small-scale egalitarian societies.[11] Still Weber is useful here for his insight that, unlike the rational/bureaucratic authority that seems to us so axiomatic, traditional authority refers for its legitimacy only partly "in terms of *traditions* which themselves directly determine the content" of a leader's "command and are believed to be valid within certain limits that cannot be overstepped without endangering the master's traditional status." It also refers to "the master's discretion in that sphere which tradition leaves open to him; this traditional prerogative rests primarily on the fact that the obligations of personal obedience tend to be essentially unlimited." Because it is not a matter of "formal principles, as in the case of legal authority," the exercise of a traditional leader's prerogative and power is "oriented toward consideration of how far master and staff can go in view of the subjects' traditional compliance without arousing their resistance. When resistance occurs, it is directed against the master or his servant personally, the accusation being that he failed to observe the traditional limits of his power."[12]

Crucial to our purposes is Weber's turn from an objective approach to tradition or culture to the situational, dynamic constitution of traditional or cultural authority in social life. Cultural authority does not rest simply on those with an authoritative command of something called "culture" but the prerogative of people invested by the community with the authority to articulate culture. To be sure, the authority of elders has to do with the acquisition over time of both cultural knowledge and judgment, augmented and tempered over years of life experience, but eldership in the sense that Anishinaabe people tend to speak of it is less a function of biological age than of community recognition. It is the prerogative of an elder to improvise, within bounds, on cultural knowledge to address new circumstances facing the community.

In turn, the measure by which successive generations of elders determine what is "within bounds" makes reference not so much to some fixed content of tradition that can be isolated independently from the utterances of elders, but to the standards established by *their* elders who entrusted the teachings to them. In other words, the claim of *cultural* fidelity to tradition is in truth a *social* fidelity to the elders' own elders. As Deborah Davis Jackson puts it, "Basically what Native people mean when they refer to the old ways or Indian ways" "is not that it was done exactly this way before Columbus landed, but simply that it is the way things are (or used to be) done in Anishinaabe communities by the elder generation."[13] This dynamic is crucial to consider, both in terms of the way that authority is fashioned ideally according to consensus and in terms of how fragile such a consensus-based authority can be in light of social distinctions and factionalism that colonialism and missionization have done so much to exacerbate.

While the mechanics of oral memory would suggest what Ong calls inherently conservative psychodynamics of orality, the social constitution of that memory in ephemeral moments of spoken exchange suggests that tradition may have more to do with the practices of speech (who speaks, when, to whom, and how) than with the plain fact of orality.

Speech Practices of Deference and Sagacity

The primary arena for the exercise of elders' prerogative has been formal speech, namely through a complex of practices that can be distinguished in terms of practices of decorum that privileged what elders had to say, and practices of sagacity through which elders' authority was staged and ceremonialized and thus conformed to established tradition. Elsewhere I enumerate in greater detail of practices of deference (chapter 2) and practices of sagacity (chapter 5) The crucial point here is that such practices do not simply *recognize* an authority that is already there, but that the constellation of practices themselves *constitute* the authority by virtue of ritualization.

Anthropologist Maurice Bloch comes to terms with the exercise, albeit not wholly conscious, of the political authority of a Madagascar people in the socialization of children into "polite" patterns of speech and through the ritualized oratory by elders. Attending less to the content of things than to the stylized form and gestural matrix of their saying, Bloch notes how the placement of speakers in a room, their cadences and their silences and their comportment, constitute authority.[14] Bloch considers the examination of speech conventions to be a crucial quarry for political anthropology, since it is in and through such everyday speech acts that the power we call "political" finds its exercise, and this in a manner that is so taken for granted that it is only partly conscious. For example, Bloch notes that the Merina people repeatedly stress learning polite speech in their socialization of children and through such manners encode a hidden restriction for social control down the road. Whatever the content of a challenge to authority, Bloch suggests, at the purely formal level it "appears mere rudeness, that is, not substantial but *ad hominem* and irrelevant."[15]

In primarily oral traditions, those whose speech commands an audience perforce exercise authority, and this is borne out consistently in ethnographic observations from various moments in Ojibwe history, A German traveler in northern Wisconsin in the 1850s noted how respected elders were seated in places of honor in lodges and deliberations, framing their utterances by virtue of a spatial ex cathedra.[16] Attending an annuity payment at which tribal business with the federal government was aired, the same observer wrote that he had heard that "a very old and celebrated speaker was interrupted by a young impudent fellow in a most improper manner. The old warrior was so incensed at it, that he drew his tomahawk, split the young man's skull open, and then quietly continued his harangue as if nothing had happened." The story was introduced as an example of how "strict" were the convictions about "the long-lasting minority of the young men."[17] A century later, E. S. Rogers made a typical observation that among the Round Lake Ojibwe of Canada, "elders are listened to in silence no matter what they may have to say. No one interrupts."[18]

Elders have been welcome to speak whenever, wherever, and however they wish. Interruptions—even follow-up questions—have been considered more than bad manners; they are disrespectful in a fundamental sense to the structures of cultural authority. Deference, then, has been no mere matter of "politeness" or etiquette, but a set of practices that have ceremonialized elders' privileged stature. The listeners were not to presume to know what questions to ask, much less the answers, and even if it seemed to them that an elder had strayed far afield from the matter at hand, or from her or his competence, the burden was on the listener to appreciate what might no less be learned.

Elders' authority to speak has extended in Ojibwe tradition to the prerogative to grant permission for others to speak. Indeed, though much public speaking has come from younger leaders of Anishinaabe communities, their authority has derived from elders, who have watched their words and actions carefully and intervened when necessary.

Those speaking at the direction or pleasure of an elder or group of elders could gain authority by making reference to their delegated authority. On the one hand, such a speech practice delimits the authority of the speaker by referencing "this is how I was taught by ———" or "my elder ——— always did this. . . ." On the other hand, such conspicuous references can be a plain appeal to the authority of one's pronouncement or position to identify her or his understanding or view with an influential or recognized elder, in turn lending further credence to that elder's authority. Indeed, where disputes arise over what constitutes traditional teaching, such specific phrasing can help establish claims in terms of particular lineages to generally recognized elders.

Even outside the arena of public address, elders' authority can be referenced and constructed in the ways that others speak deferentially about them with third parties. Codes of respect involve speaking about "that old man" or "that old woman" rather than specifying which important person is in question. The conventions of referring to such people with indirection reinforces the social restrictions on how someone regards an authoritative elder. The convention may strike outsiders as a kind of imprecise, even vague, way to attribute knowledge or practice, but for those living in tight communities, deferential circumlocutions can augment the reputation of certain figures in the community.

Speech Practices of Sagacity

At various points in this study, I have distinguished eldership as a function of performance worthy of eldership as it is a straightforward indication of age or cultural competence. Here sagacity brings together the intellective content of "wisdom" with the disciplines and embodied practices of speaking and thinking from a position of sagacity, by knowing when, and when not, to speak, by appealing to rhythms and stylizations of speech that conform what one says (and what one thinks) to agreed upon canons of tradition. Sagacity also has been exercised through formalized practices of deliberative listening, conspicuous introspection in the tempo of formal interchanges, and even protracted silence.

Lisa Philips Valentine's sociolinguistic research among Severn Ojibwe in northern Ontario also reveals the patterning of social position through speech practices. In the small community of Lynx Lake, a great deal of status is attached to those who speak well. Prestige comes to those who have the facility to orate for long, continuous utterances, and good speakers are those who conform to the highly stylized, and in some cases almost musical, ritualizations pertinent to public speech and prayer genres.[19]

And when the Wisconsin elder Archie Mosay related stories of his elders' teachings concerning traditions of respect, he referred in the Ojibwe language to their authority by making specific reference to their form of address: *akiwenziiyag gaa-pi-gaagiigidojig*, a phrase that Anton Treuer glosses as "the old men that gave the lectures."[20]

The shape and texture of such "lectures" is similar to the genre of Swampy Cree public address by community teachers and elders, *kakêshih-kêmowina*, which H. C. Wolfart designates as "counselling discourses," speeches teaching about traditional Cree ways that have a "homiletic character," delivered in an elevated register and framed with an "apologia declaring that the speaker speaks neither at his own initiative nor on his own authority but at the urging of those who called on him and as instructed by others older and wiser than him."[21] Again, conspicuous, if genuine, deprecation is a kind of humility characteristic of sagacity rather than its opposite. Wisdom need not call attention to itself.

As Bloch found in addresses of the Merina elders' councils, the speech practices of Anishinaabe sagacity similarly make appeals to authority that are often purely formal, having little to do with the content of what is said. In an Ojibwe version of speaking ex cathedra, elders make appeal to conventions expected of elders: lengthy remarks, punctuated by long silences that dramatize one's recognition to speak even as they ostensibly indicate how the utterance is coming honestly from the heart and not from some other calculus. Remarks often begin with preambles that establish authoritative lineages of knowledge: "I was given this pipe and the right to pray with it by ——"; or more general appeals to the authority of previous generations: "Our elders used to say...." In many cases long litanies of thanksgiving cast the particular points of an address in an authoritative, because spiritually responsible, light. In turn, poetic images and familiarly intoned formulaic phrases such as "our elders taught us" or "we are all related" or "looking after the land" are indirections that establish the basis for specific assertions or suggestions, rather than extensive arguments persuading an audience of the validity of a position. "The first point to notice" of such authoritative speech, writes Bloch, is that "formalised language, the language of traditional authority, is an impoverished language; a language where many of the options at all levels are abandoned so that the choice of form, or style, of words, and of syntax is less than in ordinary language."[22] This is true also of the cadence, register (often elevated from ordinary talk), and volume (often much louder than ordinary speech) that punctuate the choices of words and phrases.

This palette of formal conventions of Ojibwe sagacity enables the adept speaker to ground her/his point of view poetically, even musically, in what the community knows as an authoritative traditional past. And, of course, there has been in the twentieth century a very strategic appeal to the Ojibwe language, either for an entire address, at the outset, or at certain key moments, where "code switching" from English to Ojibwe underscores the sovereignty or sanctity of a point. Indeed masterful appeal to these conventions can constitute the principal contribution of an elder's position: reframing a particular political debate in shared, timeless images of an Ojibwe past that also shore up the speaker's authority by virtue of that move. Speech practices that refer to tradition can constitute traditional authority in their saying. As Bloch memorably puts it, "You can't argue with a song."

Still, it should be remembered, as much as they help constitute the authority of eldership, speech practices alone cannot fabricate it. Regna Darnell astutely observes that "speaking well" in Native communities is about more than the actual practices of speech itself, since from her analysis Cree interaction patterns incorporate so much more than the exchange of words. "Even in the case of the grandfathers' teachings," which Darnell sees as paradigmatic of proper use of words, "verbal messages are validated by accumulated experience which is largely non-verbal. The grandfather is respected for that experience rather than for his skill with the words themselves."[23] A recognized elder is not merely a persuasive performer of authoritative speech, but a personage known to walk their talk and thus have something to say.

The Distinctive Political Contours of Ojibwe Traditional Authority

Weber's contrast between rational/legal authority and traditional authority can also be useful in appreciating the difficulty of distinguishing what is political, religious, economic, and/or cultural in systems based on traditional authority. On the one hand, as Theresa Schenck points out, leadership in "band societies" is "informal and ephemeral." Citing Morton Fried, she writes that band leadership is characteristically "transient, moving from one competent person to another, the locus of leadership being associated with a situation, not with a person." Among the Ojibwe, Schenk continues, leadership "rests on authority, but lacks the connotation of power and declines with the territorial expansion of the group" that has characterized seasonal patterns of winter for all Ojibwe and that has characterized northernmost Anishinaabe communities especially.[24] On the other, elders in Ojibwe tradition through the prereservation years, and in improvised ways since, have been regarded as figures of an authority that spans modern Western distinctions between religion, politics, economics, and culture. This is unsurprising from a perspective informed by Weber's typology of traditional authority prior to the modern processes of rationalization and differentiation that split these facets of common life into discrete categories. But in the case of the Ojibwe, this public authority emerges from the complex relationship between the authority of age and the authority of dreams.

In fact, "authority" is not the first word in the ethnographic and interpretive literature on the Ojibwe; "power" is. Scholars have spilled much ink coming to terms with a concept of power that is at once sociopolitical and religious, which becomes a social fact in the figure of the *ogimaa* ("boss") and *ogimaakwe* ("boss woman") but which remains rooted in relations with the supernaturals who gift individuals with power through dreams and songs/dances charged with dream power. As discussed in the first chapter, the honorific "old" could apply with particular force to one evidencing dream power.

In this regard, there is not only a combination, but a conflation of Ojibwe terms of forms of authority distinguished by Weber as traditional and charismatic. In her book-length study of Northern Ojibwe social organization, Ruth Landes tellingly devoted only four pages to the category "political organization," which at any rate revolved around the "most important" figure in any *odena* ("village"), the "Medicine Man," or what she cited in Ojibwe as *nigichi anishinaabeminan* ("our wise man"). The latter formulation, one should note, is not gender specific and could perhaps better be translated as the honorific "our elder." Landes noted: "He is recognized as preeminent because he is on favored terms with the supernatural," which is to say exceptionally gifted by powerful *pawaganag* ("dream helpers or spirits"). It was respect (Landes terms it "fear") for this person's power that accorded him honor, but she added that it was "a matter of individual recognition, and the medicine man held no official position."[25]

In northerly reaches of Anishinaabe territory, social groups have tended to be smaller and more spread apart in keeping with the work of the seasonal round and the fur trade. In such communities, the authority of leadership involved community recognition of situational leadership. That is, people would take as their *ogimaa* or in certain cases *ogimaakwe* a leader who was recognized with the authority to conduct or lead at a certain time and often for a particular task, military, economic, ritual, or otherwise. An early-nineteenth-century source concerning Northern Ojibwe reported:

> The Indians of certain Districts, which are bounded by such and such Rivers, have each an Okimah, as they call him, or Captain over them, who is an Old Man, considered only for his Prudence and Experience. He has no Authority but what they think fit to give him upon certain Occasions. He is their Speech-maker to the English; as also in their own grave Debates, when they meet every Spring and Fall, to settle the Disposition of their Quarters for Hunting, Fowling, and Fishing.[26]

Because "political" leadership could accrue to one evidencing the power of dreams, it is instructive to discuss one of the more storied leaders in the written record of the prereservation Anishinaabeg, in this case an *ogimaakwe*.

Netnokwa was the matriarch of a far-ranging family group that adopted the Anglo-American captive John Tanner (born ca. 1780) and the most prominent character in his travel narrative of the fur-trade border country between Minnesota, Ontario, and Manitoba. Tanner was captured in his native Kentucky by a roving Odawa party led by Manito-o-geshik, who was seeking to replace a lost son. Manito-o-geshik later exchanged Tanner with a kinswoman, Netnokwa, who "notwithstanding her sex, was then regarded as principal chief of the Ottawwaws (Odawas)" in Michigan. Her husband, seventeen years her junior, was an Ojibwe man from Red River who, Tanner reports, "was but of secondary importance in the family, as every thing belonged to Netnokwa, and she had the direction in all affairs on any moment."[27]

Tanner refers to Netnokwa every so often as his mother, but typically he speaks of her as "the old woman," surely an English rendering of the Ojibwe honorific *mindimooyenh*. Her precise biological age is unknown, but since she wanted Tanner to replace a dead son of her own about the same age, it is doubtful that she was beyond her 50s. While Netnokwa's authority was thus described in terms of "age," it seemed to rest less on chronological years than on the fact she was an uncommonly capable person, with wit and woods sense galore, and a demonstrated capacity of ritual knowledge and morally upright living, to call effectively on spirits for help in dire circumstances. Tanner's narrative tells of a group's peripatetic search for game and beaver skins to stave off the cold and hunger that continuously stalk them. Netnokwa cobbles together displaced and orphaned people into her fold of largely fictive kin and, ever on the move, keeps them together by rebuking the lazy and inspiring the discouraged to continue in their survival against odds. Her power to do so, and thus her ability to command their respect, hinges on the strength of her ties with the supernaturals.

In at least four watershed moments in the narrative, when all seems lost, Netnokwa quietly takes her leave for the cold and remote to sing and pray to the spirits and returns with medicine bags and instructions received in dreams of where to find a moose or bear for meat.[28]

In such moments, while she does not figure in Tanner's narrative as a specialist healer, she clearly enjoys considerable reputation for successfully gaining the regard of the spirits when needed. At the same time, it is clear that Netnokwa's charisma is as mundane as it is extraordinary, her knowledge and access to power running seamlessly from this world to the other. One might justly argue that the honorific "old woman" issues as much from her reputation as a woman of impressive judgment and woods wisdom, earned over years of successful survival and band leadership, as it does from her ability to show results when it counts most from commerce with the spirits.

Exceptional as she was, Netnokwa was not unique among those taken as *ogimaag/ogimaakweg*. Chiefs were often referred to as "aged and intelligent," as William Warren did in his discussion of Wa-won-je-gnon of Red Lake.[29] The Parry Island Ojibwe in the early twentieth century similarly took for an *ogimaa* an individual of uncommonly respectable character and personality but with fairly limited powers that existed only at the pleasure of the community. Jenness wrote:

> The entire population of the island constituted a single band (kwinoak), nominally governed by a chief (ogimma). His power depended on his character and ability; an unpopular chief often wielded less influence than one of the medicine-men, and at his death the band might follow the leadership of another family, preferably one that was closely related. As his powers were limited, so his duties too were not onerous. He was expected to take the initiative in all public matters, to receive delegations from neighbouring bands or tribes, and to summon and preside over council meetings of all the adult hunters of his band, or of such families as were directly concerned in the matter at issue. He had no means of enforcing his wishes unless the principal men in the band endorsed them and the remainder were content to acquiesce.[30]

At least among the village-based Ojibwe communities of southern Ontario and what is now the United States, such elders' councils played a large role in community governance. At Parry Island "the informal council of all the hunters, presided over by the chief, was not only the chief legislative and executive body in the band, if we may apply these terms, . . . but also the chief court of judicature. There were, of course, no codified laws or statutes, merely a body of rights and practices handed down from one generation to another by word of mouth."[31]

Vernon Kinietz cited Ojibwe elder John Pete about the traditions at Michigan's Lac Vieux Desert community: "Councils would occasionally be called by the chief to deliberate on matters in which he wished to determine the will of the village, but then the chief went ahead and did what he thought best in view of these expressions of opinion. All the older people of the village could take part in these councils. In the old days, Pete said, a young man had to be 25 or 26 years old before he was considered able to manage his own affairs and also, presumably, to speak in the council."[32]

Harold Hickerson identified a "clearly reflected age status differentiation" among elder men and the "young men" or "warriors." Elder men sitting in councils were charged, in Hickerson's reckoning, with the wisdom for dip-lomatic, legislative, and judicial functions of Ojibwe communities, while the warriors or young men were charged with the energy and tactical skills for military and police responsibilities. The two circles existed, ac-cording to Hickerson, in an important, if sometimes precarious, balance aboriginally, a balance that was challenged considerably with the advent of treaty making and missionization.[33]

Importantly, the traditional authority of elders to which these sources bore witness was not constituted in an aboriginal vacuum, outside time, cul-tural encounter, contestation, or politics. As other chapters make repeatedly clear, we cannot content ourselves with a discussion of traditions of the au-thority of eldership clearly distinguished from the history of what happens to those traditions over time. Still, we can attend to the cultural history of eldership by focusing more intently on key moments in Ojibwe history where the traditional authority of elders came under clear challenge and pressure: at the moments of treaty making in the early nineteenth century, later that century in the reservation-era encounter with missionaries and formal poli-cies of assimilation, and in the rekindling of tradition in the 1970s.

· · ·

The Modern History of Traditional Authority

TREATY MAKING

Johann Kohl observed the protocol and apparent tensions between genera-tions at a northern Wisconsin treaty negotiation:

> The old people always sat in the center of the circle, close to the place where the American agents have their table, and where the speakers stand. Some of them, who were very old, were allowed chairs to sit on. The other old men sat together in the grass near them. Further out the young fellows lay about in groups. Among them were men of twenty and twenty five years of age, but they never interfered in the discussions, save by now and then uttering a loud "Ho, ho!" or some other cry of applause. The opinions of the Indians as to the long lasting minority of the young men are very strict, and if they latter do not act in accordance with their views, they are very roughly re-minded of their position.[34]

Although clan and kin relations stitched communities together, the segmentation along lines of age that Kohl saw was not only spatial. Developing Hickerson's insight, Rebecca Kugel has made much of the accentuation of age distinctions in the wake of colonization. Kugel documents how the traditional authority of male elders who were *ogimaag* had become deeply challenged in the 1850s and 1860s by younger generations of more militantly anticolonial "warriors" following charismatic leaders like Hole-in-the-Day.[35] Kugel notes that traditional Ojibwe society had always involved some balance between the civil authority of the *ogimaag*, elder male leaders typically referred to in English as "chiefs and head men," and the military authority of warriors, comprised of younger men. Times of peace and times of hostility had called for different kinds of community leadership, and Ojibwe society had seen wisdom in such a balance. But in the 1850s and 1860s, militant warriors criticized elder leaders for their accommodations and alliance seeking with Euro-Americans. After considerable deliberation and consultation, they signed treaties, invited missionaries to live among them, and sought the agricultural capital and schools they judged to be indispensable to their community's future. Kugel refers to their approach as one of "creative accommodation" geared toward the survival of their communities and the maintenance of core values and practices.[36]

Elder *ogimaag* were not uniformly aligned in opposition to the warriors and in favor of accommodationist positions with respect to the treaties and missionaries. Madweganonind is today celebrated by Red Lake enrollees like Wub-e-ke-niew for his rebuffs to federal overtures in the 1860s, 1870s, and 1880s. Even though Madweganonind became closely affiliated with the Episcopal mission, he joined other Red Lake *ogimaag* in rejecting the allotment policies of the 1880s and left a legacy at Red Lake of Minnesota's only "closed" reservation, where all reservation land continues to be communally held. Wub-e-ke-niew cites a stirring speech to treaty commissioners by another elder *ogimaa*, Little Rock, who told Governor Ramsey they had no right to alienate the land: "The Master of Life placed us here, and gave it to us for an inheritance. The Master of Life gave us the river and the water thereof to drink, and the woods and the roads we depend on for subsistence, and you are mistaken if you think we derive no benefits from them."[37]

Even those elder *ogimaag* who took accommodation positions claimed their authority in marked ways. Kugel observed:

Elders invoked the imagery of their age to validate their right to speak and make decisions: "I am not a new man," Bizhiki of LaPointe told treaty commissioners Lewis Cass and Thomas L. McKenney in 1826—an interesting literal translation by the unknown interpreter of the word "oshki" as "new" in place of the more usual "young." And the redoubtable Flat Mouth stated the obvious reason for his presence in Washington, DC, at the negotiation of the Treaty of 1855. "My old head and gray hairs tell for themselves." He also pointedly drew a comparison between his age and experience and the lesser qualifications of the Commissioner of Indian Affairs, George Manypenny, with whom the Ojibwes were negotiating. "My father, as I must call you, although from the differences of our ages, I might call you my son."[38]

Still, there remained a generational facet to the tensions of those years: a pattern of cautious engagement if not accommodation on the part of elder *ogimaag*, and this to the consternation of emerging blocs of warriors increasingly restless with the decisions of the civil leaders.

When Episcopalian Bishop Henry Benjamin Whipple told a council of Ojibwe elders in 1862 that the Ojibwe must transform their lifeways or else be doomed by the encroachment of civilization, one elder agreed in this regard: "You have spoken true words—we are poor—we are growing poorer. We feel the Great Spirit must be angry with us or our people would not fade away—our young men used to take advice of our old men and our old men spoke good words, but they don't do it now."[39]

This was more than a perennial complaint of an older generation for the loss of respect; the elder observes that part of social breakdown is on account of elder men abandoning their customary responsibilities. A balance that recognized the occasional importance of the authority of warriors but that in general privileged the circumspection, diplomacy, and less ideological judgment of elders had become polarized into competing structures of authority with respective factional alignments and had privileged the warriors' rigid approach to asserting a boundary between tradition and change. The warrior leaders claimed followers largely from among the Métis descendants of Ojibwe unions with French or English fur traders, most of whom identified with Roman Catholic missions. By contrast, the *ogimaag* drew followers largely from the ranks of "full blood" Ojibwe, who as a consequence largely identified with the accommodations of treaty making and the program of the Episcopalian mission. "The civil leader/

warrior split," Kugel concludes, "seems to have fractured the Ojibwe along the two more compelling status distinctions in their society, namely, kinship and age. The Ojibwe supported their relatives, although age was also significant in determining a person's allegiances; younger Ojibwe favored the course pursued by the warriors and older people supported the civil leaders."[40]

MISSIONIZATION AND ASSIMILATION POLICY

But the emerging generation gap was more than political or strategic. The structures of Ojibwe cultural and religious authority were deeply challenged by missionary Christianity and the social dislocations that accompanied it, even if they ultimately were not replaced as missionaries had hoped. Indeed, the continued practices of deference and sagacity provided Ojibwe Christians with key integuments between their tradition and their practice of the Christian tradition. The reservation era marked more than the diminution of Ojibwe lands. Its social structures cleared the ground for a fuller Ojibwe engagement with the Christian tradition and sedentary, agrarian life and fostered a problematic relationship between subsequent generations of Anishinaabe, their collective past, and the elders who represented it.

Plainly, assimilation policies served to undermine the traditional cultural authority of elders as the emblems of the very traditions such policies were meant to eradicate. But it was less the content of assimilation policy than the ensuing social chaos that proved to be the deeper challenge to eldership. Displacement, dispossession, poverty, and diseases like tuberculosis associated with these conditions brought alarming social fragmentation and violence to Ojibwe communities, taking their toll, in turn, on the very kinship structures on which the traditional authority of elders rested. One is tempted to view the elders who did remain in the midst of this social chaos as dogged adherents to tradition, bulwarks against change. Instead, as has been shown by Kugel, it had been elders who had accommodated and even invited important changes in the first place as strategies to secure the survival of community and tradition.

Ironically, elder *ogimaag* who had cast their lot with the new tradition of Protestant Christianity found still further challenges to their authority from within the Christian tradition itself, at least as it was promoted by missionaries.[41] Along with federal Indian Agents, these missionaries maintained that Ojibwe tradition and "Christian civilization" were incompatible. And they viewed elders as the standard bearers of those problematic traditions. For missionaries, the task of making Christians out of Natives would require hierarchical configurations of authority: educated young converts over their unschooled elders, men over women, and especially clergy over laity. To this end, missionaries hastened to wed their clerical authority with the power of the reservation agents and the annuity payment systems on which Ojibwe people increasingly depended.

Crucially, however, Ojibwe Christianity was no straightforward outcome of missionary design. Time and again, a distinctively Ojibwe Christianity would slip through the cracks of missionary discipline, and this distinctive Christianity was fashioned through the medium of practice.[42] Ojibwe Christians spoke of Christianity itself in terms of practice; they called it *Anami'aawin* ("prayer"). Likewise, their term for Ojibwe Christians, *Anami'aajig* ("those who pray"), identified that community with its practice of prayer, presumably the spoken prayers that lacked drum and dance. Despite the sharp boundary between Christianity and Ojibwe "paganism" that missionaries preached and maintained by their discipline, it is clear that the Anami'aajig did not conceive of this new complex of practices and beliefs as a clearly bounded system, antithetical to the beliefs and practices of Ojibwe tradition.[43] Put another way, in a time of rapid change, some Ojibwe people came to construe *Anami'aawin* as a form of Ojibwe tradition, one that took its place among other Ojibwe ceremonial complexes. Although these Ojibwe surely had their critics in the community, for them, *Anami'aawin* endorsed core value commitments of Ojibwe tradition while sanctioning innovations necessary for the community's continued material and cultural survival.[44]

To the extent that *Anami'aawin* could both endorse tradition and sanction innovation, this was so in no small part because its articulation took place soundly under the authority of elders. Again, what at first glance seems a rather predictably conservative force, eldership was identifiably involved with cultural change. It will be important, then, to examine the contours of Ojibwe Christian regard for the aged and their authority constituted in visible practices of deference and sagacity. The particulars of this decorum are often quite subtle—ironically most apparent in the missionary archives when their unstated rules have been violated. The practices of sagacity have largely to do with oratory—ways of speaking and remaining conspicuously silent that bespeak deliberateness, command an audience, and set the terms for public discussion. The Ojibwe Christian practices associated with deference include ways of speaking and listening that privilege elders' voices and their authority to delegate powers to speak. Deferential decorum also involves complex codes of the extension of hospitality and formalized gift-giving, offerings of tobacco for elders' counsel, and practices of decision making that take the needs of elders and children first into account. Again, such practices seem at first glance less consequential, less remarkable, than they have proved to be. But where the authority of Native elders meets challenges of clerical and bureaucratic authority from without, and prophetic authority from within, one can clearly see how such practices of decorum markedly ceremonialize their authority.

To be sure, missionaries noted the influence of prominent *ogimaag* in the mass conversion of those band members following their leadership. At Red Lake in the 1870s, for example, an entire village followed Madweganonind into baptism and affiliation with the Episcopalian mission. Within three years of the baptism of the "old chief"—*akiwenzii* ("old man") is an honorific, but it also applied to the *ogimaa's* biological age, for he was born around 1800—ninety of the one hundred fifteen villagers had become baptized, and forty-five became Episcopalian communicants. One missionary boasted that this was "a larger number proportionately by far than in any other place in the U.S."[45]

But if missionaries recognized they had to contend with certain prominent elders, and while a number of the infirm Ojibwe aged routinely stayed under the care of the mission stations when their families had left for seasonal round activities in the bush, missionaries dismissed older Ojibwe in general as intractably bound by force of habit, custom, and language and consequently poor candidates for the cultural revolution they saw necessary to the Christian life. Instead, Episcopalian missionaries sought to cultivate an indigenous church by identifying promising young Ojibwe men, removing them to boarding schools for English-language and Christian education, and eventually ordaining them as deacons to evangelize their own kin, under the supervision of a non-Native diocesan official. Churchmen and historians alike have found in these important efforts the answer to why Episcopalians outperformed a range of other Protestant missions efforts among Minnesota's Ojibwe.[46] But here it is clear that it was certain key elders in the late nineteenth century—both men and women—who were at the center of indigenous efforts to make the tradition their own in more familiar Ojibwe idioms of religious practice.

Practicing Deference and Sagacity in Anami'aawin (Ojibwe Christianity)

Sustained practices of deference and sagacity may have been familiar to Ojibwe who became involved in the Christian movement, but they carried a new charge of contestation in reservation environments circumscribed by missionaries and agents who equated the Christian life with the "civilized" life. These practices and their charged implications are visible in at least three contexts: as lay Christian sodalities articulated anew familiar forms of kinship organization, as key lay elders asserted their leadership, and as Ojibwe clergy regarded their elders.

The distinctive Ojibwe Christianity produced by the Anami'aajig took shape not so much in the chapels and schools of the mission but rather in the semiautonomous spaces in which indigenous sodalities of men and of women repaired a torn Ojibwe social fabric through new, distinctively Christian, improvisations on old kinship structures. Importantly, these were spaces of orality, out of earshot of the missionaries who determined the written record. As a result, we have precious little documentary evidence of their activities, but with trained eyes, we can appreciate the fuller force of the subtle practices that missionaries did note, if often only in passing.

In the early 1870s, Ojibwe elders at White Earth suggested to Bishop Whipple that lay societies of men and women respectively should be formed for the purposes of "encouraging one another in the faith." Whipple agreed, authorizing and directing his field missionaries to promote them and to foster a rich devotional life in prayer meetings that served as the primary occasions for their exercise. In this, Whipple and his staff drew on established Methodist and Wesleyan models to nurture lay devotion, and in this fashion they called the men's groups "Singing and Praying Bands" and the women's, "Industrial Societies."

In 1881, the Odawa priest at White Earth, John Johnson Enmegabowh spoke of having two classes of "young men," numbering between twenty-five and thirty, joined by "some of our chiefs," referring to the elder *ogi-maag*. There were also at this time two bands of women at White Earth Village. Enmegabowh said that each band had its own spiritual "chiefs," elder men and women who undertook to direct the ritualized exchange of songs and ideas, to give counsel, and to settle disputes that arose.[47] It is here that we can best see the continuation of eldership practices in Ojibwe Christianity.

Consider the case of the elder advisor to the young men's sodality at White Earth Village. It was Shaydayence (Little Pelican) who sought Bishop Whipple's endorsement of the Singing and Praying Band idea in the first place, and the sequence here is revealing. The societies were encouraged by the mission church on the model of the Wesleyan lay devotional associations; but clearly they were established under elders and, it seems, at the initiative of key elders like Shaydayence. Indeed, in a funeral eulogy, Whipple identified Shaydayence as the "real, recognized leader of the Christian community as he had before been of the heathen."[48] Clearly this elder was an exceptional leader among the Anami'aajig, representative more of the ideal of eldership than of elders generally. Still, he perhaps best exemplifies the way that elders could finesse a transition to Christian practice with integrity on Ojibwe grounds.

Prior to their removal to White Earth in 1868, Shaydayence served the Gull Lake Band as its principal spiritual leader. He was the preeminent leader of the Midéwiwin there and a *jiisakiiwinini*, a healer/diviner engaged in a shamanic ceremonial complex colloquially referred to as the "shaking tent."[49] Episcopalian missionaries remembered Shaydayence as the onetime "prime minister of Satan," a bitter opponent to James L. Breck's initial 1852 establishment of the St. Columba mission at Gull Lake.[50] But even the one-time "antichristian" leader had committed his son Nabiquan to the care of the mission in order to become, as he would later put it, "learned in the learning of the Egyptians."[51] Nabiquan, born in 1850, was baptized Samuel Madison and enrolled in an Episcopal school in southern Minnesota. Ordained deacon in 1873, Samuel Madison Nabiquan was a member of the first class of indigenous clergy.[52]

After being removed with other Gull Lakers to White Earth, several days' journey away, Shaydayence reported he became "excessively devoted to . . . to firewater. I was very quarrelsome, and was repeatedly cut and stabbed by my fellow Indians in drunken quarrels, when I knew nothing about it."[53] He recovered, however, and in 1875 became baptized at the estimated age of sixty-four (as for most of his generation, age was not reckoned precisely in biological years). For the remaining eleven years of his life he became the principal male spiritual elder of the White Earth Anami'aajig. The Episcopalian Archdeacon Gilfillan observed that "the laymen of the Church soon accorded him the place of leader, for which his zeal, his holiness, his words of power eminently fitted him."[54]

Now with a Christian affiliation, Shaydayence continued a full-time practice of spiritual counsel and healing. His plain assertion in practice of the continuity between Ojibwe and Christian traditions of leadership bespeak the continued recognition of his authority by Ojibwe and missionaries alike as well as the nondogmatic nature of his religious idiom. Even as a spokesman for the Anami'aajig, he relied extensively on the herbal knowledge he had mastered, along with specific ritual and musical knowledge, as a Midéwiwin initiate. His visits to fellow Ojibwes, either alone or with the Young Men's Band, typically took place at sickbeds or deathbeds. And although he formally parted ways with the Midéwiwin, his healing as a Christian was hardly limited to spiritual prayer. Gilfillan noted that Shaydayence is "also a great believer in the efficacy of medicine accompanied with prayer, and gives many instances of the wonderful recoveries it has caused; but to give medicine without prayer he abhors."[55] His Christian message, herbal knowledge, and confident bearing became part of the same healing art.

Shaydayence was an exceptional elder, but by no means the only elder carrying influence among the Anami'aajig. The bishop chartered sodalities under the express direction of elder men and women at White Earth's Pembina Village and at communities on the Leech Lake and Red Lake Reservations. And the presence of *ogimaag* as leaders to sodalites further suggests their import as reconstituted Ojibwe social units. A group calling itself the "Committee of Mazigishik's Band" at White Earth reported they had taken as their advisors the *ogimaag* Waubonoquod, Tecomigizhik, and Joe Critte (Charette).[56]

These "bands" made celebrated expeditions to preach and exhort near and far, visited the sick and dying, and pooled resources and labor to make their communal way in their new agrarian world. A leader of the Young Men of White Earth Village reported they had "visited to the sick man

Tecomigizhick and to our fallen friend Makaque and to another fallen man John Hanks." They also visited "Gahgige ash, sick man, and five acres of land was planted for him."[57] The sodalities most regularly assembled in evening prayer meetings as often as four nights per week. In their meetings, they ate, prayed, sang, shared food and clothing, organized mutual aid, and served as professional mourners for others in the community.

Missionary accounts of the devotional meetings noted their ritualized nature, especially the stylized nature of the oratory, its pacing, its sequencing with hymn-singing and prayer, and consistently noted the prominence of elders:

> In all these meetings the method of procedure is the same; meet about nightfall, begin with singing a Chippewa hymn, then prayer, then another hymn, then the leader names the one who is to speak, after he or she sits down another hymn, then another speaker is named and so on until 9 or 10 o'clock when the meeting is closed with prayer. The speakers are nearly all middle aged or elderly men or women. There is never any excitement or extravagance . . . but solemnity. In these meetings they seem to find most of their joy—they have no other parties nor meetings but only those connected with religion.[58]

As their moniker indicates, the "Women's Industrial and Devotional Societies" were the mission's vehicle for schooling indigenous women in the virtuous habits and practices of what it considered "true womanhood." Be that as it may, the guilds worked tirelessly for their wider communities' material and spiritual well-being. They took in textiles, beads, and other donated materials and transformed them into clothing; they pledged to come to one another's mutual aid, and did so often in these lean years, pooling resources at planting time and at harvest, taking their place at sickbeds and deathbeds, and mourning those old and young who failed to beat the odds. Guild activities addressed whatever issues befell the community at large, as evidenced in their frequent—again sometimes thrice weekly—meetings. Pauline Colby recalled:

> Our Indian church women have their weekly women's auxiliary meeting in an unoccupied house which has a spacious room and a good heater. . . . The

women come sometimes in the morning, bring their children and the blanket hammocks for the babies and generally stay until dusk. They love to make quilts or comforts and do some very nice quilting, also braid rag rugs, and make sweet grass and birch bark baskets. Of course they lunch little and big, off and on, all day, but the real meal of the day comes just before the little service which closes the day's work, and for that I always provide some provisions that are not made after Indian recipes, which they enjoy as a pleasant change. Our little services are sometimes conducted by our Indian deacon, Nashotah, and sometimes by myself. Frequently some women will rise and make an address and this always has the respectful attention of the other women. Our women look forward to these gatherings as the chief social event of the week.[59]

Whatever the occasion for their gathering, the guilds were expressly committed and apparently successful at bringing their number "into one mind" on matters spiritual, economic, and political. This was no easy task in the space of a reservation like White Earth, itself an assemblage of settlements consisting of members of various Ojibwe bands removed from various parts of northern Minnesota. Melissa Meyer has chronicled the factionalism that afflicted the White Earth Reservation and that was exploited in this period by outside timber and land speculation interests, some with the approval of the children of Métis traders who became White Earth enrollees in a contested bureaucratic move.[60] Speaking of his wife, Madjigishik told the bishop in 1889, "If any of them were at enmity between themselves there was she standing in the midst trying to bring them together again."[61]

Kugel has identified these societies as key to the "process of social regeneration." They were more than narrowly religious confraternities. In the new world of reservation and mission, they reiterated familiar structures of Ojibwe kinship, not least of which was eldership, that made a new life possible. Without them, Kugel writes, "the experiment with Christianization and agriculture would have amounted to little."[62] In the context of these sodalities, the authority of Ojibwe elders persevered despite the challenges of social dislocations, assimilation policies that undermined the value of traditional ways, and clerical authority. I turn now to specific, if subtle, practices of sagacity and deference that maintained the structures of Ojibwe eldership.

PRACTICES OF SAGACITY

Missionaries consistently reported the centrality of elder Christians' oratory in their attempt to show the vitality of Ojibwe Christian life. Shaydayence's stature rested on his ability to speak well, from the heart and with the bearing of an elder. "Talking had always been his forte," Gilfillan averred.[63] He was hailed not because he took on the aspect of an evangelist, but because he continued to speak with pacing, ceremony, and authority befitting an Ojibwe elder. "In whatever company he was, the conversation was sure to take a religious turn," it was said about Shaydayence. "He persuaded so spontaneously and almost unconsciously and with such a genuine enthusiasm that it seemed perfectly natural, and just the proper word in the proper place. All people—even heathen—unconsciously looked for it from him and would have felt a lack had they not heard it."[64] The archdeacon even expressed unusual regard for those Ojibwe speech practices, such as ribald humor, that would ordinarily provoke a missionary's rebuke: "He frequently gravitated towards spiritual things having first established his conversations with a joke and a laugh," Gilfillan observed, "What would have sounded strained and forced and would have been disgusting from anyone else sounded as natural as breathing from him."[65]

To speak well was not just to have something important to say but to have demonstrated a mastery of the decorum that gave importance and authority to whatever was said. Even a non-Indian missionary could sense Shaydayence's mastery of ceremonious social interaction: "His manners are exceedingly polite, almost courtier like; I marvel at the gracious words which proceed out of his mouth."[66] We learn from Bloch's observations of elders' councils in Madagascar, however, that the formalization of speech can mean much more than good manners; it betokens an appeal to elders' traditional authority that one cannot meaningfully challenge, because the authority is constituted in the form, not the content, of what is said.[67] To his Native auditors, Shaydayence's mastery of the practices of oratory framed *whatever* he said in terms of a recognized traditional authority.

This capacity to speak well on Ojibwe terms included the authority to delegate public speech, and Shaydayence ritualized the exercise of this authority to tangible effect as well. At devotional meetings of Ojibwe Christians, Gilfillan observed, "held in their houses in rotation two or three nights every week, he soon took the place of leader, speaking first himself, naming the speakers in succession, correcting any wild statements made, and being the life of the whole meeting. He always had the right word to say; it did not seem as if they could have any meeting without him."[68]

The rhythms of the ritualized delegation are clear in the case of a missionary excursion down the upper Mississippi in the autumn of 1880. Shaydayence, the "Young Men," and three Ojibwe deacons entered a Midéwiwin lodge where a ceremony had convened. It was Shaydayence, not the ordained clergy, who controlled the proceedings:

> The old veteran Shay-day-ence . . . told them that the young men were Christian Indians and ministers of God from White Earth, who had come . . . to speak to them about their salvation. Then he named the clergyman who should first address them. Another hymn followed; after its close the clergyman named stood up. . . . That young man had the gift of utterance given to him and preached powerfully. Then the old veteran named the next clergyman, who should speak, and another Christian hymn resounded through the dance house. The same inspiration was upon the next speaker; he did well. Another hymn followed and another speaker, who was pitched in no lower key. Last of all old Shay-day-ence addressed them.[69]

The authority of a speaker's words was not always in proportion to the quantity of those words. In fact, the measure of oratorical authority had much to do with an elder's cultivated art of maintaining silence and listening well. Madweganonind of Red Lake, for example, "spoke but few words. No one ever heard him make a speech. He listened to all that was said, and when at the end of it he summed it up in a few words and told them what ought to be done, his decision was final."[70]

In Shaydayence's case, listening was a cultivated art because it reflected a profound Anishinaabe commitment to humility, especially as it concerns knowledge of the sacred. "He never could read a word but he had listened so attentively to the Bible when it was read that though he could not give chapter and verse, the soul of the message was in his heart, and in his eloquent way he made it seem real to his listeners."[71] Indeed, prior to the reservation era, missionaries frustrated by a lack of Ojibwe conversions no less routinely observed the polite measured ways through which Ojibwes listened to the Christian message. In his earlier days, Shaydayence

Madweganonind, the aged Red Lake *ogimaa*, was widely respected for his wisdom and oratory. He is pictured here in a ca. 1894 studio portrait by A. H. Indrelee. Note the pipe in his right hand and his moccasins. *Courtesy Minnesota Historical Society*

may have challenged Episcopalians at Gull Lake, but even then it was clear that he took seriously his dialogue with them. This is largely because of the commitment on the part of certain Ojibwe elders to the Episcopalian mission, evidence itself of a cultivated pragmatic wisdom with little room for dogmatic thinking. Here again, the traditional authority of elders relied less on the content of tradition than on the formally constituted authority of elders to determine what tradition was to be in a particular circumstance. Constituted through practice rather than tethered to content, this authority was no automatic mechanism for the conservation of tradition, but left considerable room for improvisation.[72]

In this light, we can appreciate that those elder *ogimaag* who "converted" did not do so hastily or merely as a byproduct of a strategic alliance decision. The sincerity of conversion, however, did not bespeak a doctrinaire repudiation of all things non-Christian for all things Christian.[73] The deliberation, the listening, and the discernment were perhaps indicators of quite the converse: a cultivated ability to do a novel thing well on Ojibwe terms. For example, in 1869, a Gull Lake *ogimaa*, Nabuneshkung, respectfully "offered his house for services . . . even though he was not converted." Enmegabowh urged him to "renounce his heathenism and Grand Medicine (Midéwiwin)," and the *ogimaa* made clear his intention to convert, but told the deacon "I am preparing for it. I do not want to go into it half hearted, and unprepared for the great battle. When I wanted to follow the warpath I have never gone unprepared. I studied and imagined the hard battle before me."[74] Part of this cultivated ability to do a novel thing well involved proceeding according to Ojibwe patterns of discernment and decision making that inspired consensus. While there was certainly dissent and division in these years as in others, elder Ojibwe *ogimaag* did not lead by decree; they led by listening and persuading groups of the wisdom of a given course of action. A missionary at LaPointe observed out of frustration in the 1830s that "constantly you hear individual Indians in new potential mission territories, declining to render an opinion until they meet in council."[75] At the helm of such councils were elders. "The headman [*ogimaa*] acts more as an advisor than as a king, if he is a man of energy and independence, he often acquires considerable influence. But if he is not, or if for any reason he is unpopular with his band, they do not much regard him."[76]

Such cultivated practices of listening and discernment gave to Ojibwe Christian sagacity a broad-minded posture that stood in contrast to missionaries' more dogmatic views conflating Christianity and Anglo-American culture. In the early 1880s, for example, a millennial movement emerged at White Earth and Red Lake around a prophet and self-declared Ojibwe incarnation of Christ. The prophet, Abitageshig, taught a transformative ceremonial dance around a "Prayer Drum" spelled out to him in a vision. This movement did not incite violent anticolonial action, but it did pose a considerable challenge to the Anami'aajig movement, as many Ojibwe Christians themselves became swept up in its practices despite disavowals of drumming and dancing. It involved a "Prayer Dance" prefaced by a Christian prayer, whose choreography and musical accompaniment were the fruit of the prophetic vision. It thus had received a policy of engagement if not support by the Benedictine missionaries there. Enmegabowh even reported that the abbot in charge of the Ojibwe mission had himself blessed the drum.[77] According to Gilfillan, even the Ojibwe deacon at White Earth's Pembina Settlement, where Abitagezhig's movement was afoot, was being "utilized" by the prophet and the Roman Catholic missionary supporters "for their own purposes."[78] Importantly, broad-minded elders affiliated with the Episcopal mission joined Roman Catholics in their refusal to view this dance tradition in dogmatic terms. The young men's sodality at Pembina approached their "advisor," the elder Meshakikizh, about how best to respond to the inducement among "our young people to attend and join in [the dances]." With the elder's advice, the sodality "thought it politic to allow the other young people to dance at stated intervals, always of course, keeping the two ideas, devotion and amusement, distinct." Meshakikizh, in turn, sought the advice on the matter of the Métis Episcopal priest C. H. Beaulieu, who took issue with the elder and opined "strongly and clearly against any heathenish practices whatsoever."[79]

The authority of an elder's integration of Christian and Anishinaabe ways in the late nineteenth century is not unlike, I think, that which impressed Valentine among the Ojibwe of Lynx Lake, Ontario, in the late twentieth century. Of a discourse by Anapat Memekwe, a "highly respected elder who had no difficulty in reconciling Christianity and traditional Severn cosmology," Valentine wrote, "the explanation was not provided by a member of the religious hierarchy; rather, it was volunteered by an elder whose expertise was in telling traditional stories and who was speaking in that capacity." Valentine adds: "An important factor in this revised

The wife of Meshakikizhig, along with her husband, was an elder in the Anami'aajig community and was identified in this ca. 1895 photograph to be "very intelligent" and "a great medicine woman and doctor." *Courtesy Minnesota Historical Society*

worldview is that the traditional elements have been reconciled within Christian eschatology rather than the other way around. This is no thin veneer of Christianity laid over an older system: the changes represent a basic restructuring of an older worldview within a new framework." And this transpires, as Valentine's discourse analysis shows, in and through the authoritative speech practices of an authoritative elder.[80]

PRACTICES OF DEFERENCE

It perhaps goes without saying that such public expressions of sagacity imply deference. Still, one can find visible the ritualization of deference in the ways that Ojibwe Christians approached their elders and extended hospitality to them. And the continued relevance of such practices of deference are clearer still in the ways that non-Native missionaries reflected on their breach of such social codes.

Offering tobacco to elders, as we saw in chapter 2, ritually established a relation of deference and pity and apparently remained a consistent practice of the Anami'aajig community, if one that made missionaries so uneasy that they seldom wrote of it, given its association with "pagan" offerings to spirits. In 1897, a Red Lake Christmas involved the annual giveaway by the church. "The sick and the aged were not forgotten, but each received a warm piece of clothing or a packet of tea, and some of the old men a pipe and packet of tobacco."[81] Evidently, it was deemed unbecoming for elder women to thus receive tobacco, although tobacco smoking and chewing remained an important part of older women's lives. Colby, an Episcopalian missionary at Leech Lake, wrote of sending as a gesture of respect and care "a ration of flour, sugar, salt, and tobacco to an old pagan woman, grandmother of some Christian Indians."[82]

Preliminary to a formal council with Ojibwe Anami'aajig leaders and *ogimaag* while visiting the missions, Bishop Whipple handed out cigars. Such actions were long known as social lubricators for such events by treaty-making parties, but they did honor the authority of the Ojibwe dignitaries in attendance.

Codes of hospitality to elders and others may have been so axiomatic to Ojibwe life that their practice within the Ojibwe community receives little mention in the missionary record. It is implied in the complex of "visiting" that developed in reservation years, a social practice that enabled the Anami'aajig to fashion a broader community consciousness that extended beyond local ties of kin, village, and reservation.[83] The continued practice of hospitality to elders is most visible in the frequent reports that non-Native missionaries made of their own breaches of such conventions.

Gilfillan himself recognized his learning curve concerning Ojibwe hospitality. When the Red Lake *ogimaa* Madweganonind came to White Earth Village, some sixty miles to the south, Gilfillan took pains to provision him and put him up in a nearby Ojibwe home, "installing him, as I thought, comfortably, there." Several hours later Gilfillan noticed "a long thing like a log, lying on the snow in front of my woodpile—it was the depth of winter and it was cold—and found it was the Old Chief lying there wrapped in his blanket. He had taken that way of apprizing me that his quarters, or else the food, in the one room log cabin of the Indian were not altogether satisfactory. I took the hint, and for the remainder of their stay, he and his brother were my honored guests, as they ought to have been from the first."[84] According to a detractor, such conduct was more a pattern than an exception with Gilfillan, owing to the reported fact that Gilfillan's wife did not abide having Native people as guests in her home.[85]

Colby, by contrast, seemed to treasure her role as caretaker of elderly Ojibwe at Leech Lake. When a policy change dictated that a civil servant must direct the Home for the Aged that she had established, she wrote, "I lay [my position at the home] down rather reluctantly, for though I have more work than I can do justice to, I have found a vast deal of satisfaction in making the old creatures as comfortable as it is possible for them to be."[86]

BEYOND WOMEN'S SPHERE: DEFERENCE TO OJIBWE CHRISTIAN WOMEN ELDERS

Colby was an exceptional missionary who related with Native women as "sisters" and not just as "Indians," but she shared the broader Episcopal mission's agenda of promoting Victorian ideals of true womanhood, domesticity, and women's sphere that stood in stark contrast to Ojibwe traditions of deference that extended to the public authority of women elders no less than to men.[87] In fact, Colby drew her paycheck from Sybil Carter's celebrated lace-making project, a scheme that typified the mission's approach to advancing Ojibwe women by reducing them to domesticity. But here, we can also come to appreciate the creative leadership of women elders, documented ever so subtly in the missionary record, especially if we place it in relief to what was expected of them in the vision of the lace project.

Moved by a visit to a lace-making operation at a mission station in Japan, and "deeply impressed by the utter idleness of the lives of many of the Indian women," Carter resolved to begin schooling Native American women in lace making for their own improvement.[88] With Whipple's enthusiastic endorsement, she opened a school at White Earth in 1890, later expanding to other nearby reservations and, by 1904, forming a national "Indian Mission and Lace Industry Association" that would last until her death in 1926. "The lace teachers," she wrote, "show the Indian women how to make lace, and pay them when it is made, so that they not only learn to make the lace well and keep it white and clean, but they can also by it make their own living and be more comfortable in their homes."[89]

Keeping lace white and clean was clearly what most captured Euro-American imaginations about the project. For her part, Carter was eager to publicize her project so as to confront racist images of Indians as lazy and dirty. She marketed their wares among women of influence in New York City and Philadelphia and entered their work in the Chicago World's Fair and in exhibitions in St. Louis, Paris, and Milan.

Judging from the awards, the lace was of excellent quality, but the project's conceit clearly rested on its irony, and Carter enjoined her staff to protect the product from soiling even as they sought through industry to redirect the producers away from what she considered the contaminating influences of Ojibwe tradition. In a story that he repeated before numerous audiences, Whipple related the refining influence of lace making by quoting an Indian woman as saying, "[Me] have to wash hands, or lace'll get dirty; have to wash apron or hand'll get dirty; have to wash dress, or dress'll get dirty. Me like lace; make everything clean."[90]

The notion of J. Pierpont Morgan buying White Earth lace in a Fourth Avenue gift shop suggests a complete circuit of cultural revolution, where Carter's project had made Ojibwe women into something they supposedly weren't: industrious, hygienic, Victorian "true women" who left the woods, the fishnets, and the council ring for the parlor. But back on the reservation, the story of true womanhood in lace-making circles was far more complex.

For starters, Carter was less a pioneer than a relative latecomer: she built her lace-making project atop the existing foundation of women's guilds functioning for years. Crucially, the women's guilds that generated the lace had for fifteen years prior to Carter's arrival became viable social institutions because they were led by esteemed community women. Like the men's societies, which were sanctioned and organized expressly under the leadership of elder men, the women's guilds had been chartered by the bishop under the leadership of key Ojibwe elder women. With time, it was clear to Gilfillan that the leaders were more than expert seamstresses; they were *spiritual elders* in the traditional Ojibwe sense of the term. "Those who were most active in getting it up, and in having their fellow Indian women join in it," he wrote the bishop, "were the leaders of the bands of women, whom you appointed many years ago, each to have several Indian women enrolled of whom they were to have a sort of *spiritual* charge. Then names of these leaders are Cornelia E. Boardman, Mrs. Alex [Suzanna] Roy, Mrs. Maendjiwena, [Many Bird] Kakabishigwe, Emma Whitefisher."[91]

These lay leaders of the various guilds even came together to agree upon Suzanna Roy as an *ogimaakwe* "to take general leadership" of their efforts, apparently to promote unity and to make more effective their relations with Bishop Whipple and the charity and influence he could bring to bear on their behalf.[92] Equay-me-do-gay, baptized Suzanna Wright, was one of the initial Christians at Gull Lake prior to removal to White Earth. She could be regarded as a matriarch of the Anami'aajig, a powerbroker in the Episcopal mission and the Ojibwe community generally. Her leadership, and apparently that of the other *ogimaakweg*, was hardly confined to the women's meetings alone. Roy reported in 1882 that she had shared the "life giving effects" of "pointing" others "to life," "speaking to the women in the women's meeting and to the men in their meeting."[93]

Would that the documentary record revealed more of these remarkable lives and leadership. As it is, we must follow the subtle references, listen to the silences, and think with dexterity and creativity about their significance. Kugel pieces together from the same sparse archival materials a story of Suzie Bonga Wright's political leadership that appreciates how women's guilds were more than the quaint success stories that lace-making promoters made of them.[94] As "the Ojibwe sought to turn the Euro-American civilization program to their own advantage," the guilds taught Ojibwe women new skills and allowed them to bring in the cash necessary to make a living where clear-cut reservation lands could no longer. But where assimilation policies encouraged Ojibwe people toward market agriculture and the accumulation of private property, the guilds also "affirmed their commitment to the traditional Ojibwe redistributive economy."[95]

If these *ogimaakweg* functioned as community spiritual leaders in a manner that was consistent with Ojibwe tradition, their leadership was problematic to the mission hierarchy in at least two respects. The first concerned the shape that Ojibwe women's spiritual presence was to take within a patriarchal church. When the Pembina Band village sought to replicate the example of Suzanna Roy's women's meeting in White Earth Village in 1881, the nascent Anami'aajig community requested "a paper" from the bishop authorizing the formation of a men's band under Wa-ge-ji-ge-zhick as their "chief" and "leader of the meetings" and a women's band under Oge-shi-ya-shik, his wife. Their request, dictated to deacon George Johnson, was glossed for the bishop by Gilfillan with a stipulated concern about keeping the elder woman's leadership in its place under male authority, in this case under a Native deacon within his own superintendence: "If you merely write: *I hereby authorize the women of Pembina settlement to form a women's band under Mrs. Waygidjigizig under the superintendence of Rev. Geo. B. Johnson* that will be sufficient."[96] In actuality, it seems that such ordained clergymen as Deacon Johnson, like his father Enmegabowh, did not understand their authority in such patriarchal terms. On my reading, the Ojibwe clergy appear to have construed their authority as derivative of, not superceding, the authority of key *ogimaag and ogimaakweg.*

In 1887, Suzanna Roy appealed to the bishop to reverse an earlier policy that apparently forbade women to publicly exhort one another, presumably on account of the mission's paternal regard for them as women of a Native community not yet mature in its faith. Roy dictated a letter to the bishop in Gilfillan's hand, and apparently with his newfound approval:

> When two of my company died . . . so I thought, come now, let me start off fast in "religion"; but now there is something which repels me back. Is that indeed what we should do we who are Christian, not to exhort each other mutually? As for me, I think extremely useful mutual exhortation in the religion. So my head is full of asking you . . . that the women who have been forbidden to exhort each other in their women's meeting may hear your answer.[97]

But if Gilfillan had been convinced of the piety of these elder women, he was deeply concerned when Ojibwe women's leadership went beyond "women's sphere" to engage the economic and political questions facing the community. Colby reported that the Leech Lake guild meetings involved opportunities to "discuss all affairs of interest to them," and these could enable women to air grievances, organize efforts, and ally with other Ojibwe communities on other reservations. The guilds they led were more than narrowly religious confraternities. In the new world of reservation and mission, they reiterated familiar structures of kinship and mutuality that made a new life possible. Leaders like Suzanna Roy enjoyed considerable community stature by reputation as well as birth. She was a daughter of the eminent Gull Lake leader Waubojiig (White Fisher), the sister to the *ogimaa* Waubonoquod (White Cloud), and aunt of deacon Charles Wright Nashotah. Similarly, bringing spiritual unity in the community amounted to ecclesiastical work that was also crucial political work. Keeping together the various *ogimaag* affiliated with the Episcopalian missions on White Earth and on the nearby reservations of Red Lake and Leech Lake was important work in the maintenance of a united Ojibwe front in the 1880s, especially in light of the factionalism that had plagued those communities to the benefit of external colonial interests. These *ogimaakweg* also took vocal part in formal Ojibwe councils, and this to the consternation of Gilfillan. Enmegabowh reported that Gilfillan considered women's participation in politics as "an injury to the cause of [the] mission," but importantly welcomed the public voices of the Anami'aajig women in councils himself.[98] "Where Gilfillan insisted on separate spheres and female subordination," Kugel observes, "Enmegabowh emphasized women's integral importance to community rejuvenation. He urged that Ojibwe women 'not keep silence' regarding community concerns" and understood them to be "more unflinchingly committed to community well being than men."[99]

THE ORDAINED AUTHORITY OF DEACONS AND
THE TRADITIONAL AUTHORITY OF ELDERS

If Anishinaabe practices of deference to women elders continued even in the context of the mission's gender agenda, evidence of the improvised practices of deference is also visible in the way that Ojibwe Christians squared the ordained authority of deacons with that of lay elders. Although the younger Ojibwe deacons who were trained in English and in the Bible were stationed in each reservation village and credited by Episcopalian sources as the main engine of evangelism, the final authority in these Anami'aajig communities rested, as it long had, upon the shoulders of key elders. Ojibwe clergy appear to have construed their own authority as derivative of, not superceding that of, community elders. Indeed as was past practice in Ojibwe communities, the younger clergy seemed to hold authority within the community that was delegated by *ogimaag* and other elders.

And clearly the clerical authority of young male deacons presented a challenge to traditional religious authority in their exchanges with elders within and without Anami'aajig circles. In 1880, a "Sunday School for the aged" was conducted by "the young men." Gilfillan wrote, "When the young Indian clergymen spoke to the old men on the subject of religion, they were very often surprised by the reply: 'You are only a child; you do not know anything; I ought to teach you, instead of your setting yourself up to teach me; I have lived a long time and learned a great deal.'"[100] Gilfillan added that "this was in accordance with Indian notions and did not take into account the fact that knowledge of books and some other things had something to do with obtaining wisdom, as well as age. Latterly, as the Indians begin to perceive this, that rejoinder has not been so common."[101] But within the sodalities of the Anami'aajig, deacons complemented and deferred to the authority of their elders.

Indeed, almost to a person were the deacons sons, nephews, or close cousins of the aging prominent *ogimaag* and were thus possibly cloaked, in Kugel's reckoning, in a "quasihereditary" authority.[102] Perhaps this hereditary authority could have been an accentuated kind of authority in light of the dearth of elders and the assault on the clan/kin system at the time. Each of the deacons was trained in the English language by Gilfillan and Enmegabowh with the Bible as their sole text, but their scant correspondence suggests that the deacons worked in an Ojibwe-language world. Most wrote their official correspondence in Ojibwe; only Charles Wright's correspondence goes beyond broken English.

Scattered in various villages throughout the White Earth, Red Lake, and Leech Lake communities, the leadership network of Ojibwe deacons helped foster a shared consciousness across traditional band lines and more recent reservation lines that proved strategic under U.S. Indian policy. Still, their leadership was soundly woven into the fabric of the leadership of *ogimaag* and elders in their respective communities.[103]

CLERICAL AUTHORITY AND THE DEACON'S STRIKE OF 1882

If the Anami'aajig imagined the clerical authority of Enmegabowh and the deacons as delegated by that of elder men and women, Episcopalian

The physical stature of the esteemed *ogimaa* Madweganonind, photographed here in 1895 alongside an Ojibwe deacon identified as John (Charles?) Wright at Red Lake, is suggestive of the way that the Native clergy exercised authority that was delegated to them by elder leaders. *Courtesy Minnesota Historical Society*

missionaries understood it in terms of a missions hierarchy and took pains to ensure that men's authority trumped that of women and that clerical authority trumped that of lay elders and, in the crucial case of Enmega-bowh, of diocesan authority over elder clergy. In 1882, tensions came to a head when the Ojibwe deacons staged a "strike," leaving their posts and conspicuously canceling worship for months. At first glance, the affair appears to be about wages and unequal treatment of Native clergy, but a closer look reveals how seriously the Ojibwe community regarded what it construed as the mission's disrespect for elders, especially Enmegabowh.

At the center of the strike was the bishop's archdeacon for Ojibwe missions, J. A. Gilfillan, who was charged with financial, pastoral, and disciplinary oversight over the deacons and their mission stations. Perhaps it was canonically appropriate that Gilfillan referred very few matters up the chain of command to the bishop, but the Ojibwe *ogimaag* and elders came to view Gilfillan as an obstacle rather than an asset in terms of their access to Whipple, who had earned their respect and could bring his national influence to bear on their behalf.

Gilfillan took what he might have considered a "tough love" approach to supporting the work of his Ojibwe deacons, taking pains to discipline what he viewed as their constitutional proclivity toward idleness, pride, and backsliding. As the bishop's gatekeeper, Gilfillan did not hesitate to exercise paternalistic judgment that, among other things, considered elders to be the more intransigent and stubborn of a whole people he deemed children. This became clearest in the pattern of belittling or even subverting the requests of Native elders for support. In 1881, Gilfillan clarified for the bishop the broken English of a letter penned for the *ogimaa* of White Earth's Pembina Settlement by the Ojibwe deacon George Johnson: "He wishes a paper from you to Waygidjigizig, the chief of that settlement, authorizing him to hold that part of the reservation against white intruders, settlers. That of course does not amount to anything, but it is well to gratify him."[104] When Suzanna Roy appealed to the bishop for financial support, Gilfillan added a cover note urging Whipple otherwise, "You are exceedingly kind to Mrs. Roy in sending her the $10 . . . I almost fear she is imposing on your too great goodness of heart. . . . [The Roys] were better able to earn everything they want than almost any other family." When the highly esteemed *ogimaa* Manidowab appealed to the bishop to secure the "fitting" of his house as Washington officials had promised, Gilfillan glossed the letter, which he himself had transcribed for the elder, as follows: "If Isaac [Manidowab] were not very lazy he could fix up his own house. He is nothing of a worker nor ever will be and the only thing is to keep him gently alive till he dies."[105] Gilfillan added that Manidowab's wife had recently defected to the "Romish Church, the only defection of that kind we have had for some years, so *that* does not make for their being very worthy of help."[106] As personal as these glosses seem, if we situate them in the mission's larger concern to foster habits of accumulation of private property, we can view them as instances of disrespect for elders and traditions of gifting and largesse expected of them.[107]

It follows that Ojibwe Christians took seriously Gilfillan's conduct. More than bad manners, it challenged the continued practice of Anishinaabe community within the Christian tradition. Ojibwe deacons voiced this concern with their bodies. With the support if not instigation of the elders cited above, they withdrew from their posts to protest Gilfillan's inappropriate exercise of power. By no means inconsequential was Gilfillan's culturally offensive misconduct toward the lay elders, especially insofar as he consistently blocked their access to the bishop. In addition, he vied for authority as the clerical leader of the Anami'aajig with Enmegabowh, by then an ordained priest and therefore outside the archdeacon's canonical oversight, and also by this time an elder in his own right.

Tensions had been rising between Gilfillan and Enmegabowh for some time. In a letter to the bishop dated December 10, 1880, the Native priest expressed his contrition for "what I have done to the great injury of our poor missions" and promised "never to write any more letter." Enmegabowh had apparently been soliciting support for the missions directly from contacts he had made on his various travels in the East, and this without the authorization of Gilfillan. The fund-raising controversy points to deeper tensions of the autonomy of Anami'aajig affairs, for these appeals were often for clothing, food, and capital purchases necessary to survival.

For his part, Enmegabowh also had been stirring animus against Gilfillan. Whipple had several months before received a letter from the mission-supported physician, Dr. Thomas Parker, who warned the bishop "how deceived you have been in Mr. Gilfillan. We have NEVER heard a white man, half breed, or Indian speak respectfully of him. . . . The leading Indians at White Earth, Wild Rice River, Red Lake, and Leech Lake all have the same name for him—liar. And the influence of his wife who has been his pain from the first becomes constantly stronger for the church's injury."[108]

In November 1882, Charles Wright Nashotah, the deacon at Leech Lake, notified Gilfillan that he had left his post, citing a double standard concerning the stern treatment of Ojibwe deacons found in common-law marriages while accusations of an Anglo-American priest's sexual misconduct with Ojibwe women at Leech Lake fell on deaf ears.[109]

Gilfillan explained the matter to the bishop in terms of Wright's own idleness and his having had "too much prosperity" so soon after having been a "blanket Indian."[110] Several weeks later, he suggested that the bishop dismiss a letter from Wright's brother-in-law, an influential Leech Lake trader, George Bungo, because it "is Chas. Wright all over. It is dictated by Chas Wright's jealousy, who wishes to force out Mr. Benedict that he may be sole lord there."[111]

In the ensuing months, however, as all but two of the deacons left their posts, Gilfillan admitted to the bishop that the deacons had "held councils" the previous fall at White Earth, during the great gathering for the annuity payment distribution, and that the stated objectives were more pay and advancement to the priesthood. Importantly, advancement to the priesthood meant much more than a bump in pay that could allow the Ojibwe deacons to cease hunting and gathering to provide for their families. As priests, the Anami'aajig leaders would be free of Gilfillan's supervision. And in his representations of the affair, Gilfillan discloses the significant threat to his own clerical authority posed by Enmegabowh, by this time clearly an elder as well as a priest:

> Of course when a man of the age and influence of Rev. Mr. Johnson [Enmegabowh] leads astray his younger brethren, it is hard to make headway against it. It is a pity to see the aged Aaron, the priest of the Lord, fashion the idol calves to lead the people back to Egypt, but so it is. He does it through an unfounded jealousy of me, thinking if they all resign it will force my resignation as the cause.[112]

Gilfillan did not emphasize such a crisis of authority. At least in his official accounts to the bishop, he continued to explain away the strike in these terms: "The immediate object is more pay, and they think that I stand in their way and that if I were removed they would have it all their own way."[113] Gilfillan also viewed the strike in terms of "the natural want of perseverance, and stick-to-it-ive-ness of the Indian."[114] He urged the bishop to say nothing of such correspondence to Enmegabowh, whose personal relationship with Whipple had several decades on Gilfillan's. His concern recognized Enmegabowh's implicit authority over Ojibwe missions and the precariousness of his own relative authority: "I hope also that you will not write anything severe to Rev. Mr. Johnson," Gilfillan wrote, "as it would make him bitter against me as the author. It is his nature to be in conspiracies and it is better to look on it just as a natural foible."[115] Ironically, Gilfillan reported that he and Enmegabowh had not yet even talked about the matter "and our friendly relations remained undisturbed, though I still have the same opinion as to what caused all this. I have confidence that he can undo all this if he wish, but forbear speaking to him about it."[116] Indeed, in his fourth attempt that January to contain the fallout from the matter, Gilfillan revealed that much of the strike may indeed have stemmed from his blocking Enmegabowh's role as elder and priest: "I

Rev. John Johnson Enmegabowh (1807–1902), first ordained Native American Episcopalian priest, was typically photographed in clerical garb as a celebrated emblem of
the potential success of converting Indians to Christianity. Here, instead, he sits as an
elder. His authority among the many Ojibwe who affiliated with the Episcopal tradition rested not only on his ordination but also, with time, on his stature as a seasoned
veteran of struggles to survive inside and outside the church. Note the brass spittoon
concealed by the hat. *Courtesy Becker County Historical Society*

have never attempted to exercise the least supervision or superintendence over Rev. Mr. Johnson in anyway shape or manner, considering him entirely exempt from me, and he receives his salary direct. I have not even known for, I believe, three years past what it is."[117] A year previously, Gilfillan had confessed his own reluctance to follow the bishop's directions to "forbid" Enmegabowh to write unauthorized appeals for funds to contacts he had made for fear that "it might hurt his feelings for a younger person to rebuke him."[118]

The next month, Gilfillan eagerly reported that he had finally broached the topic with Enmegabowh and that the elder priest assured him the deacons would return to their posts. "He acknowledges the counciling with the young men on the subject," Gilfillan wrote, "but said he did not advise them to leave but only told them, 'If [they did], then they should seek a living elsewhere.'"[119] Gilfillan later added how others had assured him that Enmegabowh had been the cause all along.[120]

In the end, Whipple stood by Gilfillan, who was allowed to keep his job. But Gilfillan was clearly constrained to view the deacons, Enmegabowh, and the elders who stood behind them as a force to be reckoned with and not simply a problem to be managed.[121] Even after the dust of the strike had settled, the archdeacon reported continued misgivings among the White Earth Anami'aajig. Perhaps not coincidentally on the very day of a visit to the reservation by Sybil Carter, Gilfillan wrote: Enmegabowh's "entire sermon . . . was a passionate call upon the congregation to throw overboard all white people connected with the mission, . . . and for the Chippewas to take all into their own hands."[122]

Elders' Authority and a Twentieth-Century Rekindling of Tradition

For another fifty years, and arguably longer, Ojibwe Christians had few choices but to continue in the delicate task of negotiating a life, sometimes challenging and sometimes accommodating assimilation policies and missionary churches bent on what George Tinker has called "cultural genocide."[123] Still, a 1928 report commissioned by the United States roundly declared assimilation policy to have been a complete failure. In response, Roosevelt's administrations reversed those policies with the reforms of the "Indian New Deal," restoring an official endorsement of the rights (if not completely effective in practice) to hold communal property, speak Native languages, exercise Native traditions, perform ceremonies, and exist as distinct sovereign nations, constituted in federally recognized tribal governments.

But in many respects the damage was already done, and deeply so. A generation of Native people who came of age after the Indian New Deal had already been powerfully shaped by boarding school childhoods. Many boarding school veterans lost their language to the experience and the shame that went along with it, some still speaking English with an Odawa or Ojibwe accent.

In addition to the deep interruption of language fluency and the consequent dispossession and/or concentration of the cultural knowledge carried deftly in and though the Anishinaabe languages, Native experience in the latter twentieth century was deeply conditioned by a second wave of less overt, but no less assimilationist, policies of relocation and termination and by the pervasive proliferation of American culture through popular media of radio and television.

ELDERS AND THE REKINDLING OF TRADITION

In these new conditions, it was only with great cultural dexterity that twentieth-century Anishinaabe elders exercised their authority to ensure the survival and even flourishing of Anishinaabe communities and cultures. Having wintered no few nights in Larry Cloud Morgan's little cabin on Ball Club Lake, where a barrel wood stove was all that stood between us and –30°, I came to appreciate the deft art of banking the few coals that remain by three a.m., choosing the right wood combination for ignitability and slow burning qualities. I commend the nuances of the image of rekindling to describe the artfulness and integrity with which elders maintained traditions they knew, but in many cases only partially.

We could begin with the turn by high-profile urban Indian activists in the Minneapolis-based American Indian Movement (founders of which were Anishinaabe and Lakota) to reservation elders and spiritual leaders at Pine Ridge and in Minnesota's Ojibwe homelands, a weighty appeal by militant activists for meaningful traditional grounding and spiritual direction that complemented the important ways that younger activists catalyzed elders to assert their traditional roles, but that story will occupy much of the subsequent chapter. Here, I'd like to focus on that same generation of elders in the years prior to that story. The years following World War II marked a crucial, if largely unsung, period for Native Americans when the infrastructure for a broader rekindling of pride in Native ethnicities and cultures characteristic of the later twentieth century met a generation of elders who had grown up speaking Ojibwe and Odawa at the feet of nineteenth-century elders, but who came of age in boarding schools and attained their own eldership at a time of a pronounced and widening generation gap. Even as early as the late thirties, Hilger found White Earth elders who "had had the benefits of tribal social controls so effective in that day; and who taught them to their children, but who [were] saddened by the failure to persuade their grandchildren and great grandchildren to accept them."[124]

But this was not wholly the case, as at least certain elders continued to relate their knowledge in these new times. Evidence abounds in the profiles of elders in Michigan's Odawa and Ojibwe communities in the 1940s and early 1950s, and this I take to be representative for Minnesota and Wisconsin Anishinaabeg, that numbers of elders saw in the folklorization of culture in pageants and powwows a crucial if limited opportunity to extend and embody the performance of cultural traditions.

ELDERSHIP IN CONTRAST TO FOLKLORIZATION

It is counterintuitive that elders should play such a role. According to most narratives about the American Indian Movement, it was the vocal youthful activism and organizing of its founders in Minneapolis and elsewhere that catalyzed elder generations of Anishinaabeg, Lakota, and other Native communities to reclaim with pride languages, cultures, and traditions that had been deeply submerged by assimilation.[125] But there was a still subtler manner in which certain Anishinaabe elders kept their languages and cultural repertories afloat, quickening them as living traditions of practice and embodied memory, rather than allowing them to harden into the amber of folklorization, cut off from both change and from the communal ethic and integrative vision that would more forcefully call into question the norms of dominant society.[126]

An emphatic instance of this process can be seen in the storied Ojibwe-language *Song of Hiawatha* pageants that began in the straits between

Lakes Superior, Huron, and Michigan in the first decade of the twentieth century, that traveled to entertain Indian and largely non-Indian audiences at "powwows," "ceremonials," state fairs, and in urban venues in the East, and that, oddly, continued through the early 1960s at Garden River, Ontario. The original poem on which the libretto was based was published in 1855 as the *Song of Hiawatha*, though Henry Wadsworth Longfellow had submitted it to the publisher under the title *Manabozho*, for the Ojibwe trickster. Although Longfellow himself never stepped foot in Anishinaabe territory, the poem was based on the voluminous collection of Ojibwe narratives by Henry Rowe Schoolcraft, the Indian Agent in Michigan Territory who married into the Ojibwe community and remained a prolific enthusiast of its language and culture, but who also brokered treaties and removal schemes that would confine the "real Indian" to the past in a folklore owned by the American people. Longfellow's poem was widely regarded as among the most influential representations of the "vanishing Indian," translated into many immigrant languages and performed by several generations of American schoolchildren as a script of Americanization.[127]

Elsewhere, I develop more fully an argument that, in Michigan, such performances of culture for paying audiences enabled resourceful Anishinaabeg to earn needed cash but also to retain their memory of important narrative, especially drum, song, and dance repertories by means of their continued embodied practice, and importantly jokes encoded in Ojibwe language, song texts, and even reversed dance steps, which served to buffer such performances from the memory of their "truer" forms.[128] Especially prior to the 1930s, but to some extent through the late 1960s, when the resurgence of tradition centered around the American Indian Movement began to enable more "sovereign" continuation of these repertories, such seemingly impure stages as early powwows, ceremonials, and Indian villages served as important venues for the public claiming of Indianness in ways that subtly defied, even as they took place within, the structures of folklorization and romanticization.

Folklorization interrupts the flow of living culture from elder to younger generation and calcifies it into something that is seen in increasing contrast to living communities and oral traditional knowledge. But the continuation of oral traditions and the embodied dances and musical repertories that are also handed down properly through word of mouth and continued performance depend on the continuity of their exercise, and what happened in such venues in the 1930s, 1940s, and 1950s made all the difference for that generation who could have something to teach the youthful activists of the American Indian Movement. Two Odawa performers of the pageant at Petoskey were also political leaders of their community and went on to become esteemed elders in northern Michigan, repositories of cultural knowledge that they nimbly sustained, and even gained, through the pageants.

Joe Chingwa was born in a log house near Petoskey, Michigan, on land subsequently owned by the railroad that later promoted the pageants. His mother was an Ojibwe woman from Manistique, Michigan; his father, an Odawa from Petoskey. It was said that his grandfather, Mkkwuniwi, "had the power to call the bears from the dens at Midwinter."[129] During his total of three years in boarding school at Mount Pleasant, Chingwa said, "he forgot what his mother looked like." He returned to northern Michigan and was a laborer for the city of Petoskey for years, where he became a storied fisherman and raconteur. When the Hiawatha pageant came to Petoskey in 1905, Chingwa took the role of Chibiabos, the sweet singing tenor, and doubled as Gitche Manitou ("Great Spirit") in the opening scene, a role that doubtless brought a touch of mirth to the celebrated tales he told as an old man.[130]

His sense of humor notwithstanding, Chingwa took the pageant seriously, remembering it fondly as a site for the regular performance of important dance and song repertories, repertories that continued to be tied closely to a sense of peoplehood and sacred power. One of the songs in the pageant, for example, was found to be "a really old Ottawa song, perhaps not known to the Chippewa," that Chingwa told Jane Ettawageshik had been taught him by his mother. Its performance in the pageant was not inimical to its performance in other, less folkloric, contexts. Ettawageshik noted that the song could be sung "when the pipe is being smoked, perhaps by a welcoming delegation, at court trials, when asking for rain, at social meetings, etc." But even on stage in front of tourists, "solemnity pervades most of the performances" of the song.[131]

Off stage, Chingwa proved to have been a player as well. In 1930, he was elected chief of the Michigan Indian Defense Association, which continued to sponsor the summer pageants.[132] Odawa leaders had formed the organization in the 1930s in a pronounced attempt to unite Michigan's Anishinaabe communities under an autonomous organization. Leaders like Chingwa were asserting autonomy to protect cultural continuity, land, and community interests without formal incorporation under the tribal government plan devised by the Bureau of Indian Affairs under the 1934 Indian Reorganization Act.[133] Here, cultural events reminiscent of the pageants continued well into the 1950s under the sponsorship of a Native-led organization that was advancing the interests of Native communities in whatever ways were available.

While Whitney Albert never appeared as a cast member, he told Gertrude Kurath and Jane Ettawageshik that he learned a number of songs from watching the Hiawatha pageant, in addition to ones he learned more directly through the oral tradition from his grandfather. His repertory of tradition, then, relied considerably on the pageants without being derivative of them. Born in Hart, Michigan, he became in youth a lumberjack, an expert in logrolling. In the 1940s he worked on the highway that linked northern Michigan with Detroit. But Albert was deeply involved with cultural performances like the powwows at Mount Pleasant and Hastings in central Michigan. Kurath regarded him as having had "the largest and most varied repertoire of Indian songs in the state." He took the show business name "Chief Blue Cloud," although he freely admitted he was neither chief nor Blue Cloud. Whatever his stage name, Albert's Odawa name was Zhagezhin, and he knew it. "He knows both Catholic and Protestant hymns," Kurath wrote, "yet he is a pagan at heart, . . . little worried about his individual position and is poised, content, and affable."[134]

According to Kurath and Ettawageshik, for such Anishinaabe people, the pageant was not simply a job; it was also a rare occasion for the public performance of a cultural repertory.[135] To be sure, the Hiawatha stage was not exhaustive of contemporary performances of Anishinaabe tradition in Michigan. Even in that era of formal assimilation policy, Native people continued to practice their traditions with firm resolve. Still the pageants played a remarkable role in continued public performance of that repertory and apparently gave occasion for the subsequent renewal of pride in performance that emerged with the powwow tradition.[136] We should not underestimate the potential loss that a whole generation of disuse could bring to a primarily oral tradition—and in the case of this particular generation a disuse that was officially encouraged and even enforced by assimilation policies and intense social pressures on and off reservations.

At Harbor Springs, the Hiawatha pageants yielded to "ceremonials" that increasingly came to reflect the autonomous control that the Odawa community was asserting over them. While the events still drew large crowds of non-Native summer people, they were now held in a large amphitheater in the Native community of Harbor Springs, across Little Traverse Bay from Petoskey and Bayview, the tourist centers. With time, they also changed the content, incorporating a "large number of genuine Ottawa songs and dances still in their repertoire . . . into a coherent and entirely indigenous program" that were nonetheless still directed toward a paying non-Native audience.[137] In this part of Michigan, there appears to have been a trajectory that led from these festivals rather directly to the contemporary powwow tradition.

These ceremonials, like the Hiawatha pageants before them, brought needed income—about ten dollars per participant per day. But, according to Kurath, they also made leaders "more conscious of the value inherent in their non-Christian heritage. In this they have been encouraged by realization of increased white interest and appreciation. With better pay they have given more time to research and to improvements. Thus any permanent rejuvenation is a project for the White audiences as well as their Indian proteges."[138] It seems also clear that the exercise of control over the ceremonials brought its own reward, as "the effort of cohesion drew the Indians together" in such a way that Kurath thought would "grow into a permanent organization truly for the revival of their arts and lore."[139]

ELDERSHIP AND CONTESTATIONS OVER TRADITION

As assimilation policies discouraged, and then criminalized, overt public performances of Native ceremonies, many Anishinaabe traditions were retained underground, their safekeeping in no small part a function of the traditions of guarded orality and the wise stewardship of reservation elders. But in other communities like these Michigan communities, the policies created conditions that threatened these traditions to such an extent that elders like Chingwa, Albert, and others were constrained to engage whatever means were available to continue the practice of those sacred repertoires. In a word, these policies and the partial internalization of their assimilative intent created varied conditions that gave rise to various strategies of eldership.

Even as communities have sought consensus in their regard for elders and elders' teaching, and even as elders have continued to use one another as sounding boards for talking tradition over lunches at senior centers, feasts at powwows, long car rides to activities on adjacent reservations, or in visits over coffee at each other's homes, conditions of dispossession and social fragmentation have ensured there would be heightened tensions among competing articulations of tradition by different elders. As we have seen, demographic and cultural realities have exacerbated such tensions and have made consensus—or, better, indigenous procedures for negotiating such a consensus—more difficult still.

This, too, is part of the story. In no small part, the tensions have concerned the appropriate relationship between Christianity and Ojibwe traditions: whether they are mutually exclusive, "dangerous" to mix, or integratable teachings. But it would be wrong to infer that factionalism and differences over tradition, as heated as they could become, were completely novel in Anishinaabe history. For while there might be broad agreement about nonnegotiable aspects of narratives, ritual knowledge, and other oral traditions, variations could also be accommodated, or at least held in nondestructive tension, to encompass distinct lineages of teaching, and the idiosyncrasies of locality and visionary direction. In this respect, the posture of fluid "liberalism" that anthropologists like A. I. Hallowell called "Ojibwe individualism" was not inaccurate.

One concrete way to understand these tensions and appreciate the continued exercise of eldership in the face of them is to consider the life stories of several twentieth-century Anishinaabe figures who became, if not universally, then at least widely regarded as elders. In their cases, navigating the difficulties of assimilation, boarding school, poverty, and the like involved no small amount of resourcefulness,

First consider David Kenosha, a Michigan Ojibwe who impressed Ettawageshik and Kurath as a leader of traditional ways in the 1940s and 1950s when they recorded many of his songs and stories and considered his life story.[140] Born in Cross Village, Michigan, in 1892, Shawenimiki, Yellow Thunder, was baptized David and attended a Catholic school in that village. He learned Odawa, Ojibwe, and German from his parents and Latin in high school and went on to make a living in whatever ways were possible, first locally at a lumber camp and sawmill and commercial fishing along the Lake Michigan coast. He served in World War I on Great Lakes vessels as a quartermaster. After the war he worked to build the Detroit Express Highway and also picked up work, as Chingwa and Albert had done earlier in the Hiawatha pageants, performing several summers at the Wisconsin Dells Winnebago ceremonials and, in other summers, organizing an "Indian Show" himself with Margaret Gilbert at Cross Village, where he served as director, dancer, "chief choreographer," and singer.

If it weren't for a good knowledge of the historical context and difficulty facing Native people in these lean years, one might conclude that Kenosha was an assimilated "sellout." But that would be wrong from Kurath and Ettawageshik's perspective, and certainly from the perspective of subsequent generations at Cross Village and Little Traverse Bay, where his deft carriage of cultural knowledge in unlikely places made all the difference in subsequent efforts to revitalize those traditions. Kurath and Ettawageshik wrote, "He is one of the few Michigan Indians with a knowledge of native dances and songs. He claims to have learned most of these from his grandfather, also some dances at the [Wisconsin] Dells. He knows Odawa hymns, can read music, and sings in the Holy Cross choir. He used to fiddle for square dances and, just for fun, has danced Indian style to jazz." "He stands between the two cultures, the native and the white, the pagan and the Christian," their profile continues:

He knows every inch of the ground on the beach and in the woods between Sturgeon Bay and Harbor Springs. He knows where to find arbutus, wild strawberries, blueberries, choke cherries, sand cherries. He can hear the slightest rustle of a deer in the leaves or sees a herd approaching the lake far across the bay. He knows the native skills, can improvise a box from birch bark, a "tomahawk" from sticks and stones on the beach. He made a birch bark tipi which now stands on the new dance grounds, and is highly skilled in bead work. Yet he has a hard time making ends meet during the long winter months and finds work on neighboring farms or wherever he can. He is an individualist and for that reason never married. For he likes to wander. He lives in the bygone days and subconsciously seems to hold the ancient beliefs and attitudes. Yet he must fit his activities into the present day and adjust his faith to that of the church of which he is a good member.[141]

Kurath and Ettawageshik went on to remark that "this conflict is both his charm and his tragedy," but based on what we know about the history of the authority of eldership in previous generations of Anami'aajig, I'm not so sure that the conflict they saw—through a lens ground by standards of the 1950s social science so concerned to set off the "traditional" from the "acculturative"—was to Kenosha, his family, and the following generations of Little Traverse Bay Odawa who considered him a gem of cultural knowledge a "conflict" worthy of the qualifications of "charm and tragedy."

A generation later, consider the example of Earl Nyholm, a retired educator and go-to Anishinaabe elder who, among other things, is known for his compilation, with John Nichols, of the Ojibwe-English dictionary of record for the Minnesota dialects.[142] He is also highly regarded as a canoe maker and master of many traditional Anishinaabe arts. According to Wisconsin folklorist James Leary, participation in performances was important to his learning Ojibwe culture.[143] Nyholm told Leary that in the early 1950s at Escanaba, Michigan:

> They decided to start up an Indian village over in the fairgrounds, where they have that U.P. fair. They brought over a whole contingent from Odanah, Wisconsin.... My Aunt Julia Bennett was in charge of that whole business down there ... pretty much for the tourists and the white people, these Indian dances ... [but] they lived that whole summer in those wigwams ... so that was a good session too. I helped them on those wigwams. I had quite a bit of experience making those wigwams.

Like the Hiawatha pageants, and those directed by David Kenosha, these encampments were occasioned as amusements for paying customers in the mid-twentieth century. But it was in such spaces that elders like Aunt Julia passed on traditions and the value systems associated with them to the young, who would later become elders ministering to the revitalization of Anishinaabe language and culture. It was here, Leary learned from Nyholm, that the renowned Anishinaabe figure had leave to make wigwams and canoes, to tell stories, and to become practiced and fluent in an Ojibwe language whose embodied performance was occasioned by the unlikely venue. Such is the resilience of Anishinaabe eldership in the authority of tradition.

Representing not quite the next generation, in the years before he died, Larry Cloud Morgan offers another good example of this qualitative eldership. Unmarried, in his early 50s, a man whose friends were often much younger than he, Larry became increasingly regarded as an elder over the eight years I knew him. As his esteem in the community grew, so too did his comportment as an elder. His gait, saddled as it was with the amputations well known to those with advanced diabetes in Indian country, became more measured; his silences longer; his words fewer and more reflective, more poetic. As Larry himself took on the role, the community, especially the urban Indian community in Minneapolis, increasingly sought his Ojibwe-language prayers and blessings at child-naming ceremonies, weddings, and especially funerals. Larger circles of people waited until he ate before they ate, waited until he had finished speaking before they spoke, cited his permission to do so, and brought their dreams to him.

Larry was neither an ordained Catholic priest nor a recognized Ojibwe Midéwiwin medicine man. He had little working knowledge of healing plants or how to live the seasonal life in the bush. He had spent most of his adult life in urban Chicago, a luggage-department buyer for Marshall Fields, living with his longtime companion. Most Ojibwe people knew him for a courageous civil disobedience action he undertook with three other Catholic peace activists in 1984. They broke into a nuclear missile silo within earshot of a Kansas City area public school and spent four years in federal prison for it. Upon his release, he pieced together a modest living as an artist, political activist, and perhaps most especially a spiritual leader, called on to ground grassroots activist campaigns in indigenous Ojibwe ways of valuing land and community, to offer prayers and songs in the Ojibwe language, to preside at funeral ceremonies that were neither officially Ojibwe tradition nor officially Roman Catholic but that met the needs of a grief stricken community in an extraordinarily effective way.

Because of my close relationship with this friend in the last eight years of his life, I witnessed both the improvisation and the tradition at play in his articulation of culture. For a considerable circle of Native people in the Twin Cities and at White Earth who honored Larry by calling him one of their spiritual leaders, what he said was tradition carried weight. In no small part this was shaped by his youngest years at Red Lake and Leech Lake Reservations, summers spent with grandparents who spoke only

Larry Cloud Morgan gathering roadside sage for ceremonial use. *Author photo*

Ojibwe, and an adult life often spent articulating/interpreting his tradition to others. But in such moments when Larry was testifying before legislative committees or speaking in public, he would often clothe his points with "our elders tell us that . . ." or "our elders say. . . ." Larry and I often joked about "the elders say." "Who are those elders that say that, Larry?" I would ask. His gentle chuckle revealed both his mastery and his art in the rehearsal of tradition. Although Larry took his role as elder very seriously, he didn't take himself so seriously that this could become a difficult contradiction to live with. For he knew full well that his authority rested on the community's regard for his integrity and that his stewardship of tradition was under continuous scrutiny of other elders who could keep him in line. Years out from his death, it still astounds me how widely respected are his name and his words.

Until she died in 2001, Josephine Degroat spoke English with a distinctly Ojibwe accent. She was born at the Gull Lake Band settlement on the White Earth Reservation, her grandparents among the reservation's original settlers removed with Shaydayence and others. In tarpaper shacks, vernal maple-sugaring camps, and autumnal wild-ricing camps, Josephine grew up in the world of the Ojibwe language. An eighth-grade English-only education in a Catholic boarding school and a life as a farmwife off the reservation isolated her from many in her community, all the more so as a stern husband forbade her access to a car. When he died, she moved back to the reservation and became increasingly active in the public life of the community.

In 1983, she joined a dozen others gathering weekly in the basement of the Episcopal Church to learn the tradition of Ojibwe-language hymn-singing. Based on their vivid memories of all-night singing in their childhood, little phonetic hymnbooks handed down in their families, and a tape recording made by singers from an adjacent reservation who had maintained the tradition continuously, this group was gradually invited, as had singers in the previous generations, to "sing" at funeral wakes in their community. Emphatically, this was not just singing. This circle of people, none of whom took themselves too seriously, was soon recognized as "the White Earth Singers," distinguished by their commitment to bringing language and indigenous values back to their community in times of particular need, when the old were gathering all too often to bury the young. Later in the 1980s, they were singing at three wakes weekly, addressing through their music, speeches, and example how the community would continue in spite of the untimely deaths.

In 1991, they formed the backbone of elders that cast a sense of integrity on a grassroots movement protesting what they saw as a fraudulent land settlement agreement between the United States and the then tribal council, the secrecy and flippancy with which that council conducted the tribe's affairs, and the development of a casino with the Philadelphia mob. This movement was emphatically more than political activity. Named "Camp Justice" for a six-month encampment on the lawn before the tribal headquarters, it was a bold experiment in traditional Ojibwe community and spirituality, erected and practiced to call to account its tribal council. In meetings each night, the elders sang hymns, passed the pipe, and spoke publicly about the urgency of renewed spiritual commitment.

As with others of this singing group, Josephine was in this practice, in this singing, becoming an elder. People increasingly looked to her for guidance, sought her advice on "the old ways." She attended a Minnesota Council of Elders and took its proceedings very seriously, more seriously perhaps than did its organizers, whose purposes were more therapeutic and geriatric than deliberative toward identifying community direction. She traveled to the annual Kateri Tekakwitha gatherings of Native Catholics, exchanging indigenous ideas and traditions across cultures even while affirming the sainthood of that seventeenth-century Mohawk woman. She made and gave away jingle dresses to honor other elders in her community. She danced proudly in the jingle dress tradition, only at "traditional" powwows that involved no money. All the while she sought out her own elders, notably Winnie Jourdain and a centenarian German-American nun who had been Josephine's teacher in boarding school. She eagerly accepted Ojibwe tapes and went to sleep listening to her old language. She enjoyed whiling away the hours in conversation with other elders trying to piece together the old ways, often with a quilting project underway on her lap.

The singers with whom she was identified and whom she drove around, having the only reliable car among them, were also increasingly distinguished. In obedience to what was understood to be a vision, a drum maker from Wisconsin brought them a ceremonial drum and eagle staff to honor them and bless their continuing work with these highly charged Ojibwe symbols of the sacred.

Josephine Degroat with fellow White Earth Ojibwe Singers Ethelbert "Tiggums" Van-wert and Charles "Punkin" Hanks, 1994. *Author photo*

Curiously, crucially, respect for these elders and their own spiritual practice did not recognize as unequivocal the boundaries between Catholic and Protestant or even between Christianity and Ojibwe tradition. A visit to Josephine's house involved passing a portrait of John Paul II prominently displayed in her kitchen, a black-light poster of an Indian, and bundles of sage wrapped in red yarn. Sitting distinguished in her chair, Josephine might mute the televangelist's Bible study on cable. The padlock on her bedroom door kept even family members out of her most precious things, so it was anyone's guess what bundles of medicines were hanging in there along with trinkets from her travels around the country. Until the tribal council changed hands and regained control of its gaming operations, she refused to enter the casino, but she never hesitated to use the little plastic buckets for slot machine coins; she stored rendered lard in them.[144]

These may not make for a representative sample of Anishinaabe people recognized as elders, and to be sure, one could identify other recognized elders whose life stories suggest far more cultural continuity. Still, I think these examples are more representative than not of the way that cultural continuity has been maintained and secured by Anishinaabe people-become-elders whose own lives bespeak the extent of the interruptions to those traditions. It would be wrong to deny that real conflicts about what constitutes tradition have emerged, in no small part because missionization, boarding schools, factionalism, racism, and demographic realities of shorter lives lived hard have made consensus much more difficult to reach around who is authorized to speak as an elder and to articulate tradition. In particular, the boundary between Christian affiliation and Anishinaabe tradition, largely collapsed in the lives of these particular elders, remains a clearer, less ambiguous one for many, who may as a consequence look to others for their cues about what constitutes Anishinaabe tradition.

But it would also be wrong to conclude that there is no ambiguity in Anishinaabe communities about such boundaries, especially because even for many of their critics, elders whose lives bring indigenized Christianity and Anishinaabe tradition into binocular focus are often highly respected for their exemplary moral conduct and the linguistic and cultural knowledge that is, for them, conjoined with their Christian affiliation in a seamless life.

Scott Lyons, an Ojibwe literary-studies scholar who hails from Leech Lake and whose father is a singer with the Cass Lake Ojibwe Singers, spoke of the palpable tension he has seen as younger people privately and sometimes publicly question the traditional credentials as of the women and men, and perhaps especially the men, most of whom have short hair and who sing Ojibwe-language hymns.[145] As cited elsewhere, Valentine has found similar generational tensions among the Lynx Lake Ojibwe in northern Ontario. Still, such criticisms are themselves not unequivocal and must often be squared with community norms about respect for elders, even those with whom one disagrees. And although individuals speaking as elders, too, can voice criticisms that create firm boundaries between Christianity and Native traditions, as I'm told that some individuals have come down hard on attempts by some Minnesota Episcopal communities to inculturate traditional Anishinaabe symbols and practices into Christian liturgy, others have viewed this as a kind of untoward self-proclaimed claim to eldership that is not wholly credible because it stands in tension with what other recognized elders say.

Conflict happens, to be sure, and has presented no small challenge to what many regard as a time-honored consensus concerning the authority of eldership; but even the conflict is not without a particular configuration in terms of protocols and traditions of eldership that help withstand conflict's destructive force.

While eldership is determined communally, not biologically, it is also true that those who came to exercise eldership in the twentieth century (and perhaps earlier) do so in creative and partial ways that defy a conventional notion of eldership as performed competence in the unbroken content of Ojibwe tradition. In *Ojibwe Singers*, I begin to develop a notion of tradition as the rehearsal of culture rather than the performance of it, accentuating the partial, conjunctural, creative elements of cultural practice. For where performance implies mastery, rehearsal implies a process of learning while performing.

This is crucial to consider, for Ojibwe communities that practice eldership and respect for it do so in an audacious countercultural assertion of identity. In a society that considers old people obsolete and that denies and delimits women's public authority, the practices of eldership and ceremonialized respect for it become emboldened statements of identity and distinctive values. What is more, for those who claimed their authority as Ojibwe elders after lives lived in boarding schools, urban ghettos, American culture, and the English language, there is considerable gumption at work. Larry Cloud Morgan, Josephine Degroat, and the elder hymn-singers of White Earth each took their place as elders amid profoundly interrupted traditions and these linguistic and demographic interruptions marked "language," "tradition," and the elders said to carry if not embody this precious cultural knowledge, with a heightened sense of urgency and prestige.

Their examples show clearly that respecting elders today is not, as is conventionally understood, a matter of deference to the old out of rigid allegiance to a body of tradition that they conserve as "wisdom-keepers," but a principled respect, rooted deeply in notions of Anishinaabe sacred community, that honors the agency of recognized elders to wisely direct the flow of tradition.

In their case—and I think they are representative not only of respected elders today but in earlier times as well—we can see how the fluid dynamics of tradition and the authority of eldership come together. In short, tradition on Ojibwe terms is what a broad circle of elders *agree it to be* at particular moments in time, informed to be sure by long-standing customs of the past but with a posture toward survival with integrity in the present and future that authorizes change. Because of a community's recognition of them as elders and therefore authoritative voices in the articulation of tradition, elders are the crucial link that grounds improvisations in tradition. Like the ancient woman who sews day to night and night to day with bone needle and sinew, it is elders who seal the seams of continuity and change. In their articulation of it, elders are agents of, not just mouthpieces for, tradition.

A SENSE OF TRADITION

To understand more precisely how this works as something far more complex than either the rote repetition of custom or the contrivance of invented traditions, we can appeal to Pierre Bourdieu's rendering of the theory of practice and more specifically to the range of practical "senses" Bourdieu identifies that we develop in addition to the five with which we are endowed, like the sense of humor, direction, or timing. In his famous critique of subjectivist and objectivist debates about the gift, Bourdieu speaks about the "sense of honour" that is in play in the gifting tradition of the Kabyle people of north Africa, which is patterned, to be sure, but defies easy systematization in terms of "norms and rules."

Even "grammarians of decorum" like authors of etiquette books are "able to state what is right to do and say" without "presuming to encompass in a catalogue of recurrent situations and appropriate conduct, still less in a fatalistic model, the 'art' of the *necessary improvisation* which defines excellence." Far from the rules, Bourdieu writes:

> The point of honour is a permanent disposition, embedded in the agent's very bodies in the form of mental dispositions, schemes of perception and thought, extremely general in their application ... and also, at a deeper level, in the form of bodily postures and stances, ways of standing, sitting, looking, speaking, or walking. What is called the sense of honour is nothing other than the cultivated disposition, inscribed on the body schema and in the schemes of thought, which enables each agent to engender all the practices consistent with the logic of challenge and riposte.[146]

Catherine Bell uses Bourdieu's model to understand the "sense of the sacred" that is developed and exercised in ritual.[147] I suggest that we might speak of a "sense of tradition" that is highly developed among certain Ojibwe elders and that equips them to be improvisers of tradition without losing the beat or the key. It is the development of this practical sense of tradition, which is articulated more in actions than in narratives, exemplified in elders' lives and comportment rather than in fixed blueprints about the traditional life, that distinguishes certain elders able to inflect received tradition with subtle changes without interrupting its continuity. Such a practical sense accounts for the suppleness with which tradition changes, a meeting place of social expectation and an individual's artful creation that begs few if any contradictions in invented traditions. And it is this practical sense of tradition that combines with the authority of elders to situate tradition not in its theoretical content, but in its practice by those authorized and fit to improvise upon it in ways that remain viable and meaningful.

As Charles Long suggested in remarks about this project, the exercise of Native elders' authority is associated with their mastery and deployment of a sense of time that is syncopated with the natural rhythms of tradition.[148] This was clearly the principal accomplishment of Archie Mosay at the meeting with Senator Paul Wellstone described in the introduction. Taking the gavel of eldership, he reclaimed the space of a meeting where the senator, Bureau of Indian Affairs director, and their aides were elevated on a dais and whose time was demonstrably more important than that of those attending as Anishinaabe space through a masterful exercise of a speech practices that syncopated the gathering to cadences tied to the language and to tradition and to culture. What was important, one might say, was inverted: the senator was a guest in the American Indian community center, the time that was important was the time of reconnecting through prayer to the spirits and to the land. The change was palpable to me as an outsider, and if it may have been seen as an imposition on the good graces of the senator and officials taking time from their busy schedules to hear from the community, perhaps from the perspective of other Anishinaabe in the audience, they received the more important hearing.

In its aspect as a means for innovation, the sense of tradition can be likened best perhaps to a sense of timing that a good comedian or singer can exercise. One recognizes such a sense of timing in a Sinatra, an ability to take liberties with scripts in ways that enhance them rather than eclipse them. Perhaps one can think through the relationship between the traditional authority of elders and the content or scripts of tradition using this analogy of musical liberties. In performance, the liberties can work if the singer takes them persuasively in synch with the song and with an audience's expectations; at the same time, few things sound worse than an amateur lounge singer taking inappropriate liberties. It just fails.

If I'm right that such a sense of tradition has brought together the regulating effect of the objective inheritance of past traditions with the improvised performances of recognized elders, I think the analogy can help understand the perplexing way that continuity and change have come together in the authority of Ojibwe elders in history. The notion of a sense of tradition, cultivated perhaps by all, but enviably highly developed only in some, can account for the way that stewards of the past can variously make room for new circumstances in a way that still promotes consensus. Without insisting "there's no there, there" in terms of the objective content of inherited tradition, the cultivation of a sense of tradition shows how fidelity to the regulation of objective tradition proceeds to secure meaningful stability of tradition while enabling the breathing room necessary to its continuance in circumstances hostile to it. And while consensus has been increasingly difficult to realize concerning traditions intentionally interrupted by colonialism, the sense of tradition, like the sense of timing in musical or comedic performances, lends itself to scrupulous and ongoing criticism that makes the authority of eldership more than a convincing performance.

DIFFERENTIATION OF AUTHORITY

If the traditional authority of Ojibwe eldership cohered in an effort to keep religion, politics, economics, and other facets of cultural life in a meaningful integrated whole, and if on this basis such a posture commanded the respect of Joe Chingwa, Larry Cloud Morgan, and the like, the posture they took toward tradition, spirituality, and culture took on new valences as a result of a process of differentiation of those realms, even in Native communities. Communities that rejected (and to a large degree still reject) the discrete concept of "religion" as applied to their integrative ways of life came increasingly to use the term in their efforts from the late 1970s on to secure constitutional free-exercise protections for access to sacred lands, eagle feathers, sweat lodges in prisons, and the like.[149] Similarly, ethnographic and museum representations of Native cultures as well as American popular culture's desire for the otherness of Native cultures have served to folklorize the culture they have endeavored increasingly to define. On the other hand, the traditional authority of eldership as I have identified it has been less about fidelity to the purity or orthodoxy of the content of tradition than about fidelity to one's own elders and the prerogative granted to recognized elders for the nimble application of tradition to everyday life for the well-being of community.

But despite verbal commitments to the all-encompassing authority of eldership, the purview of even highly recognized elders' authority has diminished in scope. In matters cultural, they can be considered key arbiters; but in matters political or economic, their place and voice in decision making has been reduced dramatically. Political leadership in Minnesota's Ojibwe communities since the 1930s has alighted on elected officials, often younger "politicians," in keeping with tribal and reservation constitutions modeled, originally, on representative democracy. That is, in principle; in practice, it produced highly centralized executive powers relatively unlimited by constitutional checks and balances. Now, communal decision making takes place largely in the bureaucratic structures of reservation and tribal governments. Perhaps Max Weber was right, as it concerns Ojibwe history, in his characterization of the social process of modernization in terms of differentiation and a concomitant rationalization and bureaucratization of authority once traditional.

Ethnologists working with twentieth-century Ojibwe communities remarked on this differentiation and rationalization of authority. Edward Rogers discussed the transition of authority away from medicine men/ *ogimaag* to elected political "chiefs" in northern Canadian reserves. "Formerly the roles of shaman and band leader were often linked, but today these positions have been separated," Rogers writes:

Formerly the shaman had great influence and control over community affairs. As well as religious duties and rights, he also had economic sanctions, and since he was usually a band leader and/or *nintipe'ncike'win*

223

head, exercised some political control. With contact, his political authority and economic control became altered. He lost and in some cases, it appears, divested himself of political authority.[150]

Ojibwe communities did not embrace these processes without equivocation. It is telling that the language of Canadian Ojibwes registers such elected figures, along with the bureaucratic authority they represent, by inflecting the traditional word for leader/boss, *ogimaa*, with the suffix *-kan*, which places dubitative inflection on what it modifies, such that the chief is *okima'haka'n* ("bosslike" or "substitute boss").[151] One contemporary Canadian Ojibwe dictionary distinguishes *ogimaakan* ("chief") from *ogimaa* ("boss").[152]

A good example of the process was documented at a Northern Ojibwe community in 1950 by R. W. Dunning. The elder *ogimaa*, Old Birchstick, who had led the Pekangikum, Ontario, community for forty years, was "almost unanimously defeated in the government-instigated democratic election by a man of little prestige and even less self-confidence." By "prestige," Dunning meant the "old man's spirit power." "Whereas Birchstick had persuaded and almost forced his will upon the people," Dunning wrote, "the new chief talked and reasoned." The new *ogimaakan* "functioned as an attenuated version of the old chief, moving around society, visiting and talking and trying to represent opinion and keep ahead of it."[153]

Dunning found this story indicative of sea changes in Northern Ojibwe life. Where "the basis of authority in earlier time was primarily the uncertainty and fear of the uncontrollable areas of life," Dunning saw increasing education, knowledge, and modern rationality clearing room for authority to rest on more bureaucratic foundations.

This process, which also applied to an extent among Ojibwe communities to the south in the United States, had an exaggerated effect in terms of restricting the scope, or at least the public mode, of elder women's authority in the community. As the credential of exceptional spiritual power declined in importance in an era of Canadian and American political intervention that fostered the rise of the elected *ogimaakan*, so too did the possibility for exceptional women like Netnokwa to assume community leadership as public elders of the sort that shaped Anishinaabe political life form positions of acknowledged public authority. It was not until the

1990s that Marge Anderson from the Mille Lacs Band became the first Anishinaabe tribal chair in Minnesota.

But the gender implications of this history are complicated, for observers like Dunning also noted the concentrated impact of the increasingly localized Ojibwe family in Anishinaabe community life in the twentieth century, and this has tended to foreground elder women's authority. Jeffrey Anderson noted in the case of Wyoming's reservation-era Northern Arapaho how such a social change there brought the exchange of ceremonial authority away from the public ritual initiations of age-sets into the more private domain of family networks. Anderson writes: "The family, which has been more durable than age structure in reservation history, has become the center for shaping or reshaping the life movement of individuals . . . and at the center of that action there is typically a core of women."[154]

In his consideration of the debates among Ojibwe at Lac du Flambeau in the 1980s over whether to accommodate Wisconsin's interest in "buying out" treaty rights to take game fish by spears out of seasons regulated by the state or whether to assert those treaty rights, Larry Nesper found a divide that was as generational as it was identifiably anything else. "For the most part," Nesper writes, "members of the oldest living and active generation . . . were political realists and accommodationists; they sought and counseled cooperative relations with the surrounding non-Indian communities." Nesper observes their upbringings in the era of the Indian Reorganization Act (IRA), their wage labor in local economies, and their inclination toward "individualizing the meaning of Flambeau Ojibwe cultural identity. Their accommodation did not resist the loss of some significant cultural forms, such as fluency in the Ojibwe language, the Midéwiwin, fasting, and the Big Drum. Their strategy, however, has also permitted the continual redefinition and endurance of other aspects of Ojibwe culture, like hunting and fishing, and it has fostered a social coherence and continuity that made a cultural revival thinkable in the late 1980s."[155]

By contrast, Nesper found "some of the children of the eldest living generation who formed the core of those who actively criticized the accommodation strategy." Most were nearing fifty, having emerged as "young adults when a worldwide cultural revolution began to challenge long standing power relations between the dominant and the dominated."

But as generationally divided as these concluding statements seem, Nesper also documents the manner by which the latter challengers conspicuously appealed to the authority of certain elders in their own appeal to tradition, suggesting not only that the generation of elders was not in full agreement as an age-set, but also that listening to elders did not necessarily mean heeding what perhaps a majority of older Ojibwe at Lac du Flambeau were saying.

Contemporary Efforts to Institutionalize Elders' Authority

As court judgments and economic development have enabled federally recognized tribes to assert their sovereignty more fully in the waning years of the twentieth century, some tribal governments have tried to reintegrate the traditional authority of elders into bureaucratic structures of modern tribal governance. Such efforts are important directions in the claiming of sovereignty through revised tribal and reservation constitutions, codes, and rules, and to be sure, they can proceed at the behest of certain traditional elders as steps necessary to bring continuity and change together in important ways.

As active as elders can be in tribal election results, their votes count only as much as any adult. To some White Earth Anishinaabeg, like Marvin Manypenny, who criticizes the IRA tribal government system as a foreign imposition, restoring the place of elders in community governance is a necessary step to achieving cultural and political sovereignty. "We need the elders to stand up and tell the federal government, tell the state government that we've got a foreign system you've imposed on us," he told a reporter. Jim Ironlegs Weaver at that time had resolved to meet weekly at his home with others to establish a circle of elders. "If we can get a council of elders to run this reservation, they can hire the business committee," Weaver said, referring to the now-elected tribal government. "The people themselves will tell the council what they want." he said. "If we vote 'em in, we can't get rid of 'em." According to the same reporter, George Earth "argued that traditional spiritualism could replace political self-interest as the basis for a new form of government, leading the people back to unity and self-determination." "The people are the power," Earth said; "leaders that don't belong in there will leave. A good spiritual chief didn't dictate— he listened." Earth added that "elders are rarely consulted and tend to refrain from discussions about the well-known inadequacies of the existing system."[156]

Perhaps it was this same approach that underlay a reproof I received from a politically savvy Anishinaabe teacher and healer from a Canadian community in my attempt to solicit ideas of how the present study could be helpful in such attempts to document and incorporate traditional authority of elders into contemporary tribal political and educational institutions: "Incorporate?" he replied, "why do we need to *incorporate* elders?" adding that Ojibwe eldership has at least forty thousand years of successful history going for it and that incorporation is part of the problem.

He's surely right insofar as the institutionalization of elders' traditional authority changes its texture and, very possibly, its substance. For example, attempts to define eldership in legal codes and constitutions must appeal to objective, rationalized criteria like biological age instead of informal criteria like community recognition. Frequently also, institutional authority of eldership is shaped in terms of culture or tradition, where elders' councils are summoned not to make political, judicial, or economic decisions but to make determinations in matters of otherwise uncodified terrain. Among Arizona's San Carlos Apache, for example, elders comprise an advisory council on history and cultural matters.[157]

Still, communities like Minnesota's Mille Lacs Band of Anishinaabe have reconstituted government to recognize the authority of its elders in a number of codified ways. For matters that pertain to its tribal courts, the community has framed its code by a "judicial philosophy" that is "a product of the terms and conditions of our customs of life since time immemorial":

> Peace and harmony between the people of the Band is necessary to ensure the continued survival of the Anishinaabe. At times the circle of peace and harmony amongst the people will be disrupted. This circle of life needs to be restored in a manner that permits the integrity of the individual to be maintained so that the community will continue to grow and prosper. It shall be the judicial philosophy of the Court of Central Jurisdiction to promote the traditional teachings of our elders that have served the people so well since the beginning of time; to apply these principles of life to resolve conflicts between individuals; to strengthen and help those who come before the Court so that they may experience a good life. To this end, proceedings in

the Court of Central Jurisdiction shall not be adversarial but shall be a search for truth and justice.

In particular, the code bases its "theory of law" on "a high regard for the concept of sha wa ni ma. It is one of our ways of life according to custom. The purpose of sha wa ni ma [zhawenimaa-, "pity, mercy"] is to keep the people together as one. This purpose is good for all people. It serves to balance the forces of life and brings stability to the people. To achieve this way of life, the laws of the Band shall be construed to balance the rights of the individual with the need to continue to coexist in peace and harmony with one another."[158]

Elders factor into the code at a number of points. Candidates for tribal judge must be people of recognized "honor, integrity and good moral character as evidenced by letters of recommendation from four elders of the Band who are not related."[159] Also, panels of elders are consulted to provide guidance on legal issues that arise that neither tribal, state, or federal statutory or common law can determine. In "cultural causes of action between Band members," a decision of such a panel of elders is authorized to be entered as a judgment by the tribal court.[160] In its definitions, the code determines that "an elder for purposes of this statute shall be an enrolled Mille Lacs Band member who has reached the chronological age of 55."[161] But this in itself doesn't completely rationalize the authority of eldership in contrast to more traditional norms of community recognition, for only recognized elders who are enrollees over 55 would presumably be called upon for such a panel.

Conclusion

Notwithstanding such notable efforts at integrating traditions of eldership into political charters, codes, and constitutions or establishing institutional elders' councils to hear certain matters, the realities of tribal governance since the Indian Reorganization Act nearly a century ago have meant a narrowing of the reach of the authority of eldership qua eldership. An elder is a vote that can surely swing many other votes, but these are votes among votes. But this chapter has considered the traditional authority and exercise of community leadership across a range of realms: political, religious, and cultural. In this, narrowing of the authority of eldership in the political realm has been offset perhaps by an intensification of the authority and prestige of elders as elders in the religious and cultural realm. Put another way, since the mid-twentieth century, there has been an intensified sacralization of Anishinaabe language and tradition. Elders have emerged as the elemental leaders of what has come to be seen more clearly as Anishinaabe religion. And it is to that story we now turn.

5

THE SACRALIZATION OF ELDERSHIP

In the time of the Seventh Fire an Osh-ki-bi-ma-di-zeeg (New People)
will emerge. They will retrace their steps to find what was left by the trail.
Their steps will take them to the elders who they will ask to guide them
on their journey. But many of the elders will have fallen asleep. They will
awaken to this new time with nothing to offer. Some of the elders will be
silent out of fear. Some of the elders will be silent because no one will ask
anything of them. The New People will have to be careful in how they
approach the elders. The task of the New People will not be easy.
                                        —Edward Benton-Banai, *The Mishomis Book*

 In *The Role of the Aged in Primitive Society*, Leo Simmons
locates the chief relevance of the elderly in terms of their religious presence. "Not all magicians have been old nor have
all aged persons been shamans," Simmons writes, "but superannuation and the supernatural have been very commonly linked."
Because of their role as ritual leaders, "the aged have been afforded an excellent means for continued participation in the vital affairs of community
life, to the mutual advantage of themselves and younger generations."[1]

In a sense this has been true for Anishinaabe people for some time.
Although the difference between the charismatic authority of visionaries
and the traditional authority of age ought to be acknowledged as well as
the similarity, it was elders *qua elders* and not *qua shamans*, who have
classically held a privileged role as ritual specialists in the naming ceremony, in spiritual direction and mentorship, in dream interpretation, and
as intercessors.

In another sense, the spiritual authority of eldership has become even
clearer and more forceful still from the mid-twentieth century until today,
a function of a documented decline in the numbers of traditional dreamers and a decline in the authority of such medicine people as a result of
Christian missionary efforts, assimilation policies, and urbanization. But
it is also a function of an awakened consciousness from the 1970s on of the

threatened nature of Ojibwe language, culture, and traditions and a conscious turn to tradition that produced what I'll call a *sacralization* of tradition, of language, and of elders whose knowledge of tradition accentuates their authority and status, even as it limits that authority to cultural or sacred matters.

By one reckoning, the qualifications of an elder may as a result have less to do with length of years and generational position than with demonstrated knowledge of traditions and language, even virtuosity, or a particular hereditary lineage. Or in the context of urban communities, prisons, or even certain reservation communities like White Earth, where assimilation did more than elsewhere to upset traditional structures of sacred teaching and ceremonial practice, perhaps chronological years matter even more, as the authority of eldership rests on whomever is present, active, and able to place contemporary life in the context of tradition and language, whether or not they are deemed fully versed in language and/or traditional knowledge. In either case, the traditional role of elders as mentors and spiritual directors has remained, but this time not simply through informal or ceremonial relationships with individuals within families or proximal units, but through organized elders' councils that very deliberately cast the ominous struggles that face Native people in their individual and corporate lives in the broader context of returning to traditions, to language, to ceremonies, to communal economic and social and environmental ethics. In this regard, the sacralization of elders' authority may in part be a function of an internalized modern distinction between sacred and secular. Still, as I will show, the spiritual direction that Ojibwe elders bring to bear is hardly a matter of religion alone but about a return to an integrated way of life.

The Maturation of Power and Its Implications for the Spiritual Authority of Age

I observed in earlier chapters that even while early observers and ethnographers focused on the place of dream power in the configuration of indigenous leadership (especially among the Northern Ojibwe), Anishinaabe people thought and spoke of the spiritually powerful in terms of age. Dream power took shape in the song melodies and texts, dance steps, and revelatory herbal and ritual knowledge believed to be the personal gift of *pawaganag* ("dream helpers"), was made manifest in an individual's prowess in healing, divination, or capacity to deliver food, shelter, and other basic needs to family and followers, and could endow an individual with a power at once spiritual and social. While all Ojibwe, women and men, classically were encouraged to seek dreams and visions, to empty themselves in order to draw the pity of spirits and engage their support and power, certain individuals came to exercise charismatic authority through demonstrated virtuosity in this regard. Although Ruth Landes and others in the early twentieth century argued that social order among the Ojibwe rested on an irrational fear of the harm that such medicine people could do with their power, indeed suggesting a kind of unhealthy situation where the drive to accrue spiritual power perforce resulted in its eventual abuse, I think it significant that such people were called "that old man" or "that old woman" out of deference to their considerable spiritual power, in some respects regardless of how aged they were.

In chapter 1, I showed how a traditional Ojibwe understanding of the life passage considered old age, and especially extreme old age, as a kind of spiritual attainment, evidence of right living in proper relation to other persons—human, natural, and spiritual—and of physical well-being. Because it takes power to live, and right living to continue to function with power, old age signaled the realization of an ethical and religious "great person," *gichi anishinaabe* ("elder").

I also noted that an individual's power itself has been seen to mature with age. Although such observations do not abound in the ethnographic record, Robert Ritzenthaler found that, in the case of Wisconsin's Ojibwe, "for some, old age was the time when their spiritual power reached its acme. It was a common pattern that a man in his vision quest be told that he had the power to cure, but it must not be used until he had white hair."[2] Although Diamond Jenness's observations about the maturation of power took place in a discussion of the dream fast at puberty, he notes a correlation between maturation through the life course and the maturation of dream power:

> Every boy, the Indians say, received a vision and a blessing of some kind or another. One would acquire knowledge of a certain medicine-herb, another skill in hunting, and a third the ability to become a great medicine-man.

None of these blessings took effect, however, until the boy reached manhood; and they were never transferable to other Indians. Indeed, so strictly individual were they that no Ojibwa might even declare his vision until he reached old age, under penalty of losing the blessing altogether. Only when death was near, and the blessing no longer useful, might he communicate the vision to his children, if he wished; although most Indians carried the secret with them to their graves.[3]

Perhaps related to this understanding of power's maturation is an Ojibwe understanding of the spiritual work of old age, referred to in chapter 1 as an age of sacred learning, an intentional search for spiritual truth and ritual knowledge, and a focus on the proper use of spiritual power. It will be the purpose of the concluding chapter to come to terms with the precise nature of Ojibwe elders' ways of knowing and to inquire into the social location of those approaching the known end of life. For now, it is important to note that traditional Ojibwe imaginings of the life course look to all elders with expectations of their assuming a spiritual vocation.

Spiritual Leadership in Traditional Ojibwe Religion

Insofar as all Ojibwe men and women were encouraged from youth to seek visions and special relationships with spirits and believed in the revelatory possibilities of dreams and visions seen as "gifts" of the supernaturals, the authority of Ojibwe traditional religion has been profoundly democratic. To be sure there have been recognized religious specialists: *mashkikiiwininiwag* (herbal healers), *jiisakiiwininiwag* (shaking tent "diviners" or "conjurors"), *nanaandawi'wininiwag* ("doctors"), or Midéwiwin "priests" distinguished by their demonstration of uncommon power.[4] But such people, exceptional as they might be, are not decidedly set off from the general community as religious specialists by virtue of celibacy or the wearing of different clothing. On the tradition's terms, it has been incumbent on all Ojibwe people, men and women alike, to seek out the spirits and live in right relation to them.

It is fitting at this point to observe the gendered implications for this democratization of religious and cultural authority. In her 1938 study *The Ojibwa Woman*, which has come under recent critique, Landes made an impressive effort to document patterns of traditional gender norms. The "traditions" were based on concrete interviews and interactions in the 1930s with Ojibwe women of an Ontario reserve, most of whom considered themselves Christian. Landes argued that Ojibwe people regarded women's and men's roles as distinct but complementary, not hierarchically valued. Women's work was quite variable and highly visible: rearing children, distributing and preparing food, making clothing, shelter, and utensils, gathering wood, fishing, maintaining gardens, berrying, gathering herbs, making maple sugar, and harvesting wild rice. Ojibwe people were frequently on the move from village to camp and back to camp in their seasonal round, and, as Priscilla Buffalohead points out, this had implications for the authority of Ojibwe women in community affairs.[5] In winter, when Ojibwe traditionally retired in smaller family units to scattered hunting and trapping territories, women came to exercise fuller decision-making authority than in summer months when assembled in larger groups.

Landes did not note the implications of this seasonal sociology. But she did not frame her study of gender patterns in the context of the exceptions to every structured rule she seemed to find. Landes saw the fluidity of gender roles as a function of "Ojibwa individualism," a characteristic she took to be the "keystone of their culture," which was itself the cumulative fruit of religious convictions about how a person's role and status amounted to a "calling" by the spirits through her or his dreams and visions.[6] Although such revelations came to women and men alike, Landes began with an observation that men alone were expected to make a life's work the seeking of such visions and status. Landes undertook to identify clear distinctions in status, power, and public accolades paid to men and women: men's lives alone were regarded as "careers" of developing "personalities" concerned to accrue power, reputation, and influence; women's lives by contrast were not thus a matter of much public comment and concern. But Landes also concluded that, for these same reasons, women were even less constrained than men to fulfill rigid gender expectations. Since "the same culture that has laid down a glamorous course for men has provided no distinct line of conduct for women," she wrote, "women therefore attempt nearly everything available in the culture—and by so doing, alter the formulated nature of much that they engage in, heedless of the occupational demarcation so painstakingly taught to the men."[7]

Given such a dynamic, it is not surprising how much equivocation accompanies Landes's effort to typify gender patterns related to traditional Ojibwe religious leadership. "To women," she wrote, "are allotted the quiet, sedentary, and domestic operations that are not considered dependent on supernatural gifts," such as hunting, making war, and doctoring.[8] Thus women are "given little consideration culturally." Nevertheless, while she found that women in the communities she visited were generally not fulfilling the shamanistic vocation that she regarded as the key office of community leadership (both religious and civil), she had also to account for the "numerous women with an aptitude for pursuits that are culturally defined as masculine," taking recognized places as hunters, warriors, and doctors/shamans as well as more feminine roles: midwives, herbalist healers, nurturers of children in culture and tradition.[9]

Chief among these supposed exceptions was Maggie Wilson, Landes's principal consultant, who among other things was regarded as a bear-dreamer, one who had been visited by Bear in a dream and gained considerable status thereby. Also among them was Two Skies, an initiate of the Midéwiwin and a practitioner of a healing complex called *nanaandawi'iwe*, as well as a ceremonial innovator in her own right. An entire community performed the "Feast for the Dead" ceremony that she introduced to it after a vision in which the spirits instructed her on the steps, songs, and attendant teachings. Also among them was Kita, who "undertook shamanistic practice when, in Native thought, she was quite an old woman" of 50 years old.[10] Interestingly, Landes tells us—though only in passing—both Wilson and Kita were also Christian.

Although Landes herself did not take notice of the fact, the women claiming these roles of public leadership were, unlike many of their male counterparts, almost uniformly elders. This is significant because eldership itself carried an authority that could trump other orthodoxies, a prerogative claimed regularly by women as well as men. Perhaps the authority of eldership itself could not settle for orthodoxies, as is illustrated in the way that these women elders were able to hold traditional Ojibwe healing and ritual practices and associated beliefs in common with Christian commitments.

That elders in particular are regarded with an expectation of having a spiritual vocation does not contravene the democratized nature of Anishinaabe religious authority. Because ideally everyone attains old age some day, age stratification does not assert the same kind of social distinction as do charismatic or gender distinctions. I turn now to the number of significant ritual roles pertaining to elders, especially the privilege of naming.

In addition to the general discussion of power maturing among male medicine men, several early ethnologists reported a typical role of elder woman healer, who in some cases brought together that medicine of the medicine man and herbalist knowledge, itself a function of study, attention, apprenticeship, and dreaming. Of Northern Ojibwe and Cree at the turn of the twentieth century, Alanson Skinner wrote: "Beside the shamanistic doctors, there is a second class of healers, generally old women, who so far as could be learned use no supernatural means whatever in performing their cures. They rely on purely physical boluses, both internal and external."[11]

But Frances Densmore observed that many of the practitioners of herbal *materia medica* at White Earth and Red Lake in the 1920s, including perhaps many of the women, were initiates of the Midéwiwin whose herbal healing knowledge owed in part to their formal training in the repertory of that society. Although Densmore, too, distinguished these practitioners from those of the *jiisakii* and *nanaandawi'iwe* traditions relying on ritual (Densmore: "mental") means, she did note that healers of both classifications involved the singing of songs and herbal practices particular to that craft.[12]

Midwifery was decidedly "a woman's practice," according to Landes's consultants in Ontario. "Only during difficult labors" were Midéwiwin medicine men called in, and then only "entering briefly."[13] Likewise, A. I. Hallowell observed, the midwife does not dream in order "to be able to deliver women in case labor is prolonged: she would get the woman's husband to get medicine from one of the men. A midwife does not have any medicine apparently for such care."[14]

Still, Landes's more careful attention to the roles of Ojibwe women, and also her access to women consultants, suggested that midwifery was hardly without religious significance or requiring religious power. "The midwife," Landes wrote, "is called kakanaweenimit, nurse or guardian, and the practice is called Ki:shki disijige, cutting the navel cord."[15] Younger women were involved as well, attending births and "assisting experienced midwives, who usually are a senior relative," but it was more typically elder women who presided at all but the more difficult births.[16] In 1932, Landes noted that there were eight midwives functioning on the Manitou Reserve in Ontario, most of them in their late 60s and older, with only one younger than 50.[17] The seniority of midwives owed much to the fact that "midwife fundamentals are learned by experience only. One learns partly by having gone through several childbirths oneself and been treated by others."[18] But Landes also indicated that old age promoted the requisite bearing and, at least in some cases, the mature dream power, for successful navigation of this often difficult life passage: "The midwife should be a woman of mature years, preferably not under thirty five. . . . She should be of calm temperament. She is fortunate if she has had favorable dreams, such as bless her with the childbirth powers of a bitch, mare, or cow."[19] Again, the charismatic authority of dream power and the bearing and accrual of practical knowledge associated with old age were part of the same package.

MENTORS AND INTERPRETERS OF DREAMS

Certain elders were also crucial to the ritualized mentoring and interpretation of the dreams and visions of their juniors. Dream experience was— and still is today—regarded as more than "real"; dreams were potentially revelatory in nature, the privileged medium for exchange with spirits, or even the Great Spirit, of ritual power and knowledge. "Every dream, however insignificant it might appear, carried a meaning or a warning," Jenness wrote of Ontario's Parry Island community, "for the soul had undergone some experience, and everything that affected the soul had its influence on the individual's life." But the dream's "interpretation generally remained obscure," requiring that young people offer tobacco to gain the symbolic and ritual knowledge, but also the wisdom and confidence, of one's esteemed and trusted elders.[20]

Lee Irwin has demonstrated how the Lakota vision quest relies on the ritualized practices and mentor relationships that undergird this ritual, for as personal as the content and power of dreams was, it was clearly in relationship, in conversation with one's mentors and interpreters, who themselves exercise considerable art in the doing, that dreams became meaningful and powerful existential and social facts.[21]

This is equally true among the Anishinaabeg. Intergenerational mentoring was particularly ritualized in the boys' and girls' dream-fasting. Maude Kegg of Mille Lacs, for example, told of how her grandmother sent her off as a girl from the maple sugar camp to fast for several days.[22] The dream fast, or simply "fast," involved making oneself "pitiable" through a period of humble self-examination, self-abnegation, fasting, and painting the face with black charcoal. Depending on the direction specific to an elder's discretion, initiates would ascend promontories, retreat to certain places associated with spirits, or in some cases climb to "nests" made in the crests of tall trees to make themselves as baby birds, waiting for the spiritual food of the spirits. From four to ten days, according to Inez Hilger's White Earth consultants, the boys would fast in this position, visited daily by a "father or some older man who brought him a little food and some water, and instructed him in all things that were expected of him as a man."[23]

Inasmuch as "vision-quests" have become, in the American popular imagination, cliché peak moments of vivid solitary religious experience—ones that even many non-Native people have sought for themselves—a longer and closer view reveals a highly ritualized structure that patterned individual experience as much as they enabled individuals to have their own personal visions. As Hilger and others pointed out, it was precisely at this time of puberty that elder men and elder women—typically grandparents—would educate the young men and women respectively in the "moral code" and expected responsibilities and behaviors of adulthood.[24]

Elders drew on repertories of ritual knowledge, but doubtless also on good judgment about the needs and promise about particular young people, to help their young charges prepare emotionally and spiritually for their ventures, teaching them the appropriate conduct and responsibility of adulthood, purifying them in sweat lodges, guiding them in fasting and earnest self-examination, preparing them to how to receive certain *pawaganag* ("dream visitors"), helping (upon return from the fast) to discern whether the experiences were visions or mere self-deception, and interpreting the experiences.[25] Because the particular content of, or spiritual characters appearing in, such ceremonialized dreaming could shape the subsequent life of a dreamer, calling them to become one thing or another in the life of the community, the interpretation process worked out in confidence with an elder mentor played an enormous role, nearly as important as the dream itself. In this process, the authority of dreams and the authority of eldership worked hand in hand to secure the transitions in the key rite of passage into adulthood. Jenness wrote of one instance in the early twentieth century at Parry Island in Lake Huron:

> Pegahmagabow's elder boy, aged nine, dreamed about a flood, and an old man of whom the father took counsel interpreted it to mean that the boy would receive a present. He offered the same interpretation for a second dream, and warned Pegahmagabow that the boy would shortly receive a visitation and a blessing from the supernatural world. Dreams had an influence at every period of life.[26]

Sources spoke readily to Jenness and others of failed dream fasts, which were also part of an individual's moral and spiritual growth. Failure to dream effectively, to win the blessing of a spirit, in these ritualized dream fasts also required the mentorship and direction of elders whose wisdom and judgment enabled them to encourage and reshape moral or spiritual behavior for a better outcome in the future.

Importantly, intentional dreaming was encouraged throughout life, not simply in the fast at puberty. So, too, was bringing one's dreams to trusted elders to determine a meaning and gauge its significance for the course of an individual's life. Whether ceremonially solicited as a mentor in the puberty fast or otherwise solicited with tobacco to offer interpretation and guidance in light of a significant dream, it was the wisdom of elders that one sought in the dialogic process of spiritual direction and mentorship. Again, elders were sought out who were further along the path of intentional lifelong spiritual learning, but it was not simply narrowly ritual knowledge sought by supplicants in these mentoring relationships. More than their ability to decode symbolism or frame the specifics of an individual's dream in a larger matrix of ritual knowledge, what distinguished elders as being of good counsel—some more than others, of course, but in any event all of them elders—was the character insight, judgment, and practical experience that ripened with years of living.

The Sacralization of Eldership

Although the particulars of the Midéwiwin will not occupy this study, it bears mention that a form of age and eldership held sway in that initiatory context.[27] In his description of Midéwiwin initiation, Peter Marksman referred frequently to elders. The ordination includes an elder sponsor who speaks for the initiate. But eldership in this context pertained even less directly to biological age in the context of Midéwiwin than it did in traditional Ojibwe life generally. One's "age" in this context was ritually determined, a matter of duration from the point of one's initiation into the society and progress through several stages or "degrees." The title *Midewakiwenzii* ("Midé old man"), appealing to the honorific *akiwenzii*, refers to leaders of the Grand Medicine Society, again a reference to age that has more to do with power and initiatory status than with chronological age itself, though both senses of age can converge.[28] Ceremonial authority and seating arrangements pertain to initiation degree and initiation age. At the conclusion of a discussion of initiation, Marksman wrote, "I was only a boy when I was classified as an elder."[29] In the context of Midéwiwin ritualizing, and indeed beyond the confines of the ceremonies themselves, eldership status pertained not to one's biological age, but one's recognition. But its observance was consistent with that of eldership generally. As discussed in chapter 1, the White Earth Midé initiate Maingans told Frances Densmore about seven temptations in life that included violations of codes of respect for one's Midé elders. Today in Minnesota, the Midéwiwin has enjoyed a considerable revival, with the continuous leadership from Red Lake and elsewhere extending to the other reservations.

While midwifery, herbal healing, and dream interpretation were all associated with the authority of eldership, the most significant ritual leadership of elders has involved the ceremonial *wiindawasowin* ("giving of names"), along with the ceremonialized mentorship that the "namer" provided over time to the "namesake."

As typically has been the case in Ojibwe ritualizing, the details of the ceremony could vary considerably, but the basic structure involving an elder has remained the same. When a parent deemed it time to seek an "Indian name" for their son or daughter, or in some case where an adult sought a name, they approached an elder they respected with a ceremonial offering of tobacco and a request for a name for their child. The elder, male or female, was perhaps in the old days chosen for his or her reputation as a dreamer, gifted by certain spiritual sources with the power to dream and the power of dreams. Classically the elder would fast or seek a vision in which the child's name would itself be bestowed as a gift from the spirits or, in some cases, confer his or her own name on the child. After some measure of time, a feast was prepared, relatives and friends were gathered, and the honored elder presented the person with their name publicly. The elder who names bestows not simply a name, but also the blessing power associated with the name, and a very special sponsorship or "namesake" relationship becomes effective between namer and named and between their families.

Jenness described a typical early twentieth-century naming ceremony at Parry Island, Ontario:

In nearly all cases . . . the parents commissioned an old man, whose age indicated that he had enjoyed the favor of the supernatural world, to discover a suitable name for their child while they themselves accumulated the food necessary to entertain relatives and neighbors at the naming feast. The old man generally devised a name from some incident in the vision that had come to him during his boyhood fast, but occasionally he sought a special dream for the occasion, or accepted the name suggested by some dream of the baby's parent or relative. Yet it was not absolutely essential, in recent times at least, that he should derive the name from a dream; he might simply resuscitate the name of any notable tribesman, since the very distinction of its original bearer attested its virtue.

Several weeks often elapsed before the parents were ready for the naming feast, because the father always tried to secure a deer or a bear for the occasion. Relatives and friends gathered at the wigwam, and the old man who was to bestow the name danced and sang, holding in his hand the animal's head. Then, laying it aside, he took the child in his arms and said: "All you manidos in the east, all you manidos in the south, all you manidos in the west, all you manidos in the north, all you manidos in the earth, all you manidos in the air, bear witness that I give this child the name of ———."

He then kissed the child and handed it round to the encircling crowd, when each person in turn embraced it, imparting with the kiss an iota of his strength. Sometimes the old man made a speech about the significance of the name; if he had named the child after an animal, for example, he described the power of that animal. Sometimes, too, he gave the infant some object to wear that would represent its name, although the parents themselves often depict the name by patterns on its clothes. The ceremony concluded with a feast.[30]

From these reported details at Parry Island it would be wrong to extrapolate a rule for all Anishinaabe naming ceremonies. Fixed traditions of naming did not determine the choosing of a name but rather the prerogative of the elder ritually approached to give the name. Jenness cited consultant Jonas King's narration of a ceremony:

One baby whom I was asked to name I called "Eagle swoops down from the sky," after an incident in my adolescent vision. I cannot tell you the vision, because that would destroy its potency and the potency of the name. Names seem to have lost their power today, but formerly a good name ensured a child long life. Dreams for the sole purpose of securing names had little value; the really good names came from visions at adolescence. An old man still living on Parry island, North Wind, has been asked to name two or three babies. To one child he gave his own name, North Wind. Most of us think this was foolish, for he himself has never been remarkable in any way, and his name can have little power.[31]

It would also be wrong to extrapolate a rule that only male elders were called upon to name. From the circumstances of his experience in localities in northern Manitoba, Hallowell described the naming ceremony as "almost entirely a male prerogative," and he and other ethnographers characterized it in terms of an elder man selected as the namer.[32] But as was noted about midwifery, women ethnographers like Landes could witness a different social reality. Her main consultant at Emo, Ontario, had given names. Maggie Wilson "dreamed about the gleaming body and wings of a Thunderbird. . . . So she named her infant daughter, the Shining of the Thunderbird."[33] Likewise, Hilger, whose fieldwork in the mid-twentieth century spanned northern Minnesota and Wisconsin, observed no rule concerning the sex of the namer or the named:

> A man might name a girl; a woman, a boy: there are no fixed rules as to the sex of the namer. Windawas'siwinini—man namer; windawas'sikwe—woman namer. Nor was there a limited number of children that any one person might name. No namer gave the same name twice. "I have named about 20 children and all have different names. I dreamed each name: dreamed them as I needed them," said an informant on the Vermilion Lake Reservation.[34]

Again, what was consistent amid all these variations was that the namer be an elder. Hilger found it an "unfailing rule" that the namer "be an old person and one that had not been sickly during his life, the belief being that the child would then be healthy." She related that "a 53-year-old informant was not old enough to name a child, but was old enough to be invited to the feast at which a child was named."[35]

THE MEANING OF NAMES

In his nineteenth-century narrative of the traditional life of his Ojibwe people in Michigan and Ontario, clergyman Peter Marksman described a typical ceremony in considerable detail, underscoring its importance:

> In our language, all the personal names have some meaning. We obtain our names when young, by our parents making a feast to the elder of our tribe, or some man or woman who professes knowledge of the gods of the heaven or of the earth or of the waters, and have blessed him or blessed her; and these persons receive the feast prepared and offered to their god, whoever he is . . . and after the offering is over, the guests of the feast answer the person, who pronounces with a loud voice, saying, "He shall be called by his generation." The guests say, Ha, which means Amen. . . . Then the food is distributed to every person who was called to this feast. After the child receives a name, he is known by that name.[36]

It is hardly novel to suggest the significance of names for the construction of identity. But in their continuous intention toward and behind names,

Anishinaabe people distinguish themselves in terms of how they assign meaning to names. "A name was not merely an appellation, or a term of address," writes Basil Johnston, "it was an identity at the time it was bestowed, merging later into reputation." Johnston called the ceremony "the most important event in a person's life: the receiving of an identity through ceremony and name" and the gaining of respect on account of the name's origins from dream spirits.[37] When names were not of immediately spiritual origin, as in the case of a namesake conferring his or her name on a child, or the name of some other influential personage, the name could carry significance by association.

THE POWER OF NAMES

If names *meant something* by reference to a dream or namer, they also were understood to *do something* by reference to that power of that dream or namer. In a discussion entitled "Supernatural Power as a Private Resource," Victor Barnouw wrote that naming was the only noticeable sharing of personal power in Wisconsin Ojibwe life and that the conferral of power on an infant could mean life or death:

> Babies were considered to be particularly in need of supernatural support, being weak, exposed, and frail; but they were naturally too young to acquire guardian spirits of their own. Parents would therefore solicit the aid of some elderly person, believed to be strong in supernatural power, who would condescend to share some of his guardian spirit's protection with the child until the youngster was able to fast for his own guardian spirit vision. Except for this namesake relationship there was no sharing of power among the Chippewa. . . . Every man had his own private pipeline so to speak to his own guardian spirit, and he retained the monopoly of those resources.[38]

According to Densmore, "the child or person receiving the name was supposed to receive a definite benefit from it, but he could not transmit this acquired power to anyone else," until perhaps he or she might name.[39]

Supernatural power could be crucial to the survival of the baby. Of Parry Island Ojibwe, Jenness wrote that "the bonds uniting the shadow, soul, and body of a young baby" were considered so weak that they "refrained from spreading the news of its birth until it had received a name, through fear that an evil manido might steal and destroy its soul. A good name, they believed, focused the attention of the baby's shadow on its significance and thereby gave it strength and power throughout the duration of its owner's life. A poor name correspondingly weakened it and sometimes caused the child's death."[40]

But power was not merely supernatural in that it was also more plainly associated with material well-being, with life. Ceremonial naming had everything to do with conferring well-being and the promise of a long life on a child. In this respect, it made sense that the namer would be an older person because they had attained old age by virtue of personal power. As Thomas Peacock relates, the one given tobacco to confer a name was "always an old person who had not been ill during his or her life, . . . because it was believed the child would then be healthy. Children who were sickly were sometimes given two or more names from different namesakes for this same reason."[41]

Perhaps it is Johnston's semifictional style of published narrative teaching that best conveys the inside story of a southern Ontario naming ceremony. After making a speech about the chosen name, a namer pressed the baby, wordless, to his chest:

> This was the most solemn and profound moment in the ceremony. Cheengwun was about to give his N'Kweemiss a name. But first he was to give part of himself, to transmit a portion of his own potential to the child. There was no word for this potential; no word to describe its character; no word that could cause it to pass from one person to another. Because it was an act that was consummated between souls no words were necessary. Touch, flesh to flesh, was the way in which spirits met and became one. By holding his N'Kweemiss close, Cheengwun was letting part of his being enter the child. He willed his dream and his dream power to well out into the child to form part of the child's being and potential.[42]

In no case was a name merely a casual denotation; in certain cases under certain ritual directions, names were not to be shared. Naawigizis, Jim Clark, of Mille Lacs recalled that "there are some names you wouldn't discuss. I've heard of some people whose names they couldn't use, like an old man who gave a name so sacred that his immediate family couldn't use it out in public."[43]

If the power of names ritually transferred through a naming ceremony is significant for an appreciation of the spiritual vocation of eldership, so too is the relationship ceremonially created by namer and named. In fact, sources make more voluminous reference to the preparations leading up to the moment of naming itself, suggesting the larger significance of the ceremony in terms of social relationships.

The *we'enh* relationship, by which both namer and named are *we'enh* ("namesakes") to one another, is one of equals. Perhaps this harks back to an era when it was more consistently the case that namers conferred their own name to the named. In this case, both would carry the same name and could in so many respects be construed as the same person.

In her reckoning with the sociology of Ojibwe kinship, Landes found that "anomalous situations arise" from the *we'enh* relationship. Hilarious as well as anomalous, for the identity of the two in a *we'enh* relation could and did make for ironic boundary crossings of gender, marriage, and generation:

> If Ego [that is, the named child] is female and the namer is male, Ego's parent calls Ego's namer "daughter" and regards him in the parental respect-jesting way [properly accorded a child]. The namer answers reciprocally. But the namer's spouse calls Ego by the term for spouse—a coeval, joking term according to which female Ego is now addressed as male.[44]

Because such pronounced exceptions to the rules were "incomprehensible in terms of behavior or associated with the kinship system," Landes concluded that the *we'enh* relation was primarily a matter of the flow of supernatural power. "The identity of the namer and named," she wrote, "results from native theories of the transfer of this power; that it has been taken into the kinship terminology is in keeping with Ojibwa forms of thought, but its application proves very difficult."[45]

Still the *we'enh* relationship suggested more than that supernatural power had once flowed in a ceremonial moment, for the choosing of a namesake and the continued mentorship of the same formed an important part of a young person's life. Not always was it the parents who chose the namer, according to Hilger:

> Occasionally an old person asked to name it or announced that he would do so. When a child is born an old lady might say to the parents, "Now, you give me that child for my namesake." Another would say, "Let it be my namesake." Parents select one then and give a feast at which the child is named. A retention of this old custom survives on the L'Anse Reservation where many others no longer exist. An old Indian will announce himself as the namer of a child, and will name it; but no feast is given.[46]

An Ojibwe consultant from L'Anse, Michigan, told Hilger of two incidents when the prerogative to name was claimed by the elders themselves:

> When my sister was a mere baby, a very old man from the neighborhood came into our house and said, "I want the baby for a namesake." Mother didn't know what to think of it. He took a red ribbon from his pocket, pinned it to the baby's pillow, and started to smoke. "Your little girl's name is going to be Batawa'sigikwe, meaning Two clouds and sunshine between the clouds," he said. That's how my sister got her name. Another old man who was at a certain home where a child was born asked the mother if he might have the child for a namesake. He called her Bugonageshikwe, which means A-hole-in-the-sky [woman]. After he named her this he hit the ground with his cane as many times as the years of his age, saying he wanted the child to live that long.[47]

That the naming ceremony should be so central to Ojibwe religiosity is ultimately unsurprising, for with each naming, with each interpersonal flow of power from namer to named, has been accomplished the great intergenerational flow of power that can keep *bimaadiziwin*, the circle of life, in healthy motion. Naming here stands in contrast to the emphasis on originality and individuality of the name that obtains in most segments of contemporary American society.

As Mille Lacs elder Naawigiizis (Jim Clark) recently put it, when it comes to our names, "we have no choice." Such associations surround and inform the contemporary power and significance of Anishinaabe names. If the naming ceremony differs from here to there and according to the dictates of a particular *namer*, be it a dream name, a namesake name, or some other powerful name, what matters is the authority recognized in the elder giving the name and therefore the authority, power, and significance of that name. This significance has carried well into the present day, and the history of Anishinaabe naming traditions as they became integrated with other naming practices is an instructive example of the suppleness and resilience of the authority of elders in and through that history.

THE POWER OF OJIBWE NAMES IN THE CONTEXT OF MISSIONS AND ASSIMILATION

Because it had been elders ceremonially approached with tobacco who conferred names in Ojibwe tradition, it is noteworthy to compare how such Ojibwe names fared in light of baptismal names conferred by Christian priests, most of whom were white, and "agency names" conferred by Indian Bureau and boarding school officials. Indeed one finds a range of ways that members of the Anami'aajig community chose to identify themselves or were identified in common parlance, but missionary documents suggest that the Ojibwe names, conferred by elders ceremonially in their capacity as conduits of sacred dream knowledge, stuck, and remained significant registers of an abiding distinctive Ojibwe identity among Christian converts.

The first thing to observe is the play of multiple names in the early twentieth century. Consultants at White Earth in the first decade of the twentieth century led Densmore to distinguish six "general classes" of names:

a "dream name given ceremonially by a "namer"
a dream name acquired by an individual
a "namesake name given a child by its parents"
a common nickname
the clan name
a "euphonious name without any significance"

"In recent years," she wrote, "there are also translations of Chippewa names into English, the adaptation of English names into Chippewa, and the mispronunciation, in English, of Chippewa names."[48]

As Densmore's observation suggests, there was ample precedent, even in prereservation Ojibwe life, for multiple names. And there are numerous Anishinaabe people who proudly hold a number of Ojibwe names. But a practiced way of thinking about many names proved useful indeed to a people whose lives and livelihoods hinged on multiple allegiances, moving in and out of various spheres—missions, boarding schools, kin networks, and so on.

Pauline Colby wrote in 1893 of a baby born to a Christian couple at Leech Lake, Thawenigesik and Owenibequa. "The baby will soon be baptized and receive a Christian name," Colby wrote, "but of course he will also have an Indian name, which will be the one he will be known by until he goes to a church or government school."[49] In the 1920s, one of Hilger's Minnesota or Wisconsin Ojibwe consultants told her how baptismal and Anishinaabe namings could complement, not exclude, one another: "Each one of my children was given its Indian name a few days after baptism."[50]

Naming practices were anything but politically neutral matters. As Jean Comaroff discusses in the context of missions to indigenous South Africans, baptismal naming practices were an instance of "linguistic colonialism." Colby observed how Ojibwe names would not suffice in the official world of the mission or schools: "If the children have no Christian name when they enter . . . the principal or some other official registers them on the roll arbitrarily, and we have a George Washington, Benjamin Harrison, Grover Cleveland here right now. The girls seem to be named most frequently after some of the employees."[51]

By Ojibwe standards, baptismal naming was often no less arbitrary. Indeed, baptismal names offered an important fund-raising opportunity. For instance, James Breck baptized a Gull Lake Band Ojibwe girl Selma Dimock, after a benefactress from St. Luke's, New York City. To the elder Selma Dimock, Breck wrote, "May this be some reward to you, madam, for your gracious deeds done to us from year to year. May your prayer follow this little one, and may God prosper her." Ojibwe deacons also exercised a canonical authority within the Episcopalian tradition to baptize. Although missionary documents make few references to such practices, John Coleman and George Smith at St. Antipas mission in Redby chose for their first baptizand the name Theodore Reilly, for a priest in Minneapolis, who had examined them for orders.[52]

Baptismal Christian names were wedded to patrilineal surnames by force of U.S. policy. In 1903, the Commissioner of Indian Affairs decided that "it was necessary to require Indians to adopt family names in view of the confusion in connection with heirship and transfer of property which had prevailed under the present system." "A name is one of the most sacred privileges accorded to any person," the White Earth newspaper run by mixed-blood enrollee Gus Beaulieu declared, "and even the Indians will resent any interference by the officials of the government with this right. Even if an Indian is not named Tom Smith or John Jones there would not be any less confusion if his Indian name should be translated into English, for he would probably not recognize it. The government officials may arbitrarily replace Indian names on allotment and pay rolls, but they cannot compel the Indians to make use of them in their daily intercourse with each other or to do business in their English names."[53]

In this light, the practice of continuing to use one's Ojibwe name was more than force of habit; it indicated a charged assertion of Ojibwe identity and charged recognition of the process by which names became meaningful and powerful, a process that hinged on the authority of eldership. For many, the baptismal name seems to have become a second name, itself not uncommon in Ojibwe tradition, an indicator of the Anami'aajig's affirmation of a basic congruity between the Christian life and the Ojibwe.

More striking still is how stubbornly Ojibwe deacons, supposed paragons of the Christian life, retained Ojibwe names granted them ceremonially by their elders. Although the more official diocesan correspondence of Gilfillan and Whipple made reference to the Reverends Charles Wright or George Smith, Colby's rich memoir of mission life spoke routinely of Nashotah (Two Heart, Twin) and Kichi Nodin (Big Wind), respectively. Seldom if ever did the name Rev. John Johnson appear in print without Enmegabowh attached to it. Colby even mentioned that a Leech Lake "lad" had been named Kichi Nodin as "a namesake of our Indian deacon of that name," adding that "Benjamin Harrison is the name he was given in school."[54] While the deacons were still known by their Ojibwe names, they did not disparage their baptismal names. Indeed they put them to good use. John Coleman craftily applied to the son of his own baptismal namesake in England in order to secure for the Red Lake Anami'aajig a donation of a yoke of oxen. How significant, indeed that a son of Enmegabowh, Deacon George Johnson, had for an Indian name, Waubunoquod, a clear indication that the old *ogimaa* had been the boy's *we'enh*.[55]

Given the power that Ojibwe names owed to their origin in the dream gifts from the spirits to namesake elders, and the continued association of kinship between the namesake and the named, the continuation of Ojibwe naming practices demonstrated a subtle but significant regard for the spiritual authority of those elders and, without dismissing the importance of baptism's conferral of an additional identity, challenged the missionaries' understanding that baptismal names marked the death of the old self and its adherence to obsolete traditions. Perhaps because in certain instances revealing a dreamed name could diminish its power or the valor of the one so named, the very secrecy within an assimilative context conferred particular power on the Ojibwe name.[56]

To be sure, in the twentieth century, the conferral of an Ojibwe name would have further consequence as a newly powerful form of subtle resistance and assertion of identity. Today, for example, it is a relative rarity for one to have an "Indian" name, and it is a mark of very conscious affirmation of an Indian identity. In public speech, people today, as perhaps of old, say with pride who they are in Ojibwe, "———— *indizhinikaaz*." Such words are often the first steps one takes in an Ojibwe class and often frame public addresses in English with a bold assertion of identity.

Similarly, a number of Ojibwe people speak of the urgency of having an Ojibwe name so that upon death, one is known by spirits that speak only Ojibwe. This urgency was not felt in 1770 like it is in 1970, but in both cases, names carry a powerful charge, and the gaining of a name confers a sense of power and identity.

· · ·

The Implications of Twentieth-Century History for Eldership

If traditions of naming have remained profoundly continuous through the changes of assimilation, boarding schools, and Christian missions, in important respects the spiritual leadership of Anishinaabe elders has been dramatically reshaped by that history. But this is not a story of interrupted traditions, at least traditions of eldership; indeed the story I wish to tell is one of an accentuated spiritual leadership of older Anishinaabe men and women as elders. It is, I think, a story of the *sacralization of eldership*, of elders coming into their own as spiritual leaders of their communities and of an accentuated marking of the spiritual authority of old age that has resulted in part from the dramatic loss of language and the generational concentration of linguistic and oral traditional knowledge on the age-set of those who could still claim an Anishinaabe language upbringing.[57]

As previously discussed, the era of formal assimilation policy from the 1870s through the 1930s involved mandatory English-language boarding school education and suppression—sometimes overt, sometimes subtle— of Native ceremonies and giveaways. Even when legislation in the 1930s sought to reverse the wrongs of assimilation, the policies had already begun to accentuate generational divides by language and education and were grimly effective in destroying lives, families, communities, and the languages, practices, and beliefs that had formerly knit them together with their land base, itself gutted in size and health. The eldest members of today's Anishinaabe communities in the United States and even in Canada are typically survivors of these abuses and losses, who had generally been shamed out of daily use of their language. By the 1960s, in Minnesota, Wisconsin, and Michigan, Ojibwe and Odawa were indeed still spoken, but less in public, less as languages of daily life, and by fewer people increasingly defined by generational position.

At the cusp of the twenty-first century, the fluency rate among southern Ontario's Ojibwe was estimated at 3%, with most speakers over age 60. By Mike Chosa's reckoning, only six fluent speakers lived at Lac du Flambeau and Fond du Lac Reservations. White Earth has a fluency rate of 1%; Leech Lake 4%. Even the communities of Neyaashiing (Mille Lacs) and Ponemah (Red Lake), which have higher fluency rates than most of their neighbors, have very few young people who speak fluent Ojibwe. At Mille Lacs, all fluent speakers are reportedly 45 or older.[58]

To judge by linguist Michael Krauss's four categories of indigenous language health, only the Lac la Croix Ontario dialect of Ojibwe joins Inuit Cree, Dine, Hopi, and Zuni as "Category A: Most Stable," where the language is being learned as a first language by significant numbers of children. Category B, "languages still spoken by the parental generation but not most young people," includes Red Gut and White Fish Bay in Ontario and Ponemah, on Minnesota's Red Lake Reservation. Category C, languages spoken solely by people 50 and older, "includes most of the Ojibwe dialects in the United States and southern Ontario." Category D, where only a few of the oldest tribal members speak the language, applies to Ojibwe dialects at Lac du Flambeau and Fond du lac.[59]

In addition to the deep interruption of language fluency and the cultural knowledge carried deftly in and though the Ojibwe language, Native experience in the latter twentieth century was deeply shaped by the second wave of assimilation marked by policies of relocation and termination, which brought more than one half of the U.S. Native population to cities, and subsequent developments that have further incorporated reservation communities into the American economy and culture.

These circumstances, perhaps especially the dramatic loss of language fluency, did much to intensify the ritual role of eldership. Among contemporary Ojibwe people, the relationship between language, culture, and traditional religion is clear. Larry Smallwood, director of an Ojibwe-language immersion camp at Mille Lacs said, "ceremonies must be conducted in Ojibwe language, because that is the way that was given us to use by the Creator as Anishinaabe people. We were given ways to communicate with the Creator. And that's why it's important, not only in this world, but when we move on to the next world, go to the spirit world. We need that language."[60] Smallwood's views are widely shared: many contemporary Ojibwe people speak about the language, its potential loss, and its potential rebirth in spiritual terms. Anton Treuer points out what amounts today to only the "handful of elders" with the requisite linguistic knowledge that enable Ojibwe ceremonial traditions to remain practicable. "Most others believing in Ojibwe culture," Treuer continues, "depend entirely upon those elders."[61]

Such elders are also distinguished by a kind of lineage of language authority. They grew up speaking the language, absorbing it through the oral tradition alone, rather than through the mediations of college classrooms, orthographies, workbooks, or language tapes appropriate to some other dialect. This is not to besmirch such worthy media for the rekindling of language learning, but it is to recognize a kind of particular authority in the present day to the source of one's language knowledge, an authority perhaps accentuated by the very presence of alternative means of language learning. Here the authority is less that of age as such than it is the authority of a particular generation of elders whose age happens to place them in proximity to this authoritative lineage of learning.

There are plenty of examples in the history of religions of languages undergoing a transition from the quotidian to the liturgical or the sacred. Latin and Sanskrit, for example, have survived in a ritualized sphere amid other vernaculars and have been associated with hierarchical elites (e.g., the

Roman provincials in late antiquity who came to people much of Church hierarchy). In those cases, however, the privileged class had access to the sacred language in and through textual literacy, and in time, the sacralized language became further removed from its local origins, associated with decidedly nonlocal replicable ritual practices that could happen anywhere.

Importantly, I do not here mean to suggest that the Ojibwe language is a sacred language only in this restricted sense, or that it is destined to become such. There is too much vitality surrounding contemporary efforts to make it happen, and too much intention about keeping the language alive and vibrant in culturally and ecologically relevant contexts. For example, a 2003 Ojibwe Language Society calendar is representative of the effort to keep the connection between the significant meanings of teachings, proverbial sayings, and lore with the practices (berrying, ricing, trapping, fishing) of an age-old seasonal round tied to a particular landscape. The Ojibwe language itself is comprised of numerous dialects whose very distinctions are associated with distinctive landscapes and waterscapes within Anishinaabe territory.

Still, the play of possibilities for language learning in print and educational institutions has served to accentuate the authoritative lineage of linguistic and cultural knowledge to today's elders via oral tradition, even as it has construed them as authoritative sources of linguistic and cultural repertoire. If Ojibwe has not become wholly a liturgical language, its use by elders has accrued accentuated meanings we might recognize as sacred, in contrast to the sometimes felt profanation of other media.

SACRALIZATION OF LANGUAGE, TRADITION, AND THE PRIESTLY VOCATION OF ELDERSHIP

Amid these circumstances, persisting practices of "honoring elders" carry new valences of resistance, agency, and urgency. It follows that eldership becomes an even more distinctly religious role. In a word, my argument is that tradition and culture have become reified and more sacralized precisely because they were so interrupted and potentially threatened with oblivion, that the Ojibwe language has gone from being an everyday language to an everyday language that is also a *holy* language, and that elders who still speak it, even some of it, and who are esteemed by virtue of their access to these traditions have become something like "priests."

If today's elders, distinguished as they are in terms of this access to oral tradition and language fluency, have grown into a sort of priestly role. I mean this not in narrow Weberian terms of the restricted access to priestly authority based on exclusions by gender, ethnicity, learning, or even in strict terms of age, since age alone does not indicate access to this linguistic and cultural knowledge. In fact, I wish to suggest that priestly authority of eldership marks a kind of democratization of religious authority over time. In prereservation years, medicine people, men and women, distinguished by degree in the Midéwiwin, or by the dream authority/power tangible in the healing and divination arts of the *jiisakii* shaking tent or *nanaandawi'iwe* doctoring traditions, were recognized for their commerce with the spiritual world. At least in the context of the shaking tent tradition, effective *jiisakiiwininiwag* demonstrated their ability to "talk supernatural" *manidookaazo*, to interact on behalf of ordinary Anishinaabe with the spirits. This fashion of religious specialty, broadly denominated "shamanism" and directly so in John Grim's work, continues in certain pockets of Anishinaabe life today, but certainly with less frequency.

At White Earth today, for example, Joe Bush is the most prominent and respected "spiritual elder" who is called, along with the distinguished pipe he carries, to confer names, perform "weddings," preside over wakes and funerals, offer invocations for powwows and community meetings, or sanctify important passages in the life of the community. "I travel wherever I'm wanted," he told a reporter. "I'm trying to get people to look at themselves, be proud of who they are and where they're going."[62]

It is clear, particularly in the funeral moments when White Earth people most often encounter his spiritual work, that Joe Bush (whose given name, though almost never used, is George Fairbanks) carries on with the bearing and authority and linguistic competence, as well as the compassionate, pastoral presence that is characteristic of the most highly esteemed elder. He is distinguished by his association with Jimmy Jackson, a storied spiritual leader who gave Joe Bush his pipe. In his own words:

> Jimmy was getting on in years and asked me to carry on for him. He handed me this pipe and said, "You're going to do a lot of helping and healing with this pipe." The medicine man gets his powers, his medicines from the creator. I'm a spiritual elder, a helper with the medicines. I get my

powers from this pipe. It has taught me that anything you really need you can get from Mother Earth.[63]

Today, elders with the specialized knowledge and training of Joe Bush are key presences in the lives of Native communities, perhaps increasing in esteem because decreasing in numbers. But if numbers of such traditional spiritual leaders have declined, another dynamic has emerged that is significant to appreciating the force of contemporary eldership. In the context of language loss, language proficiency itself can distinguish an elder woman or man as one worthy of going between the spiritual and ordinary world, in a manner consistent with previous generations' distinction of dream power. When elder men and women are called on to offer an invocation before a graduation, feast, powwow, or health center dedication, they are called on at least in part because they speak a language that the spirits can comprehend.

One can justly argue that a public address or prayer in the Ojibwe language on the part of an elder whose authority is recognized as being consistent with the oral tradition provides a functional equivalent to yesterday's *manidookaazowin* ("talking supernatural"). If such utterances are less specific to the ritual spaces and times effected in the shaking tent or in the Midéwiwin, and more specific to invocations and blessings that begin or end community events that one might not recognize as conventionally ceremonial, their very occurrence suggests the importance of framing ordinary community events in the context of Ojibwe language, tradition, and spirituality and can take on a life of their own that suggests their urgency. Recall, for example, Archie Mosay's invocation for the community meeting with Senator Paul Wellstone described in the introduction. Mosay stood and uttered his lengthy invocation in a rapid cadence, high register, and garbled manner that would have gone unrecognized by most of those in attendance—even those who could understand spoken Ojibwe. Judging from the respect maintained by Native people in the gym, it was clearly enough that Mosay was praying on their behalf in a language and idiom recognizable to the spirits.

If eldership has accrued a more demonstratively priestly role in such moments, there was ample precedent in tradition for elders functioning as general intercessors. Peter Jones noted that the Ojibwe of his early-nineteenth-century southern Ontario boyhood "have no regularly appointed

White Earth pipe carrier and spiritual leader Joe Bush is frequently asked to conduct funerals, give invocations at powwows and other community events, and offer various ceremonial blessings. Here, he offers a prayer at the release of sturgeon fingerlings in the Wild Rice River during a 2008 sturgeon restoration project. *Courtesy Judy Olansen*

priests among them. The powwows, conjurors, and gifted speakers, act for them, as any ambitious Indian, by cultivating the talent of public speaking, may become the mouthpiece of his ... brethren." He noted, for example, that at a feast of offering for first game, "an aged man, previously engaged, offers up a prayer, consisting of vain repetition," and made several references elsewhere to some "old man" who prays on behalf of people.[64]

But "old man" in Jones's 1861 parlance probably made reference to an *akiwenzii* who was thus distinguished by exceptional shamanic dream power. Thus it was perhaps Shaydayence's shamanic power, connected with his former leadership of the Midéwiwin at Gull Lake before removal, conversion, and becoming a "spiritual elder" among the White Earth "Episcopalian" Anami'aajig. Shaydayence's speech commanded audiences, but clearly it was also regarded as particularly effectual. In missionary accounts of this elder, the language used is that of intercession. Shaydayence was hailed as having taken prayer extremely seriously. Shaydayence's healing practice rested on the esteem given him as one who prays over the sick; and his whole life as a Christian seemed to involve conspicuous acts of intercessory prayer. "This only I think and desire," Shaydayence dictated in a thank you letter to a supporter in the East, "oh that I may be permitted to live all winter to intercede for [you], that is what I think. I believe in intercession, and so that is what I have set before me if I am spared this winter. Always I shall intercede for you and your husband."[65]

A century later still, such an *akiwenzii* or *mindimooyenh* would surely refer as well to someone esteemed for their moral uprightness, but would more likely characterize such an elder with the requisite linguistic fluency characteristic of her or his age-set. And the social position of old age, newly configured under these circumstances, has put elders at the forefront of efforts to reclaim Anishinaabe traditions of language, culture, and religion.

ELDERS AND THE REKINDLING OF TRADITION

While elders have always been viewed as custodians of tradition, a conscious attempt to rekindle it relies on today's elders in historically specific ways. Reflecting on his mortality, Lac du Flambeau elder and language teacher Joe Chosa says: "I feel a kind of urgency in myself. I'd hoped more people would carry on our language. We're reaching that stage now where people are interested enough they're going to want to carry it on. Do you realize how many people we have on the reservation that can talk the language; how few there are?"[66] Although they speak the language with varying degrees of proficiency, today's elders grew up listening to their grandparents speaking Ojibwe as a living language. They recall, to varying degrees, the sequences of ceremonies, the tunes of dream songs, the uses of plants in healing. What is more, since these elders have had to rely on their own resourcefulness to survive boarding schools, racism, and shifting winds of Indian policy through the turbulent twentieth century, they know how to move well within the racism, poverty, and bureaucracies that structure lives on reservations like White Earth and in urban ghettos.

Such people swiftly became key figures for the conscious return to tradition led by the Indian power movement in the 1970s, which was fueled in large part by the zeal of younger Anishinaabe who were hindered from access to tradition by urban, in some cases, adoptive, upbringings and mediated through the politicized intensity of the American Indian Movement in Minneapolis (AIM). Clyde Bellecourt, a cofounder of AIM, underwent a kind of conversion experience to a profound sense of Anishinaabe identity in the Stillwater, Minnesota, prison when Edward Benton-Banai tried to minister to him during a hunger strike with books about Anishinaabe traditions.[67] As AIM gained momentum through actions protesting police brutality, treaty violations, and other ills borne by Native people and became the public face of the resurgence of tradition among the Anishinaabeg and other Native people, its young leaders actively sought out for direction, and indeed emboldened, older Anishinaabe people who had endured the assimilating experiences of boarding school, military service, and relocation programs to cities.[68]

That's how I understand the moment in historical and sociological terms; in the idiom of Anishinaabe teachings, particularly the Seven Fires Prophecy, the period from the 1970s to the contemporary day marks the watershed where, after several generations of oppression, younger Anishinaabeg must turn away from the seductions of the present day to elders and to traditions and, importantly, where elders who had "fallen asleep" to the urgency of their vocation must "wake up" and teach traditions and values. Waking up to tradition is an apt image here; it is a rekindling of something there all along but a rekindling that takes place in a new day all the same. That new day is characterized by a dramatic differentiation of an integrated Anishinaabe way of life into religion, politics, and economics that came with the territory of linguistic, cultural, and economic incorporation into dominant North American society. But the zealous call to wake up to tradition is at least in part a gesture to reintegrate the lifeway (we don't have a religion, we have a way of life) and to consciously privilege the authority of elders, not ethnographies, about what tradition has been and can be for the moment.[69]

Theresa Smith noted how the authority of eldership became accentuated at Manitoulin Island as an alternative to thorough assimilation into Euro-American culture, society, and economy:

> Elders have status, prestige, and power. Joseph Cahill suggests that the current cultural/religious renaissance found among various North American tribes is borne out of a conflict between "two symbolic systems." In their effort to resolve this conflict, Amerindians have turned toward a source of authority—the tribal Elders, who are understood to be keepers of wisdom and tradition. Neglected in recent years, these people are now being sought out both individually and under the leadership of various band councils. Elders conferences are held regularly, usually at the instigation of younger members of a group.[70]

Indeed this historical moment has breathed new life into intergenerational complementarity and also marked it in new ways. To Jeffrey Anderson, late-twentieth-century circumstances among Wyoming's Northern Arapaho generate something of a contradiction: "To adapt and revitalize traditions, the tribe has allowed younger people more frequent participation and greater access to knowledge and authority once reserved for older age groups . . . concurrently, adaptations and collectivizations of ceremonies has proposed competing definitions for doing things in a good/correct way that are divided at times along generational lines." Where "one side defends practices needed on the basis of expediency, . . . another presses for the old ways of doing things."[71]

OVERT SACRALIZATION OF ELDERSHIP

AIM and similar grassroots neotraditionalist efforts could train the public attention that followed them on elders in new and strategic ways that framed those elders' utterances and privileged them even while the elders were being mobilized as symbols of legitimacy and tradition. Doubtless such elders knew what they were doing in granting their presence, but the strategic nature of the appeals to elders and elders' circles played chords with new resonances.

Larry Nesper's study of contested notions of community, leadership, and identity among northern Wisconsin Ojibwe during the spear-fishing protests in the late 1980s attends to how dramatic appeals to the authority of elders had become part of a traditionalist strategy. The Wa-Swa-Gon Treaty Association distinguished itself from elected Lac du Flambeau tribal leadership through its opposition to "accommodating the state's interests through leasing off-reservation subsistence rights," but also in its orientation to "consensual democracy and egalitarianism" and traditionalist efforts to, among other things, "preserve our native heritage" and "provide for elderly, children, and shut ins."[72] The Wa-Swa-Gon Treaty Association, Nesper added, "also drew upon historical modes of recruitment by attempting to win the support of elders through feasts and gifts of fish and game. In so doing the group grounded its politics in the authority of tradition by displaying its respect for community elders, who are still valued on the reservation."[73]

This respect was conspicuous—even staged—at a May 1989 rally drawing many Indian organizations, including AIM, and non-Indian supporters to encourage those Lac du Flambeau members spearing fish in a bold assertion of their treaty rights. Edward Benton-Banai, who had become the "spiritual leader" of the movement, had arranged a liturgical space in a community gym. Nesper remembered:

> Drawing attention to his Indian features, Benton-Banai began by introducing himself as Burt Reynolds, to the mild amusement of those gathered. He asked the elders of the community to come close and sit nearby on chairs being set in an arc around the altar. Pipe carriers were then invited to stand behind the elders. Treating the elders with honor and recognizing their knowledge and experience signaled Benton-Banai's cultural credibility to the audience.[74]

In many such moments, conspicuous honoring of elders has become a highly symbolic way of being traditional in the contemporary era. But the place of eldership can be more complicated than even Nesper's astute analysis suggests. I turn now to a movement not unlike the Wa-Swa-Gon Treaty Association with which I was involved at White Earth. This 1992 movement was known as Camp Justice, for the encampment outside tribal headquarters that resulted in three rounds of civil disobedience arrests and that lasted more than seven months. Arguing from "traditional" Anishinaabe values, Camp Justice challenged the values and positions of the tribal government, particularly alleged government secrecy, cronyism, and embezzlement surrounding the creation of the tribe's casino. Like the Wa-Swa-Gon movement, the place of elders in its work was conspicuous, but also quite substantive in important if subtle ways.

IMPLICIT SACRALIZATION OF ELDERSHIP:
OJIBWE SINGERS AND CAMP JUSTICE

The story of these dozen or so elders doesn't start, though, with the public framing of their authority at Camp Justice, when I first came to know them. It starts earlier, with their formation as a circle of elders through their work as "Ojibwe Singers," their term for a group that sang Ojibwe-language hymns in highly ritualized ways. Indeed, as I came to know them, their example occasioned this book project, for from having been rather unremarkable people, they became elders in the process of their hymn-singing.

Since the core group of White Earth singers were in their 60s and 70s, they were members of a generation spanning a major transition in Ojibwe history. Most of them grew up in Ojibwe-speaking households, or at least grew up hearing people who spoke Ojibwe first and English only incidentally. These elders were raised with a strong sense of distinctive Anishinaabe values and a good command of Anishinaabe oral wisdom for how to make a living on the seasonal round. At least one of the singers remembered a grandparent who had been born at Gull Lake and had moved to White Earth with the first generation.[75]

And yet born in the 1920s and 1930s and coming of age in the 1940s, these elders were of a generation whose assimilation to American social norms had been encouraged to an unprecedented degree. The women attended either St. Mary's Catholic school or the government boarding school. Military service in the 1940s and massive federal relocation programs of the 1950s brought several of the men singers to seek work in the cities and on the railroads and lumber camps far away from White Earth.

I know of no White Earth singer who had not had to struggle to survive, to keep his or her children fed and household healthy and safe. Survival had meant traveling long distance for work; it had also depended on resourcefulness in living off the land at White Earth: ricing, sugaring, berrying, canning, and gardening. It had meant seasonal work: doing hard manual labor of farm work or lumbering, picking up seasonal jobs thrashing wheat or picking sugar beets on the plains to the west. It had meant setting and checking trap lines to earn some extra cash selling muskrat pelts. It had meant long hours in the wild rice fields, or berrying, or hunting deer and ducks. Survival had depended on one's willingness to share what one had when others were in need and being able to call on others in moments of one's own family's need. Survival had meant providing the stability to hold households together against the fracturing forces of dispossession, alcohol, domestic violence, and poverty.

It would be a stretch to call these elders spiritual leaders, as they surely would not have referred to themselves as such; those distinctions are for particularly influential pipe-carriers or drum-carriers or those degreed with Midéwiwin credentials. But it is thoroughly reasonable to claim the special status they came to have as the moral, spiritual, and often economic and physical backbone for extended families and for wider circles of the White Earth community, not the least of which was Camp Justice.

It began in 1983, in the basement of St. Columba's Episcopal Church, where up to seventeen people then in their 50s and 60s assembled each Thursday night to sing hymns. Not just to sing hymns, of course, but to sing them in the Ojibwe language, according to a ritualized practice that they all remembered as being traditional at White Earth. After decades of English-only education and widespread relocation to cities for jobs, a hundred-year-old tradition of singing these hymns all night long at funeral wakes had burned down to an ember or two, but with the help of a "lead singer" from a neighboring reservation, a cassette recording of the songs, and well-worn hymnals (with the phonetic words in Ojibwe), these people brought the practice back.

The singers didn't take themselves nearly as seriously as this discussion does, and their Thursday night meetings were filled with laughter, coffee,

Marge McDonald, one of the elders who joined the White Earth Ojibwe Singers, being arrested for a July 1992 Camp Justice civil disobedience action in an occupation of the tribal headquarters. *Author photo*

and hearty potluck dishes, but they were resolved nonetheless to do some important cultural work. These singers were rising to fill what they saw as a vacuum of traditional leadership in White Earth Village, a vacuum that went unaddressed by a tribal government that they viewed as having lost traditional Anishinaabe ethics of placing community good over private gain, a vacuum that was registering itself in an alarming number of funerals mourning victims of violent and untimely deaths.

By the time I met them eight years later, White Earth's Ojibwe Singers had become something of a fixture in nearly every community occasion of mourning and had brought a ministry of healing to wakes—highly charged events in a community that rued how often the old were burying the young. They did so through their music, sung so slowly as to resemble chants or laments rather than hymnody. They did so through the formal addresses that they made during the silent pauses between hymns, where they would fold the particulars of mourning a particular youngster into larger questions of resolve to keep surviving as a community. But they also did so merely in their presence as recognized elders, singing/praying on behalf of their community in the original language. For their music making was intricately related to an honorable way of life expected of them according to Ojibwe idioms of music-making and eldership.

Elsewhere, I have already treated their making as elders in and through the practice of funerary hymn-singing.[76] Here, I want to shift attention to their exercise of eldership in the context of Camp Justice. Because of their singing, the Ojibwe Singers had become a de facto elders' circle in the community, their determined, if gentle, leadership coalescing wider circles of White Earth people concerned about a tribal government that they believed had compromised sovereign Anishinaabe ways of valuing community, people, and land in its calibration to the ways of dominant American society. The result had been a raging, bitter factionalism on the reservation, together with dramatic inequities between haves and have-nots. Their work of funerary singing brought them to public prominence when the grim realities of violence, suicide, or alcohol-related deaths struck close to home.

Camp Justice became news statewide as three large civil disobedience actions dramatized how some Indians were calling for a federal investigation into their own tribal government and its casino plans. Fully one third of those arrested were not angry young people but elders, comporting themselves with the gravity and respectability becoming their station. But the local issues were less obviously political, and the healing that began in and around Camp Justice was less directly tied to demonstrable political gains.

Camp Justice itself was constituted as a kind of daring assertion of Anishinaabe community right in front of a tribal headquarters that was criticized for its loss of Anishinaabe values. It was a protest camp to be sure: press releases were written, civil disobedience actions planned, pro bono lawyers consulted, elected officials summoned. But the camp explicitly tried to calibrate its political work to Anishinaabe time and Anishinaabe ways of valuing land and community. Crucially, this involved placing the visions and tactics of political change firmly on a spiritual footing, treasuring elders and their authority, and trying to bring healing through the process of Camp Justice itself, and not simply the product or fruit of its political activity.

At opposite ends of the camp were two fires, one for cooking, the other ceremonial. The cooking fire was the primary gathering place, and people were always fed somehow. Some came to the camp not to protest, but just to eat, but nothing dishonorable was inferred thereby, for in Anishinaabe community, everyone's needs are to be met. The ceremonial fire was the site of quiet reflection and the offering of prayers made visible with cedar and tobacco pinches. Pipe ceremonies were held regularly around the fire, the pipe-keeper lighting his prayer-laden tobacco with an ember from it. Atop it was an ironwood arbor and boughs of quaking aspens that made a continuous and eerie rustling noise as the rising heat animated the dried leaves. The ceremonial fire burned continuously well into the next winter, maintained by vigilant fire-keepers who protected it from thundershowers and snowstorms with an old pickup hood from "Toad" Bellanger's salvage yard on the other side of the knoll.

With time, Larry Cloud Morgan became recognized as a kind of spiritual leader for the movement, called upon to conduct pipe ceremonies, pray in Ojibwe, address the camp to remind it of the spiritual context that placed its actions in a long history of Anishinaabe people standing up for the land and summoned to mediate the more difficult tensions within the group. It was indeed largely in and through Camp Justice that Larry (then in his mid-50s) became an elder, assuming the carriage and bearing befitting eldership and using the measured speech of a contemplative, more poetry than prose.

People gathered with coffee cups around the picnic table or around the ceremonial fire to speak about old ways, ceremonies, recent dreams. The Ojibwe language was at home in the camp in a way that it did not seem to be within the tribal headquarters or the casino or other public spaces on the reservation. Elders conversed with one another in Ojibwe; those who did not speak the language fluently made a practice of listening and exercising a bit of sovereignty on their English by seasoning it with important Ojibwe terms like *Anishinaabe, miigwech* ("thank you"), *akiing* ("land"), *ogimaa,* and *niijii* ("adoptive cousin" or "comrade"). As with well-timed appeals to Yiddish terms that fit certain situations like a glove, these Ojibwe words could bring warm chuckles.

It was in the context of such discussions that political visions were forged. People did not content themselves with just "throwing the crooks out" but tried to rethink the official constitution of the tribe in terms of Anishinaabe idioms of community, land, and authority. Among the specific concerns was how elders of the community, hereditary chiefs, and the clan system would be integrated into the decision-making processes established by a revised constitution.

At its height, the camp commanded fifty or sixty people living in tents and tipis, with another two hundred people attending the evening meetings, each of which began with Ojibwe-language prayers and a pipe ceremony or Ojibwe hymn-singing. After all were fed and the prayers uttered, a circle gathered to hear the movement's leaders' update on the day's progress. The three leaders of the movement brought together three or four different constituencies loyal and supportive of them, different villages, and different angry groups in a fragile coalition.

It was precisely because of the sanction of community elders that the Camp Justice coalition could form in the first place across the tense factional lines at White Earth. The presence of elders in the arrests, around the cooking fire, and on their lawn chairs in the meeting circle conferred an imprimatur that made this effort much more effective than the scattered protests of previous years, which were regarded as being driven by frustration or the ambitions of leaders seeking personal gain. Camp Justice earned the confidence of a critical mass of people who came out of the woodwork to join at risk of losing reputations, jobs, and even family loyalties.

The elders' authority was inconspicuous in the daily activities and meetings of the camp, but it was no less understood by all to be the binding force. The singers were more typically quiet, attentive, watching the leaders and goings-on with care and gravity, ensuring that this effort would remain nonviolent, reliably rooted in a concern for the common good, and free of alcohol or drugs, ever a danger among poor, frustrated, and disenfranchised people like many supporting Camp Justice. No doubt out of respect for the circle that the elders honored, the camp remained clean. If someone had been drinking, even with clouded judgment they found it within themselves to steer clear of Camp Justice. More surprising were the Camp Justice participants who credited the camp and all it represented as an occasion to dry out or to assert pride in their identity. In the Camp Justice circle, grown men cried like babies in sweat lodges and recommitted themselves to lives of Anishinaabe responsibility toward community, tradition, and land. Some whose public voices had been effectively silenced stood proudly to speak on behalf of their people and the land.

For the rest of that year, Camp Justice continued to nourish a beleaguered community with its vision of rekindled Anishinaabe community. Shortly thereafter, a long-sought federal investigation brought convictions on corruption charges and imprisonment for three of the four tribal officials. A reform government was elected and, several configurations and many disappointments later, still shows signs of promise: cleaning up financial wrongs, conducting public business in the clear light of day, and seeking to rewrite the tribal constitution to institutionalize reform. But many of the old fracture lines that Camp Justice had brought together are active again, and two successive chairmen who had been among Camp Justice's spokespersons have been voted out apparently for replicating the very wrongs they saw in the previous regime.

And yet the tangible sense of agency that Camp Justice planted continues today to root and grow in its participants, remaining a kind of yardstick to gauge the effectiveness of subsequent efforts to put Anishinaabe community more fully into practice. This has certainly been the case among those elders still living, who continue to exercise their prerogative to lead the community and lead vital and proud lives despite the difficulties of aging. But even larger circles of Camp Justice members, even those at political loggerheads today, refer to the power generated through the camp's assertion of Anishinaabe community.

SACRALIZATION OF TRADITION DOES NOT
MEAN ITS FOLKLORIZATION

The way that Camp Justice elders did their work of memory, through their hymn-singing and through their political activity as well, did more than serve as an emblem of a particular view of tradition, for their work brought to bear a moral presence and a notion of traditionalism that defies any boundaries of emblem or folklorization. In *Ojibwe Singers*, I described the place of their hymn-singing at funeral wakes as work of cultural criticism against those who would identify with tradition everything that predates the colonization. Their resource in this was a kind of "memory" in the sense that French sociologist Michel de Certeau has used the term. For Certeau, the memory of oral traditions of dominated peoples can constitute a kind of "antimuseum" rife with possibilities for resisting the stereotypical representations of folklorization. Certeau's "memory" "is in decay when it is no longer capable of its alteration.... It constructs itself from events that are independent of it, and it is limited to the expectation that something alien to the present will or must occur. Far from being the reliquary or trash can of the past, it sustains itself by *believing* in the existence of possibilities and by vigilantly awaiting them, constantly on the watch for their appearance."[77]

That the bringing together of Ojibwe and Christian traditions into a seamless ethical and communal whole was part of these elders' memory work at Camp Justice is an indicator of the way their eldership took shape. Lisa Philips Valentine found something similar in eldership at Lynx Lake in northern Ontario. Anapat, an elder whom Valentine depicts as integrating Anglican Christianity and the Ojibwe way through seamless integration of the repertories in her storytelling, is the source of an Ojibwe phrase *Anohkaatamok kaa-ishi-nantawentamek weti niikaan* ("work to create the future you want"), which became a slogan for an airline advertisement, a business venture of the Lynx Lake Band trying to control technology for its own benefit. "The attitude which Anapat so eloquently summarized," Valentine writes, "was precisely that which I found in Lynx Lake: the future begins now; one must work to create the future that is wanted. These people *are* creating their own futures by making considered decisions about the importation of technology and ideas.... These changes continue in the lives of the Lynx Lake community, but these are changes that arise out of a solid understanding of what it means to be and live as an *Anishininiwak*. They are making the future their own."[78]

Valentine contrasts such a view with an article written in a Native newspaper by a "younger person who called for a combination of Christian and Native religions." Valentine contrasts this folklorization of ethnicity with that determined by local structures of religious and cultural authority, where "to be Anglican in Lynx Lake is to be a Native, and to be a Native is to be Anglican."[79]

> Here a young man (or perhaps a group of young adults) is turning to sources outside the home community to define identity. The focus among anthropologists and others on studying the "traditional" elements of Native religions has led to a situation in which "Native" aspects of religion are defined as essentially, "not white." Using such an external standard which insists that "Christianity cannot be Native," those Natives who adopt

Christianity as their primary religious affiliation are categorized as enculturated at best and deluded at worst. The external observers look to what they consider a more pristine religious state and declare that any memory of such activities indicates that this is the "true religion" for the Native people.[80]

Now, to be sure, Valentine does not draw this line in terms of a contrast in the authority of eldership and the authority of external articulations of culture, but she does point out that a folklorization of ethnicity emerges from Lynx Lake communications with other Native communities to the south "who have had their ethnic identities threatened" and who, in their understandable resistance against centuries-old policies of subjugation, have "inadvertently begun to plant seeds of ethnic insecurity among younger, more mobile sectors of the Severn Ojibwe community." "The tension between being Anglican and being Native seems to be a problem only for the youth."[81]

ELDERSHIP AND PRINT TECHNOLOGIES

If oral traditional memory as antimuseum can characterize the work of contemporary elders, I should also mention a number of contemporary elders whose public authority has been amplified by their writing in print media. One could even call them "superelders" to distinguish the reach of their authority beyond individual reservation or urban communities.[82] Unlike the ethnographic imagination of most non-Native writers, however, these elders' writing and oratory bespeak a form of memory more in keeping with that of the Camp Justice elders than with Densmore or Hallowell.

Basil Johnston is notable in this regard. The Ontario Ojibwe educator and author's many book titles include *Ojibway Ceremonies* and *Ojibway Myths*, but their style is decidedly narrative, as much a kind of ethnographic fiction—playful even—as it is disciplined documentation or analysis. From these books it is difficult to emerge with a definitive sense that Ojibwe tradition dictates this or that; instead one reads stories that bear the intimate feel—but in some respects also the distance—of a fluid oral delivery fixed in print. The published newspaper columns, volumes, recordings, and live performances of Minnesota activist and storyteller

Anne Dunn carry a similar authority—one that doesn't claim ultimate knowledge of Ojibwe language but rather, as one of her poem titles suggests, an eclectic assemblage of materials of various provenances caught in windswept "uncombed hair." The political and philosophical ruminations of one-time long-haul truck driver and Red Lake elder Wub-e-ke-niew (aka Frances Blake) similarly bear the imprint of a sovereign mind, even as they engage linguistics and political philosophy from the sovereignty of an "Ahnishinahbaeotjibway" perspective.[83] A similar edge—at once humorous and profoundly sincere—characterized White Earth elder Maynard Swan's *Ojibwe News* column in the 1990s. Jim Northrup's column, *Fond du Lac Follies*, similarly reaches wide circles who regard it as a kind of humorous wisdom from a self-described "apprentice elder."

In addition to these particular elders whose commentary in print (and recently on the internet) as newspaper columnists or writers has augmented the reach of their authority as elders, there are also a number of notable oral history projects in print and on the internet that document the stories, teachings, and perspectives of a broader range of respected elders, carry them to wider audiences, and establish their authority in between the authorship of literacy and the immediacy of the oral narrative. Indeed the current study has relied greatly on the transcripts and translations of oral history projects collected and edited in the past decade by Anton Treuer, Elizabeth Tornes, John Nichols, Vance Vannote, and Jennifer S. H. Brown, among others.[84] Though these documented oral narrative resources frequently work against the linear elaboration typical of print, and while easily accessible audio recordings enable the student to encounter the voice and person of the elder, not just their words flattened to a translated transcript, their very accessibility removes the elders' knowledge from the relational context of a student-teacher relation so important, as we have seen, to traditional Anishinaabe eldership, though to be sure, these elders mostly related their narratives to microphones held by family members or trusted students.

IMPLICATIONS: THE SACRED, THE SECRET, AND THE UNIVERSAL

That their words ultimately might be used in unauthorized ways clearly did not go unnoticed by the astute elders who committed their time and wisdom to the tape recorder in these projects. Most oral history projects require informed consent through signatures on legal releases. And clearly controversy and disagreement have arisen in discussions among elder leaders about the risks and worth of such projects, akin to the discussions about teaching Anishinaabe languages through linguistics and technology.

Cecilia Defoe related in the project *Memories of Lac Du Flambeau Elders* how the reticence of elders of her generation owed to a mistrust borne of years' experience in boarding schools and other highly regulated environments where shared cultural knowledge could be used against them: "What you learned, the teaching—you keep that to yourself. And when you get to be a woman, you teach only your family. You don't go out telling everybody. That's why a lot of people when they go around, they don't say anything. You're supposed to save the culture." Still she was persuaded when Joe Chosa approached her and fellow elder Reva Chapman and said: "You know, if you don't tell everything, there's things if you don't want to tell, its too sacred, you just keep it in your family. But there's some things you have to tell because who's going to know after we're gone."[85] In the end, Defoe joined her fellow elders in a variety of efforts to extend their knowledge to wider circles within Lac du Flambeau and in other Ojibwe communities and, indeed, inevitably, beyond Anishinaabe circles to any curious reader.

Others, like Edward Benton-Banai, appear less concerned with misuse of their knowledge by unauthorized readers than they do with the precarious state of a world out of balance.[86] This may be more characteristic of Native elders functioning in urban centers and away from the close quarters, guarded secrets, and highly local contexts of reservation communities. "It is time," he writes, "to talk with our Brothers and Sisters of other nations, colors and beliefs. The ideas and philosophies of yesterday may be the key to the world family's future."[87]

Still, other elders have remained reticent, even guarded, concerning the sharing of knowledge outside circles of family and long-established relationships of trust with sincere students. In my experience, what Defoe enunciated as a concern is the rule, not the exception, at places like White Earth. There are no small number of non-Native seekers of the New Age or related movements soliciting information for purposes that do not have the well-being of Anishinaabe communities as their first concern.

Here again, the primary orality of the Anishinaabe tradition has secured a certain prestige for the religious and cultural authority of elders who can choose, or not, to relate their knowledge depending on the circumstances and intentions of the student. And that prestige, though local, can still be maintained precisely by not participating in such projects that commit knowledge to posterity through technologies of print, recording, publishing, and the internet.

By contrast, the authority and stature gained by engaging such technologies in order to prevent cultural extinction can involve a sea change in the structure of the indigenous tradition, as Paul Johnson has ably shown in the context of the transformation of Afro-Brazilian Candomblé, traditionally an initiatory ritual complex that hinged on secretism, on the power and prestige of those adepts reputed to hold secretive knowledge.[88] Johnson's work joins others in noting the "more than etymological" relationship between the secret and the sacred, both in a Durkheimian sense relying for their power on a relational opposition from the profane, or the public, the known. Following Johnson's analysis, secretism can be distinguished from other secret-society materials in terms of its being a strategic, conscious promotion and circulation of the "reputation of secrets." In the case of the African-derived New World religion of Candomblé, secretism emerges as a strategy especially as the workings of public religions in the modern nation-state and the desiring eyes of the metropolis threaten the loss of control of culture and tradition. What remains secret gains purchase the more it is threatened with open knowledge, appropriation, and the like. Again, though Johnson goes little further than suggesting the secret is "rather like" the sacred in this Durkheimian sense, in this case we can see a clear correspondence between the sacralization of tradition and an Anishinaabe secretization of oral traditional knowledge vis-à-vis the accessible knowledge of print and electronic media and the searching gaze of New Age seekers of Native American spirituality.

At the same time, the extension of their reach that some key elders feel is necessary to preserve their languages, practices, traditions, and landscapes, or that others feel is necessary to the continued survival of the human race on planet earth, extend the matters of Anishinaabe religion from the local to the universal in ways that are similar to the process that Johnson observes in the recent history of Candomblé in Brazil and in a Brazilian diaspora.

ENCIRCLEMENT: PAN-INDIAN ELDERSHIP AND ELDER COUNCILS

As print media amplified the reach if not the authority of certain key superelders and extended the authority of others beyond family networks, newly created institutional niches have provided certain chosen or appointed elders a new platform from which to teach and advise their communities. While drawing on continuous traditions of authority, eldership in the late twentieth century also began to take new corporate forms, less a function of the authority of particular elders than on an age-set organized as members of organizations that assumed traditional roles of eldership but through more bureaucratic means. To be sure, the organizations to which I refer are movements more than bureaucracies proper. By and large they involve no paid staff members and are really occasional gatherings of particular elders. But the organizations together cohere around the spiritual vocation of the elder more than around other functions. While reservation communities frequently have circles of elders who are convened on occasion to share food, knowledge, and the like, the groups of which I am speaking here are organizations or councils formed for the express purpose of giving guidance to Native communities that is considered "spiritual" in nature.

The National Indian Council on Aging sponsored a gathering of hundreds of "spiritual Elders" (note both "spiritual" and the capitalization of Elder) who convened for ten days at Nambe Pueblo in New Mexico in 1998 "to discuss problems facing the world community and especially Indian Peoples." The leadership made clear it was "not a political organization. 'We are a spiritual entity, working on a spiritual cure for the illness and violence, which has been inflicted on our Mother Earth, our cultures and our peoples for the last five hundred years.'"[89] When the same event convened in Duluth, Minnesota, in 2000, it consisted of more than one thousand elders from 105 different tribes and produced a "spiritual message from our elders" that they asked to be widely circulated to Native and non-Native people alike.[90] I include the declaration in its entirety to show the texture of this new form of eldership.

SPIRITUAL MESSAGE FROM OUR ELDERS

As we stand before the dawn of a new millennium, we pray for America's survival, our survival.

We pray that we will be given strength by the Creator to follow the footsteps of our forefathers to share our love, respect and compassion for one another. There is good in everyone because our Creator has put a little of Himself in all of us.

We pray for forgiveness for the pain and suffering we have caused one another.

We pray that our children will not repeat our mistakes.

We pray that we can respect the diversity of America; all life is sacred. Every child born is a precious gift of our Creator. It is our sacred trust to embrace children from all walks of life because we are part of the same family.

We pray that children will honor and respect their elders—that is where the wisdom comes from. This respect will not allow forgotten elders. We are all equal, with each having our own special gift to contribute. These values allow our youth to become leaders and workers in our society. Children, you are our future and our hope for the people. Stand and be courageous.

We pray to learn and use the wisdom of all that has come before us, to achieve personal successes and to contribute to those of others. Only when our young ones learn respect for everything can they evolve.

EARTH

We pray for respect and love of Mother Earth because she is the foundation of human survival and we must keep her pollution-free for those who will travel after us. Protect her water, air, soil, trees, forests, plants and animals.

Do not just take and waste resources. Make it a priority to conserve.

The land is given to us by the Creator to care for, not to own. If we take care of the land, the land will take care of us.

UNITY

We should have respect for each other. We pray for commitment and responsible behavior in order to help those in need and to give them support and friendship. Be an example in life that others may follow; serve people, community and country.

We should all strive to be leaders and contributors. Do not sit back and let others plan and do all the thinking.

Let us unite together so that we may have the strength to protect our future. Strength comes from working through trials and tribulations.

HEALTH

Spiritual health is the key to holistic health.

We pray to have the discipline to set healthy examples for our children to follow.

Respecting everyone and everything in the universe starts with self-respect.

Take time to listen and take care of your body and spirit.

FAMILY AND YOUTH

Family is important and precious. Always let them know that they are loved.

Let your children and grandchildren know you are always there to love and support them and that they mean the world to you no matter what they do or say. Children are of infinite value.

Live what you teach. Spiritual values, honesty, and integrity start in the home.

We pray for the youth. We must teach the youth to work together and respect all that is living on our Mother Earth.

We need to convey to our younger generations that the survival of our people lies in spirituality.

PEACE

We pray to learn ways to settle differences peacefully.

Teach respect for each other's ideas. Value honesty on all levels, from children to parents to community to governments. We will be happy when we create peace with each other.

TO THE 7TH GENERATION

- Survive
- Keep hopes and dreams

- Take care of yourself
- Remember your spirit
- Be there for each other
- Respect courage
- Share knowledge
- Always keep learning
- Remember your true values

. . .

Note the stress on the inner and spiritual well-being of younger Native people as key to physical and economic and societal success, intended as a mass-mediated spiritual direction from one entire generation to another generation.

The National Indian Council on Aging is hardly the only encirclement of elders across traditional tribal lines. Many have appeared, often assembling occasionally as resources become available to bring older people together from different Native communities. One notable and more durable gathering occurs every summer in conjunction with the emerging Native Catholic devotional movement centered on Kateri Tekakwitha, the Mohawk woman beatified by the Vatican. Annual Kateri gatherings are not formally about elders, but if the one I attended in Bemidji, Minnesota, the White Earth Ojibwe Singers is representative, this assembly could be said to be a great council gathering of intertribal elders with workshops and numerous informal conversations about spiritual matters both Catholic and indigenous. It was largely comprised of elders from around the nation, many of whom have developed relationships annually sustained across boundaries of geography and tribe. Of the people I knew in attendance, they were largely elders who were anchoring their local parishes as lay leaders.

Whither Sacralization

An open question concerning any sacralization of eldership is to what extent it bespeaks an internalization of modernity. Does its differentiation as sacred authority mean some diminishment of its social/political power?

To a degree, one must appreciate that a spiritual proclamation of an elders' council may entail prestige, but it doesn't carry the force of a tribal council action or federal policy. But the spiritual direction that most Anishinaabe elders bring to bear is hardly a matter of religion alone but about a return to an integrated way of life. Theresa Smith's field research at Manitoulin Island in the 1980s showed that "elders have in recent years, been actively turning people away from foreign value structures and back to traditional ways in an effort not only to preserve culture but to ensure the continuance of life itself."[91] The lesson sought from elders, Smith elaborates, "is how may one adopt, readopt, or simply remember the Anishinaabe tradition so that one may *bimaadiziwin* (live well) in a changed world."[92]

Indeed part of what confers this accentuated authority on today's elders is the fact of their survival to old age, not just in the classic terms of their having succeeded in living well on the land—though that may still ring true—but in the sense that they have accrued the wisdom to survive conditions and experiences that could annihilate persons without that demonstrated wisdom. Perhaps as well, the fact of this age, of the maturation of power and social position, gives rise to an integrative perspective that is increasingly treasured in an Anishinaabe community under siege.

During my initial research at White Earth in the 1990s, I encountered posthumous photocopies of a 1980s utterance by the late Mille Lacs Ojibwe elder George Aubid posted on many kitchen refrigerators:

> We do not own the land upon which we live. We do not have the basic things of life which we are told are necessary to better ourselves. We do not have the tools to be self-sufficient. But today, I want to tell you that we do not need these things what we do need, however, is what we already have. . . . We need to realize who we are and what we stand for. . . . We need to be as one again. We need to work again for the common good of all of us! We the Anishinaabeg are the human beings of this land. We are the keepers of that which the Great Spirit has given to us. . . . If it is to be destroyed, only we can do it, by turning our backs on our language, our culture, our traditional drums and our religion; then and only then do we lose because we cease to exist as Anishinaabeg. Remember what the object of the game is. Don't be enticed by their almighty dollar. Never allow them to forget the injustices. And always my friends, remember the suffering of our Anishinaabeg.[93]

For George Aubid, as for those who considered him or other contemporary figures as spiritual elders, a sacralization of eldership has not decidedly diminished the reach of their authority. If such elders have been put on a pedestal in ways that have confined them, many have successfully claimed their voice in ways that collapse any clear distinction between politics and economics on the one hand and religion and culture on the other. Clearly chapters 4 and 5 of this study are part of a continuous discussion; the wisdom recognized in the authority of eldership and the traditions for which they are recognized stewards address the very core of contemporary Anishinaabe life, not just its cultural trappings. As the next chapter will show, Anishinaabe people broadly feel that the wisdom of elders is the key to the very survival of healthy communities.

6

THE SHAPE OF WISDOM

My rule is anyone who says they are an elder isn't.

—Richard Vedan

I'm gonna live a good life, the rest of my days, I plan to do that, you know. I'm just gonna live it the way the Great Spirit wants me to live. I pray every day, I try to pray. Offer my tobacco, I pray for the kids, I pray for the people that are sick, and then I pray for myself. You know, please don't let me say anything unkind. But its hard to raise kids without saying . . . [laughs]. You've got to discipline 'em. So sometimes I just say, oh forgive me.

—Reva Chapman

 In each of the previous chapters I have endeavored to denaturalize Anishinaabe eldership, to put it into historical motion in order to see the different uses and meanings it has accrued over the years and also to claim how consistently the practices of deference and sagacity that constitute eldership have been the stuff of disciplined thought and action, of hard work. Anishinaabe tradition and Anishinaabe history show that honoring elders comes anything but naturally or easily.

In this chapter I want to ask why it has remained such an urgent priority for Anishinaabe people to continue the practices of eldership as they have become further and further integrated into a Euro-American society that does not privilege the authority of the aged. Acknowledging the importance of the historical changes I've attended to, here I want to pose questions that might apply to any moment in that history and perhaps pose questions of wider North American society today, in turn: if elders have wisdom to offer, then what is the shape of wisdom in Anishinaabe thought and practice? How might this wisdom compare and contrast with knowledge? Or more precisely, what traits distinguish the exercise of wisdom from the exercise of other knowledge forms? How is wisdom, or its exercise in what I've regarded as practices of sagacity, related to the religious?

While it seems fitting to ponder such "big" questions, I must acknowledge the artifice in the task of formulating fluid practices of eldership into transposable, translatable "ways of knowing." I should also admit how daunting is the challenge of answering them from my own social position. On Ojibwe terms, it is an audacious thing indeed for a forty-something to presume to comprehend the shape of elders' wisdom. I feel not unlike the young Ojibwe man in the 1880s who, as an ordained deacon, was directed to lead Sunday schools for his elders, only to receive the rebuff, "You are only a child; you do not know anything; I ought to teach you, instead of your setting yourself up to teach me; I have lived a long time and learned a great deal."[1] In my case, the issue is not solely one of age or maturity, and maybe not even simply an added matter of outsider and insider. The issue is the authority of different ways of knowing: the practices of argument, substantiation, and elaboration that pass muster for the award of a PhD—or a university press monograph, for that matter—as we have seen, stand in sharp contrast to the authority of eldership, and even to the authority of books crafted by Native authors recognized as elders.[2] Put another way, the wisdom exercised by eldership is credentialed in dramatically different ways than the knowledge practices I've used to illuminate it. The practices of elders' sagacity are different in shape, context, and urgency from the practices of theoretical knowledge identified by Pierre Bourdieu and others as specific to the social position of academics.

Sociologically, the shape of Ojibwe wisdom is *credentialed knowledge*. Chapter 4 identified tradition as that which elders say it is, so wisdom might be seen simply in sociological terms as knowledge that is socially recognized because its knower is socially recognized as authoritative. It ought to be added that the social recognition of an elder is always provisional, always subject to the ongoing scrutiny of a circle of elders. But on what basis, one can ask, is that scrutiny based? Here, the sociological shape of wisdom relies on the exercise of ways of knowing particular to Anishinaabe understandings of eldership but that can also perhaps provide some suggestive categories for a broader religious studies appreciation of the *elder* in other cultural and historical contexts.

After revisiting the contours of sagacity as the *practice* of wisdom, I will explore how age actually is seen by Anishinaabe people to matter in eldership's authority, considering the elder as old person. With an insistence on lifelong learning, associated with wisdom, and a particular humility that goes along with that, I will then consider the elder in her/his aspect as sage. Since much of the learning of an Anishinaabe elder makes reference not just to the content of many accrued oral traditional exchanges but perhaps more elementally to spiritual knowledge generated in and through practices of silence and contemplation, I will consider the elder in his/her aspect as seer. But Anishinaabe eldership relies upon ethical even more than mystical discipline, and so I consider the elder as moral exemplar and prophetic voice. Finally, following the cue of an Anishinaabe term that regards peppiness as a virtue, I consider the elder as a life exemplar, a model for the saucy, witty, passionate affirmation of life. Again, my purpose is not to naturalize wisdom, but to nonetheless account for Anishinaabe understandings of the wisdom befitting eldership that defies its reduction to its social constitution.

Sagacity: The Practice of Wisdom

If wisdom is credentialed knowledge, and if such credentials are constituted in a community of persons, there is an important sense in which wisdom is a practice: a performance whose worth may be judged by the community but is also a product of the mastery of gestures, postures, and ways of speaking that bespeak and perform wisdom. A Blackfeet scholar remarked that, in her language, there is even an expression that describes an elder "sitting holy."[3] As I have endeavored consistently to show throughout this book, a way of knowing commonly referred to as wisdom is not simply an intellective matter, but a practice in the fullest sense of that word: an embodied, social, situational mastery of dispositions that gives rise to particular kinds of wisdom but that cannot be reduced to the non-situational, disembodied, theoretical propositions that can be understood as knowledge.

If it makes good heuristic sense here to distinguish wisdom from knowledge, I should caution that any such weighty distinction is not indigenous to the Ojibwe language, where a cluster of concepts stemming from the root *gikend-* encompass the entire semantic field designated by both "wisdom" and "knowledge" in English (even Anishinaabe English) parlance. That said, it still makes sense to distinguish an Anishinaabe understanding of wisdom from an understanding of a conventional sense of knowledge as that which can be efficiently segmented from its context in books, lectures, and classroom exercises and "acquired" or even "produced." In fact, the unity of the Ojibwe expression suggests no opposition between experiential knowledge that matures along with the body, mind, and souls of an individual and the kind of knowledge acquired and owned by an individual.

It follows that practices of sagacity modeled by elders are not unique to the aged in biological terms: they model a discipline for conduct and relationship that is suggestively referred to in English as doing things "in a good way" and typically signaled in Ojibwe parlance by the term *weweni* ("carefully," "in a good way"). Ruth Landes described this way of proceeding in her observation of a conversation between a supplicant and an elder sponsor concerning the former's dream:

> All important communications were acknowledged slowly and stonily, with great preliminaries, interspersings, and sequences of tobacco, food and yard goods. Haste was disrespectful and irresponsible; all matters had to be pondered over and questioned, skeptically or fearfully; nothing was taken for granted or accepted on a permanent basis.[4]

In chapter 2 I identified the practices of deference that partly constitute the authority of eldership, and in chapter 4 I discussed the particular speech practices that give shape to sagacity in return. The effort has been to show how much learning and discipline has gone into the making of these virtues over the years by both older Anishinaabeg and their juniors. If such a view of eldership as constituted by practices makes sense in terms of Anishinaabe sources, it has made good interpretive sense in the ways it draws on the insights of ethicists and intellectual historians Pierre Hadot and Alasdair MacIntyre, who have sought to understand moral virtues as conjunctions of thought and practice, as cultivated mental disciplines where the knowing and the doing are mutually constructive.[5] In the social sciences, following Pierre Bourdieu and Catherine Bell, there has been emergent attention to the significant cultural work performed in and through the great embodied practices of ritual, but also in the ritualized gestures, interactions, and habits of everyday life.[6]

These intellectual currents lead to an understanding of Anishinaabe elders' wisdom not as a theoretical thing but as a disciplined play of practices. But more than some of his interpreters perhaps, Bourdieu himself recognizes that practices as such are not mere performances empty of determinative content. Here I want to refine a sense of the practice of sagacity as something more than the mere performance of the assumed postures and practices of speech discussed in chapter 4. For even in her thoroughgoing sociolinguistic analysis of authoritative speech practices among the Cree—what she calls more generically "interaction patterns"—Regna Darnell has argued for the central importance of nonlinguistic criteria for authority. "The speaking which is most highly valued," Darnell observes, "is a monologue by someone who is wise (old) enough to have something to say that is worth listening to. . . . Even in the case of the grandfathers' teachings, verbal messages are validated by accumulated experience which is largely non-verbal. The grandfather is respected for that experience rather than for his skill with the words themselves. The asymmetrical structure of the interaction, giving the grandfather great control over what is said, is a manner of preserving and reflecting upon that knowledge which makes him a man to be listened in the first place."[7]

The Age of Wisdom: Elder as Elder

Wisdom is credentialed knowledge, and its credential is recognized eldership, an elder's way of knowing. As we have seen, eldership is a function of community recognition, not merely a function of biological age. At the same time, I have observed that no Elder capital E is not also old, either biologically or in terms of performance and perspective.[8] As we did briefly in chapter 1, it will be helpful to examine the ways in which eldership is tied, on Anishinaabe terms, to the maturity of age. What does seasoned knowledge look like, knowledge that is matured with age?

First, it is useful to think of age as a function of the gathering of life experience, and this is no doubt a major source of the authority of wisdom. Lac du Flambeau elder Cecilia Defoe emphasized being good to the older people "because they came a long way, you know. They were on a long road." That credential leads directly, in Defoe's train of thought to a strong admonition: "You don't answer them back. If you want to answer them back, keep it to yourself. It's always good advice. I don't care what you say, or what anybody else says."[9] Similarly, according to White Earth Anishinaabe activist Diana Osborn-King, "We were taught to listen to our elders and to anyone who had earned the right through the wisdom of experience. . . . I have an elder whom I listen to. I may debate with her, but I always listen to what she says."[10] On Anishinaabe terms, one may disagree with an elder but may not gainsay the greater experience that one's elder brings to a discussion.

Second, it is important to acknowledge that wisdom is understood in Ojibwe myth as a *gift* whose realization is tied to the process of maturation of the aging person, rather than a mere acquisition of an adept. In its self-representation of its culture at the Smithsonian's National Museum of the American Indian, the Sagkeeng Ojibwe community regards *wisdom* as one of seven cardinal gifts of seven spirit grandfathers. Wisdom takes its place beside (and thus distinguishable from as well as correlative to) love, respect, courage, honesty, humility, and truth.

In Edward Benton-Banai's Wisconsin Ojibwe version of the same sacred narrative of the gifting of the seven virtues, "The Seven Grandfathers and the Little Boy," the innocent boy who receives the gifts on behalf of the people is seen to grow very old dramatically by virtue of his acquired knowledge. Indeed in this account, wisdom is not merely one seventh of the teaching gifts, but their sum total as well. After the flood, Benton-Banai's account goes, an emissary from the seven spirit grandfathers, after six previous attempts, finally finds a baby boy who alone is worthy of their instruction about how to live. The baby was the one because "he was innocent. His mind was untouched by corruption and pain of the world. This baby was still fresh from inside where he stayed before he came to his mother's womb. He had not yet opened his eyes and ears to the world."

Then the seven grandfather spirits rub seven substances as gifts on the boy and get otter to accompany him home, along with a huge bundle. At seven stops on their way home, spirits told them the meaning of seven gifts "that were given to him out of the vessel of the Grandfathers":

1. To cherish knowledge is to know *wisdom*.
2. To know *love* is to know peace.
3. To honor all of the Creation is to have *respect*.
4. *Bravery* is to face the foe with integrity.
5. *Honesty* in facing a situation is to be brave.

6. *Humility* is to know yourself as a sacred part of the Creation.

7. *Truth* is to know all of these things.

The boy "would have to be careful to instruct his people in the right way to use each gift." At each stop returning back from the spirits, he picks up a shell, and during the trip home he grows into manhood. When they come to a big lake across which are the people, and while the otter goes to swim and show the people the four directions, the boy becomes an old man. "Then, [the otter] escorts the old man to his people. The old man carried a huge heavy bundle. It was a great power that he was to share with his people."[11] In this story, wisdom is clearly more than a human attainment; it is a divine gift.

Third, the spoken Ojibwe language offers linkages between wisdom and maturity going hand-in-hand. If there is not a historically etymological one, there is surely a sonic association or folk etymology between the Ojibwe term for being old (the verb root *gikaa-*, "to be elderly") and for being learned or wise (from the verb root *gikendam-*, "to know something").[12] Following elder Melvin Eagle's cue, Anton Treuer glosses the term *gekend-aasojig* as "learned elder," joining together the two concepts.[13]

As is central to Confucian spirituality, maturation involves a disciplined seeking after wisdom, with a close association of the later stages of the life passage with the accrual of wisdom. And it suggests something of the generational exchanges of wisdom for respect discussed in the first two chapters. Still, there is an important sense in which this conviction is predicated on the facts of physical maturation implied in old age. Without suggesting that any old person by virtue of their age issues in beneficent wisdom—recall the cautionary tales in Ojibwe oral tradition of the elder Frog Woman who is not benevolent with her knowledge—there remains a sense that the aging of body and mind produces something about wisdom that cannot be had by shortcut.

In her consideration of the ways that concrete Cree speech practices are formed by the stature of the speaker, Darnell writes, "No one can comprehend more than their own understanding allows at a given point in the life cycle." For this reason, she continues:

> Words spoken by a teacher/elder/man of power are retained for future consideration, for growing into to the greatest degree possible. The Cree believe

that there is time for things to come to fruition, that there are cycles both in the natural world and in individual human life (beginning with birth and ending with death). Wisdom and understanding are the natural consequences of living and attempting to maintain harmony of oneself with the world of livingness.[14]

By "natural consequences of living and attempting to maintain harmony," Darnell surely means something other than that wisdom is a natural by-product of biological aging but an outgrowth, a product of a living according to *bimaadiziwin*, where life movement is a process seamlessly joining the *natural* and *supernatural*, virtue and longevity, in the manner discussed in chapter 1.

If we can't allow the supernatural and moral to be eclipsed from the natural in Anishinaabe understandings of life movement, neither can we allow the natural dimensions of maturing, aging bodies to be obscured. Elder Melvin Eagle related in a series of stories to Anton Treuer that it was only once he had become an elder that he could recollect the fuller details and appreciate the significance of various teachings bestowed on him serially by "those old men" who were his *gekendaasojig* ("learned elders"). In a passage shot through with various references to honorific old age (making frequent reference to *akiwenzii* and *gichi-aya'aa*), Treuer's translation reads:

This is how I became so learned myself about what that old man told me, as he was always telling me things when I was small. I couldn't remember then. But as I am now an elder myself, maybe I remember what that old man used to tell me. It's just like yesterday or the day before when I think about what that old man used to tell me about, as he told me about all spiritual matters and everything about this road. . . . So I certainly learned, and for a long time. I didn't remember then. But as I came into my old age, I arrived at an understanding of what those old men had been telling me about. And that's why I'm so knowledgeable about this myself. I don't know everything, but maybe sometime I'll certainly come to understand that which those old men told me.[15]

Among the Northern Arapaho, Jeffrey Anderson found a necessary relationship between cultural knowledge and the maturation in the life cycle as ritually marked by initiations into a series of age-grades. "Only a few of the oldest people," Anderson writes, "possessed at any given time, knowledge of the total cosmological order."[16] As is clear in Melvin Eagle's remark, Anderson notes that among the Arapaho, knowledge could be embodied in practices, which are at first just performed and only with time, understood: "In the movement through different ways of knowing," Anderson writes, "persons acquired the 'practices' before they learned the shared meanings of those practices. . . . Doing and then knowing things 'at the right time' governed all temporal movements."[17]

These examples suggest a view toward the maturation of knowledge, an unfolding, or perhaps a deepening, of understanding that at first had been only sufficient. To be sure, these examples suggest that life experience, gained only through time, can make wisdom of other forms of knowledge. Perhaps this is linked to the notion that by the fourth hill of an Anishinaabe life course, one has shed many concerns in order to see more clearly what is of use and value.

As it became physically necessary, older Ojibwes historically withdrew from activities related to economic production (importantly, though, ethnographic sources suggest many exceptions to the rule, and elder men's withdrawal to the home/camp involved a stronger break than elder women's) and focused more on their role as custodians of memory, telling stories, teaching and caring for children, engaging in ritual activities. In this regard, Leo Simmons's observations in *The Role of the Aged in Primitive Society* are apt, for physical limitations of movement and economic activity related to old age could enable the old to focus on, and to be associated primarily with, custodianship of the religious/cultural resources of ritual, medicinal, and cosmological knowledge.

But there also appears to be something about the embodied experience of one's own physical limitations and proximity to known death that distills wisdom from a repertoire of knowledge. If the transition from adulthood to eldership was a gradual one not ritually demarcated, E. S. Rogers noted that "years and a diminution of physical ability tend to delimit this period."[18] Basil Johnston's interlocutor in the fictive colloquy discussing the marks of the "fourth hill" suggests how the finitude of old age shapes a way of knowing that cautions against ossifying orthodoxies or static notions of truth and knowledge:

In the evening of life, the aged give way to decrepitude and must accept the loss of strength, the lessening of endurance, and the wane of agility as part of life's destiny and the consequence of continuing to live. A former way of life must be forsaken; a new mode of living accepted. But to give up the old and embrace something new has always been difficult. For labors, pursuits, habits, manners, and pleasures that have become part of a man or woman are not easily cast off. The more familiar and cherished former ways, the more difficult the parting. Though former modes can no longer be exercised, they live on in memory. By their very sweetness and worth they call out for living on; they deserve to be repeated in life again and again. To resurrect the past in forms already done, is to negate survival. The same flower does not live, die, to live again. It lives, dies, and is no more. After death and passing it leaves a memory of loveliness and a promise of a renewal of that beauty in another flower in another spring. To resurrect former times and to relive them would end the fulfillment of visions and growth in the new order.[19]

By virtue of embodied experience of bodily limitation and conscious proximity to death, aged Anishinaabeg, perhaps no less than the aged of other societies, find themselves evaluating anew what knowledge, experience, and concerns are most important to them and to their communities. If, in Johnston's words, "it is the knowledge that what was can never be again . . . that renders old age most difficult," it is precisely because of this difficulty that the community recognizes the authority of this knowledge as the most mature, that prolongs the vitality of tradition, keeping it supple, in touch with life movement.[20]

As he himself was entering the latter stages of kidney failure and a regimen of dialysis, Larry Cloud Morgan spoke often of the work of elders living more deeply into silence, not just because of the fact of being increasingly removed from the bustle of life but because it was their vocation to do it. A poet, he also spoke of them figuratively and often literally bending back to earth, occupying themselves with the work of "preparing to go home."[21] Popular aging literature suggests the significance of the life review, of narrating one's own story to oneself and to others as a typical occupation of this time of life. For where there is an embodied awareness of physical limitations, there can also be a kind of moral maturity, alike part of wisdom.

But, of course, not always. And here again one must firmly distinguish the physical maturity and wealth of accrued experience that old age enables from the moral maturity that does not simply issue from age but emerges from learning and from the moral and spiritual disciplines of sagacity. There are elders and there are Elders. And again, we can draw on the more theologically elaborated Confucian traditions of the authority of old age to appreciate the subtleties of Anishinaabe understandings of moral and spiritual maturity. Confucians have regarded old age positively as a possibility, if not probability, that one had matured morally as well as physically, since life presented the opportunity to cultivate and realize humanity in the world. In *Analects* 2.4, Confucius charted what generations of Confucians have seen as the ideal relationship between the life cycle and moral/spiritual maturation:

> At fifteen, I set my heart upon learning.
>
> At thirty, I established myself [in accordance with ritual/*li*]
>
> At forty, I no longer had perplexities [self-possession, an unperturbed mind]
>
> At fifty, I knew the Mandate of Heaven [the limitations of one's own fate, fulfillment of transcendental command]
>
> At sixty, I was at ease with whatever I heard
>
> At seventy, I could follow my heart's desire without transgressing the boundaries of right.

Tu Weiming identifies what occurs at 50 as a kind of "spiritual crisis" of "adjusting to coming of old age and confronting it squarely as both possibility and limit."[22]

But making it through this realization is hardly arriving at the goal; it is merely the prerequisite to the most important stages of self-cultivation. Tu continues to gloss the level of maturation appropriate to age 60: "'I was at ease with whatever I heard' suggests receptivity. The art of listening (especially in contrast to seeing) is neither aggressive or possessive. It is an affirmation of the world in a spirit of detachment." Tu heeds what Confucius relates, rather enigmatically, about his capacity at 70, as the fullest expression of moral maturity: having so mastered the ritualized art and ethics of propriety, he was able to exercise convention fully animated by the ethical spirit of humanness, "able to bridge the gap between 'what is' and 'what ought to be.'" He was "so versed in self-cultivation that he could operate in a specific social setting with an artistic maturity."[23] This maturity can also be regarded as a kind of second childhood, "for the harmony it implies is an artistically cultivated spontaneity, a second childhood in old age."[24]

Although sagehood is a function of virtue and learning, not age directly, the concept of maturation remains crucial to Confucian ethical ideals. The *Analects* dramatize in the famous scorned image of the unmannerly old man that virtue is not coterminous with age, but it would be "misleading to suppose . . . that one's moral growth can significantly surpass one's physical maturation."[25]

A Swampy Cree elder described the relationship between the accrual of experience and learning made possible by age and spiritual maturity in terms of the "old people's" proximity to the divine. Again, because "old people" is an honorific and not just a generic reference to senior citizens over 65, his reference already incorporates this view: "Thus I would be glad if we were going to discuss this again another time, for of course, we must put our faith in the testimony of the old people; for they have reached the All Father for themselves, by that which they have accomplished, by the work of their hands, so that they might open the way for us and intercede for us; that is what I, at least, think. That is why I am greatly content that we should put our faith in the testimony of the old people in these things."[26]

The Learning of Wisdom: Elder as Sage

If "learned elder" is Melvin Eagle's construction of what could be referred to as Elder capital E—an elder who is particularly recognized and credentialed with wisdom—then we might also observe Eagle's sense that elders, like the Confucian sage, are *all about* learning, that they are not just its bearers, but the one's committed to the calling of learning. To revisit Benton-Banai's formulation, to "know wisdom" is to "cherish knowledge."[27]

The third phase of traditional Ojibwe education, according to Johnston, was "when people began a search for wisdom. This search would consume the rest of an individual's life: a quest to know the whole story of things, to know things in their simplicity and in their complexity, to know the many layers of meaning. Wisdom is the whole of these things."[28]

Learning here seems an especially apt way to characterize wisdom: it suggests a nod to an unending process, a realization that the goal will never be fully realized. It has been characteristic of the Confucian ideal of sagehood that the true sage does not claim to have achieved the goal. Confucius did not claim himself a sage, but only one trying to approximate classic ideals of a golden era. This is true of Anishinaabe eldership as well; reluctance to consider oneself an elder is, in part, an indication that eldership is a goal never completely attained, even if it becomes a social fact in a given instance. Jim Northrup, for example, ran a newspaper column that identified himself as "almost an elder." "Now that I am getting close to becoming an elder," he wrote, "I look around to see all the things I have yet to learn. I am hoping to learn from my elders and grandchildren. I could be called a junior elder, maybe an apprentice elder."[29]

This is not merely conspicuous modesty; it bespeaks a humility borne of the kind of situated and thus delimited knowledge that constitutes wisdom. The late-nineteenth-century Red Lake *ogimaa* Madweganonind was regarded highly by his people for the way he did not call attention to his eldership. He was remembered for being "very modest; he never spoke of himself or of anything pertaining to himself."[30] In part this humility concerns a continued respect among elders for those elders of theirs still alive. Josephine Degroat, herself an increasingly distinguished elder at White Earth, was still tending to those she called "my elders," including Winnie Jourdain and Margaret Hanks, to whom she was barely a junior.

This kind of humility is so deeply engrained in contemporary practices of eldership that its violation is a keen measure of imposture. "My rule is anyone who says they are an elder isn't," quipped the director of an aboriginal Canadian university center that selects and hires older Native people to serve as elders-in-residence.[31] If the comparison between the Anishinaabe elder and Confucian sage suggests itself so strongly on this key point, important contrasts should also suggest themselves as well: is not Confucian learning oriented toward textual learning according to established paradigms and institutions of education, encouragement of virtuosity recognized in processes of examinations, and the like? True, but contemporary scholars of Confucianism and neo-Confucianism hasten to point out that the shape of Confucian learning is much more than the book learning suggested by its formal focus on the study of canonical classics. Even more than talmudic studies in rabbinic Judaism, book learning in neo-Confucian tradition is a framework and springboard for a wealth of nontextual disciplines of contemplation, practical learning in the refinements of techniques of arts and ritual, disciplined observation of nature and serves as a framework for any number of nontextual practices.

Here I wish to suggest that truer forms of learning on Ojibwe terms reflect the maturation of knowledge suggested by Melvin Eagle's acknowledgment that it was only as an emerging elder that he came to fully understand the meaning and import of knowledge he had acquired earlier in life from his own elders. For Eagle, this involves a knowledge of the inner, not just outer, meanings of cultural and spiritual teachings. I suggest it also marks an ability to recognize what knowledge counts and what counts for knowledge, what knowledge can sustain communities and individuals.

The Contemplative Shape of Wisdom: Elder as Seer

Though accrued memory and knowledge constitute part of the learning of wisdom, and the performance of that memory and knowledge part of the display of that authority, it is withdrawal and silence, not conspicuous authoritative speech, that is more emblematic still of sagacity. Recall Darnell's observation that the authority of Cree elders' speech emerges more from the nonverbal than from the verbal. Carriage or bearing, and the judgment of a scrupulous community that such carriage or bearing has been earned through good living, matter.

In the early twentieth century, Frances Densmore identified the gentleness that characterized the public disposition of White Earth Midéwiwin practitioners: they were taught to be moderate in speech, quiet in manner, and not hasty in action. This directed the writer's attention to the gentle voices, the patience and the courtesy of the old people who had been trained in the Midéwiwin.[32] A disciplined gentleness has remained a key virtue. "In Gentleness Is Strength" read a hand-lettered cardboard sign outside the trailer that served as the headquarters for Camp Justice at White Earth, part of the leadership's spiritual direction away from rash and violent protest to disciplined, peaceful, but no less forceful, work. It did not come handily to members of Camp Justice to live up to such a slogan: it is tremendously countercultural, and no less among people who have not enjoyed a share in American prosperity. But rooted it has been in practices of virtue associated most clearly with elders, who among other things have sought a still center by withdrawing from the business of the world.

Less predictably perhaps, some elders earn particular respect through their demonstrated visionary or contemplative authority. Specific visions and dreams could compel community recognition of certain elders, but there is also a subtler way of viewing this source of authority. According to Cloud Morgan, the life course is laid out in such a way that one is to learn and absorb culture and tradition throughout one's life, but then, one reaches a certain maturity in which one phases out "words and diversions . . . in order to really communicate." One finds oneself becoming more reflective, more deliberate in everything one does to the point at which "saying yes to becoming nothing is really no big transition."[33] He imagined old age as a deliberate process of "preparing to go," a matter of accentuated calmness and silence.[34] Ultimately, elders are engaging in this contemplation out of necessity as they face their own losses, their own limits, and their own ultimate limit. Still, elders can engage in this for the entire community: it can be their work.

Importantly, this withdrawal—and the quiet that accompanies it—is not quietism in the sense that it eschews public life. Most of the more recognized elders today would hardly be classified as withdrawn people. Indeed, their prerogative to speak when and how they wish equips them to come front and center when need compels. At the same time, what often gives elders such public stature is what they bring to such utterances, and what they bring frequently comes from a moral or reflective vantage at some remove from the day-to-day clutter of economic and political life.

Instead, as Anderson observes of the Arapaho, a kind of quiet leadership of community activity carries the day. Of the "seven old men" who lived quietly—whose quiet lives were symbolic—at the center of the classic Arapaho camp circle, "ironically through living the quiet life, the Seven Old Men represented the 'consensus of the people,' as Fowler . . . indicated, and extended their presence to decision making."[35] Such old people were first consulted in their silence, we learn, in any important decisions for the people or for individuals.

QUIET

Theresa Smith was struck at Manitoulin Island by the close relationship between quiet, respect, and wisdom. "I found people admire," she observed, "sober, quiet, thoughtful and respectful individuals above all others for they are said to possess wisdom."[36] Indeed maintaining quiet—that is, not simply ceasing to talk, but recognizing the presence of quiet—in relations between juniors and elders is a key discipline of respect. Anderson speaks of quiet as actually "subsumed" into Arapaho respect. This relation to respect may also help illuminate an increasing emphasis on quiet in the life of Anishinaabe elders in a classical sense, giving voice through silence of their respect for spiritual nonhuman persons who are in some regards their own seniors by homology.

At the same time, I think, there is something of a generative presence of silence, as seen in other traditions. Quiet may not simply be the absence of words out of respect, but a presence, a privileged medium for relationship, and a cultivation of receptivity to wisdom.

Yao Xinzhong observes that the Chinese character for sage, *sheng*, presents a pictographic understanding that a person of achievement would "listen more than speak. The Sage listens to the calling from Heaven," "listens to the demands of the people," and "listens to the rhythm of the natural world so that he can reproduce the heavenly principles in terms of human codes and guide human activities by wisdom."[37]

Keith Basso has written the most generative work on silence in Native American communities, oft-cited perhaps because the sociolinguistic approach he models makes room within linguistic studies to say something about silence, which despite having no internal grammatical structure, can be observed to engender social structures. Basso finds six situations in which conspicuous silence governs Apache relationships: and in each case, they involve "social situations in which the status of focal participants is ambiguous" and where silence "is a response to uncertainty and unpredictability in social relations."[38] Subsequent discussions have concluded from Basso's essay that silence can be parsed in terms of such social relations; indeed in *Unspoken: A Rhetoric of Silence*, Cheryl Glenn musters Basso's six examples of social ambiguity as evidence dismissing appeals to the stereotypically quiet Indian person, concluding that for Basso, specific acts of deliberate silence are "always in response to situational uncertainty and unpredictability."[39] Following a Simon Ortiz poem, Glenn rightly interrogates the silent Indian stereotype, but hewing too closely to Basso's famous essay, as Glenn does in interviews toward her own study of Navajo silence, can eclipse a key aspect of Native silence. In fact, in a charged footnote, apparently overlooked by his readers, Basso writes that "the social situations described in this paper are not the only ones in which Western Apaches regularly refrain from speech," adding "a second set of situations in which silence appears to occur solely as a gesture of respect, usually to persons in a position of authority" and a third set in which ritual leaders "keep silent at certain points during the preparation of ceremonial paraphernalia."[40]

To be sure there are a variety of such situations in Anishinaabe social life where social situations command what might be called "the silent treatment." Indeed, as I learned in my book on Ojibwe hymn-singing, the more trenchant criticisms that Native people give an author can be silent criticisms that refuse to dignify with a response the thing disdained. One could surely proceed further in this direction.

But I wish here to suggest that, more than an appeal to a stereotype of the stoic or passive Indian, voluntary, disciplined silence can be explored for the way it provides a privileged medium for relationality. Basso's recognition of other situations where the clarity and not the ambiguity of social relations calls for silence—both situations demanding respect—is important. If the choice not to speak hastily, loosely, or first in the presence of another can indicate an active, even creative, gesture of honor or respect and not simply fear or programmatic reticence, we can appreciate the fuller senses of older Ojibwe peoples' own practices of silence. In particular, Basso's third set of situations—involving ritual specialists preparing their ceremonial paraphernalia—is suggestive of an Anishinaabe posture of silence toward nonhuman spiritual others. And while I want to underscore the creative, agentive aspects of keeping silence over the programmatic, I would suggest that ideological commitments to the virtues of quiet and the meanings of silence are important parts of the equation. Richard Bauman, for example, emphasizes that the place of Quaker theological commitments to "the experience of God speaking within" the person, unmediated by ritualism or external words, is crucial to understanding early Quaker practices of silence, even as those practices were also heavily marked subversions of social conventions. "As this most important act of speaking took place inwardly and was spiritual," Bauman writes, "it required that one refrain from speaking that was outward and carnal."[41]

Indeed, disciplines of silence can punctuate spoken words with gravity and urgency. The early White Earth spiritual elder Shaydayence, discussed in chapter 4, was known for his practices of silence. Attentive listening was related in Shaydayence's case to a regular practice of contemplative silence, another practice befitting elders that could give the few words that were spoken further esteem still. J. A. Gilfillan noted that even though Shayday-ence's Christian life occupied only his final eleven years, he had developed a "deep knowledge of spiritual things," things that "were the subjects of his incessant contemplation and prayer, and the action of the Holy Spirit on natural abilities of the very highest order enabled him to arrive at those things independently without ever having been taught them or heard them from others."[42] More than a century later, Lisa Philips Valentine remarked about how she was deeply impressed with the respectful silence that greeted her when she arrived at Lynx Lake for extended fieldwork:

> I still remember the older women, dressed in bright flower print skirts, their heads covered by colorful scarves knotted beneath their chins. These women stood, hands outstretched, as my husband and I, carrying my two year old daughter, followed the Band officials from the airplane. The image of these women was so strongly etched in my mind that I was later able to name them in the order that they greeted me and shook my hand. I was amazed at the seeming quiet, given the number of people, at least 150, at the dock that day. It wasn't until years later that I realized the reception was not for the band officials, but for us, these *kihci-moohkomaanak* (Americans) who were coming to live in their community—not as transient teachers, but simply as guests.[43]

Erma Vizenor tells of an elder man who came to visit her grandfather, sat with him over shared food in quiet stillness for more than an hour, and then left. The entire visit consisted of the exchange of but a few words. In such cases, disciplined practices of silence and contemplation lend special authority to what an elder says when she does speak.[44] In similar fashion, I recall vividly being invited into the trailer of Jim Ironlegs Weaver, a White Earth elder who wanted to honor work I'd done over several tense days during a civil disobedience action connected with Camp Justice. He and his "old woman," Judy Bellecourt, invited me ceremoniously inside their trailer, bade me sit down at a small table, poured me a cup of strong coffee, and sat in silence with me. At first I was uncomfortable, reading the silence as an awkward indicator of social distance, but being invited by their continued silence to remain in it, after several minutes I came to appreciate the wordless encouragement and affirmation and gratitude.

Stressing the dominance of nonspeech elements like silence in Cree interaction patterns, Darnell places "talking" in this context. What is salient is the idea of "co-presences, people being together and acknowledging their so being."[45] In Darnell's able reckoning, this frames Cree speech— and this would be true as well of Anishinaabe speech—profoundly in terms of the relational cycles of life:

> Meaningful talk, then, hinges less on the content of the talking than the quality of the relationship and situation of talking. For this relational reason, in Cree interactions, there is little emphasis on "topic closure," placing the interactional burden on continuity rather than novelty. Life itself is a cycle, within which individuals grow up listening to their grandfathers, come to be old themselves, teach their own grandchildren, become one of the ancestors ("nimosomipanak," morphologically "the grandfathers who have died"), expect that their teachings will be assimilated by the next generation, providing eventual closure to old teachings and open-endedness to new ones.[46]

CULTIVATING SILENCE

Lawrence Gross's formal training in the study of Japanese Soto Zen Buddhism and his training with his own Ojibwe grandmother at White Earth equip him to see how Anishinaabe people, like Japanese Buddhists, participate in a "culture of silence." Gross locates silence and concentration in the economy of a traditional Ojibwe life on the land, where silence, he suggests, could be a matter of survival, where a traditional way of life in the woods found Ojibwe people "immersed in silence," "taking in the world around them."[47]

Gross likens the tangible, reverent quiet that envelops a group of Ojibwe elders sitting down at a meal at a community center to the disciplined quiet of the Japanese Tea Ceremony, a cultural practice imbued with Bud-

dhist disciplines of quieting the mind and utterly concentrating on whatever activity is at hand in a given moment. If the Tea Ceremony is "more
refined" in Gross's view, there remains a degree of ritualized silence in
everyday Anishinaabe life.[48] Gross speaks in particular of the memorable
intentionality and concentration of his grandmother's washing and drying of dishes at her kitchen sink, wherein the practice of her "paying attention" with her whole self, body, and mind could be seen as no less intentional a realization of the sacred in the ordinary than Zen's celebrated
disciplines of ritualizing quotidian actions like sweeping or writing, toward "total exhaustion" and hence full realization of the moment.

Indeed quietness is no naturally appearing "personality trait" of Ojibwe
culture, as some have observed, particularly in the contexts of institutional
education; it is a discipline, even a spiritual discipline. Gross emphasizes
that Zen silence is more recognizably a "spiritual imperative" for "being
fully engaged with the world," whereas for the Anishinaabe, silence was
more "a matter of survival."[49] But differences in the specific function of
silence in the two traditions are eclipsed by the remarkably parallel vision
that everything is sacred, a philosophical outlook shaping and shaped by
such practices of silence and cultivated concentration. Gross glosses the
generative Soto master Dogen's insistence that everything has Buddha Nature as an insistence that "the world is sacred just as it is." Gross likens this
to the teaching of Minnesota Anishinaabe spiritual leader Tom Shingobe,
who said that "the whole world is spiritualized" with "such a tone of voice
and manner of inflection [that] it was clear he intended that phrase to be
understood just as he said it. In his mind, there were no exceptions. The
whole world, and everything in it, is spiritualized."[50]

If practices, even disciplines, of silence shape Ojibwe eldership, so does
the quiet life serve as a kind of fruition of the good life well lived. For the
late Dan Kier of White Earth, as for Cloud Morgan, aging is an opportunity for simplifying (mind you, this from lives that are built around the
virtue of simplicity), to living a quiet life. Dan's stated dream about his elder years, to have been underwritten by a kidney transplant that ultimately
would never come, was to live quietly on the reservation with his new wife,
to keep a wood stove going, to maintain an outdoor fire as often as possible, to mind a vegetable garden, cut grass, and spend time with visiting
kids (as well as their newly adopted toddler, Preston). One hears such
"ambitions" for old age frequently at White Earth.

Anderson observes that the good life for Arapaho consultants past and present is tantamount to "a quiet life." The goal for life in old age was classically a withdrawal from the business, wordiness, and craziness of earlier life stages to a quieter, simpler existence, and the knowledge of such elders was held close to the small circles of family and students who had access to them. Anderson also notes that the oldest Arapaho classically, as contemporarily, withdraw from the business of life not simply into the quiet life, but into a more intensive focus, as Cloud Morgan suggests for the Anishinaabe, on matters spiritual.[51] Densmore observed that "wisdom could be obtained through teaching of elders, through observation of 'elder brothers' the animals and plants, and 'from silence' the knowledge to contemplate and to think through things before acting."[52]

"KNOWING THERE"

Implicit throughout this discussion has been the extraordinarily local nature of the wisdom of Anishinaabe elders. And this in dramatic contrast to the universalizing nature of so much religious thought characteristic of the modern West. "Wisdom," to cite Basso's phrase, "sits in places."[53] Anishinaabe wisdom is closely tied to a way of living on Anishinaabe land. In this respect, elders' wisdom is marked by what John Grim provocatively suggested could be called a "knowing there." This does not reduce wisdom to mere woods sense—that is, instrumental knowledge toward an economy in a particular ecology—rather. The keenness of observation, reflection, and elaboration are clearly much more than that.

There are important folk etymological associations between key honorific terms for elder in the Ojibwe language and the idea of this "knowing there." Recall that Peter Jones glossed the honorific *uhkewaihsee* (*akiwenzii*) as "long dweller on the earth."[54] Although Ojibwe parlance could draw on the morpheme *akii*, what Jones glosses "earth," to contrast with the heavens, more typical usages of the term are local rather than global in scope. *Akii* more often than not implies "land," and often a particular land. If the principal honorific for elder man, *akiwenzii*, makes reference to the land or place, so too does another standard Ojibwe term translatable as elder, *gichi-aya'aa*. It might be glossed as "great-being," but the term *being* is problematic in that the Ojibwe language does not have a verb "to be" that is not already locative in nature. In the Ojibwe language, to be is to "be there" in particular. As Gross puts it, "The idea that everything in the world is spiritualized seems to be a part of a larger Ojibwe sense that wherever you are is good enough. Wherever you are, well, that is where you are, and you need to relate to the world right there, no matter what is going on."[55]

A convention of Ojibwe speech that appeared frequently in the prayers of Cloud Morgan and was present in several Ojibwe-language renditions of Christian hymns like *Ondashan, Ondashan, Giche Ochichag* is *oma aki-ing ayaayaan* ("here on earth/the land, where I am"). Cloud Morgan glossed the phrase to engage the richer spiritual associations of the term: "Here where we are on this earth at this moment, this is the greatest gift we have."[56]

If, as I'm suggesting, the "work" of withdrawal, cultivated concentration, and silence point to a kind of vocation for Anishinaabe elders as contemplatives, this is emphatically not the kind of wilderness contemplative or desert father, seeking a solitary no-place and no-when to confront the task of fuller knowledge of the self and contemplation of universal truths. Far from solitude, the "knowing there" of the elder is an immersion into a vast network of social, natural, and spiritual relations intersecting at, and in a sense occasioned by, a particular place.

I have met some elders like Margaret Hanks, who reportedly had never traveled beyond Minnesota when she joined a group of Ojibwe Singers on trips to Clergy and Laity Concerned gatherings in New York City and Wheeling, West Virginia. Although it became something of a good natured joke on those trips that she had not packed enough clothes and belongings for the trip, the chuckles were no sign of disrespect but instead respectful affirmations of her particular kind of knowledge and acknowledgements of how countercultural they would be by standards of contemporary American society. In other words, this was not a sign of her deficiency, her backwardness: it was, on the contrary, a credential in itself, and certainly for me a moment to realize that cosmopolitanism is only one way to evidence sophistication in knowledge.

Ojibwe elders' ways of knowing are tied profoundly to place and to the lifeways pertinent to that place. Mrs. Fields at wild rice harvest, Nett Lake Indian Reservation, 1939. *Courtesy Minnesota Historical Society*

DOXA NOT ORTHODOXY

That wisdom is a "knowing there" localizes elders' ways of knowing in particular ecologies and landscapes. But there is another aspect in which wisdom is situated knowledge. That is in its resistance to universalizing orthodoxies. Chapter 4 considered this dynamic aspect of tradition in considerable detail, but the situational nature of elders' ways of knowing is worth discussing here for its contrast from the ossified orthodoxy that a contemporary youth culture might pronounce as characteristic of elders they see as "set in their ways."

Jack Goody has contrasted what he calls *doxa*, the dynamics of knowing stemming from the orality of primarily oral traditions where the authority of "right thinking" resides in the lineage or social regard for the knower, with the more familiar notion (to literate societies) of *orthodoxy*, where the concern is the propositional content of right thinking more than it is the personage or station of the thinker.[57] Perhaps a distinction due to orality is what promotes a counterintuitive flexibility in the intellectual dynamics of the authority of age. But I have also suggested, in

chapter 4, that the authority of tradition references less some fixed orthodox content of tradition than it does the social fidelity an elder maintains
to her or his own elders. As pronouncements about tradition are often
framed by references like "my elders told me . . . ," we can perhaps see how
much play could emerge in reckonings of tradition.

Or perhaps orality ensures that the content of tradition and its social
constitution cannot be distinguished, much less separated. Of the Cree,
Darnell writes:

> It is understood that each particular grandfather will have his own unique
> experience and way of expressing it. Thus new wisdom is always being ac-
> cumulated and integrated with the traditional. No effort is made to ho-
> mogenize the teachings of various grandfathers, even if they appear to be
> inconsistent; individual autonomy precludes such disrespect. Part of the
> autonomy of each individual is the right to assimilate whatever combina-
> tion of available teachings fits with life experience, temperament and posi-
> tion in the life cycle.[58]

As I also suggested in chapter 4, an important occasion for contestation in
such reckonings has been the appropriate relationship that Anishinaabe
traditions were to have with the teachings and practices of the Christian
tradition. And while the authority of eldership itself has been a moving
target such that no clean, consistent generational divide has emerged, its
appears that elders of different generations have construed the problem
from different places.

In her creative telling of her own grandmother's story, Ignatia Broker
describes Oona's perplexity at her boarding school teachers' condemna-
tion of the Midéwiwin and other traditional Ojibwe ways. But in a manner
characteristic of eldership, her grandfather does not condemn the teachers, even though he recognizes it would be "easier" if the teachers bothered
to learn Ojibwe ways. Instead, he tells her, "do not be ashamed of the good
that we have taught and do not be ashamed of the good to be learned. Our
way of life is changing, and there is much we must accept. But let it be only
the good. And we must always remember the old ways. We must pass them
onto our children and grandchildren so they too will recognize the good
in the new ways."[59]

By the twentieth century, Broker writes, "the Ojibway were now a Christian people. They went to churches, were baptized, and did what was required. The old people who knew the old Indian ways could relate them to what was taught in the churches. 'Honor they father and mother,' 'Love thy neighbor as thyself,' 'Thou shalt not kill,' respect, brotherhood, 'thou shalt not covet they neighbor's goods'—these were what the Ojibway had always practiced. The Old Ones believed that Christian principles that were similar to the old ways could help the Ojibway people."[60]

The Ethical Shape of Wisdom: Elder as Moral Exemplar

Perhaps the most important manner in which wisdom is credentialed knowledge has to do with the moral stature of the elder, and not simply a matter of what is deemed worthy of belief or what gains credence by social agreement (which is also to say invites contestation). Wisdom by this measure is the utterance/perspective/pronouncement of a person with credence.

Theresa Smith wrote concerning life on Manitoulin Island, "You do not become an elder there because you have reached a certain age, but because people see that you are 'living right.' Thus not all elderly people are elders and some extraordinary middle-aged persons are, in fact, included in this honored group."[61] In this there is a kind of moral presence that elders carry. In the case of the White Earth Ojibwe Singers, Erma Vizenor had reflected it was so much more to their voices than what they said or sang: it was their moral presence that carried in and through their voices.

In some exceptional Anishinaabe people, the moral stature associated with eldership could even be said to be prophetic. Cloud Morgan's authority as an elder was clearly shaped deeply by his moral stature: what gave his words standing and what gave him presence was not his store of knowledge, rich as it was in terms of the Ojibwe language, as much as the moral esteem he had earned in the way he lived his life. His reputation as a peace activist walking his talk had preceded his return to Minnesota in the 1980s following his release from four years in federal prison for civil disobedience at a nuclear missile silo. Of course, it was not mere reputation, but a consistent pattern of ethical courage in his work on peace and justice issues, especially American Indian issues, that bolstered his credibility as an elder.

So, too, Bea Swanson, a good friend of Larry's, fellow White Earth enrollee, and an important figure in the urban Native community in Minneapolis from the 1970s through the 1990s. She would develop a long list of
causes and courageous actions that gave her credibility in the community.
An active Catholic layperson, Swanson was unafraid to speak out at a
meeting of the 1979 Tekakwitha Conference, in its early days when non-
Native clergy largely were setting the agenda. A Benedictine nun remembered the watershed moment in the transition of the Tekakwitha movement to becoming a more decidedly Native organization:

> At the back of the auditorium of Mount Marty College I stood with a lady
> from the White Earth Reservation, Bea Swanson. Let her always be remem-
> bered. Bea spoke quietly to me, "Is it possible for me to say something?" I
> said, "Of course. I'll get Bishop Dudley to call on you." A momentous
> change in the Tekakwitha Conference was about to come. The Church from
> the reservation was about to give direction to the clergy who serve them.
> Bea walked slowly to the front. She stood shy and trembling, but resolute.
> "Bishops, you are so nice." They smiled. "You always say such nice things."
> They beamed. "But you always say the same things." There was a stillness.
> Humble men, the bishops listened. "Can we Indians talk to you ourselves?
> You say you are our pastors. Can we just be alone with you? Can the priests
> and sisters go out? We have something to say to you by ourselves."[62]

A document emerged from the closed-door discussion that called for more
episcopal advocacy for Native ministers, the training of indigenous spiritual leaders, stronger roles for Native women in the church, and a commitment to discontinue placing clergy in Native communities who did not
wish to do Indian ministry, and the Tekakwitha movement in the years
since has been a center of vitality for indigenous Catholicism.[63] In her senior years, Swanson initiated a "grandmothers' circle" to support Twin
Cities grandmothers raising young children. She convened, with Roberta
Brown, Ira Sailor, and other Native seniors living in Minneapolis, an occasional elders' circle to meet with elected officials on matters of concern.
In 1991, the *New York Times* reported Swanson's protest, accompanied by
an important Minnesota drum called Peace Drum, of the First Gulf War
in Lafayette Park across from the White House.[64] In 1993, Swanson was
arrested for possessing a fishing spear during the tense assertions of treaty

rights, soon to be affirmed by the Supreme Court, at Minnesota's Mille Lacs Reservation.[65]

Swanson illustrates well how the self-described stubbornness that she and other Anishinaabe elders could show has less to do with being set in one's ways but rather committed to moral resolve. She spoke of the keen sense of justice that motivated her but also a mature vision of constructive prophetic change. "But of course," she said, "the anger is always there. If I let myself go with just the anger I would destroy myself. I have to turn that into 'what can we do to change it' and we can change it. I believe that God has called me to help make changes and then to see what I can do as a woman and as a grandmother. I know that I'm stubborn, and now I can use that to help change injustice."[66] Bea Swanson's eldership served as a platform for effective moral leadership, and her moral leadership, in turn, gave further credibility to her eldership.

One of the most moving moments I spent with the elders of White Earth's Ojibwe Singers was at the south Minneapolis home where Swanson, bedridden with advanced cancer, was receiving hospice care. Cloud Morgan, too, was there, and after an improvised feast in the sunroom-turned-bedroom and visit, Swanson asked that they sing some hymns for her. The songs had a force to them that was as much about the cumulative moral presence of the elders in the midst as it was about the music itself.

Indeed while less articulate and outspoken than Bea Swanson or Larry Cloud Morgan, the women of that same group of singers, all of them described as "the elders" at White Earth, exemplified the moral stature of sagacity in and through their visible resolve as grandmothers and elders in several civil disobedience arrests connected with Camp Justice. Marge McDonald, Ethelbert "Tiggums" Vanwert, and Josephine Degroat liked to joke about each other as unlikely "jailbirds," as they spent at least one night in the Becker County Jail, having been arrested for peacefully occupying their own tribal headquarters. In their case, they needed no microphone to speak articulately with their aged bodies on a "perp walk" to a paddy wagon. If the action augmented their own authority, it was they who gave the actions credibility as grounded in the right.

This ethical shape of sagacity, the connection between wisdom and the moral scrutiny that is expected in its exercise, is in considerable tension with a prevailing ethnographic understanding of the relationship between Ojibwe knowledge, power, and respect. In the calculus of power/knowledge observed in medicine people as elaborated by Mary Black-Rogers, ritual knowledge gifted through dreams exhibits itself not in the moral transparency of ethical living, but in its opposite: the moral ambiguity of sacred power. To some degree, the tension can be explained by the idiosyncrasies of the ethnographic record on the Ojibwe as it grew over time. The generation and interpretations of fieldwork "data" by A. I. Hallowell and his graduate students was part of their effort to challenge an assumption of collectivism in primitive societies. To make this point strongly, they gravitated toward aspects of their experience of Ojibwe culture and society driven by what they labeled "Ojibwe atomism" or "Ojibwe individualism" and in particular a social structure built not on an ethic of *respect* but on fear of the power of the "oldest" shamans to inflict harm and not just healing. Perhaps here, the shape of wisdom can be seen in some tension with a form of knowledge/power that stems from dreams. But the exercise of knowledge I've called sagacity also overlapped with the exercise of dream power/knowledge in ways that suggest the medicine person of old was never *just* morally ambivalent.

The Vitality of Wisdom: Elder as Life Exemplar

If the exercise of wisdom is characterized by moral transparency, sincerity, learning, and contemplation, sagacity is hardly humorless. In fact, part of situated knowledge in its resistance to disembodiment is its ability to not take itself too seriously. This way of knowing actually mobilizes sexuality, humor, and attendant vitality in a number of important respects. As a primary term for elder, *gichi anishinaabe* ("great person") suggests that the elder is not merely a model of the moral life or the spiritual life but the good life in all its dimensions. The ideal of eldership is thus deeply grounded in an Anishinaabe affirmation of life, an affirmation of the body, and an affirmation of the very nature that produces old age and death.

SENSUALITY

In a discussion of classic Ojibwe kinship structure, Hallowell tried to depict the full humor of cross-cousin joking etiquette. But another reading of the same incident could perhaps have taken it as evidence of an abiding—perhaps accentuating—sense of humor associated with old age. "Once when I was preparing to photograph an old man," Hallowell wrote, "several Indians gathered around":

> Among them was a very dignified old woman, a Christian and a pillar of the Church, the mother of a large family of grown children. The old man had assumed a position in which it happened that his legs were spread widely apart. Just before I was ready to snap the shutter of my camera, the old lady suddenly reached towards the old man's fly as if to unbutton it. Everyone went into peals of laughter. The old man was her cross cousin. But on other occasions I have seen this same old woman watch the departure of her husband without a gesture or change of expression and accept his return home after weeks of absence with a similar nonchalance.[67]

Nanapush and Margaret Kashpaw, elder characters of several of Louise Erdrich's novels about a fictional Anishinaabe reservation in the north, depict a similar ongoing repartee of good natured, sexualized banter, banter that literally reminds them they are alive in conditions that otherwise might give way to the alternative. Though fictional characters, I feel as though they are so true that I've either met them already or would recognize them on the street were I to encounter them. "I cheated death by never stopping talking," Nanapush memorably declares in Erdrich's novel *Tracks*.

HUMOR

Hallowell identified robust Ojibwe laughter as the "outstanding exception" to a society that he argued was greatly restrained in terms of public expression of emotion. As humorless as the functional explanation of laughter predictably turns out to be, Hallowell experienced its vitality at Berens River.[68] To illustrate its persistence, Hallowell cites Gilfillan, the Episcopalian missionary at White Earth:

> There is continual laughter, and jests flying all around the wigwam from the time they wake in the morning till the last one goes to sleep. As long as they have anything to eat, and if no one is very sick, they are as cheerful and happy as can be. The laughter and droll remarks pass from one to the other,

Fred and Mary Day making maple sugar, photographed by Monroe Killy in 1946. According to historian Bruce White, Killy indicated that at the time the photo was taken the couple were trading stories about sugar making. Fred had asked, "You didn't really do it that way, did you?" "Yeah, that's the way we used to do it." Here, growing old together, living on the land, and humor are all part of an Ojibwe elder's way of knowing. *White, We Are at Home,* 106. *Courtesy Minnesota Historical Society*

a continual fusillade all round. The old woman says something funny; the children take it up, and laugh at it; all the others repeat it, each with some embellishment, or adding some ludicrous feature, and thus there is continual merriment all day and all evening long.[69]

Hallowell continued to speak about an "institutionalization of humor" in the body of myths that further evidenced the cathartic psychological function of humor. "Tear jerking or tragic stories of any kind," Hallowell observed, "would, in fact be unthinkable" among the Ojibwe.[70]

If Hallowell was onto something important, we might make more room than his functional analysis could for the agency involved with a sense of humor. Gerald Vizenor has written extensively on Anishinaabe humor and the emblematic figure of the trickster, whose shape-shifting is always enabling escapes and undermining the ultimacy of tragic experience. This comic embrace of life evidenced in Indian humor is for Vizenor the resource for the most unrelenting resistance to the "pathetic seriousness" and "tragic victimry" of colonization.[71] More recently, Gross has written about the healing effects of a nimble Anishinaabe humor in defeating the societal equivalent of posttraumatic stress disorder.[72]

VITALITY

This book has not marked an effort to document "vital aging" as much as it has attended to the contours of healthy community insofar as they take into account the authority of eldership. At the same time, there is much to be learned about vital aging from these communities as well.

In terms of longevity, elders in the past who outsmarted the rates of life expectancy arrived at incredibly old ages. At the turn of the twentieth century, for example, Gilfillan identified a certain Gegwedjiga at Leech Lake, who at 115 was considered to be the oldest of the generation at the dawn of the twentieth century.[73] Kahbcnagwiwcns/John Smith was another example celebrated in Native and non-Native circles in the mid-twentieth century as a man who reputedly "had lived in three centuries." Smith's age, which registered on his weathered visage, had turned the many photographs and postcards of him into circulating commodities, indeed significantly shaping, at least locally, the stereotype of the aged Indian. Still, as Bruce White suggests, Smith was no dupe of the photographers who paid him to pose; it would seem that he made a living at it and even enjoyed the notoriety it brought him (see figure on p. 21).[74]

The late Jack Potter was an Ojibwe Singer at White Earth whose hip condition was so severe that he could barely walk, let alone live on his own, but who came alive late in life as a dancer in powwows. I cannot underscore just how unlikely it is that this older man would dance in the rigorous all-weather powwows. Potter explained to me how he brought an old-time understanding of dance as prayer, where his own dancing in the face of physical infirmity was a vocal act of affirming life: "When I raise that feather, I honor all the earth," he said with a great deal of gravity in his expression.

Jim Weaver, commonly referred to at White Earth with the nickname—honorific, really—"Ironlegs," is another late White Earth elder whose vitality in old age was humbling. Prior to Camp Justice, Ironlegs had established a reputation for having chained himself to a tree and staged a hunger strike on the grounds of the White Earth tribal government headquarters building to call attention to what he and many others viewed as abuses of that government under the protracted leadership of the longtime tribal chair (who was later convicted on felony counts of embezzlement and more recently charged with fraudulent evasion of DWI laws). In 1994, a septuagenarian by this time, Ironlegs took his message of abuses at White Earth to Washington, D.C.—on foot. With a motley crew of fundraisers and supporters along the way, Ironlegs walked U.S. Highway 2 through Anishinaabe country in northern Minnesota, Wisconsin, and the Upper Peninsula of Michigan, then south and east over the Appalachians over the course of three months. That he arrived (against the counsel of supporters) in the capital on the day that Congress had left town for Thanksgiving recess and as a consequence was unable to fully articulate his message there did not detract from the numerous interviews he conducted along the way, where he countered conventional narrative that tribal gaming proved a rags-to-riches panacea for Indian country's challenges. Nor did that change his larger-than-life reputation back at White Earth as an elder who had earned his authority by literally "walking his talk," not merely in the ethical sense but also in the sense of defying wider societal expectations for infirm old age with hardy, vital aging.

Anne Dunn is another example of an elder (indeed one who, like Josephine Degroat, frequently defers to *her* elders) whose vitality, passion, and humor are striking. "I was born in northern Minnesota and I'd never been to a place where the tamarack did not flourish," she writes, referring to the conifers distinguished by loss of their needles in autumn after they turn an arresting strawberry blonde. Dunn is certainly distinguished by education, career accomplishment, and notoriety as a published columnist, writer, and poet, and activist (she worked as staff to the Minnesota chapter of Clergy and Laity Concerned and formed the Northern Minnesota Religious Freedom Council, serving inmates in area prisons and bringing to public attention violations of their right to free exercise). Increasingly regarded as an elder and as a sort of public grandmother, Dunn engages that role with increasing passion, humor, and creativity.

Citing Elder Susan Jackson of Leech Lake, Anton Treuer calls attention to an Ojibwe expression, *wajebaadizi-*, that means "to be spry, peppy, and full of life." "*Niwajebaadiz* [I live spryly] she often says. Most people don't

Jim Ironlegs Weaver in the early stretches of his successful several-month-long walk from northern Minnesota to Washington, D.C., in order to call attention to abuses at White Earth. He was reportedly in his late seventies at the time. *Author photo*

believe her when she tells them that she is well over 70 years old. Her body is strong, her wits are sharp, and she rarely complains of any physical condition."[75] There is a sense in which Jackson is perhaps exceptional for her peppiness, but there is also a sense in which she represents an ideal of old age that is found in practice often enough to remain more than a distant ideal for Anishinaabeg. According to Treuer, Archie Mosay "in his retirement was more active than in his working years" as a counselor and spiritual leader, and that period of public authority continued until his death at 94.[76] This is surely true of the White Earth Ojibwe Singers, who were effectively serving as professional mourners, bringing their music and the support of their presence to as many as three wakes per week.

As is clear from the number of wakes involved, and in particular from the frequent violent and untimely deaths where the old were burying the young, there is a deep and painful irony here. These stories of late-life vitality and longevity today, impressive and inspiring as they are to an outsider and precious examples as they might be to Anishinaabeg of the cultural ideal, hardly represent the unequivocal triumph of Anishinaabe eldership over the forces of colonization, poverty, violence, and racism. Lac du Flambeau elder and fishing guide Ben Chosa speaks of the deep concern that has arisen in his lifetime over "the deteriorization of our old people":

> When I was young, there was a lot of old people—eighty, ninety years old. I remember they used to paddle in with canoes to get their mail, go shopping, come in from the village, and I'd see them all over the reservation. Old people! Eighty, Ninety years old. Active! I'd see them out cutting wood and doing everything, making wild rice and trapping and doing all these things. . . . There used to be a lot of them: a hundred, ninety years old here. And we have no old people here no more! Its of great concern to me that our ability to live a long time is gone now.[77]

As seen in chapter 1, the diminishment of life expectancy means that far too few Anishinaabe adults make it past the travails of violence, or diabetes, or heart disease, or cancer to live to ripe old age. And far too many aged Anishinaabeg are subdued by physical affliction or isolation to live as spryly or relevantly or authoritatively as they wish, effectively making elders out of younger and younger people.

Conclusion

So what can we conclude about the shape of the wisdom that Anishinaabe elders can bring to bear? Wisdom on Ojibwe terms is credentialed knowledge, that of recognized elders distinguished for their ongoing commitment to sacred learning, their spiritual maturity, moral example, and vitality. Wisdom, or sagacity, is ultimately a fruit of practice, but the consistent characteristics of the fruit of this practice can be enumerated. Wisdom is deeply involved with lifelong learning, and thus ever provisional. It is shaped by an awareness of the limits of the physical self and an awareness of just how limited is one's ability to know beyond one's place— one's place on the land or one's place in the life cycle. It is aware of how little mystery one can ever hope to comprehend. It is not given to formulations of orthodoxy, remaining instead tied to situational, perspectival, proverbial ways of knowing. It is seasoned knowledge, both in terms of the accrual of experience but also in terms of the maturation of that knowledge. It is knowledge that emerges from moral discipline and promotes the ethical and healthy life of communities. Finally, it is knowledge that builds up and enlarges life, *bimaadiziwin*, and communities of the living. Although there are considerable challenges facing those communities and their capacity to fully honor, and learn from, their elders, it is also true that Anishinaabe eldership has proved remarkably resourceful and resilient over time, and is very likely up to the challenge.

NOTES

Preface

1. The seventeenth-century Westminster Larger Catechism teaches that "by father and mother, in the fifth commandment, are meant, not only natural parents, but all superiors in age and gifts; and especially such as, by God's ordinance, are over us in place of authority, whether in family, church, or commonwealth." This point of view was incorporated in Puritan clergyman John Cotton's 1656 New England catechism, *Spirituall Milk for Boston Babes in Either England*, where father and mother specifically refer to "all our Superiors, whether in family, school, church, and Commonwealth" and where the "honor due to them" includes "reverence, obedience, and (when I am able) recompense." As to the distinctive authority of age in Jewish tradition, as well as its similarly conflicted history in the modern American context, see Myerhoff, *Number Our Days*; and Kugelmass, *Miracle at Intervale Avenue*.

2. The Anishinaabeg, like the three nations comprising them, have never been a unified political unit, but rather a congeries of groups living and migrating seasonally in the region surrounding the western Great Lakes who have shared linguistic, cultural, and clan identities and who have in many cases gathered in larger numbers for ceremonial complexes and political/military alliances. Today, their reservation communities are in the states of Minnesota, Wisconsin, and Michigan and in the Canadian provinces of Ontario and Manitoba, with several

communities who migrated with the fur trade to the Northern Plains of North Dakota, Saskatchewan, and Montana. Anishinaabe communities speak distinct, but related languages of the Algonkian language family, and northernmost Canadian Ojibwe communities are closely related linguistically and culturally with the Cree and Algonquin communities in their proximity. Even within the "tribal groups," there is considerable localized diversity of lifeway and dialect. The literature also makes reference to significant social and cultural differences between Northern Ojibwe, for a subsistence life in the bush hunting, fishing, and trapping has continued to this day, and Southern Ojibwe who, though living a traditional seasonal round, have remained in larger numbers more of the time.

3. McNally, *Ojibwe Singers*.

4. I do not mean to be as exhaustive here, as I do in placing this study in the context of literature in Native American studies and the study of religion. My purpose is to make clear to the general reader the major transformation in the place of old age in North American history and to make possible a reading of this book in light of the scholarship in American social and cultural history that has already masterfully charted that narrative.

5. Cole, *Journey of Life*.

6. This baseline itself represents a historical early modern transformation from medieval representations of lifetime as a cycle overlain with the cyclical progression of the agricultural year, where the lives of individuals are swallowed up into collective and natural cycles, a view that is more attuned to the sensibilities of Anishinaabe representations of lifetime.

7. Heyrman explores the way that even, in the eighteenth century, evangelical revivals, at least in the south, were challenging the social norms of patriarchy and age by pitting the authority of dashing young circuit preachers, combined with the interests of those women and younger men who stood to gain from the authority of the converted soul, over that of older resident clergy and the landed elders who were the leaders of local churches. See Heyrman, *Southern Cross*.

8. Cole, *Journey of Life*, 152.

9. Cole, *Journey of Life*, 147.

10. Thomas, "Age and Authority in Early Modern England;" John Demos, "Old Age in Early New England," in *Aging, Death, and the Completion of Being*, ed. Van Tassel.

11. Achenbaum, *Old Age in the New Land*; Fischer, *Growing Old in America*; Haber, *Beyond Sixty-Five*.

12. Achenbaum, *Old Age in the New Land*, 177.

13. Thomas R. Cole, review of *Beyond Sixty-Five* by Carole Haber, *Journal of Social History* 18 (Spring 1985): 502–4. European studies include George Minois, *History of Old Age: From Antiquity to the Renaissance*, trans. Sarah Hanbury-Tenison (Chicago: University of Chicago Press, 1989); and David Troyansky, *Old Age in the Ancien Regime* (Ithaca: Cornell University Press, 1989). Exceptional studies are to be found in Thane, *Old Age in English History*; Vincent Gourdon, "Are Grandparents Really Absent from the Family Tradition? Forbears in the Region of Vernon Around 1800," *History of the Family* 4 (1999): 77–91; and idem, *Histoire des grand-parents* (Paris: Perrin, 2001), which works demographic observations into meaningful interpretations of the complications of family relationships. The articles in Ottaway, Botelho, and Kittredge's *Power and Poverty* and in Ottaway's *Decline of Life*, although very much concerned with transformations in the care of the elderly, pay close attention to situating old age in relationships that were as meaningful as they were socially significant.

14. See, for example, Amoss and Harrell, *Other Ways of Growing Old*; Kertzer and Keith, *Age and Anthropological Theory*; Premo, *Winter Friends*; Buchanan, "Fall of Icarus"; Susan Ridgely Bales, *When I Was a Child: Children's Interpretations of First Communion* (Chapel Hill: University of North Carolina Press, 2005). See also recent work, surely to be published, by Masen Uliss on the White House Conference on Aging, paper presented at the American Academy of Religion Annual Meeting (November 2007); and by Taylor Hines, "The Blinding of H. Emilie Cady: The Dilemmas of Aging for a New Thought Woman," paper presented at the American Academy of Religion Annual Meeting (November 2007).

15. On the deep and troubling history of "playing Indian" in American identity formation, see Philip Deloria, *Playing Indian* (New Haven: Yale University Press, 1998).

Introduction

1. On the image of the Indian in American thought, literature, and film, see Robert Berkhofer Jr., *The White Man's Indian* (New York: Vintage, 1978).

2. Although seemingly a commonplace, the concept of a "practice" has been elaborated by Marx and used specifically by social scientists in the tradition of Pierre Bourdieu. For my purposes *practices* are embodied gestures, postures, habitual and ritualized actions, but also cultivated mental disciplines (and thus distinguished by that discipline from mere intellection). These are marked off from

nonpurposive actions either by their intention, as in explicit devotional practices, or by their formal stylization, as in the bow. Such practices are corporate in nature; that is, even when practiced in private, they are related to inherited habits and traditions of a community and in turn contribute to the process of passing on such traditions. Practices are not always—in fact, seldom are they—directed with fully conscious intention; more often they are so habituated that they become second nature, and because of this, they are, importantly, only partially narratable. In this, they are more, and less, than the sum of their intentional parts and for this reason have the possibility of shaping thought.

3. Gladys Ray, in Vannote, *Women of White Earth*, 9.

4. United Nations, A/61/L.67 (September 7, 2007).

5. In particular, see Anderson, *Four Hills of Life*; Amoss, "Cultural Centrality and Prestige for the Elderly"; and the essays in Schweitzer, *American Indian Grandmothers*.

6. Shils, *Tradition*. Significant studies also include Hobsbawm and Ranger, *Invention of Tradition*; and Hervieu-Léger, *Religion as a Chain of Memory*.

7. When Bucko references "elders," it is in the context of claims to legitimacy that in his analysis are in question: either Indian movement grandstanding, justifications for non-Native and New Age appropriations of the ceremonies, and of what he terms "ethnonosticism." Appeals to the authority of elders, in Bucko's analysis, always seem to be "reaching" for legitimacy and, although Bucko does not say so, are on my reading of his language, suggestively inauthentic.

8. Ethnohistorians include Calvin Martin and Fergus Bordewich; Native scholars include, for example, Vine Deloria Jr., Inés Talamantez, and George Tinker.

9. Blackbird, *History of the Ottawa and Chippewa Indians*, 12–13.

10. What is more, it bespeaks the bicultural position of Blackbird, a man educated in the languages and conventions of both Odawa and Anglo-America and writing strategically in English for a largely non-Native audience. Jace Weaver's notion of "communitism" encapsulates the strategic position from which nineteenth-century Native figures like Blackbird took to their literary products in English. See Weaver, *That the People Might Live: Native American Literatures and Native American Community* (New York: Oxford University Press, 1997).

11. Rosaldo, *Culture and Truth*.

12. Jones, *History of the Ojebway Indians*, 68.

13. The ethnographic record on the Ojibwe is one of the more extensive and influential, with references appearing in classic texts in the field of religious studies by Freud, Durkheim, Levi-Strauss, Eliade, Wach, and others.

14. Ritzenthaler, "Southwestern Chippewa," 752; and Rogers, *Round Lake Ojibwa*, B59: "Men and women move gradually into the period of old age. There is no ritual or event which marks the transition. Years and a diminution of physical ability tend to delimit this period. . . . Advancement to this stage does not lower the status of the individual, especially men. In general elders are loved and respected."

15. A. I. Hallowell, "Temporal Orientation in Western Civilization and in a Preliterate Society," *American Anthropologist* 39 (1937): 647–70.

16. Hilger, *Chippewa Child Life*, 74; Jenness, *Ojibwa Indians of Parry Island*, 94: "The ethical training was as rigid as the physical. Children were taught certain rules of conduct, and frequently punished for their infringement. They should never tell lies. They should be respectful to their elders and not walk in front of them."

17. Landes, *Ojibwa Religion*, 8, 11.

18. Landes, *Ojibwa Sociology*, 12.

19. Landes, *Ojibwa Sociology*, 12, 5.

20. This is the informed perspective of Jeffrey Anderson, an anthropologist whose work on Northern Arapaho age-grade societies, addresses this error to find not only a wealth of details pertaining to the ritual society of the tribe's eldest, but also wholly reconceives categories perilously taken for granted by generations of ethnologists, categories like "knowledge" and "culture," to see them as dynamic categories in motion with the life movement of the life cycle. See Anderson, *Four Hills of Life*.

21. Sam Gill, *Mother Earth: An American Story* (Chicago: University of Chicago Press, 1987).

22. In Landes's reckoning, "individualism" made more sense in understanding the world of Ojibwe men than that of Ojibwe women.

23. Hickerson, "Some Implications of the Theory of Particularity."

24. Hallowell, *Culture and Experience*, 147.

25. Landes, *Ojibwa Religion*, 37.

26. Rogers, *Round Lake Ojibwa*, D4: "With time, an individual's power is said to become dissipated. Young men, it is thought, have the greatest amount. It is of interest in this connection that the native preachers who are considered to have the most Christian power are young men. By the age of forty or fifty individuals begin to lose their power. One shaman in the village who was in his late sixties was reported to have said he was losing his power."

27. Rogers, *Round Lake Ojibwa*, D4: "Further information is needed on this point. The idea that power is lost with increasing age conflicts with the idea that

the older males were leaders in former days because of their religious power. It also conflicts in part with the idea that one could continuously seek power. . . . A further complication is, of course, due to the fact that the religious system is undergoing violent change."

28. Dunning, *Social and Economic Change Among the Northern Ojibwa*, 184.

29. Jenness, *Ojibwa Indians of Parry Island*, 91–94.

30. Landes, *Ojibwa Sociology*, 23.

31. Barnouw, "Acculturation and Personality," 24.

32. Anderson, *Four Hills of Life*, 160. "Advancing through life required increasingly giving one's own life for others. As one's power for life movement was given away and therefore diminished, the next generations received momentum and direction" (198).

33. A. I. Hallowell, "Northern Ojibwa Ecological Adaptation and Social Organization," in *Contributions to Anthropology: Selected Papers of A. Irving Hallowell*, ed. Raymond Fogelson (Chicago: University of Chicago Press, 1976), 349.

34. An extensive entry on "Elder" in Eliade's encyclopedic forebear, the *Encyclopedia of Religion and Ethics*, ed. James Hastings (Edinburgh: Clark, 1912), focused on the place of the elder in Israelite religion and elaborated on the biblical term in light of nineteenth-century philology, with little attention to racial or cultural significance.

35. Weber, *Economy and Society*, 1.231.

36. Weber, *Economy and Society*, 1.230ff.

37. Wach does note that "the seer" is almost invariably aged, but the authority of the seer, like that of the diviner—the two closest figures in Wach's scheme—is charismatic, not traditional. "The seer is held in great reverence and honor, part of which may be due to his age or psychological peculiarities. Like the prophet, this type of *homo religiosus* may be visited by ecstatic states, visions, auditions, and even cataleptic trances. There have been few young seers; the experience of a long life seems to be necessary. Moreover, the seer is credited with a particularly close connection with the past which enhances his prestige and is often regarded as the keeper and guardian of tradition. Whereas the bard and the scribe hand down the literal content of the oral and written lore, the seer guarantees in his person and message the spirit of this heritage. Like the magician and pronouncer of charms, the seer speaks solemnly, and emphasis is placed on each of his words and utterances" (*Sociology of Religion*, 352).

38. Simmons, *Role of the Aged in Primitive Society*, 79.

39. On the history of anthropology, see, for example, James Clifford and George Marcus, eds., *Writing Culture: The Poetics and Politics of Ethnography* (Berkeley: University of California Press, 1986); and Johannes Fabian, *Time and the Other: How Anthropology Makes Its Object* (New York: Columbia University Press, 1983). In the case of Anishinaabe ethnology, Simmons relied fairly extensively on the work of Frances Densmore and William Hoffman.

40. Simmons, *Role of the Aged in Primitive Society*, 142.

41. Simmons, *Role of the Aged in Primitive Society*, 176.

42. See, for example, the literature review and introductory essay to *Other Ways of Growing Old*, ed. Amoss and Harrell; Fry, *Dimensions*; Kertzer and Keith, *Age and Anthropological Theory*; Rubinstein et al., *Anthropology and Aging*; Sokolovsky, *Cultural Context of Aging*; and Fried and Fried, *Transition*. This literature emerged around the same time as a cluster of American social historians, discussed in the preface, began publishing in the field.

43. Amoss, "Cultural Centrality and Prestige for the Elderly."

44. In the ethnographic literature on Africa, there are a number of helpful works, though as Lilian Dube observes in her research on Shona elders' place as caretakers during the HIV/AIDS pandemic, much of the literature focuses in cultural gerontology terms on the quantitative data and the needs of aged Africans rather than on their authority or place in traditional societies and in history. See Lilian Dube, "African Healers and Prophets: The Dynamics of Healing as Trajectories of Power and Piety among the Zimbabwean Women Elders," paper read at the American Academy of Religion 2007 annual meeting; and also John Mbiti, *African Religions and Philosophies* (New York: Praeger, 1968).

45. Schweitzer, *American Indian Grandmothers*; Anderson, *Four Hills of Life*.

46. Anderson, *Four Hills of Life*, 118.

47. Anderson, *Four Hills of Life*, 162–63.

48. Some recent efforts in the history of American religion are studies of religiosity: Susan Bales, *When I Was a Child: Children's Interpretations of First Communion* (Chapel Hill: University of North Carolina Press, 2005); and Robert Orsi, *Between Heaven and Earth: The Religious Worlds People Make and the Scholars Who Study Them* (Princeton: Princeton University Press, 2005).

49. Hallowell, *Ojibwa of Berens River*, 82. An analogy in the literature on Native Americans that receives more sustained attention is that of the Navajo concept of *bikeh hozho sa'ah naaghai*. See Gary Witherspoon, *Language and Art in the Navajo Universe* (Ann Arbor : University of Michigan Press, 1977).

50. Black-Rogers, "Ojibwa Power Belief System," 147n2.

51. See again, Anderson, *Four Hills of Life*.

52. Orsi, *Between Heaven and Earth*.

53. Weber, *Economy and Society*, 1.227.

54. As Jackson puts it, "basically what Native people mean when they refer to the old ways or Indian ways" "is not that it was done exactly this way before Columbus landed, but simply that it is the way things are (or used to be) done in Anishinaabe communities by the elder generation" (*Our Elders Lived It*, 125).

55. On the demographics, see Thornton, *American Indian Holocaust and Survival*. On the new social frameworks, see White, *Middle Ground*.

56. See Kugel, *To Be the Main Leaders of Our People*.

57. The concept of "culture in motion" is found in Rosaldo, *Culture and Truth*.

58. Jeffrey Anderson (personal communication, February 2006).

59. Benton-Banai, *Mishomis Book*, 91–93.

60. Benton-Banai, *Mishomis Book*, 91–93.

61. Benton-Banai, *Mishomis Book*, 91–93.

62. Wub-e-ke-niew, *We Have the Right to Exist*, 7.

63. I am grateful to Robert Orsi for first posing this question of me.

64. Broker, *Night Flying Woman*; Pflüg, *Ritual and Myth in Odawa Revitalization*; Smith, *Island of the Anishinaabeg*.

65. Jerry Morgan (personal communication, March 1994).

1. Aging and the Life Cycle Imagined in Ojibwe Tradition and Lived in History

1. "*Bagag Dibadj-mowin* (The Story of Bagag, the Skeleton)" is paraphrased from a version written in Odawa and translated roughly by Fred Ettawageshik in the 1950s; found in Kurath, Ettawageshik, and Ettawageshik, *Art of Tradition*. One could also consult Joe Chingwa's story of his grandfather's dream of old age from the same collection: "When he was a boy of twelve, he went to a little lodge to fast. He dreamed of his future life and saw an old man with a long beard. The man looked at him a long time and smiled at him. He had white hair and a wrinkled face. The man looked familiar. It was himself. Because of this, [he] always said that he would have a long life. He died at about 86 years in 1910."

2. Vecsey, *Traditional Ojibwa Religion*, 59–60, citing Åke Hultkrantz, *Conceptions of the Soul Among North American Indians*, Ethnographical Museum of

Sweden Monograph Series 1 (Stockholm: Ethnographical Museum of Sweden, 1953), 208.

3. Vecsey, *Traditional Ojibwa Religion*, 61, citing Hultkrantz, *Conceptions of the Soul*.

4. Jenness, *Ojibwa Indians of Parry Island*, 48–49.

5. See Black-Rogers, "Ojibwa Taxonomy and Percept Ambiguity."

6. Vecsey, *Traditional Ojibwa Religion*, 60–61.

7. Vecsey, *Traditional Ojibwa Religion*, 61, and citing Densmore, *Chippewa Customs*, 52–53.

8. Vecsey, *Traditional Ojibwa Religion*, 59.

9. Importantly, this grammatical usage also, according to Pat Ningewance, indicates a built-in empirical humility that rarely declares anything is as it appears, making room perhaps for the consideration that among the visible people in the room is a spirit. It admits of multiple interpretations.

10. Grim, *Shaman*.

11. Tu, "The Confucian Perception of Adulthood," in *Humanity and Self-Cultivation*, 35.

12. Fingarette, *Confucius*.

13. Grim, *Shaman*, 197.

14. This point was affirmed almost verbatim in the case of the Northern Arapaho. In *Four Hills of Life*, 160, Anderson's specific wording follows on the heels of a particular observation that the oldest men, that is members of the most senior lodge in the Arapaho age-grade system, traditionally wore red paint nearly all the time and that the color red was tied to humanness/maleness.

15. Hallowell, *Ojibwa of Berens River*, 82. An analogy in the literature on Native Americans that receives more sustained attention is that of the Navajo concept of *bikeh hozho sa'ah naaghai*. See Witherspoon, *Language and Art in the Navajo Universe*.

16. Black-Rogers, "Ojibwa Power Belief System," 147n2.

17. Vecsey, *Traditional Ojibwa Religion*, 4.

18. Hallowell, *Culture and Experience*, 171.

19. Anderson argues that classically for the Arapaho, "life movement does not emanate from natural processes or from an automatic inculcation or enculturation. It is a process generated by proper relations toward other persons, extended through kinship and age hierarchy and into the realm of other-than-human persons" (*Four Hills of Life*, 85).

20. Densmore, *Chippewa Customs*, 87.

21. Barnouw, "Acculturation and Personality," 24.

22. Carl Starkloff, *The People of the Center: American Indian Religion and Christianity* (New York: Seabury, 1974), 74.

23. As Anderson writes of classic Arapaho, "achieving longevity is symbolic of having lived in a good/correct way and therefore receiving blessings from above. In turn, those who have a long life have the power to give life movement to others" (*Four Hills of Life*, 113).

24. Hallowell, *Culture and Experience*, 230–31.

25. Rebecca Kugel, "Young Dogs and Gray Hairs: Considering Age and Gender Inequalities in 19th Century Ojibwe Society," paper presented at the American Society of Ethnohistory, October 2006.

26. Of mature men and women, Hallowell wrote that there are "only terms for married man, *onabemimaa*, and married woman, *wiwimaan*." While "bachelors and spinsters are rare," Hallowell noted, such unmarried adults were referred to with a kind of "temporal paradox," by joining the prefix for "old" or "great"— *giche* or *kete*—to the terms for unmarried male and female youth; thus *gete oshkiniige* and *gete oshkiniigikwe*.

27. Hallowell, *Culture and Experience*, 231.

28. Rogers, *Round Lake Ojibwa*, B59.

29. Buffalohead, "Farmers, Warriors, Traders."

30. On the accentuation of seasonal activities as markers of ethnic identity, see Nesper, *Walleye War*.

31. Such community self-representation distinguishes the newly created Smithsonian National Museum of the American Indian from traditional museum representations of Native cultures.

32. Tobasanaquod, Remarks at St. Cloud State University (September 2003).

33. See diagram in Densmore, *Chippewa Customs*, 89.

34. Densmore, *Chippewa Music*, 1.24, cited in Densmore, *Chippewa Customs*, 88–89. Densmore indicates that Walter Hoffman had written of a Midé scroll with a similar diagram concerning the path of life. Maingans was taken to task by Midéwiwin leaders for his disclosure and photographed mock performance in Washington, D.C. of Midé ceremonializing and secret knowledge.

35. Johnston, *Ojibway Heritage*, 109–10.

36. Johnston, *Ojibway Heritage*, 110.

37. Johnston, *Ojibway Heritage*, 111–12.

38. Johnston, *Ojibway Heritage*, 117–18.

39. Johnston, *Ojibway Heritage*, 118.

40. Anderson, *Four Hills of Life*, 99.

41. Anderson, *Four Hills of Life*, 106.

42. Anderson, *Four Hills of Life*, 113.

43. Jenness reported how the Parry Island Ojibwe of Lake Huron regarded this life movement in the heavens: "The Milky Way, to the Parry Islanders, is an enormous bucket-handle that holds the earth in place; if it ever breaks the world will come to an end. The 'life-line' (madjimadzuin: 'moving-life') is a human Milky Way; it is the chain connecting those who have gone before with those who follow, the line of ancestors and descendants together with all the inheritance factors they carry with them. There are two strands in this line or chain, a right and a left, a male and a female; and they are joined but loosely. It is woman's duty, therefore, to preserve the line intact, to bear many children lest the family, the clan, and the whole human race itself perish. Just as a tree has many branches, some of which flourish and some die, so it is with the clan and family; if all the branches die the tree, the family, or the clan perishes. To the Parry Islanders, therefore, the preservation of a strong life-line was the primary concern of every man and woman in the community. It demanded from them upright lives, for the parent who sinned might so shame his infant children that they would refuse to live; or else he might reap some disability that would descend to his children and grandchildren" (*Ojibwa Indians of Parry Island*, 90).

44. Smith, *Island of the Anishinaabeg*, 180.

45. Richard Vedan, in "Debate Continues over Canadian Universities' Elder-in-Residence Programs," *Indian Country Today*, August 2, 2006, B3.

46. Leroy Valliere, in Tornes, *Memories of Lac du Flambeau Elders*, 55.

47. Ningewance, *Talking Gookom's Language.*

48. Baraga, *Dictionary of the Ojibway Language.*

49. Nichols and Nyholm, *Concise Dictionary of Minnesota Ojibwe.*

50. Landes, *Ojibwa Sociology*, 86.

51. Jones, *History of the Ojebway Indians*, 164–65, cited in Simmons, *Role of the Aged in Primitive Society*, 133.

52. Hallowell offers examples of how "reincarnation is possible, even if occasional" in his essay "The Ojibwa Self and Its Behavioral Environment" in *Culture and Experience*, 172–82.

53. Hallowell, *Ojibwa of Berens River*, 57–59.

54. Hallowell, *Culture and Experience*, 162.

55. Hallowell, *Role of Conjuring in Saulteaux Society.*

56. Smith, *Island of the Anishinaabeg*, 56.

57. Clifford Geertz's generative discussion appears in his essay "Religion as a Cultural System," reprinted in *The Interpretation of Cultures* (New York: Basic Books, 1973).

58. Landes, *Ojibwa Sociology*, 7.

59. Hallowell speaks of this term as it applies to those ancestors living in *ji-ibayakiing* ("land of the ghost-spirits") to the south; *Culture and Experience*, 155.

60. Simmons, *Role of the Aged in Primitive Society*, 142.

61. Again, Anderson is to be credited with extending this insight; see *Four Hills of Life*.

62. A. I. Hallowell, "Northern Ojibwa Ecological Adaptation and Social Organization," in *Contributions to Anthropology: Selected Papers of A. Irving Hallowell*, ed. Raymond Fogelson (Chicago: University of Chicago Press, 1976), 349.

63. Hallowell, *Culture and Experience*, 147.

64. Thornton, *American Indian Holocaust and Survival*, 39. For example, late-eleventh-century Mississippian populations had an estimated life expectancy of 33, compared with 35.3 for the English in the same year. I am indebted to Professor Thornton for much of the historical demographic discussion that follows.

65. Thornton, *American Indian Holocaust and Survival*, 39. Posing the question why Native American life expectancies before contact were only comparable to, and not dramatically higher than, those for Europeans, Thornton offers the explanations that higher infant mortality and/or childbirth-associated deaths, accidental deaths, and less reliable stores of food may have been responsible (41).

66. Thornton, *American Indian Holocaust and Survival*, 43.

67. Henry Dobyns, *Their Numbers Became Thinned* (Knoxville: University of Tennessee Press, 1983), 15–23, cited in Thornton, *American Indian Holocaust and Survival*, 45.

68. Dobyns, *Their Numbers Became Thinned*, 15–23, cited in Thornton, *American Indian Holocaust and Survival*, 45.

69. E. Wagner Stearn and Allen Stearn, *The Effect of Smallpox on the Destiny of the Amerindian* (Boston: Bruce Humphries, 1945), 44–45, cited in Thornton, *American Indian Holocaust and Survival*, 78–79.

70. White, *Middle Ground*.

71. A contrary aside: in the case of smallpox, Thornton refers to studies that suggest this particular disease struck disproportionate numbers of people aged 14 to 40.

72. See Dowd, *Spirited Resistance*.

73. Enmegabowh blamed this in large part on the "impurity of the water used on the reservation," but he also blamed the social stresses and "firewater" for an epidemic of premature death; *Minnesota Missionary* 3.7 (April 1880).

74. Thornton, *American Indian Holocaust and Survival*, 100.

75. *Commissioner of Indian Affairs Annual Report* (Washington, D.C.: Government Printing Office, 1902), 634–35.

76. Reddy, *Statistical Records of Native North Americans*, 10.

77. Thornton, *American Indian Holocaust and Survival*, 181.

78. Thornton, *American Indian Holocaust and Survival*, 181. In 1901, Hallowell tallied the distribution of population by age at Berens River and Little Grand Rapids and found the following statistics to be fairly consistent with national distribution of population as a whole:

	<6 yrs	6–15	16–20	21–65	>65
Berens River	64	83	39	108	8
Little Grand Rapids	21	29	17	51	7

79. See Jane Lamm Carroll, "Dams and Damages: The Ojibway, the United States, and the Mississippi Headwaters Reservoirs," *Minnesota History* 52 (Spring 1990): 2–16.

80. Thornton, *American Indian Holocaust and Survival*, 171.

81. *Trends in Indian Health, 1997* (Washington, D.C.: U.S. Indian Health Service, 1997), http://www.ihs.gov/publicinfo/publications/trends97/trends97.asp.

82. Thornton, *American Indian Holocaust and Survival*, 171.

83. *Trends in Indian Health, 1997*.

84. *Trends in Indian Health, 1997*.

85. *Trends in Indian Health, 1997*.

86. McCabe and Cuellar, "Aging and Health," 4.

87. Reddy, *Statistical Records of Native North Americans*, 387. Reddy's survey included 23,686 Ojibwes between ages 5 and 17, of which 1,059 reported speaking Ojibwe at home. The same study finds more than 70% of Navajo children aged 5–17 speak their Native language at home. Among Lakota Sioux children of the same age, the figure is 15%.

88. White Earth Land Recovery Project, Occasional Report (1994).

89. John Pietezel, *Life of Rev. Peter Marksman: An Ojibwa Missionary* (Cincinnati: Western Methodist Book Concern, 1910), 41.

90. Pietezel, *Life of Rev. Peter Marksman*, 32.

91. Kohl, *Kitchi-Gami*, 113.

92. William Warren, *Collections of the Minnesota Historical Society* (Saint Paul: Minnesota Historical Society Press, 1885), 5.270.

93. Densmore, *Chippewa Customs*, 27.

94. Jenness, *Ojibwa Indians of Parry Island*, 94.

95. Landes, *Ojibwa Sociology*, 2.

96. Hilger, *Chippewa Families*, 74.

97. Hilger, *Chippewa Child Life*, 170.

98. Rogers, *Round Lake Ojibwa*, B39.

2. Eldership, Respect, and the Sacred Community

1. Peacock and Wisuri, *Ojibwe Waasa Inaabidaa*, 24.

2. Landes writes, "The keystone of their culture, the bias which molds all personal actions and reshapes the cultural details that have been borrowed from neighboring tribes—is individualism" (*Ojibwa Woman*, 178).

3. Hallowell, *Culture and Experience*, citing Ruth Landes, "The Ojibwa of Canada," in Margaret Mead, ed., *Cooperation and Competition Among Primitive Peoples* (New York, 1937), 489, 491, 498.

4. Hickerson, "Some Implications of the Theory of the Particularity."

5. Schenck, *Voice of the Crane Echoes Afar*.

6. Rohrl, *Change for Continuity*, 133.

7. Rogers, *Round Lake Ojibwa*, D29.

8. Landes, *Ojibwa Sociology*, 11.

9. Landes, *Ojibwa Sociology*, 14.

10. Further ethnohistorical research remains to be done concerning the connection between eldership and clan organization. The extension of the kinship terms *grandmother* and *grandfather* to include everyone of one's grandparent's generation, discussed at length in chapter 3, suggests that clan affiliations alone would not be responsible for such special relationship beyond one's local kin group. Still, one's elder who is also one's *doodem* or fellow clan member may have been marked a social tie of particular importance. There is a passing reference in Broker's *Night Flying Woman* to "elders of the dodaim," but any distinction between kin and clan is not developed. Although Theresa Schenk does not make this observation in her ethnohistorical study of the Crane *doodem*, perhaps clan

elders served particular leadership purposes within the division of labor that the *doodem* system represented.

11. Again, "life movement" is Jeffrey Anderson's gloss on the Arapaho counterpart to the Ojibwe term.

12. See Richard Nelson, *Makes Prayers to the Raven* (Chicago: University of Chicago Press, 1983), for an evocative examination of analogous Koyukon views and practices with respect to the nonhuman persons of the northern forest.

13. Larry Cloud Morgan (personal communication, 1994).

14. Larry Cloud Morgan (personal communication, 1994). Cloud Morgan is, among other things, known for his part in designing and implementing a series of thirty units of Ojibwe-language tapes entitled "Learn to Speak and Understand Ojibwe with Pimsleur Language Programs," published by Simon and Schuster.

15. Ningewance, *Talking Gookom's Language*, xvii–xviii.

16. Ningewance, *Talking Gookom's Language*, xvii–xviii.

17. Actually, a classic Confucian cosmology involves three realms—heaven, earth, and humanity—and those farthest along the path of human self-transcendence (in human relations) are said to become "one body with Heaven and the myriad things."

18. Fingarette, *Confucius*.

19. In his *Introduction to Confucianism*, Yao suggests how this reorientation of ancestor worship to filial piety includes a ritual regard for ancestors within the ethical regard for one's filial seniors.

20. Tu, "The Creative Tension Between Jen/Ren and Li," in *Humanity and Self-Cultivation*, 27.

21. In answer to twentieth-century critics of Confucian social thought for its implication in authoritarian, patriarchal regimes, Tu Weiming, Rodney Taylor, and other contemporary scholars of the Confucian tradition have paid increased attention to the religious dimensions of its thought and practice, in part to distinguish the majority of Confucians over time from the legalistic "Confucianism" to which Chinese regimes from the Han and T'ang dynasties through the nineteenth century variously appealed in their attempts to consolidate state power.

22. Tu, "Creative Tension Between Jen/Ren and Li," 14.

23. *Classic of Filial Piety*, trans. James Legge, in *The Sacred Books of the East: The Texts of Confucianism*, 2nd ed. (Oxford: Clarendon, 1899), 3/1.465–88.

24. *Classic of Filial Piety*, 3/1.14.

25. Thomas Berry, "Affectivity in Classical Confucian Traditions," in *Confucian Spirituality*, ed. Tu and Tucker, 1.105–6.

26. Yao, *Introduction to Confucianism*, 201.

27. Berry, "Individualism and Holism in Chinese Tradition," 47.

28. Mary Evelyn Tucker, "Introduction," to *Confucian Spirituality*, ed. Tu and Tucker, 1.9.

29. Cited in Berry, "Individualism and Holism in Chinese Tradition," 48.

30. Contemporary scholars of that tradition like Tu Weiming assert that the tradition's insistence on the authority of age is a license to neither authoritarianism nor blind obedience. And even here Tu's insights are helpful to understanding Anishinaabe eldership. "Old age in itself commands little admiration," notes Tu, but instead the ethical maturity that can only come from, but does not simply follow from old age. "Respect for the old is actually based on the assumption that, in the long and unavoidable journey of self-improvement, an old man ought to have forged way ahead in furnishing his life with inspiring contents. . . . Simply being old and not dying does not get one very far." Confucius has what Tu calls a "shockingly un-Confucian regard" for an unmannerly old man who was, according to the *Analects* 14.46: "In youth, not humble as befits a junior; in manhood, doing nothing worthy of being handed down; and merely to live on, getting older and older is to be a useless pest." Given Confucius's own conviction that few, if any, fully arrive at the ultimate goal of sagehood, Tu reminds us that this indicates a not un-Confucian view that the unmannerly old man is himself only on the way. Still, Tu adds, it would also be misleading "to suppose that one's moral growth can significantly surpass one's physical maturation" (Weiming Tu, "The Confucian Perception of Adulthood," *Daedalus* 105 [1976]: 114).

31. Ben Chosa, in Tornes, *Memories of Lac du Flambeau Elders*, 145.

32. Kâ-Nîpitêhtêw, *Counselling Speeches*, 55.

33. Kâ-Nîpitêhtêw, *Counselling Speeches*, 93.

34. Buffalohead, "Farmers, Warriors, Traders," 242, citing as her evidence Harold Hickerson, ed., "The Journal of Charles Jean Baptiste Chaboillez, 1797–98," *Ethnohistory* 6 (Summer 1959): 275, 299.

35. Buffalohead, "Farmers, Warriors, Traders," 243, citing as her source Henry Rowe Schoolcraft, *The Indian in His Wigwam*, 169–73.

36. Rebecca Kugel, "Young Dogs and Gray Hairs: Considering Age and Gender Inequalities in 19th Century Ojibwe Society," paper presented at the American Society of Ethnohistory (October 2006).

37. Benton-Banai, *Mishomis Book*, 64.

38. Nichols and Nyholm, *Concise Dictionary of Minnesota Ojibwe*; and Ningewance, *Talking Gookom's Language.*

39. Baraga, *Dictionary of the Ojibway Language.*

40. For an analysis of the distinctive contours of Native American English, see William Leap, *American Indian English* (Salt Lake City: University of Utah Press, 1993).

41. In Kurath, Ettawageshik, and Ettawageshik, *Art of Tradition*, ms. p. 321.

42. Benton-Banai, *Mishomis Book*, 22.

43. A. I. Hallowell Papers, Series V (Research Notes), 18 boxes Ser V Folder: Ojibwe Indians #2, American Philosophical Society (Philadelphia).

44. A. I. Hallowell Papers, Series V (Research Notes), 18 boxes Ser V Folder: Ojibwe Indians #2, American Philosophical Society (Philadelphia); John Nichols (personal communication, August 2005).

45. Treuer, *Living Our Language*, 259. The association with respectful regard here could be circumstantial in the narrative, for the speaker, Archie Mosay, was telling of a respectful way to think about fish.

46. Rogers, *Round Lake Ojibwa*, B59.

47. Kâ-Nîpitêhtêw, *Counselling Speeches*, 63.

48. Black-Rogers, "Ojibwa Power Interactions," 54.

49. Black-Rogers, "Ojibwa Power Interactions," 45.

50. Black-Rogers, "Ojibwa Power Interactions," 45.

51. Black-Rogers, "Ojibwa Power Interactions," 45.

52. Black-Rogers, "Ojibwa Power Interactions," 57.

53. Translation from Treuer, *Living Our Language*, 93–95.

54. Treuer, *Living Our Language*, 94–94.

55. Hilger, *Chippewa Child Life*, 98.

56. Rogers, *Round Lake Ojibwa*, B59.

57. Darnell, "Implications of Cree Interactional Etiquette."

58. Valentine, *Making It Their Own*, 112.

59. Nesper, *Walleye War*, 114.

60. Cecilia Defoe, in Tornes, *Memories of Lac du Flambeau Elders*, 197.

61. Baraga, *Dictionary of the Ojibway Language.*

62. Translation from Treuer, *Living Our Language*, 93–95.

63. Bell, *Ritual Theory, Ritual Practice.*

64. Kohl, *Kitchi-Gami*, 66.

65. Kohl, *Kitchi-Gami*, 110–11.

66. Hilger, *Chippewa Child Life*, 98.

67. For example, Barnouw, *Wisconsin Chippewa Myths and Tales*.

68. See, for example, the malicious old man in Barnouw, *Wisconsin Chippewa Myths and Tales*; and in Overholt and Callicott, *Clothed-in-Fur and Other Tales*, 40ff.

69. Author's paraphrase of story found in Kurath, Ettawageshik, and Ettawageshik, *Art of Tradition*, ms. p. 468.

70. Wub-e-ke-niew, *We Have the Right to Exist*, 7.

71. Ritzenthaler, "Southwestern Chippewa," 752.

72. Alanson Skinner, *Notes on the Eastern Cree and Northern Saulteaux*, Anthropological Papers of the American Museum of Natural History 9 (New York: American Museum of Natural History, 1911), 1.

73. Peter Grant, *The Saulteux Indians, 1791–1804* (London, 1890), 365–66.

74. Kohl, *Kitchi-Gami*, 310.

75. F. J. Long, *Voyages and Travels, 1777–1781* (London, 1904), 110–11.

76. Kohl, *Kitchi-Gami*, 110–11.

77. Hilger, *Chippewa Child Life*, 98.

78. Hilger, *Chippewa Child Life*, 98.

79. Hilger, *Chippewa Child Life*, 98, citing Gilfillan, "Ojibways in Minnesota," 96. Of his prejudice against the old, see the extensive discussion in chapter 4.

80. So goes the argument of Thomas in "Age and Authority in Early Modern England."

81. Dunning, *Social and Economic Change Among the Northern Ojibwa*, 184.

82. Hallowell, *Culture and Experience*, 141.

83. See Berkhofer, *The White Man's Indian*.

84. Schweitzer, *American Indian Grandmothers*, 18.

85. Office of Indian Affairs, Circular No. 1665 (April 26, 1921).

86. See Melissa Meyer, *The White Earth Tragedy: Ethnicity and Dispossession at a Minnesota Anishinaabe Reservation, 1889–1920* (Lincoln: University of Nebraska Press, 1994).

87. Pauline Colby, *Reminiscences*, 65, Minnesota Historical Society (hereafter MHS). Colby is referring to reverence accorded Indian elders in *Ramona*, a fashionable reform novel that highly romanticized noble savages.

88. J. A. Gilfillan, Undated Notes and Fragments, J. A. Gilfillan Papers, Box I, MHS.

89. Hilger, *Chippewa Families*, 58.

90. Hilger, *Chippewa Families*, 57,

91. Dunning, *Social and Economic Change Among Northern Ojibwa*, 40.

92. McCabe and Cuellar, "Aging and Health," 4.

93. McCabe and Cuellar, "Aging and Health," 4.

94. U.S. Department of Health and Human Services, "Report of the Secretary's Task Force on Black and Minority Health," 2.287–29, cited in McCabe and Cuellar, "Aging and Health," 25.

95. U.S. House of Representatives, Select Committee on Aging, "Hispanic and Indian Elderly: America's Failure to Care" (Committee Publication No. 101-730), 70–76, cited in McCabe and Cuellar, "Aging and Health," 6.

96. Edwin Walker, "The Needs of Indian Elders," Statement in a Hearing by the Senate Committee on Indian Affairs (July 10, 2002) http://www.nicoa.org/policy_walker.html (accessed June 2006).

97. American Association of Retired Persons, "A Portrait of Older Minorities" (Washington, D.C., 1987), cited in McCabe and Cuellar, "Aging and Health," 7.

98. R. John, "The State of Research on American Indian Elders' Health, Income Security, and Social Support Networks," in *Minority Elders: Longevity, Economics, and Health: Building a Public Policy Base* (Washington, D.C.: Gerontological Society of America), 38–50, cited in McCabe and Cuellar, "Aging and Health," 7.

99. D. Buchwald et al., "Physical Abuse of Urban Native Americans," *Journal of General Internal Medicine* 15 (2000): 562–64.

100. National Indian Council on Aging, "Elder Abuse in Indian Country, a Review of the Literature," 2004, http://www.nicoa.org/elderabuselitreview.pdf (accessed July 2006).

101. Chris Horvath, "Addressing Elder Abuse with American Indian Tribes: A National Teleconference" (September 24, 1995), http://www.elderabusecenter.org/pdf/publication/telecon.pdf (accessed July 2006).

102. Saraphine Martin, in Vannote, *Women of White Earth*, 75.

103. F. L. Johnson, E. Cook, M. Foxall, E. Kelleher, E. Kentopp, and E. A. Mannlein, "Life Satisfaction of the Elderly American Indian," *International Journal of Nursing Studies* 23 (1986): 265–73, cited in McCabe and Cuellar, "Aging and Health," 27–28.

104. Despite widespread public opinion that Indians are vastly enriched with payouts from gaming, in Minnesota, the vast majority of Ojibwe people are enrolled at White Earth, Leech Lake, and Red Lake, far from the more profitable gaming reservations nearer the cities.

105. http://www. aoa.gov/ain/97report/default.htm (accessed June 2006).

106. For example, the Sault Tribe of Chippewa Indians sets 55 as the threshold for many benefits, though elders' benefit checks are available solely for members

aged 60 years or more; http://www.saulttribe.com/index.php?option=com_sim plefaq&func=display&Itemid=285&catid=148 (accessed February 17, 2006).

107. http://www.glifwc.org/pub/winter01/elder_hunt.htm (accessed May 2000).

108. McCabe and Cuellar, "Aging and Health," 31.

109. National Indian Council on Aging, "SSI Search Program: Access Model" (Albuquerque, 1993), cited in McCabe and Cuellar, "Aging and Health," 7.

110. National Indian Council on Aging, "SSI Search Program: Access Model" (Albuquerque, 1993), cited in McCabe and Cuellar, "Aging and Health," 7.

111. National Indian Council on Aging, Testimony, The Needs of Indian Elders: A Hearing by the Senate Committee on Indian Affairs (July 10, 2002), http://www.nicoa.org/policy_baldridge.html (accessed June 2005).

112. National Indian Council on Aging, Testimony, The Needs of Indian Elders: A Hearing by the Senate Committee on Indian Affairs (July 10, 2002), http://www.nicoa.org/policy_baldridge.html (accessed June 2005).

113. Treuer, *Living Our Language*, 208–9.

114. Constitution of the Little Traverse Bay Bands of Odawa Indians, article I.B, http://www.ltbbodawa-nsn.gov/tribal_council/OdawaRegister.htm (accessed February 17, 2006).

115. Sue Bellefeuille, in Vannote, *Women of White Earth*, 109.

116. Cecilia Defoe, in Tornes, *Memories of Lac du Flambeau Elders*, 197.

3. Elders as Grandparents and Teachers

1. Northrup, *Rez Road Follies*, 1.

2. Barnouw, *Wisconsin Chippewa Myths and Tales*, 237.

3. Paul Levy, "Spirit of White Earth, I" *Minneapolis Star Tribune* (April 25, 1999).

4. Landes, *Ojibwa Sociology*, 41.

5. Landes, *Ojibwa Sociology*, 12.

6. Landes, *Ojibwa Sociology*, 12.

7. Rogers, *Round Lake Ojibwa*, B15.

8. Rogers, *Round Lake Ojibwa*, B13.

9. Landes, *Ojibwa Woman*, 14.

10. Dunning, *Social and Economic Change Among the Northern Ojibwa*, 86.

11. Greg Skrypek (personal communication, November 19, 1996), paraphrasing a radio interview broadcast on Minnesota Public Radio.

12. Ben Chosa, in Tornes, *Memories of Lac du Flambeau Elders*, 132.

13. Northrup, *Rez Road Follies*, 21–22.

14. Jones, *History of the Ojebway Indians*, 164–65.

15. Johnston, *Ojibway Ceremonies*, 118.

16. Broker, *Night Flying Woman*, 56.

17. Peacock and Wisuri, *Ojibwe Waasa Inaabidaa*, 68.

18. Buffalohead, "Farmers, Warriors, Traders," 241.

19. Hilger, *Chippewa Child Life*, 74.

20. Hilger, *Chippewa Child Life*, 74.

21. Jenness, *Ojibwa Indians of Parry Island*, 94.

22. Tanner, *Falcon*, 39.

23. Ben Chosa, in Tornes, *Memories of Lac du Flambeau Elders*, 145.

24. Ben Chosa, in Tornes, *Memories of Lac du Flambeau Elders*, 145.

25. Cited in Peacock and Wisuri, *Ojibwe Waasa Inaabidaa*, 68.

26. Kâ-Nîpitêhtêw, *Counselling Speeches*, 48.

27. Densmore, *Chippewa Customs*, 60.

28. Kinietz, "Chippewa Village," 139.

29. Tanner, *Falcon*, 72.

30. *Jesuit Relations* 62 (1681–83): 197 (Thwaites translation)

31. Blackbird, *History of the Ottawa and Chippewa Indians*, 103.

32. Kinietz, "Chippewa Village," 111.

33. Northrup, *Rez Road Follies*, 67.

34. Hilger, *Chippewa Families*, 98.

35. George Copway, *The Traditional History and Characteristic Sketches of the Ojibway Nation* (Boston: Benjamin Mussey, 1851), cited in Hilger, *Chippewa Families*, 98.

36. Densmore, *Chippewa Customs*, 62n.

37. Broker, *Night Flying Woman*, 3.

38. Miller, *Shingwauk's Vision*, 18.

39. Northrup, *Rez Road Follies*, 3.

40. Kimberly Blaeser, in Vannote, *Women of White Earth*, 5.

41. Transcript of Louis Bird English-language interview on September 8, 2001, http://www.ourvoices.ca/filestore/pdf/0/1/2/0/0120.pdf (accessed February 16, 2006).

42. Ong, *Orality and Literacy*, 141–42.

43. On this feature in other Native American communities, see also Keith Basso, *Wisdom Sits in Places: Landscape and Language Among the Western Apache*

(Albuquerque: University of New Mexico Press, 1996); and Robin Ridington, *Trail to Heaven: Knowledge and Narrative in a Northern Native Community* (Iowa City: University of Iowa Press, 1988).

44. Darnell, "Implications of Cree Interactional Etiquette," 71.

45. Darnell, "Implications of Cree Interactional Etiquette," 73–74.

46. Darnell, "Implications of Cree Interactional Etiquette," 77.

47. Anderson, *Four Hills of Life*, 113.

48. Anderson, *Four Hills of Life*, 113.

49. Schweitzer, *American Indian Grandmothers*, 10.

50. Schweitzer, *American Indian Grandmothers*, 8.

51. Gladys Ray, in Vannote, *Women of White Earth*, 9 (emphasis added).

52. Shkilnyk, *Poison Stronger than Love*.

53. Hilger, *Chippewa Families*, 89.

54. Kinietz, "Chippewa Village," 120.

55. Hilger, *Chippewa Families*, 89.

56. See Frederick Hoxie, *The Final Promise: The Campaign to Assimilate the Indians, 1880–1920* (Lincoln: University of Nebraska Press, 2001).

57. Child, *Boarding School Seasons*, 17.

58. Child, *Boarding School Seasons*, 27.

59. Cited in Child, *Boarding School Seasons*, 48.

60. Child, *Boarding School Seasons*, 100.

61. Broker, *Night Flying Woman*, 94.

62. See, for example, Joan Weibel Orlando, *Indian Country, L.A.: Maintaining Ethnic Community in Complex Society* (Urbana: University of Illinois Press, 1991).

63. Jackson, *Our Elders Lived It*.

64. Jackson, *Our Elders Lived It*, 147.

65. Paul Levy, "Spirit of White Earth, V: Winnie Jourdain Takes in City Life," *Minneapolis Star Tribune* (April 29, 1999).

66. Levy, "Winnie Jourdain Takes in City Life."

67. Darryl Zitzow, "A Comparison of Time Ojibway Adolescents Spent with Parents/Elders in the 1930s and 1980s," *American Indian and Alaska Native Mental Health Research* 3 (Spring 1990): 7–16 (abstract).

68. Corbiere, "Reconciling Epistemological Orientations," 3.

69. Corbiere, "Reconciling Epistemological Orientations," 5.

70. Corbiere, "Reconciling Epistemological Orientations," 6.

71. Corbiere, "Reconciling Epistemological Orientations," 8.

72. Akan, "Pimosatamowin Sikaw Kakeequaywin."

73. "Debate Continues over Canadian Universities' Elder-in-Residence Programs," *Indian Country Today*, August 2, 2006, B3.

74. "Debate Continues."

75. "University College of the North Act," Legislative Assembly of Manitoba, 2nd Session, 38th Legislature, Bill 20, http://web2.gov.mb.ca/bills/38–2/b020e.php (accessed August 2006).

76. Tom Robertson, "Reviving the Language" (radio broadcast), Minnesota Public Radio (August 20, 2003), http://news.minnesota.publicradio.org/features/2003/08/20_robertsont_languagecamp/ (accessed August 2006).

77. Alan Corbiere (personal communication, January 15, 2008).

4. Elders Articulating Tradition

1. Simmons, *Role of the Aged in Primitive Society*, 176.

2. The Ojibwe language has remained primarily oral, even with an aboriginal writing system on bark scrolls that served to prompt mnemonic rehearsal of narrative, herbal, and sacred knowledge, and with the influence of a nineteenth-century syllabary developed in northern Canada by neighboring Cree Anglicans.

3. Jones, *History of the Ojebway Indians*, 164–65.

4. Abby Goodnough, "Survivors of Tsunami Live on Close Terms with Sea," *New York Times*, January 23, 2005.

5. See, inter alia, Vansina, *Oral Tradition as History*.

6. Ong, *Orality and Literacy*, 41. Ong does not deny that narratives, cosmologies, and religious practices can change in oral traditions. Citing Goody's notion of the "intellectuals" in oral society, Ong notes that new shrines and "new conceptual universes" can emerge, but "these new universes and the other changes that show a certain originality come into being in an essentially formulaic and thematic noetic economy. They are seldom if ever explicitly touted for their novelty but are presented as fitting the traditions of the ancestors" (*Orality and Literacy*, 42, citing Goody, *Domestication of the Savage Mind*, 30).

7. Ong, *Orality and Literacy*, 49–50.

8. This is true of Ningewance's *Talking Gookom's Language*; Rhodes's *Eastern Ojibwa-Chippewa-Ottawa Dictionary*; and Nichols and Nyholm's *Concise Dictionary of Minnesota Ojibwe*. Interestingly, however, one can find them in Baraga's

Dictionary of the Ojibway Language, invested as he was in a missionary project of conveying thought generated in European languages into Ojibwe.

9. Nichols and Nyholm's *Concise Dictionary of Minnesota Ojibwe* does not even include English to Ojibwe entries for such abstractions as culture, tradition, or knowledge.

10. Weber, *Economy and Society*, 1.215.

11. For Weber, traditional authority is less a complex subject of analysis in its own right than a sort of premodern foil to the contrastive modern processes of differentiation, bureaucratization, and the emergence of market capitalism (*Economy and Society*, 1.231).

12. Weber, *Economy and Society*, 1.227. But Weber understood the capacity of traditional authority to sanction innovation. "Deliberate creation by legislation" is impossible, but "rules which in fact are innovations can be legitimized only by the claim that they have been 'valid of yore,' but have only now been recognized by means of 'Wisdom' (the *Weistum* of ancient Germanic law)" (*Economy and Society*, 1.227).

13. Jackson, *Our Elders Lived It*, 125.

14. See Bloch's "Introduction" to *Political Language and Oratory*, esp. 5–13.

15. Bloch, *Political Language and Oratory*, 6.

16. Kohl, *Kitchi-Gami*, 66.

17. Kohl, *Kitchi-Gami*, 273.

18. Rogers, *Round Lake Ojibwa*, B15.

19. Valentine, *Making It Their Own*, 70, 125, 141.

20. Treuer, *Living Our Language*, 44–45.

21. Kâ-Nîpitêhtêw, *Counselling Speeches*, 141.

22. Bloch, *Political Language and Oratory*, 13.

23. Darnell, "Implications of Cree Interactional Etiquette," 75.

24. Schenck, *Voice of the Crane Echoes Afar*, 71, citing Martin Fried, *The Evolution of Political Society* (New York: Random House, 1967).

25. Landes, *Ojibwa Sociology*, 1–2.

26. Jenness, *Ojibwa Indians of Parry Island*, citing *Documents Relating to the Early History of Hudson Bay*, ed. J. B. Tyrrell (Toronto: Champlain Society, 1931), 382.

27. Tanner, *Falcon*, 16.

28. Tanner, *Falcon*, 36, 47, 54, 57.

29. Warren, *History of the Ojibway People*, 289.

30. Jenness, *Ojibwa Indians of Parry Island*, 2.

31. Jenness, *Ojibwa Indians of Parry Island*, 2.

32. Kinietz, "Chippewa Village," 82.

33. Harold Hickerson, "The Southwestern Chippewa: An Ethnohistorical Study," *American Anthropological Association Memoirs* 64 (1962): 57.

34. Kohl, *Kitchi-Gami*, 273.

35. Kugel, *To Be the Main Leaders of Our People*.

36. Kugel observes that the many "full-blood" Ojibwe who aligned with the Episcopal mission had basically followed their elder civil leaders' strategic alliances with the missionaries and their power network for an accommodationist future. In sum, for Kugel, becoming Episcopalian was a religious repercussion of strategic political choices made by the elders whose authority they recognized. And this in stark contrast to a faction, many of whom were of mixed descent (and thus more closely affiliated with the Roman Catholic mission heritage during the fur trade), drawn to the militancy of the warrior leaders.

37. Wub-e-ke-niew, *We Have the Right to Exist*, 47.

38. Bizhiki quoted in "Journal of the Commissioners appointed to hold a treaty with the Chippeways, on Lake Superior in 1826," in Documents relating to the Treaty of 5 August 1826, National Archives Records Administration, Record Group T 494, Roll 1, pp. 825–69 at 840; Flat Mouth quoted in "Interview between the Commissioner of Indian Affairs and the Pillager and Winnepec band of Chippewas on Saturday morning, Feby 17, 1855," in "Transcription of the record of the negotiation and signing of the Treaty of February 22, 1855, made and entered into at Washington, D.C., by and between George W. Manypenny, Commissioner of Indian Affairs, on the part of the United States, and the chiefs and delegates of the Mississippi, Pillager and Lake Winnibigoshish bands of Chippewa Indians," 74–75, in James F. Sutherland Papers, MHS—both cited in Rebecca Kugel, "Young Dogs and Gray Hairs: Considering Age and Gender Inequalities in 19th Century Ojibwe Society," paper presented at American Society of Ethnohistory (October 2006).

39. H. B. Whipple, Account of 1862 Visitation, H. B. Whipple Papers, Box 3, MHS.

40. Kugel, *To Be the Main Leaders of Our People*, 73.

41. Christian missionaries made inroads among Ojibwes, beginning with French Jesuits in the late seventeenth century. But it was in the mid- and late-nineteenth century, as the Ojibwe were increasingly confined to reservations and as necessity forced a traditional lifeway based on the seasonal round to keep time with the unfamiliar rhythms of sedentary agriculture and annuity payments, that

Ojibwe people became more demonstrably Christian in more demonstrable numbers. In 1879, Episcopalians claimed one fourth of White Earth's population as communicants, not to speak of Roman Catholics. Among Minnesota's Ojibwe in this era, the most heavily ramified encounters among full-blood Ojibwe were with Episcopalian missionaries, and this discussion will focus on that encounter.

42. On the dexterity of practice in missionary encounters, see John and Jean Comaroff, *Of Revelation and Revolution: Christianity, Colonialism, and Consciousness in South Africa* (Chicago: University of Chicago Press, 1991); and idem, *Of Revelation and Revolution: The Dialectics of Modernity on a South African Frontier* (Chicago: University of Chicago Press, 1997).

43. I develop this theme in the introduction to *Ojibwe Singers*.

44. See McNally, *Ojibwe Singers*, 81–122.

45. J. A. Gilfillan, "Some Indians I Have Known," in *The Red Man by Red Men*, J. A. Gilfillan Papers, MHS.

46. Bonnie Sue Lewis, *Creating Christian Indians: Native Clergy in the Presbyterian Church* (Norman: University of Oklahoma Press, 2003).

47. Enmegabowh to Samuel Hollingsworth, December 30, 1878, Enmegabowh Papers, MHS.

48. Gilfillan, "Indian Notes," *Minnesota Missionary* 10.1 (January 1886).

49. For a discussion of his shaking tent, see Gilfillan to Rev. E. W. Cook, August 3, 1882, Gilfillan Papers, Folder 5, MHS.

50. Gilfillan, "Indian Notes," *Minnesota Missionary* 10.1 (January 1886).

51. *The Red Man* (December, no year), Gilfillan Papers, Box 7, MHS.

52. It is tempting to credit, as missionaries did, the conversion to the influence of his son the deacon, but Gilfillan revealed in passing that Shaydayence's "conversion" was due largely to the "burning exhortations" of his friend and fellow elder Nabuneshkung, baptized shortly before, after considerable deliberation on his own part (Gilfillan, "Shaydayence" in *Woman's Work* [July 1882], Gilfillan Papers, Scrapbook, Box 2, MHS).

53. Gilfillan, "Shaydayence."

54. Gilfillan, "Shaydayence."

55. Gilfillan, "Shaydayence."

56. Committee of Mazigishik's Band via Henry Selkirk to H. B. Whipple, August 14, 1881, H. B. Whipple Papers, Box 15, MHS.

57. Committee of Mazigishik's Band via Henry Selkirk to H. B. Whipple, August 14, 1881, H. B. Whipple Papers, Box 15, MHS.

58. Gilfillan, "Indian Notes," *Minnesota Missionary* 10.5 (May 1886), MHS.

59. Pauline Colby, *Reminiscences*, 65, MHS.

60. Melissa Meyer, *The White Earth Tragedy* (Lincoln: University of Nebraska Press, 1994).

61. Madjigishik to H. B. Whipple, January 5, 1889, Whipple Papers, Box 18, MHS.

62. Kugel, *To Be the Main Leaders of Our People*, 123.

63. Gilfillan, "Shay-Day-Ence," Gilfillan Papers, Box 1, Folder 1, MHS.

64. Gilfillan, *Minnesota Missionary* 3.6 (March 1880).

65. Gilfillan, *Minnesota Missionary* 3.6 (March 1880).

66. Gilfillan, "Shaydayence."

67. Bloch, *Political Language and Oratory*.

68. Gilfillan, "Shaydayence."

69. Gilfillan, "Some Indians I Have Known," 463–68.

70. Gilfillan, "Some Indians I Have Known," 463–68.

71. Gilfillan, "Shay-Day-Ence."

72. On this point, I take issue with the gist of Bloch's and other anthropological analyses of traditional authority. Concerned merely to document how formal elders' speech acts, and the formal expectations of deference that follow, bespeak social control, Bloch does not make room for the considerable improvisational possibilities that elders enjoy. See Bloch, *Political Language and Oratory*; Simmons, *Role of the Aged in Primitive Society*; and Kertzer and Keith, *Age and Anthropological Theory*.

73. Kugel argues persuasively that the elder civil leaders alignment with the Episcopal mission beginning in the 1850s was in large part a matter of a strategic alliance, one that resulted in considerable disillusionment in the 1870s when non-Indian Episcopalian authorities supported policies that further undermined the sovereignty of Ojibwe leadership. See *To Be the Main Leaders of Our People*, esp. 143ff.

74. Enmegabowh, January 13, 1874, to *Spirit of Missions* (April 1874) 222, Gilfillan Papers, Box 2, MHS.

75. Sherman Hall's Diary, July 22, 1832, in Grace Lee Nute Collection, Box 2, MHS.

76. Grace Lee Nute Collection, Box 3, Folder 1, MHS.

77. C. H. Beaulieu to H. B. Whipple, September 17, 1881, H. B. Whipple Papers, MHS.

78. Gilfillan to H. B. Whipple, September 12, 1881, H. B. Whipple Papers, MHS.; Grace Lee Nute Collection, Box 11, Folder 7, MHS.

79. C. H. Beaulieu to H. B. Whipple, September 17, 1881, H. B. Whipple Papers, MHS.

80. Valentine, *Making It Their Own*, 217, 138.

81. Francis Willis Jr., "Red Lake Mission," *Minnesota Missionary and Church Record* 21.2 (February 1897), MHS.

82. Colby, *Reminiscences*, 29.

83. In this respect visiting among the Anami'aajig may have reiterated the expectations of clan membership, where Ojibwe travelers could always claim the hospitality of members of their clan or *doodem*.

84. Gilfillan, "Some Indians I Have Known."

85. Dr. Thomas Parker to H. B. Whipple, March 12, 1880, H. B. Whipple Papers, Box 14, MHS.

86. Colby, *Reminiscences*, 105.

87. For prereservation-era examples, see the case of Netnokwa discussed in this chapter or that of Ruth Flatmouth, an *ogimaakwe* at Leech Lake in the mid-nineteenth century.

88. Robert Neslund, "Native American Lace: An Experiment in Mission and Self Help," *The Historiographer of the National Episcopal Historians and Archivists and the Historical Society of the Episcopal Church* 41 (Pentecost, 2003), 18.

89. Sybil Carter, "Opitchi-Bimisay" (Hartford, CT: Junior Auxiliary Publishing, 1894), MHS.

90. Neslund, "Native American Lace," 18–19.

91. Gilfillan to H. B. Whipple, December 3, 1875, Whipple Papers, Box 11, MHS.

92. Suzanna Roy to H. B. Whipple via Gilfillan, July 25, 1875, Whipple Papers, Box 11, MHS.

93. Suzanna Roy to H. B. Whipple via Gilfillan, April 13, 1882, Whipple Papers, Box 16, MHS.

94. Rebecca Kugel, "Leadership Within the Women's Community: Susie Bonga Wright of the Leech Lake Ojibwe," in *Midwestern Women: Work, Community, and Leadership at the Crossroads*, ed. Lucy Eldersveld Murphy and Wendy Hamand Venet (Bloomington: Indiana University Press, 2002), 17–37.

95. Kugel, "Leadership Within the Women's Community," 24–25.

96. Gilfillan to H. B. Whipple, September 12, 1881, H. B. Whipple Papers, MHS (emphasis original).

97. See McNally, "Honoring Elders."

98. Enmegabowh to H. B. Whipple, September 23, 1878, Whipple Papers, Box 13, MHS, cited in Kugel, "Leadership Within the Women's Community," 25.

99. Kugel, "Leadership Within the Women's Community," 26.

100. Gilfillan, *Minnesota Missionary* 3.6 (March 1880), MHS.

101. Gilfillan, *Minnesota Missionary* 3.5 (February 1880); 3.6 (March 1880) MHS.

102. Kugel, *To Be the Main Leaders of Our People*, 142. Samuel Madison Nabiquan was the son of Shaydayence of the Gull Lake Band; Charles Wright Nashotah was son of Waubunoquod, one of the more powerful *ogimaag*; George Morgan Kakagun, the son of Ayabe of the Mille Lacs Band; Mark Hart, the son of Obimweweosh; and George Johnson, the son of Enmegabowh. By contrast, Fred Smith Kadawabide was the orphaned son of Bugonegeshig's Hole-in-the-Day's principal warrior. For more detail about their lives, see McNally, *Ojibwe Singers*, 96–99.

103. See McNally, *Ojibwe Singers*, 98–99. At Leech Lake, another *ogimaakwe* emerged with influence enough to appear with some clarity in a documentary record penned by missionaries who otherwise rarely remarked on the activities of the women. Leech Lake women met under the "spiritual charge" of Susan Bonga, daughter of an influential trader and granddaughter of a runaway African American slave. Clearly, Bonga was no elder: she led the guild beginning in her thirties. Her esteem appears to have involved her ability to navigate the American and Ojibwe worlds, though savvy alone would not command respect of her Ojibwe sisters and brothers. In the 1880s, she married Ojibwe deacon Charles Nashotah Wright, making Suzanna Roy her aunt, in a union that showed how the Anami'aajig were fashioning an important religious and political network across lines of band and reservation to answer the divide and conquer agenda of colonizing interests ("Notes from the Indian Field," *Minnesota Missionary* 4.6 [March 1881], MHS).

104. Gilfillan to H. B. Whipple, January 30, 1883, H. B. Whipple Papers, MHS.

105. Gilfillan to H. B. Whipple, September 23, 1882, H. B. Whipple Papers, MHS.

106. Gilfillan to H. B. Whipple, September 23, 1882, H. B. Whipple Papers, MHS.

107. "The people demanded from their chiefs liberality above all things. If a family were in need the chief had to provide for it from his own resources, as well as levy contributions from other families in the band; and in times of plenty he maintained his popularity and prestige by a bountiful distribution of the fish and

game that he secured through his own exertions" (Jenness, *Ojibwa Indians of Parry Island*, 2).

108. Thomas Parker to H. B. Whipple, March 2, 1880, H. B. Whipple Papers, Box 15, MHS.

109. Nashotah called for a renewed investigation into the sexual misconduct of a non-Native priest there and for the replacement of the sub-Indian Agent and schoolteacher at Leech Lake, a retired missionary named S. G. Wright whose wife left for their native Oberlin and who also had allegedly harassed Ojibwe women. Nashotah's claims also concerned the double standard being applied to the Native clergy, for Gilfillan had made haste to discipline deacons John Coleman and George Johnson (Enmegabowh's son) for fathering children deemed illegitimate by Anglo-American reckonings of marriage (Kugel, *To Be the Main Leaders of Our People*, 149). By the conventions of Ojibwe marriage, men and women could come and go from marital relationships with an ease and frequency that greatly irritated missionaries.

110. Gilfillan to H. B. Whipple, November 21, 1882, H. B. Whipple Papers, MHS.

111. Gilfillan to I I. B. Whipple, January 23, 1883, H. B. Whipple Papers, MHS.

112. Gilfillan to H. B. Whipple, January 10, 1883, H. B. Whipple Papers, MHS.

113. Gilfillan to H. B. Whipple, January 10, 1883, H. B. Whipple Papers, MHS.

114. Gilfillan to H. B. Whipple, January 4, 1883, H. B. Whipple Papers, MHS.

115. Gilfillan to H. B. Whipple, January 10, 1883, H. B. Whipple Papers, MHS.

116. Gilfillan to H. B. Whipple, January 23, 1883, H. B. Whipple Papers, MHS.

117. Gilfillan to H. B. Whipple, January 30, 1883, H. B. Whipple Papers, MHS.

118. Gilfillan to H. B. Whipple, February 8, 1882, H. B. Whipple Papers, MHS.

119. Gilfillan to H. B. Whipple, February 6, 1883, H. B. Whipple Papers, MHS.

120. Kugel notes (*To Be the Main Leaders of Our People*, 150–51) that it was Clement Beaulieu Sr., a key figure of the old "warrior-mixed-blood-trader coalition," who informed Gilfillan of Enmegabowh's involvement and thus disclosed that he was privy to the affairs of Enmegabowh and the deacons. Kugel argues suggestively that the strike indicated a realignment of the old civil leaders and the Episcopal deacons with their former adversaries.

121. In the aftermath of the affair, Gilfillan ironically argued against Edwin Benedict's proposal that Charles Wright Nashotah receive exemplary punishment (Gilfillan to H. B. Whipple, May 4, 1883, H. B. Whipple Papers, MHS).

122. Gilfillan to H. B. Whipple, July 19, 1886, Whipple Papers, Box 17, MHS.

123. George Tinker, *Missionary Conquest: The Gospel and Native American Cultural Genocide* (Minneapolis: Fortress, 1993).

124. Hilger, *Chippewa Families*, 57.

125. Vernon Bellecourt (personal communication, July 2006); Benton-Banai, *Mishomis Book*.

126. McNally, *Ojibwe Singers*, 177. I gained my understanding of folklorization from the ethnomusicologist Thomas Turino's thick description of urban performances for audiences of highland Indian panpipe repertories in *Moving Away from Silence* (Chicago: University of Chicago Press, 1993).

127. On the influence of Longfellow's poem, see Alan Trachtenberg, *Shades of Hiawatha: Staging Indians, Making Americans, 1880–1930* (New York: Hill and Wang, 2004).

128. For a detailed discussion of these pageants, see Michael McNally, "The Indian Passion Play: Contesting the Real Indian in *Song of Hiawatha* Pageants, 1901–1965," *American Quarterly* 58 (March 2006): 105–36.

129. Kurath, Ettawageshik, and Ettawageshik, *Art of Tradition*, 13.

130. Michigan Indian Foundation, *Annual Review*, 1948, Bentley Historical Library, Ann Arbor.

131. Kurath, Ettawageshik, and Ettawageshik, *Art of Tradition*, 63.

132. Kurath, Ettawageshik, and Ettawageshik, *Art of Tradition*, 13.

133. James McClurken, *Gah-Baeh-Jhagwah-Buk/The Way It Happened: A Visual Culture History of the Little Traverse Bay Bands of Odawa* (East Lansing: Michigan State University Press, 1991), 83–84.

134. Kurath, Ettawageshik, and Ettawageshik, *Art of Tradition*, 18.

135. Kurath, Ettawageshik, and Ettawageshik, *Art of Tradition*, 104.

136. On the cultural history of powwows, see Tara Browner, *Heartbeat of the People: Music and Dance of the Northern Powwow* (Urbana: University of Illinois Press, 2002); and William K. Powers, *War Dance: Plains Indian Musical Performance* (Tucson: University of Arizona Press, 1990).

137. Kurath, Ettawageshik, and Ettawageshik, *Art of Tradition*, 38.

138. Kurath, Ettawageshik, and Ettawageshik, *Art of Tradition*, 46–47.

139. Kurath, Ettawageshik, and Ettawageshik, *Art of Tradition*, 38.

140. All the details that follow are found in Kurath, Ettawageshik, and Ettawageshik, *Art of Tradition*, 15–16.

141. Kurath, Ettawageshik, and Ettawageshik, *Art of Tradition*, 15–16.

142. Nichols and Nyholm, *Concise Dictionary of Minnesota Ojibwe*.

143. James O'Leary, "We Chose to Go That Way: Tradition and Volition in the Lives of Algonquian Artists," paper presented at the Algonquian Conference, Madison, Wisc. (October 2004).

144. The discussion of Josephine Degroat can be found in McNally, *Ojibwe Singers*.

145. Scott Lyons (personal communication, April 2008).

146. Pierre Bourdieu, *Outline of a Theory of Practice*, trans. R. Nice (Cambridge: Cambridge University Press, 1977), 15.

147. Bell, *Ritual Theory, Ritual Practice*.

148. Charles Long (personal communication, November 2005).

149. For more on the relationship between Native traditions, religion, and the law, see www.nativereligion.org.

150. Rogers, *Round Lake Ojibwa*, E5.

151. Rogers, *Round Lake Ojibwa*, B90.

152. Ningewance, *Talking Gookom's Language*.

153. Dunning, *Social and Economic Change Among the Northern Ojibwa*, 184–85.

154. Anderson, *Four Hills of Life*, 208.

155. Nesper, *Walleye War*, 202–4.

156. "Elders to form Council on White Earth," *Ojibwe News*, May 15, 1999.

157. http://www.ksg.harvard.edu/hpaied/hn/hn_2000_elder.htm (accessed April 1, 2005).

158. Mille Lacs Band Statutes 24 MLBSA Sec. 2002.

159. Mille Lacs Band Statutes 24 MLBSA Sec. 2003.

160. Mille Lacs Band Statutes Title 5, ch. 2, Sec. 103.

161. Mille Lacs Band Statutes 24 MLBSA Sec 2001.

5. The Sacralization of Eldership

1. Simmons, *Role of the Aged in Primitive Society*, 142.

2. Ritzenthaler, "Southwestern Chippewa," 752.

3. Jenness, *Ojibwa Indians of Parry Island*, 50.

4. Even the Midéwiwin, with its clearly demarcated "degrees" of initiation and leadership, is open to women or men willing to make the commitment and seek initiation.

5. Buffalohead, "Farmers, Warriors, Traders."

6. Landes, *Ojibwa Woman*, 178.

7. Landes, *Ojibwa Woman*, 177.

8. Landes, *Ojibwa Woman*, 125.

9. Landes, *Ojibwa Woman*, 135.

10. Landes, *Ojibwa Woman*, 159–60, 161.

11. Alanson Skinner, *Notes on the Eastern Cree and Northern Saulteaux* (Anthropological Papers of the American Museum of Natural History 9; New York: American Museum of Natural History, 1911), 160.

12. Densmore, *Chippewa Customs*, 44.

13. Landes, *Ojibwa Sociology*, 140.

14. Hallowell, field notes, n.d., A. I. Hallowell Papers, folder entitled "Saulteaux Indians—Social Organization," American Philosophical Society.

15. Landes, *Ojibwa Sociology*, 140.

16. Landes, *Ojibwa Sociology*, 140.

17. Landes, *Ojibwa Sociology*, 141.

18. Landes, *Ojibwa Sociology*, 140.

19. Landes, *Ojibwa Sociology*, 139.

20. Jenness, *Ojibwa Indians of Parry Island*, 48.

21. Lee Irwin, *The Dream Seekers* (Lincoln: University of Nebraska Press, 1994).

22. Kegg, *Portage Lake*, 22–25.

23. Hilger, *Chippewa Families*, 74.

24. Hilger, *Chippewa Families*, 74.

25. Johnston, *Ojibway Ceremonies*, 55.

26. Jenness, *Ojibwa Indians of Parry Island*, 48.

27. Here, I take seriously the strong direction of my Native teachers, who consider this domain to be privileged initiatory knowledge.

28. The term appears in a discussion of Archie Mosay in Treuer, *Living Our Language*, 18.

29. John Pietezel, *Life of Rev. Peter Marksman: An Ojibwa Missionary* (Cincinnati: Western Methodist Book Concern, 1910), 32.

30. Jenness, *Ojibwa Indians of Parry Island*, 92–94.

31. Jenness, *Ojibwa Indians of Parry Island*, 92.

32. Hallowell, field notes, n.d., A. I. Hallowell Papers, folder entitled "Saulteaux Indians—Social Organization," American Philosophical Society.

33. Landes, *Ojibwa Woman*, 14.

34. Hilger, *Chippewa Child Life*, 38.

35. Hilger, *Chippewa Child Life*, 37.

36. Pietezel, *Life of Rev. Peter Marksman*, 41.

37. Johnston, *Ojibway Ceremonies*, 15.

38. Barnouw, "Acculturation and Personality," 24, E-5.

39. Densmore, *Chippewa Customs*, 52.

40. Jenness, *Ojibwa Indians of Parry Island*, 91.

41. Peacock, *Forever Story*, 292.

42. Johnston, *Ojibway Ceremonies*, 20–30.

43. Clark, *Naawigiizis*, 103.

44. Landes, *Ojibwa Sociology*, 23.

45. Landes, *Ojibwa Sociology*, 23.

46. Hilger, *Chippewa Child Life*, 37–38.

47. Hilger, *Chippewa Child Life*, 37–38.

48. Densmore, *Chippewa Customs*, 52.

49. Pauline Colby, *Reminiscences*, 65, MHS.

50. Hilger, *Chippewa Child Life*, 37–38.

51. Colby, *Reminiscences*, 65; John and Jean Comaroff, *Of Revelation and Revolution: Christianity, Colonialism, and Consciousness in South Africa* (Chicago: University of Chicago Press, 1991), 219.

52. Charles Breck, ed., *The Life of the Reverend James Lloyd Breck* (New York: Young, 1883).

53. *Annual Report of the Commissioner of Indian Affairs: 1903* (Washington: Government Printing Office, 1903).

54. Colby, *Reminiscences*.

55. Fragment, n.d., Whipple Papers, box 1, MHS.

56. Kohl, *Kitchi-Gami*, 275.

57. I should be clear that this process arguably has not been uniform across Indian country. In the context of Northern Arapaho communities in Wyoming, Anderson found evidence that the religious authority of old age had decreased, not increased, through the twentieth century. Anderson refers to an "incipient traditional monotheism" where the relationship between individual and Creator eclipses an older set of relationships with numerous spirits "mediated by elders" (*Four Hills of Life*, 207). Still, one must recognize that Anderson's concern was not eldership in the Ojibwe sense, but in the sense of clearly marked traditional Arapaho age-sets, where only the eldest men (and to some degree, women) were eligible for initiation into the most important sacred knowledge. I think the Ojibwe case might contrast with this one, in that eldership gains religious author-

ity from shamanic/dream authority over time rather than concedes knowledge/ power/authority from an old age-grade system.

58. Mary Losure, Minnesota Public Radio (1996).

59. Michael Krauss, "Status of Native American Language Endangerment," in *Stabilizing Indigenous Languages*, ed. Gina Canton (Flagstaff: Northern Arizona University Center for Excellence in Education, 1946).

60. Tom Robertson, "Reviving the Language" (radio broadcast), Minnesota Public Radio (August 20, 2003), http://news.minnesota.publicradio.org/features/ 2003/08/20_robertsont_languagecamp/ (accessed August 2006).

61. Anton Treuer (personal communication, 2005).

62. Paul Levy, "Spirit of White Earth," *Minneapolis Star Tribune* (April 23, 30, 1999).

63. Levy, "Spirit of White Earth."

64. Jones, *History of the Ojebway Indians*, 96, 95.

65. Shaydayence to Women's Auxiliary, November 7, 1881, J. A. Gilfillan Papers, Scrapbook, Box 3, MHS.

66. Joe Chosa, in Tornes, *Memories of Lac du Flambeau Elders*, 162–63.

67. Vernon Bellecourt (personal communication, July 2006).

68. Vernon Bellecourt (personal communication, July 2006).

69. One register of these sea changes shifted political authority from the *ogimaa* characterized by old age and accrued supernatural power to the elected *ogimaakan*. From the 1940s on, anthropologists consumed with documenting acculturation in the field (e.g., Hallowell and Rogers) observed a waning of the charismatic authority of dreams and dreamers, but what they didn't note, or chance to observe prior to the 1970s, is that this religious/cultural authority had become associated more with the authority of age and moved from "shaman" to "elder," with the accentuation of the authority of eldership.

70. Smith, *Island of the Anishinaabeg*, 33.

71. Anderson, *Four Hills of Life*, 202–3.

72. The latter language comes from a 1989 letter from the organization to the Lac du Flambeau leadership. See Nesper, *Walleye War*, 113–14.

73. Nesper, *Walleye War*, 116.

74. Nesper, *Walleye War*, 141.

75. Josephine Degroat (personal communication, December 1994).

76. See McNally, *Ojibwe Singers*.

77. Michel de Certeau, *The Practice of Everyday Life*, trans. Stephen Rendall (Berkeley: University of California Press, 1994), 108.

78. Valentine, *Making It Their Own*, 217.

79. Valentine, *Making It Their Own*, 163.

80. Valentine, *Making It Their Own*, 163.

81. Valentine, *Making It Their Own*, 165.

82. I'm grateful to John Grim for this recognition of the sort of elder that has newly emerged through print (personal communication, April 2005).

83. See Wub-e-ke-niew, *We Have the Right to Exist*, or his columns in *Native American News*, archived at http://www.maquah.net/ (accessed July 21, 2007).

84. Treuer, *Living Our Language*; Tornes, *Memories of Lac du Flambeau Elders*; Kegg, *Portage Lake*; Vannote, *Women of White Earth*; Kâ-Nîpitêhtêw, *Counselling Speeches*; the Omushkego Oral History Project of the Centre for Rupert's Land Studies and organized in part by Jennifer S. H. Brown, accessible at http://www.ourvoices/ca/.

85. Cecilia Defoe, in Tornes, *Memories of Lac du Flambeau Elders*, 192.

86. Admittedly, Benton-Banai was not of age for eldership when he published *The Mishomis Book* and was active in the early years of the American Indian Movement in Minneapolis. But he has, I believe, emerged with this stature with time, as perhaps with the other AIM leaders.

87. http://www.aimovement.org/iitc/index.html#BENAI (accessed July 21, 2007).

88. Paul Johnson, *Secrets, Gossip, and Gods: The Transformation of Brazilian Candomblé* (New York: Oxford University Press, 2002).

89. http://www.geocities.com/CapitolHill/Senate/5205/ConfedBody.html (accessed May 2005).

90. "2000 Spiritual Statement," http://www.nicoa.org/message.html (accessed May 2005).

91. Smith, *Island of the Anishinaabeg*, 180.

92. Smith, *Island of the Anishinaabeg*, 34.

93. George Aubid, *Words of Wisdom*, undated typescript widely but informally circulated, ca. 1985.

6. The Shape of Wisdom

1. J. A. Gilfillan, *Minnesota Missionary* 3.6 (March 1880), MHS.

2. I think, for example, of the texture of the published books by Wub-e-ke-niew or Benton-Banai.

3. Nimaxia Hernandez (personal communication, November 2004).

4. Landes, *Ojibwa Religion*, 11.

5. See Pierre Hadot, *What Is Ancient Philosophy?* trans. Michael Chase (Cambridge: Harvard University Press, 2002); and Alasdair MacIntyre, *After Virtue: A Study in Moral Philosophy* (Notre Dame, Ind.: University of Notre Dame Press, 1981).

6. See Pierre Bourdieu, *Outline of a Theory of Practice*, trans. R. Nice (Cambridge: Cambridge University Press, 1977); Bell, *Ritual Theory, Ritual Practice*.

7. Darnell, "Implications of Cree Interactional Etiquette," 75.

8. I am taking into account the manner in which diminished life expectancy in some Native communities has meant that old age can arrive in one's 50s.

9. Cecilia Defoe, in Tornes, *Memories of Lac du Flambeau Elders*, 197.

10. Vannote, *Women of White Earth*, 21.

11. Benton-Banai, *Mishomis Book*, 62–65.

12. I am grateful to John Nichols for his confirming observation that "the transparency of the structures of *gik-end-aaso* and *gik-end-am* (and related) makes *gik-* quite prominent to a speaker and *gikaa* would be a natural association. So a folk etymology that connects" learning and elderhood (one not backed by the actual historical development of the language) "seems likely to be very strong psychologically and thus as real if not more so than any historical one" (personal communication, July 2007).

13. Treuer, *Living Our Language*, 85.

14. Darnell, "Implications of Cree Interactional Etiquette," 77.

15. Treuer, *Living Our Language*, 88–91.

16. Anderson, *Four Hills of Life*, 118.

17. Anderson, *Four Hills of Life*, 117.

18. Rogers, *Round Lake Ojibwa*, B59.

19. Johnston, *Ojibway Heritage*, 117–18.

20. Johnston, *Ojibway Heritage*, 118.

21. Larry Cloud Morgan (personal communications, 1992–99).

22. Tu, "The Confucian Perceptions of Adulthood," in *Humanity and Self-Cultivation*, 49.

23. Tu, "The Creative Tension Between *ren* and *li*," in *Humanity and Self-Cultivation*, 14.

24. Tu, "Confucian Perceptions of Adulthood," 51.

25. Tu, "Confucian Perceptions of Adulthood," 43.

26. Kâ-Nîpitêhtêw, *Counselling Speeches*, 55.

27. Benton-Banai, *Mishomis Book*, 63.

28. Johnston, *Ojibway Heritage*, 70, cited in Peacock and Wisuri, *Ojibwe Waasa Inaabidaa*, 69.

29. Northrup, *Rez Road Follies*, 12.

30. J. A. Gilfillan, "Some Indians I Have Known," in *The Red Man by Red Men*, J. A. Gilfillan Papers, MHS.

31. "Debate Continues over Canadian Universities' Elder-in-Residence Programs," *Indian Country Today*, August 2, 2006, B3.

32. Densmore, *Chippewa Customs*, 87.

33. Larry Cloud Morgan (personal communication, June 1991).

34. Author's field notes, June 26, 1991.

35. Anderson, *Four Hills of Life*, 168.

36. Smith, *Island of the Anishinaabeg*, 180.

37. Yao, *Introduction to Confucianism*, 159.

38. Basso, "To Give Up on Words," 96.

39. Glenn, *Unspoken*, 116.

40. Basso, "To Give Up on Words," 178–79n1.

41. Bauman, *Let Your Words Be Few*, 29–30.

42. Gilfillan, *Minnesota Missionary* 3.6 (March 1880). MHS.

43. Valentine, *Making It Their Own*, 19.

44. Erma Vizenor (personal communication, December 1994).

45. Darnell, "Implications of Cree Interactional Etiquette," 71.

46. Darnell, "Implications of Cree Interactional Etiquette," 73.

47. Gross, "Making the World Sacred," 6.

48. Gross, "Making the World Sacred," 15.

49. Gross, "Making the World Sacred," 5.

50. Gross, "Making the World Sacred," 7.

51. Anderson, *Four Hills of Life*, 118.

52. Peacock and Wisuri, *Ojibwe Waasa Inaabidaa*, 71.

53. Keith Basso, *Wisdom Sits in Places: Landscape and Language Among the Western Apache* (Albuquerque: University of New Mexico Press, 1996).

54. Barnouw, "Acculturation and Personality," 55.

55. Gross, "Making the World Sacred," 8.

56. Larry Cloud Morgan (personal communication, January 1997).

57. Goody, *Logic of Writing and the Organisation of Society*; and *Domestication of the Savage Mind*.

58. Darnell, "Implications of Cree Interactional Etiquette," 73–74.

59. Broker, *Night Flying Woman*, 94.

60. Broker, *Night Flying Woman*, 129.

61. Smith, *Island of the Anishinaabeg*, 180.

62. American Benedictine Academy, *American Monastic Newsletter* 29 (1999), http://www.osb.org/aba/news/992902/letters.html (accessed August 2006).

63. American Benedictine Academy, *American Monastic Newsletter* 29 (1999), http://www.osb.org/aba/news/992902/letters.html (accessed August 2006).

64. *New York Times*, January 15, 1991.

65. *Minnesota v. Mille Lacs Band of Chippewa Indians* 526 U.S. 172 (1999).

66. Gary Blair, "Minneapolis Elder Bea Swanson Passes," *Ojibwe News*, July 29, 1994.

67. Hallowell, *Culture and Experience*, 146.

68. Hallowell, *Culture and Experience*, 145.

69. Gilfillan, "Ojibways in Minnesota," 64, cited in Hallowell, *Culture and Experience*, 145.

70. Hallowell, *Culture and Experience*, 145.

71. Gerald Vizenor, *Fugitive Poses: Native American Indian Scenes of Absence and Presence* (Lincoln: University of Nebraska Press, 1998), 54–55.

72. Gross, "Comic Vision of Anishinaabe Culture and Religion."

73. Gilfillan, "Ojibways in Minnesota," 105–6.

74. White, *We Are at Home*.

75. Treuer, *Living Our Language*, 204.

76. Treuer, *Living Our Language*, 19.

77. Ben Chosa, in Tornes, *Memories of Lac du Flambeau Elders*, 136–37.

BIBLIOGRAPHY

Achenbaum, W. Andrew. *Old Age in the New Land*. Baltimore: Johns Hopkins University Press, 1978.

Akan, Linda. "Pimosatamowin Sikaw Kakeequaywin: Walking and Talking: A Saulteaux Elder's View of Native Education." *Canadian Journal of Native Education* 19 (1992): 191–214.

Amoss, Pamela T. "Cultural Centrality and Prestige for the Elderly: The Coast Salish Case." In Christine Fry, ed., *Dimensions: Aging, Culture, and Health*, 47–65. New York: Bergin, 1981.

Amoss, Pamela T., and Stevan Harrell, eds. *Other Ways of Growing Old: Anthropological Perspectives*. Stanford: Stanford University Press, 1981.

Anderson, Jeffrey. *The Four Hills of Life: Northern Arapaho Knowledge and Life Movement*. Lincoln: University of Nebraska Press, 2001.

———. *One Hundred Years of Old Man Sage: An Arapaho Life*. Lincoln: University of Nebraska Press, 2003.

Angell, Michael. *Preserving the Sacred: Historical Perspectives on the Ojibwa Midewiwin*. Winnipeg: University of Manitoba Press, 2002.

Baraga, Frederic. *A Dictionary of the Ojibway Language*. Saint Paul: Minnesota Historical Society Press, 1992 (originally 1878).

Barnouw, Victor. "Acculturation and Personality Among the Wisconsin Chippewa." *American Anthropological Association Memoirs* 72 (1950).

——. *Wisconsin Chippewa Myths and Tales*. Madison: University of Wisconsin Press, 1977.

Bass, Dorothy, ed. *Practicing Our Faith*. San Francisco: Jossey-Bass, 1997.

Basso, Keith. "To Give Up on Words: Silence in Western Apache Culture." In Basso's *Western Apache Language and Culture*, 80–98. Tucson: University of Arizona Press, 1990.

Bauman, Richard. *Let Your Words Be Few: Symbolism of Speaking and Silence Among Seventeenth Century Quakers*. New York: Cambridge University Press, 1983.

Bell, Catherine. *Ritual Theory, Ritual Practice*. New York: Oxford University Press, 1992.

Benton-Banai, Edward. *The Mishomis Book: The Voice of the Ojibway*. Saint Paul: Red School House, 1988.

Bird, Louis. Oral Historical Interviews (2001ff.). www.ourvoices.ca.

Birren, James E., and Vern Benston, eds. *Emergent Theories of Aging*. New York: Springer, 1988.

Blackbird, Andrew (Macke te be nessy). *History of the Ottawa and Chippewa Indians of Michigan*. Ypsilanti, Mich.: Ypsilantian Job Printing House, 1887.

Black-Rogers, Mary. "Ojibwa Power Belief System." In R. D. Fogelson and R. N. Adams, eds., *The Anthropology of Power*, 141–51. New York: Academic Press, 1977.

——. "Ojibwa Power Interactions: Creating Contexts for 'Respectful Talk.'" In Regna Darnell and Michael K. Foster, eds., *Native North American Interaction Patterns*, 44–77. Ottawa: Canadian Museum of Civilization, 1988.

——. "Ojibwa Taxonomy and Percept Ambiguity." *Ethos* 5 (1977): 90–118.

Bloch, Maurice, ed. *Political Language and Oratory in Traditional Society*. New York: Academic Press, 1975.

Borrows, John. "Listening for a Change: The Courts and Oral Tradition." *Osgoode Hall Law Journal* 39 (2001): 1–38.

Broker, Ignatia. *Night Flying Woman: An Ojibway Narrative*. Saint Paul: Minnesota Historical Society Press, 1983.

Brown, Jennifer S. H., and Maureen Matthews, "Fair Wind: Medicine and Consolation in the Berens River." *Journal of the Canadian Historical Association* 55–74 (1993).

Buchanan, Constance. "The Fall of Icarus: Gender, Religion, and the Aging Society." In Clarissa Atkinson, Constance Buchanan, and Margaret Miles, eds., *Shaping New Vision: Gender and Values in American Culture*. Harvard Women's Studies in Religion Series. Ann Arbor: UMI Research Press, 1987.

Bucko, Raymond. *The Lakota Ritual of the Sweat Lodge: History and Contemporary Practice*. Lincoln: University of Nebraska, 1988.

Buffalohead, Priscilla K. "Farmers, Warriors, Traders: A Fresh Look at Ojibway Women." In Roger L. Nichols, ed., *The American Indian: Past and Present*. 3rd edition. New York: Knopf, 1986.

Child, Brenda. *Boarding School Seasons: American Indian Families, 1900–1940*. Lincoln: University of Nebraska Press, 1998.

Clark, Jim. *Naawigiizis: The Memories of the Center of the Moon*. Edited by Louise Erdrich. Minneapolis: Birchbark Books, 2002.

Cleland, Charles. *The Place of the Pike Gnoozhekaaning: A History of the Bay Mills Indian Community*. Ann Arbor: University of Michigan Press, 2001.

Cole, Thomas R. *The Journey of Life: A Cultural History of Aging in America*. Cambridge: Cambridge University Press, 1992.

Cole, Thomas R., and Sally Gadow, eds. *What Does It Mean to Grow Old? Reflections from the Humanities*. Durham: Duke University Press, 1986.

Corbiere, Alan Ojiig. "Reconciling Epistemological Orientations: Toward a Wholistic Nishnaabe Education." Paper Presented at the Annual Meeting of the Indigenous and Native Studies Association, Edmonton, Alberta, 2000.

Danziger, Edmund J. *The Chippewas of Lake Superior*. Norman: University of Oklahoma Press, 1979.

Darnell, Regna. "The Implications of Cree Interactional Etiquette." In Regna Darnell and Michael K. Foster, eds., *Native North American Interaction Patterns*, 69–77. Ottawa: Canadian Museum of Civilization, 1988.

Densmore, Frances. *Chippewa Customs*. Saint Paul: Minnesota Historical Society Press, 1979 (originally 1929).

———. *Chippewa Music*. 2 vols. Bureau of American Ethnology Bulletin 45, 53. Washington, D.C.: GPO, 1910–13.

Diamond, Beverley, M. Sam Cronk, and Franziska von Rosen. *Visions of Sound: Musical Instruments of First Nations Communities in Northeastern America*. Chicago: University of Chicago Press, 1994.

Dowd, Gregory. *A Spirited Resistance: The North American Struggle for Unity, 1745–1815*. Baltimore: Johns Hopkins University Press, 1992.

Dunn, Anne M. *Grandmother's Gift: Stories from the Anishinabeg*. Duluth, Minn.: Holy Cow Press, 1997.

———. *Uncombed Hair: Poems*. Bemidji, Minn.: Loonfeather Press, 2005.

———. *Winter Thunder: Retold Tales*. Duluth, Minn.: Holy Cow Press, 2001.

Dunning, R. W. *Social and Economic Change Among the Northern Ojibwa*. Toronto: University of Toronto Press, 1959.

Fingarette, Herbert. *Confucius: The Secular as Sacred*. New York: Harper & Row, 1972.

Fischer, David Hackett. *Growing Old in America*. 2nd edition. New York: Oxford University Press, 1978.

Fried, Martha Nemes, and Morton H. Fried. *Transition: Four Rituals in Eight Cultures*. New York: Norton, 1980.

Fry, Christine, ed. *Aging in Culture and Society*. New York: Praeger, 1980.

——. *Dimensions: Aging, Culture, and Health*. New York: Praeger, 1981.

Gilfillan, Joseph A. "The Ojibways in Minnesota." *Collections of the Minnesota Historical Society* 9 (1901).

Glenn, Cheryl. *Unspoken: A Rhetoric of Silence*. Carbondale: Southern Illinois University Press, 2004.

Goody, Jack. *The Domestication of the Savage Mind*. Cambridge: Cambridge University Press, 1977.

——. *The Logic of Writing and the Organisation of Society*. Cambridge: Cambridge University Press, 1986.

Gray, Susan E. *I Will Fear No Evil: Ojibwa-Missionary Encounters Along the Berens River, 1875–1940*. Calgary: University of Calgary Press, 2006.

Grim, John. *The Shaman: Patterns of Religious Healing Among the Ojibway Indians*. Norman: University of Oklahoma Press, 1983.

Gross, Lawrence W. "The Comic Vision of Anishinaabe Culture and Religion." *American Indian Quarterly* 26 (Summer 2002): 436–59.

——. "Cultural Sovereignty and Native American Hermeneutics in the Interpretation of the Sacred Stories of the Anishinaabe." *Wicazo Sa Review* 18 (Fall 2003): 127–34.

——. "Making the World Sacred, Quietly, Carefully: Silence, Concentration, and the Sacred in Soto Zen and Ojibwa Indian Experience." Address to Harvard Buddhist Studies Forum, April 1, 1996.

——. "The Trickster and World Maintenance: An Anishinaabe Reading of Louise Erdrich's *Tracks*." *Studies in American Indian Literatures* 17 (Fall 2005): 48–66.

Haber, Carole. *Beyond Sixty-Five: The Dilemma of Old Age in America's Past*. Cambridge: Cambridge University Press, 1983.

Hallowell, A. Irving. *Culture and Experience*. Philadelphia: University of Pennsylvania Press, 1955.

———. *The Ojibwa of Berens River, Manitoba: Ethnography into History.* Edited by Jennifer S. H. Brown. Fort Worth: Harcourt, Brace, Jovanovich, 1992.

———. *The Role of Conjuring in Saulteaux Society.* New York: Octagon, 1971 (originally 1942).

Hareven, Tamara, and Kathleen Adams, eds. *Aging and Life Course Transitions: An Interdisciplinary Perspective.* New York: Guilford, 1982.

Hervieu-Léger, Danièle. *Religion as a Chain of Memory.* Translated by Simon Lee. New Brunswick: Rutgers University Press, 2000.

Heyrman, Christine Leigh. *Southern Cross: The Beginnings of the Bible Belt.* New York: Knopf, 1997.

Hickerson, Harold. *The Chippewa and Their Neighbors: A Study in Ethnohistory.* Revised and expanded edition. Prospect Heights, Ill.: Waveland, 1987 (originally 1970).

———. *The Ethnohistory of the Lake Superior Chippewa.* New York: Garland, 1974.

———. "Some Implications of the Theory of the Particularity, or 'Atomism' of Northern Algonkians." *Current Anthropology* 8 (October 1967): 313–43.

Hilger, M. Inez. *Chippewa Child Life and Its Cultural Background.* Saint Paul: Minnesota Historical Society Press, 1992.

———. *Chippewa Families: A Social Study of White Earth Reservation, 1938.* Saint Paul: Minnesota Historical Society Press, 1998.

Hill, Greg. *Norval Morrisseau: Shaman Artist.* Ottawa: National Gallery of Canada, 2006.

Hobsbawm, Eric, and Terence Ranger, eds. *The Invention of Tradition.* New York: Cambridge University Press, 1983.

Jackson, Deborah Davis. *Our Elders Lived It: American Indian Identity in the City.* DeKalb: Northern Illinois University Press, 2002.

Jenness, Diamond. *The Ojibwa Indians of Parry Island: Their Social and Religious Life.* Ottawa: National Museum of Canada, 1935.

Johnson, Paul. *The Transformation of Candomblé.* New York: Oxford University Press, 2005.

Johnston, Basil. *Ojibway Ceremonies.* Lincoln: University of Nebraska Press, 1990 (originally 1982).

———. *Ojibway Heritage.* Lincoln: University of Nebraska Press, 1990 (originally 1976).

———. *Ojibway Tales.* Lincoln: University of Nebraska Press, 1993 (originally 1978).

Jones, Peter. *History of the Ojebway Indians, with Especial Reference to Their Conversion to Christianity.* London: Bennett, 1861.

Bibliography

Kâ-Nîpitêhtêw, Jim. *The Counselling Speeches of Jim Kâ-Nîpitêhtêw*. Edited and translated by Freda Ahenakew and H. C. Wolfart. Winnipeg: University of Manitoba Press, 1998.

Kegg, Maude. *Portage Lake: Memories of an Ojibwe Childhood*. Edited and translated by John D. Nichols. Calgary: University of Alberta Press, 1991.

Kertzer, David, and Jennie Keith. *Age and Anthropological Theory*. Ithaca: Cornell University Press, 1984.

Kinietz, Vernon. "Chippewa Village." *Cranbrook Institute of Science, Bulletin* 25 (1947).

———. *The Indians of the Western Great Lakes, 1615–1760*. Ann Arbor: University of Michigan Press, 1965.

Kohl, Johann Georg. *Kitchi-Gami: Life Among the Lake Superior Ojibway*. Translated by Lascelles Wraxall. Saint Paul: Minnesota Historical Society Press, 1985 (originally 1860).

Kugel, Rebecca. *To Be the Main Leaders of Our People: A History of Minnesota Ojibwe Politics, 1825–1898*. East Lansing: Michigan State University Press, 1998.

Kugelmass, Jack. *The Miracle at Intervale Avenue: The Story of a Jewish Congregation in the South Bronx*. New York: Columbia University Press, 1996.

Kurath, Gertrude, Jane Ettawageshik, and Fred Ettawageshik. *The Art of Tradition: Sacred Music, Dance, and Myth of Michigan's Anishinaabe, 1946–1955*. Edited by Michael D. McNally. East Lansing: Michigan State University Press, 2009.

Laduke, Winona. *All Our Relations: Native Struggles for Land and Life*. Cambridge, Mass.: South End Press, 1999.

———. *Last Standing Woman*. Stillwater, Minn.: Voyageur Press, 1997.

Landes, Ruth. *Ojibwa Religion and the Midewiwin*. Madison: University of Wisconsin Press, 1968.

———. *Ojibwa Sociology*. New York: Columbia University Press, 1937.

———. *The Ojibwa Woman*. New York: Norton, 1971 (originally 1938).

McCabe, Melvina, and Jose Cuellar. "Aging and Health: American Indian/Alaska Native Elders." Working Paper no. 6, Stanford Geriatric Education Center (1994).

McNally, Michael D. "Honoring Elders: Practices of Sagacity and Deference in Ojibwe Christianity." In Laurie Maffly-Kipp, Leigh Schmidt, and Mark Valeri, eds., *Practicing Protestants: Histories of the Christian Life in America, 1630–1965*, 77–100. Baltimore: Johns Hopkins University Press, 2006.

———. "Ogimaakweg/Boss Women: Women Elders in 20th Century Ojibwe Christianity." In Fredrica H. Thompsett and Sheryl Kujawa-Holbrook, eds.,

Deeper Joy: Laywomen and Vocation in the 20th-Century Episcopal Church,
41–55. New York: Church Publishing, 2005.

———. *Ojibwe Singers: Hymns, Grief, and a Native Culture in Motion*. New York:
Oxford University Press, 2000.

Miller, J.R. *Shingwauk's Vision: A History of Native Residential Schools*. Toronto:
University of Toronto Press, 1996.

Moss, Walter G. *Humanistic Perspectives on Aging: An Annotated Bibliography
and Essay*. 2nd edition. Ann Arbor: Institute of Gerontology, 1976.

Myerhoff, Barbara. *Number Our Days*. New York: Simon and Schuster, 1978.

Nelson, George. *The Orders of the Dreamed: George Nelson on Cree and Northern
Ojibwa Religion and Myth, 1823*. Edited by Jennifer S.H. Brown and Robert
Brightman. Saint Paul: Minnesota Historical Society Press, 1988.

Nesper, Larry. *The Walleye War: The Struggle for Ojibwe Spearfishing and Treaty
Rights*. Lincoln: University of Nebraska Press, 2002.

Nichols, John, and Earl Nyholm. *A Concise Dictionary of Minnesota Ojibwe*. Minneapolis: University of Minnesota Press, 1995.

Ningewance, Patricia. *Talking Gookom's Language: Learning Ojibwe*. Lac Seul,
Ont.: Mazinaate Press, 2004.

Northrup, Jim. *The Rez Road Follies: Canoes, Casinos, Computers, and Birch Bark
Baskets*. New York: Kodansha, 1997.

Norval Morrisseau: Travels to the House of Invention. Toronto: Key Porter Books,
1997.

Ong, Walter. *Orality and Literacy: The Technologizing of the Word*. New York:
Methuen, 1982.

Ortiz, Alfonso. *The Tewa World: Space, Time, Being, and Becoming in a Pueblo
Society*. Chicago: University of Chicago Press, 1969.

Ottaway, Susannah. *The Decline of Life: Old Age in Eighteenth-Century England*.
Cambridge: Cambridge University Press, 2004.

Ottaway, Susannah, L.A. Botelho, and Katharine Kittredge. *Power and Poverty:
Old Age in the Pre-Industrial Past*. Westport, Conn.: Greenwood, 2002.

Overholt, Thomas, and J. Baird Callicott. *Clothed-in-Fur and Other Tales: An Introduction to an Ojibwa World View*. Lanham, Md.: University Press of America, 1982.

Peacock, Thomas. *A Forever Story: The People and Community of the Fond du Lac
Reservation*. Cloquet, Minn.: Fond du Lac Band of Lake Superior Chippewa, 1998.

Peacock, Thomas, and Marlene Wisuri. *Ojibwe Waasa Inaabidaa: We Look in All
Directions*. Afton, Minn.: Afton Historical Society Press, 2002.

Bibliography

Peers, Laura. *The Ojibwa of Western Canada, 1780–1870.* Saint Paul: Minnesota Historical Society Press, 1994.

Pflüg, Melissa. *Ritual and Myth in Odawa Revitalization.* Norman: University of Oklahoma Press, 1998.

Pollard, Leslie. *Complaint to the Lord: Historical Perspectives on the African American Elderly.* Selinsgrove: Susquehanna University Press, 1996.

Premo, Terri. *Winter Friends: Women Growing Old in the New Republic, 1785–1835.* Urbana: University of Illinois Press, 1990.

Rathbone-McCuan and Betty Havens, eds. *North American Elders: United States and Canadian Perspectives.* New York: Greenwood, 1988.

Reddy, Marlita, ed. *Statistical Records of Native North Americans.* 2nd edition. New York: Gale Research, 1995.

Rhodes, Richard. *Eastern Ojibwa-Chippewa-Ottawa Dictionary.* Berlin: Mouton, 1985.

Ritzenthaler, Robert. "Southwestern Chippewa." *Handbook of the North American Indian* 15. Washington, D.C.: Smithsonian Institution, 1978.

Rogers, Edward S. *Round Lake Ojibwa.* Occasional Paper 5, Art and Archeology Division. Toronto: Royal Ontario Museum, 1962.

Rogers, John. *Red World and White: Memories of a Chippewa Boyhood.* Norman: University of Oklahoma Press, 1996 (originally 1957).

Rohrl, Vivian. *Change for Continuity: The People of a Thousand Lakes.* Lanham, Md.: University Press of America, 1981.

Rosaldo, Renato. *Culture and Truth: The Remaking of Social Analysis.* Boston: Beacon, 1989.

Rubinstein, R. L., J. Keith, D. Shenk, and D. Wieland. *Anthropology and Aging: Comprehensive Reviews.* Dordrecht: Kluwer, 1990.

Schenck, Theresa. *The Voice of the Crane Echoes Afar: The Sociopolitical Organization of the Lake Superior Ojibwa, 1640–1855.* New York: Garland, 1997.

Schweitzer, Marjorie, ed. *American Indian Grandmothers.* Albuquerque: University of New Mexico Press, 1999.

Sherzer, Joel. *Kuna Ways of Speaking: An Ethnographic Perspective.* Austin: University of Texas Press, 1983.

Shils, Edward. *Tradition.* Chicago: University of Chicago Press, 1981.

Shkilnyk, Anastasia M. *A Poison Stronger than Love: The Destruction of an Ojibwa Community.* New Haven: Yale University Press, 1985.

Simmons, Leo. *The Role of the Aged in Primitive Society.* New Haven: Yale University Press, 1945.

Bibliography

Smith, Theresa. *The Island of the Anishinaabeg: Thunderers and Water Monsters in the Traditional Ojibwe Life World*. Moscow: University of Idaho Press, 1995.

Sokolovsky, Jay. *The Cultural Context of Aging*. South Hadley, Mass.: Bergin and Garvey, 1990.

Spicker, Stuart, Kathleen Woodward, and David Van Tassell, eds. *Aging and the Elderly: Humanistic Perspectives in Gerontology*. Atlantic Highlands, N.J.: Humanities Press, 1978.

Stiegelbauer, S. "What Is an Elder? What Do Elders Do? First Nation Elders as Teachers in Culture-Based Urban Organizations." *Canadian Journal of Native Studies* 16 (1996): 37–66.

Strange, Heather, and Michele Teitelbaum, eds. *Aging and Cultural Diversity*. South Hadley, Mass.: Bergin and Garvey, 1987.

Tanner, John. *The Falcon: A Narrative of the Captivity and Adventures of John Tanner During Thirty Years Residence Among the Indians in the Interior of North America*. New York: Penguin, 1994 (originally 1830).

Taylor, Rodney. *The Confucian Way of Contemplation*. Columbia: University of South Carolina Press, 1988.

Thane, Pat. *Old Age in English History*. Oxford: Oxford University Press, 2000.

Thomas, Keith. "Age and Authority in Early Modern England." *Proceedings of the British Academy* 62 (1976): 205–48.

Thornton, Russell. *American Indian Holocaust and Survival: A Population History Since 1492*. Norman: University of Oklahoma Press, 1987.

Tornes, Elizabeth, ed. *Memories of Lac du Flambeau Elders*. Madison: Center for the Study of Upper Midwestern Cultures, 2004.

Toulouse, Pamela Rose. "Sagamok Anishnawbek: The Decision Makers and Varying Conceptions of Cultural Inclusion at Beedaban School." *New Approaches to Lifelong Learning*. Toronto: Ontario Institute for Studies in Education, 2001.

Treuer, Anton, ed. *Living Our Language: Ojibwe Tales and Oral Histories*. Saint Paul: Minnesota Historical Society Press, 2001.

Tu, Weiming. *Humanity and Self-Cultivation: Essays in Confucian Thought*. Berkeley: Asian Humanities Press, 1979.

Tu, Weiming, and Mary Evelyn Tucker, eds. *Confucian Spirituality*. New York: Crossroad, 2003.

Valentine, J. Randolph. *Nishnaabemwin Reference Grammar*. Toronto: University of Toronto Press, 2004.

———. ed. *Weshki-Bmaadzijig Ji-Noondmowaad: "That the Young Might Hear": The Stories of Andrew Medlar as Recorded by Leonard Bloomfield*. London, Ont.: Centre for Research and Teaching of Canadian Native Languages, 1998.

Valentine, Lisa Philips. *Making It Their Own: Severn Ojibwe Communicative Practices*. Toronto: University of Toronto Press, 1995.

Vannote, Vance. *Women of White Earth*. Minneapolis: University of Minnesota Press, 1999.

Vansina, Jan. *Oral Tradition as History*. Madison: University of Wisconsin Press, 1985.

Van Tassel, David, ed. *Aging, Death, and the Completion of Being*. Philadelphia: University of Pennsylvania Press, 1979.

Vecsey, Christopher. *Traditional Ojibwa Religion and Its Historical Changes*. Philadelphia: American Philosophical Society Press, 1983.

Wach, Joachim. *Sociology of Religion*. Chicago: University of Chicago Press, 1944.

Warren, William W. *History of the Ojibway People*. Saint Paul: Minnesota Historical Society, 1984 (originally 1885).

Weber, Max. *Economy and Society*. 3 vols. Translated and edited by Guenther Roth and Claus Wittich. Berkeley: University of California Press, 1978.

Westmann, Clinton N. "Understanding Cree Religious Discourse." PhD diss., University of Alberta, 2008.

Westphal, Merold. *God, Guilt, and Death: An Existential Phenomenology of Religion*. Bloomington: Indiana University Press, 1984.

Wheeler-Voegelin, Erminie. *The Red Lake and Pembina Chippewa*. New York: Garland, 1974.

White, Bruce. *We Are at Home*. St. Paul: Minnesota Historical Society Press, 2007.

White, Richard. *The Middle Ground: Indians, Empires, and Republics in the Great Lakes Region, 1650–1815*. New York: Cambridge University Press, 1991.

Williams, Angeline. *The Dog's Children: Anishinaabe Texts Told by Angeline Williams*. Edited and translated by Leonard Bloomfield, newly edited by John D. Nichols. Winnipeg: University of Manitoba Press, 1991.

Wub-e-ke-niew (Francis Blake). *We Have the Right to Exist: A Translation of Aboriginal Indigenous Thought*. New York: Black Thistle Press, 1995.

Yao, Xinzhong. *An Introduction to Confucianism*. Cambridge: Cambridge University Press, 2000.

INDEX

Index

Cole, Thomas, xiv–xvi, 44
Coleman, Rev. John, 249
Commandments, Ten, xi, xin1, 5
Conflict, 29, 138, 264–65; between deacons and Gilfillan, 197–203; exacerbated by assimilation, 115, 182, 184–85, 218. *See also* Contestation
Confucius, 62, 90, 290
Confucianism, 3, 62, 83, 89–92, 107; community as holy rite in, 47, 90; cultivation of humanity in, 47–48, 90–91; disciplines of learning in, 286; filiality in, 25–26, 91–92, 95; old age idealized in, 93n30, 291; sagehood in, 290–93, 295. *See also* Filial piety
Constitutions, tribal, 32, 122, 267
Contemplation, 282, 292, 293–300; locative aspects, 301; withdrawal, 294
Contestation: generational, 112, 129, 225; of Christian leadership, 197–203, 305; of tradition, 209–10, 218–19, 260
Copway, George, 10, 139
Corbiere, Alan, 154–55, 156
Council of elders. *See* Elder councils
Counseling speeches, 136, 168
Cree, 11, 93, 97, 134, 252, 284, 291, 298; counseling speeches, 136, 168; storytelling, 142–43
Crier, 136
Cross Village, Mich., 210
Cuellar, Jose, 121
Culture, 6, 49, 163; folklorization of, 205–9, 269. *See also* Tradition
Curanderas, 3

Dance, 56, 65, 171, 179, 206, 310; *Anami'aawin* and, 189;

criminalization of, 115; Jingle Dress, 216; naming and, 241. *See also* Drum Dance
Darnell, Regna, 142–43, 169, 284, 286–87, 293, 288, 303
Day, Fred, 309
Day, Mary, 129, 309
Day, Richard, 129
Deacons, 30, 179–80, 181; elders delegate authority to, 195, 196–97, 250; namesakes of *ogimaag*, 250; relatives of *ogimaag*, 197; strike by, 197–203
Declaration of the Rights of Indigenous Peoples, 2–3, 122
Deference, 82, 165–67, 190–95, 283; ambivalence about, 106–7; avoidance of eye contact, 101; avoidance of questioning, 284; avoidance of walking in front of, 134; beyond etiquette, 14, 93; in Confucianism, 91–92; economic provision of, 103–5, 110; indirect reference as, 101; listening practices and, 100, 132, 166, 284–85; quietness and, 294–95; ritualized nature of, 96–97, 190; serving food as, 105; silence and, 295–300; speech practices and, 100–1, 166; strategic use of, 261–62; tobacco offerings and, 66, 100, 102, 191, 237; violation of codes of, 199–203. *See also* Practices; Respect; Ritualization
Defoe, Cecilia, 102, 122, 272, 284
Degroat, Josephine, 122, 215–17, 219, 292, 307, 311
Densmore, Frances, 10, 56, 136, 161; on life cycle, 11; on Midéwiwin, 50, 240; on names, 248–49; on stories, 139
Descartes, René, 43–44

Diabetes, 118, 213

Differentiation of authority, 222–26, 231, 260, 260n68

Dimock, Selma, 249

Disease, 28–29, 68–69, 72, 118, 148, 177. *See also* Alcohol

Divination, 16, 47, 181

Dobyns, Henry, 69

Dogen, 299

Doodem (clan), 84, 86n10, 108, 132, 175; names and, 46; grandparents of, 127–28

Dream helpers, 171, 232, 235, 238

Dream power, 14, 172, 207, 235; authority of, 24, 35, 170–71; erosion of, 231; fear of, 15, 16, 67; healing and, 236–37; maturation of, 16, 45, 231–33; midwifery and, 237; naming and exchange of, 17, 241, 242, 244–48

Dreams, 42, 42n1, 134, 172, 237–39; requiring interpretation, 238; life direction and, 234, 238–39; as source of names, 46, 241, 242, 244–48; as vehicle of spiritual gifts, 66, 232–33. *See also* Dream power; Mentorship; Vision fasts

Drum, 7, 41, 56, 65, 88, 178, 189, 206, 216, 305

Drum Dance, 65, 114–15, 216, 225

Dunn, Anne, 140, 271, 311

Dunn, Josephine, 156

Dunning, R. W., 111–12, 130, 224

"Duty of Elders," 87

Eagle, Melvin, 99–100, 103, 286–87

Earth. *See* Grandmother Earth

Earth, George, 226

Education: by example, 137–38; higher, 153–58, 292; incumbent on youth to ask for teaching, 135;

institutionalization of, 146–50; interruption of traditional pedagogy, 145–50; lifelong learning, 131, 142, 290–93; life skills, 133; moral, 134; more than cultural transmission, 144; religious, 134–35; repetition in, 139; search for wisdom as final phase of, 291; eldership and institutionalized, 153–58; storytelling and, 139–41; teacher/student relationship in, 135, 156; traditional pedagogy of, 133–45, 154; tribally controlled schools, 153. *See also* Boarding schools; Grandparents; Elders

Elder abuse, 37, 108, 111, 118–19

Elder councils, 12, 152, 173, 177, 188, 216, 305; eldership shaped by, 231, 274; codification of, 228; sacralization and, 227, 274–77

Elders, 61–63; abandonment of, 108–10; age of decreasing over time, 34, 74–75, 260, 313; anthropology of religion and, 19–22; as "anti-drug," 157–58; assimilation policy targets, 114–15, 177; Christianity and, xi, 18, 78, 177, 180, 188, 193–94, 197; deference to own elders, 165, 168, 311; dream interpretation of, 58–59, 135, 237–40, 283; educational attainment of, 118; as educators of young, 26, 124, 133–45; as embodiments of community, 2, 39–41, 145; English term of, 33, 40, 62, 77–81; factionalism and, 184; families revolving around, 125–26, 225; French terms for, 78–79, 138; as healers, 233–37; as herbalists, 236; health of, 118; housing of, 118, 199; humor among, 307–10; as life